BEYOND

THE

BOUNDARIES

ONE

WATER, WOODS, AND WINTER
A Special Sense of Place

There was "speculation" in their eyes; the hope of making a speedy fortune in the newly discovered mineral region of the north was uppermost in their minds. . . . Few even dreamed of making permanent settlements in that far off land, in that howling wilderness, wherein the ice king ruled with terrible severity for nearly six months in the year.

John Harris Forster, "Early Settlement of the Copper Regions of Lake Superior," 1886

On August 1, 1848, Ruth Douglass took tea with her husband, Columbus Christopher Douglass, at their residence in Detroit. The young wife enjoyed spending such moments with her thirty-six-year-old husband. On this occasion, "Mr. Douglass," as she called him, had interesting news: he had received a letter from the Ohio and Isle Royale Mining Company, offering him a position. Would he be interested in going up to Lake Superior to establish a copper smelting works on Isle Royale, located fifty miles northwest of Upper Michigan's Keweenaw Peninsula?[1]

The proposition unsettled both husband and wife. C. C. Douglass had kicked around quite a bit during his life. Born in New York state, he had moved west to lower Michigan as a child and later returned east to study geology. Starting in 1837—the year Michigan became a state—he had served as an assistant on geological expeditions headed by his cousin, Douglass Houghton, Michigan's first state geologist. In that capacity he had first journeyed north to Lake Superior to explore the region's novel deposits of almost pure, metallic copper. After a mine rush to the Keweenaw's copper district began in 1843, Douglass consulted for new companies searching for workable deposits of the native metal, and he invested in one of the region's earliest stores.

C. C. Douglass hoped to profit as settlers transformed this region from a remote wilderness into a copper mining center. Yet the prospect of relocating to Isle Royale gave him pause. He told Ruth that "he had led something of a backwoods life, and was ready to go almost anyplace." Nevertheless, he confided that "the idea of being banished to a desolate island was something that had not entered his head."

C. C. asked, in jocular fashion, if Ruth would consider joining him on such an expedition, and she responded affirmatively. But privately she hoped the idea would die. She was happy with her life among friends in a more settled and familiar part of Michigan. On August 2, she recorded in her diary: "There was nothing said about going to Isle Royale today. I abstain from mentioning it in hopes it may blow over."

It didn't blow over. The company "seemed determined to prevail on C. C. to go to Isle Royale," and one of its directors visited him on August 3. Two weeks later, on August 17, Ruth and C. C. Douglass "sailed from Detroit on the steamer *Michigan,* bound for Isle Royale."

The steamer made several short stops as it headed north, receiving and delivering passengers and picking up wood from shoreline forests to fire its boilers. It reached the top of Michigan's mitten on August 19. The next day it left Lake Huron and moved up the Saint Mary's River toward Lake Superior. The first leg of the trip for C. C. and Ruth ended at Sault Ste. Marie (the "Soo"), about four hundred nautical miles from Detroit, where rocky rapids on the Saint Mary's blocked their steamer's way. Because of an eighteen-foot drop over a three-quarter-mile run of rapids, persons and freight bound for Lake Superior had to be taken off here and put aboard another vessel plying the waters above the rapids.

The couple stayed at Sault Ste. Marie for several days. Ruth occasionally stood on the riverbank, watching Indians paddle bark canoes into the rapids to fish. When the propeller *Independence* arrived from the western reaches of Lake Superior, it came laden with "some very large masses of pure native copper." Ruth watched men unload the copper, portage it past the rapids, and load it onto another vessel bound for the lower Great Lakes.

This native copper was the stuff that had excited a mine rush a half decade before, the stuff responsible for Ruth's presence at Sault Ste. Marie. The large pieces of copper carried aboard the *Independence* were not ingots, poured of refined and smelted copper. Instead, these jagged pieces of the red metal, weighing hundreds or thousands of pounds, were being shipped just as they had been taken from the mines. Their nooks and crannies still carried inclusions of the trap rock which, before the miners had blasted it with black powder, had held the copper captive for millions of years.

Nowhere on earth, save for the south shore of Lake Superior, did native copper exist in quantities sufficient to support a mining industry. This copper had had a special allure since prehistoric times. At least five thousand years earlier, it had attracted Native Americans, who took the metal away, fashioned it into ornaments and tools, and traded it widely across North

America.[2] During the colonial era, the French and British explored and attempted to mine it. Then parties of early American geologists—supported by the federal government or the new state of Michigan—came to assess it. Despite their far-flung, remote locations, the Keweenaw Peninsula and Isle Royale, solely because of their copper deposits, were "visible" from the east coast, where many investors lived. And in the 1840s, speculators, investors, and miners determined that it was time to defy the odds. Time to try to put enough people, money, and technology into the woods to found a new industry.

As Ruth and C. C. Douglass waited for their boat to leave Sault Ste. Marie, the steamer *Detroit* arrived from the south, carrying an influential investor in the Lake Superior Mining Company who hailed from New York City. Newspaper editor Horace Greeley not only advised other opportunists to "Go west, young man"; he also heeded his own advice. In the summer of 1848 Greeley headed west to Lake Superior to check on his investment in a Keweenaw copper mine.

On August 25, Greeley, the Douglasses, and other passengers took a scow out to the *Independence* and climbed ladders to get aboard. Two days later, after a voyage of nearly 250 miles, they rounded the point of the Keweenaw Peninsula, a hook of land that curves northeastwardly as it reaches seventy miles out into Lake Superior.

Hundreds of layers of rock—some sedimentary, but most put down by volcanoes—underlay the Keweenaw Peninsula. Instead of remaining as horizontal beds, these rock strata bent into a bowl shape. One upturned rim formed the central spine of the Keweenaw, rising about six hundred feet above Lake Superior. The rock then dipped westward beneath the great lake before rising again as the outcrop forming Isle Royale. Beneath the Keweenaw and Isle Royale, a copper-bearing solution had at one time been propelled upward under great pressure from deeper in the earth. It flowed into large fissures and small cavities found in the sedimentary and basaltic rock. Then, curiously, the copper precipitated out of solution not as a compound but as a nearly pure metal, very unevenly distributed throughout the host rock. Some small specks of copper were hard to see with the naked eye. Other single masses of copper were every bit as big as the miners' cabins that now dotted the northern tip of the Keweenaw, which, in the 1840s, was the center of the early mining industry.[3]

The *Independence* skirted this northernmost tip in a fog, by passing the small village of Copper Harbor, where the U.S. government had built Fort Wilkins and established a land agency office to protect and promote the nascent copper industry. On the western shore of the Keweenaw, the lake boat stopped for a few hours at Eagle Harbor, where Horace Greeley disembarked, and then at

Eagle River. Each of the little harbors served as a commercial, trade, and transportation center for a cluster of small mines located not hard against the shoreline but two to ten miles deep into the wooded hinterland.

When the *Independence* left Eagle River, unfavorable winds kept it from sailing straight to Isle Royale. The captain abandoned that course and took his ship to LaPointe, Wisconsin, where Ruth Douglass was entertained by the sight of "some 2 or 3 thousand Indians assembled to receive their yearly payments" from the Indian agent. From LaPointe, the *Independence* sailed back eastward, arriving on August 29 at the southern base of the Keweenaw Peninsula. No good harbor existed here at the mouth of the Ontonagon River, so the *Independence* anchored some distance offshore, and small scows came out to take aboard passengers and freight.

Ruth recorded in her diary that the Ontonagon River "is said to pass through a rich mineral district." Indeed, thanks to recent discoveries made by the Minesota [*sic*] Mining Company, the southern range of the Keweenaw was just then on the verge of a copper boom. But it had long been known as home of the legendary "Ontonagon Boulder," by far the most famous specimen of mass copper ever taken from the region.

A glacier had long ago mined the Ontonagon Boulder. Moving over the land, ice scoured the upturned edge of a mineralized portion of rock and tore from its grasp this sizable piece of mass copper. The glacier carried this mass for some distance before dropping it off alongside the West Branch of the Ontonagon River, some twenty miles upstream from Lake Superior.

Native Americans were the first to discover the Ontonagon Boulder. In the 1600s and 1700s they recounted tales of the boulder to French and then British explorers (starting, perhaps, with Champlain, as early as 1610). Whether French, British, or American, all early white travelers to the Keweenaw made nearly obligatory pilgrimages up the Ontonagon River to see the famous boulder for themselves.[4]

The boulder's actual size diminished as visitors hacked off its more fragile corners and took away specimens. But its legendary size continued to swell. In 1820, the territorial governor of Michigan, Lewis Cass, headed an expedition to Lake Superior sponsored by John C. Calhoun and the War Department. As part of this effort, Captain David Bates Douglass, a West Point engineer, and Henry Rowe Schoolcraft, a multitalented mineralogist, made the difficult trek to the boulder. When they finally got there, Douglass was keenly disappointed. Expecting an awesome natural treasure, he had to settle for a piece of copper he called "a mere stone, a large pebble." Schoolcraft, too, initially found the copper boulder far less impressive than its reputation.[5] But a year later, when he published an account of his travels, Schoolcraft included a drawing of the boulder that showed it dwarfing the three canoes carrying fifteen men who came to see it. In reality, the Ontonagon Boulder was about four feet long and weighed 3,700 pounds. School-craft's drawing portrayed it as six to eight feet thick and twenty-five to thirty feet long!

The Ontonagon Boulder—this large specimen of almost pure copper, sitting right on the surface of the ground—engendered enthusiasm and optimism among speculators and investors. Knowledge of the boulder's existence helped spark the mine rush to the Keweenaw. In 1843, after being wrested from its riverbank site, it drew large crowds of admirers while being transported to Washington via Detroit, Buffalo, and the Erie Canal. The boulder still lured settlers to the Keweenaw even after it was gone from there.

The propeller *Independence* stayed only briefly at the mouth of the Onton-agon before pulling up anchor and sailing northwestwardly across Superior. On August 30, almost two weeks after departing Detroit, Ruth and C. C. Douglass arrived at Isle Royale. Ruth stood at the railing of the ship as it passed along the shoreline of this place where she had never really planned or hoped to be. Later in the day she penned a diary entry that captured her response. That response was ambiguous, even contradictory. Near the entry's midpoint, its tone changed, indicating that Ruth found this unusual place in-viting and daunting at the same time:

> Arrived . . . at 8 in the morning. Looks very pleasant. The inhabitants hoisted their flag and fired a salute on our arrival. On the whole our trip had been a very pleasant one. When I arose in the morning we were in sight of the Island about 15 miles West of our place of destination. Keeping near the shore we had a fine view of the coast with its bold rocky cliffs, small bays and fine harbors. The view . . . obtained of the Island was anything but a favorable one for me—at least, as there was nothing to be seen but barren rocks and a small growth of evergreen and birch timber, as my eyes had not the gift of magnifying every little seam in the rocks into a large vein of copper. This being the only inducement for people to settle in this remote region. As we entered Rock Harbor I was happily disappointed at the appearance of our temporary home.

The Lake Superior region was not one that men or women, explorers or geologists, entrepreneurs or miners, took for granted. For nearly everyone, it seemed a very special place. It wrung reactions out of people, both good and bad. Ruth Douglass called it "remote." An early French traveler called the Keweenaw region "the fag-end of creation."[6] In 1820, on the day his expe-ditionary crew visited the Ontonagon Boulder, Henry Rowe Schoolcraft made a similar point but expressed it in his journal in a more thorough, negative manner:

> One cannot help fancying that he has gone to the ends of the earth, and beyond the boundaries appointed for the residence of man. Every object tells us that it is a region alike unfavorable to the productiveness of the animal and vegetable kingdom; and we shudder in casting our eyes over the frightful wreck of trees, and the confused groups of falling-in banks and shattered stones. . . . Such is the frightful region through which,

for a distance of twenty miles, we followed our Indian guides to reach this unfrequented spot, in which there is nothing to compensate the toil of the journey but its geological character, and mineral production.[7]

Twenty-five years after Schoolcraft traveled up the Ontonagon River, Charles Whittlesey explored the same area, yet responded to it in a remarkably different way. On the ridge of the valley, Whittlesey ascended to the "waving top of a trim balsam" to get a panoramic view of the terrain:

The sides and bottom of the valley of the Ontonagon were brilliant in the mellow sunlight, mottled with yellow and green; the golden tops of the sugar tree mingled with the dark summits of the pine and the balsam. The rough gorges that enter the valley on both sides were now concealed by the dense foliage of the trees, partly gorgeous and partly sombre, made yet richer by the contrast, so that the surface of the wood as seen from our elevation . . . lay like a beautifully worked and colored carpet ready for our feet.[8]

Where one man saw a "frightful wreck of trees," another saw an arboreal canopy that looked like "a beautifully worked and colored carpet." One saw disorder; the other, order. Two strongly felt responses, with Whittlesey's as the infinitely more romantic and positive statement. But even in expressing his very romantic view of the Keweenaw environs, Whittlesey allowed ambiguity and contradiction to slip in: it was both "partly gorgeous" and "partly sombre."

Those who traveled through or settled on the Keweenaw Peninsula or Isle Royale were almost universally struck by its remoteness and by how greatly it differed from other places they had lived. Even after decades of settlement, residents continued to contrast the Lake Superior region with what they called the "world below." The world below meant places to the south and east: places that were more populated, civilized, and comfortable; places that were dominated by culture, not the natural environment. On Lake Superior, the environment, including the elements, reigned. Water, woods, and winter made the place seem so special, and each of these natural elements, like Whittlesey's forest, was "partly gorgeous" and "partly sombre." Each inspired, yet threatened. Each was beautiful and picturesque, yet dangerous and terrifying. The Keweenaw was a place both to love and loathe, to fancy and fear.

Charles Whittlesey, again writing of his 1845 expedition to the copper district, noted that every member of his party "was delighted with . . . the unsurpassed purity, plenty, and coldness of its waters."[9] Water was a dominant, dramatic part of the environment, especially Lake Superior. There was nothing ordinary or commonplace about Lake Superior, which was—and is—truly one of the world's grandest bodies of fresh water. Its length stretches 350 miles; its breadth, 160 miles. Its maximum depth is 1,335 feet; its average depth, nearly 500 feet. Lake Superior's water surface measures 32,000 square miles, while its shorelines, including island boundaries, runs 2,700 linear miles. Lake Superior contains 2,900 cubic miles of water, a considerably greater volume than that of the other Great Lakes (Michigan, Huron, Erie, and Ontario) combined.

This vast, inland sea—which lapped and sometimes lashed the shorelines of the Keweenaw Peninsula and Isle Royale—broadly influenced life and weather in the region. It was a transporter. It carried early waterborne migrants and their supplies to this remote destination. Importantly, besides carrying boats, the lake stirred the climate and affected the air. The lake's capacity was so enormous that its water warmed up slowly in summer and cooled down slowly in winter. Consequently, the lake moderated air temperatures year-round over the Keweenaw. Compared with settlers of, say, the northern Great Plains, who would live at about the same latitude as those along Superior, Keweenaw settlers endured less extreme high and low temperatures during summer and winter seasons. They had fewer days above 80 degrees Fahrenheit and fewer days below zero. However, these settlers paid a price for the 5 to 10 extra degrees that the lake often gave them on winter days—and that price was an abundance of lake-effect snow. Air picked up moisture in passing over Superior's open waters, then released that moisture as snow when moving over the colder land mass. On the Keweenaw, the sun could shine and the snow could fall, all at the same time.

The earliest commercial villages in the developing mine district were hard against Lake Superior's shore—Copper Harbor, Eagle Harbor, Eagle River, Ontonagon. In these locations, water and vessels were omnipresent. John Forster described the premier pioneer settlement, Copper Harbor:

> This rock-bound harbor . . . , when we first saw it, was animated by numerous sail boats, canoes, and mackinaw boats, gliding to and fro,—all craft belonging to explorers.
> During the lively summer of 1846, several thousand people must have arrived at Copper Harbor. . . . The birch woods in the vicinity . . . underwent a great transformation, and a lively town of white tents gleamed out of the green groves. It was an improvised metropolitan city; men from many nations were covered by its canvass and made merry beside the clear waters of the Great Lake.[10]

The Keweenaw's copper lodes ran not next to the shore but along the peninsula's central spine, elevated about six hundred feet above Superior. So the mining companies put their rough-hewn settlements—usually called mine "locations," rather than villages—in the hinterland, where the copper was. Although inland, the mine locations were rarely more than five or ten miles distant from Lake Superior, and if a bit removed from the great lake, they nevertheless were often sited near one of the Keweenaw's many interior streams, rivers, or lakes. Travelers and settlers often remarked about the natural beauty of these waters. Henry Hobart, an uprooted Vermont Yankee who taught school at the Cliff mine, found much to fault about pioneer life on the Keweenaw. Still, he allowed as how "there are scenes here that cannot be far surpassed of color & beauty." On September 20, 1863, he wrote in his diary:

> I imagine myself seated in a birch canoe out on the placid surface of Gratiot Lake, ten miles
> distant in the woods, the beautiful trout are busy at the hook, the sloping hills extend back
> in the distance unmarred by the ax in all the richness of their ancient beauty. Everything is
> pleasant to the eye and sweet sounds meet the ear. Yonder . . . beautiful trout of twenty
> pounds darts to the surface of the water after the hook; ducks & water fowls are seen every-
> where. What a scene for the painter. Thus it is all through this region.[11]

In describing interior lakes, Hobart and others often merged their appreciation for the water with an equal appreciation for the surrounding forest.
Geologist Charles T. Jackson passed along the largest of the interior lakes on
September 15, 1848, and recorded in his journal: "The lake is a beautiful sheet
of water. . . . We coasted along the shores of Portage Lake, viewing the beautiful autumnal scenery. . . . The hills are covered with primeval forests of maple, ash, birch, pine, spruce and fir trees."[12] But while water merged with woods
on interior lakes, water merged with sky on the great lake, Superior. Bela
Hubbard, a principal assistant to Douglass Houghton on his geological exploration of the Copper Country in 1840, described a July sunset at Copper
Harbor: "When the sun set last night, as it sank beneath the waters which
were a perfect calm, the reflection was like a pillar of fire, extending half across
the lake & gradually shaded away, the reflected light was most brilliant &
firey & the margin of the pillar very distinctly drawn."[13]

Geologist Jackson, describing Superior at Rock Harbor on Isle Royale in
1847, also connected water and sky:

> The color of the water, affected by the hues of the sky, and holding no sediment to dim
> its transparency, presents deeper tints than are seen on the lower lakes—deep tints of
> blue, green, and red prevailing, according to the color of the sky and clouds. I have
> seen at sunset the surface of the lake off Isle Royale of a deep claret color—a tint much
> richer than ever is reflected from the waters of other lakes.[14]

Finally, John Forster, reminiscing about camping on the Lake Superior
shore in the 1840s, presented an idyllic scene:

> We pioneer explorers . . . passed the whole season out of doors, sleeping under the blue
> canopy of the heavens, upon cedar boughs or the shingle beaches, wrapped in a single
> pair of blankets, with our boots or a piece of drift wood for a pillow. . . . The bright
> starry nights, as we reposed upon some lonely sand beach, with the waters of the great
> solemn Lake rippling at our feet, were beautiful beyond expression. The twilights were
> long, and the great Borealis arch, spanning the northern sky, sometimes turned night
> into day.[15]

Superior could be most gorgeous and congenial—especially if you merely
viewed it. Even in midsummer it was better to look at it than to be in it, or
on it. On June 28, 1840, Charles Penny "could not resist the temptation of
bathing" in the rolling surf, so he stripped off all his clothing and waded in.
The first breaker nearly took his breath away, and after three or four he "was

obliged to go on shore to breathe." As he got back his wind, Penny discovered that his skin had become "as red as a ripe cherry."[16] In August 1848, not long after arriving on the *Independence*, Horace Greeley, not believing tales that Superior was too cold to swim in, personally tested its waters: "Going alone to the headland west of Eagle Harbor, on a bright Summer noon, when a fresh northern breeze was rolling in a very fair surf, I stripped and plunged in; but was driven out as by a legion of infuriated hornets."[17]

The vast northern lake could be more than inhospitable. It could be terrifying or deadly when in storm, jeopardizing the lives of those aboard the smallest or largest vessels. Those who coasted the copper district in small boats, including canoes, particularly feared sudden storms erupting out of the blue that could overtake them before they could reach shore. Charles Jackson, who rhapsodized about the beautiful colors of Superior off Isle Royale in 1847, also experienced the wrath of the lake that same summer:

> We set out for Rock Harbor, hoping to arrive before the thunder squall, now gathering, should overtake us. In this we were defeated, for soon a most violent thunderstorm broke upon us, and forced us to betake ourselves to the first landing we could find. Hastening to the shore, we had just time to throw up our tent to cover ourselves, throw the India-rubber cloth over the provisions, when the rain began to fall in torrents. Our boat was drawn up on the shore, and made an excellent rain-gauge, collecting 150 quarts of rain in one hour.[18]

Douglass Houghton, the state geologist whose expeditions and published reports had done a great deal to fire up the copper fever that resulted in a mine rush, was not so lucky. In mid-October 1845, his party of five was trying to reach Eagle River after dark. Already heavy seas turned heavier. It started to snow. Houghton went past a sand beach where he might have landed safely in the early part of the storm, and then got caught off a rocky coast when conditions became critical. As Houghton tried to put the small craft about, it capsized. Two men made it to shore; three, including Douglass Houghton, drowned.[19]

Superior could be equally hard on the largest boats plying its waters, a fact driven home early in the history of the copper rush. In 1844, while the *John Jacob Astor* was seemingly safe at port at Copper Harbor, a September storm destroyed the ship by breaking it from its anchorage and dashing it against the rocks. The *Independence*, which delivered Horace Greeley and Ruth and C. C. Douglass to the copper district in 1848, had experienced a rough maiden voyage on Lake Superior in 1845:

> The seas got to running so high that it tossed our little steamer like a shell and rolled so heavy that the stoves broke loose from their moorings and tumbled all over the cabin, scattering fire all over the floor. When it is remembered that it was not generally known among passengers and crew that we had 50 kegs of powder aboard, it made rather lively work for us straightening things up.[20]

Superior not only threatened the lives of those aboard ships; it also threatened those on land who depended on waterborne provisions. Accidents and storms could sever the fragile lifeline of supply extending from the lower Great Lakes up to Superior, just when it was needed most to fill larders before the onslaught of winter. Late in the summer of 1851, an unfortunate sequence of groundings and collisions, involving three of the four steam-powered, propeller-driven ships on Superior, temporarily caused the loss of over half of the lake fleet's cargo-carrying capacity. When the navigation season closed in November, some eighteen thousand barrels of provisions and supplies, instead of being delivered to Upper Peninsula communities, were left stranded in warehouses lining the rapids at Sault Ste. Marie.[21]

In 1855, the last supply ship of the year bound for Ontonagon had to cut its voyage short to escape oncoming winter. It dropped Ontonagon's supplies off at Eagle Harbor, some seventy miles to the north, and beat it back to Detroit via the new Soo Locks, which had just opened at Sault Ste. Marie. This turn of events put the population of Ontonagon in a hard spot. A small local schooner sent for the supplies was wrecked in a storm. No passable overland road connected the two villages. The residents conserved on their supplies while waiting for Superior to freeze along the coast, thereby creating a smooth ice road. In January, teams driven over the ice from Ontonagon to Eagle Harbor and back finally resupplied the town.[22]

Lake Superior put its indelible stamp on the evolving history of the copper district. So did local woods. Dense forests of tall, thick trees ran virtually end to end on the Keweenaw and Isle Royale. Stands of virgin timber assured that this land did not look at all like the many other parts of America that had been cut over or farmed, or like Cornwall, where very few trees stood among the old villages and mines. The woods struck settlers as another key, defining component of the region's natural setting.

These woods were decidedly useful. They offered up game and fowl for food; logs for cabin construction; stulls for underground mine supports; and cordwood for fuel. They also offered up grandeur and inspiration. Impressive, untouched forests were a hallmark of the region in the early mining days. Ruth Douglass very much enjoyed the forest she found on Isle Royale in 1848. After one hiking expedition, she recorded in her diary on November 30: "We passed through a beautiful grove of evergreen trees consisting of Cedar, Spruce and Fir, standing very thick and having tall straight bodies with cone like tops, forming so thick a mass that the sun is unable to penetrate to the earth through them. The beauty of this lovely spot is still enhanced by the meandering of a small brook passing nearly through its center." An earlier time (October 4) she had written:

> We went out around the point of the Island and went ashore at a place where the Indians had camped. It is a lovely spot, & at this season the woods are beautiful. The frost has

changed the foliage to bright yellow and red colors, these mingled with the unchanged green of the Cedar, Spruce and Balsam, form a beautiful contrast for the eye to rest upon.

Sarah Barr Christian, who wintered on Isle Royale in 1874–75, never forgot the forest she found there:

> The mine was two and a half miles inland. A road of sorts had been cut through the tall pine trees. It was my first acquaintance with them; and though perhaps they might seem dark and forbidding to some, I loved them from the first moment, and a pine forest thrills me to this day and takes me back. . . . In memory I live often in the midst of their beauty and grandeur.[23]

Another unusual source documents that trees and woods were a defining characteristic of the region for settlers. In 1917, a teacher at Houghton High School had students talk with their parents and grandparents and then write family histories. Within these histories, the image of a wooded Keweenaw passes from older generations to a younger one:

> —"My grandmother came to this country when it was all woods."
> —"When my mother and father first moved here there were only a few houses. It was all woods."
> —"When she was fourteen years old she came over to the Copper Country. . . . The Copper Country was nothing but forest then."
> —"There was no street cars or railroads yet. Trees were everywhere."
> —"When they came to Houghton, West Houghton was not only a bush. There were many large trees. My mother thought it was very lovely to live here at first."[24]

The forests were lovely, but like Lake Superior, they had their darker side. They burdened workers who had to peel back a tangled forest floor to try to expose the upturned edge of a copper-bearing lode. In particular, dense woods, thick underbrush, and occasional swamps thwarted overland transportation and challenged the region's early road builders, who struggled to connect mine to mine, or coastal village to hinterland settlement.

An immense virgin forest lacking roads and signposts also offered settlers the opportunity to become profoundly lost. Father Frederic Baraga, a Catholic missionary, first to Native Americans in the Lake district and then to the fledgling mine villages, regularly crisscrossed the Keweenaw's terrain. One night in 1852, darkness stranded him in an unknown wood. Luckily, since it was early in September, the bishop did not suffer any ill effects of exposure, as he would have in colder months:

> I was on a mission tour in the Ontonagon Mining Region. On Sept. 8 I got lost in the woods and had to spend the night out in the open, without fire, without blankets.—It was my own fault.—Whatever you do, do prudently. I certainly know that I am not in a position to go straightway through the woods; I should always keep to the marked trail.[25]

In 1845, Charles Whittlesey walked himself around and around in a Keweenaw woods before finding the way out. He described feelings that no doubt overcame numerous pioneers who found themselves in similar straits:

> In this region, none but the oldest hunters and trappers feel safe when the compass begins to play false and the sun withdraws himself. . . . With the mind in a state of perplexity, the fatigue of travelling is greater than usual, and excessive fatigue in turn weakens not only the power of exertion, but of resolution also. The wanderer is finally overtaken with an indescribable sensation—one that must be experienced to be understood—that of *lostness*.[26]

Something else had to be experienced to be understood: sharing the woods, streams, and swamps with the swarms of insects that lived there—especially mosquitoes and blackflies. The bug, far from being of little consequence, was another important hallmark of life along Lake Superior. Summer insects were an omnipresent evil, especially early in the season. As a writer for *Harper's* magazine noted in 1853, the copper district was an unusual place: you could "be bitten by mosquitoes here *when knee-deep in the snow*."[27]

Mosquitoes, blackflies, and other insects often feasted on people, covering flesh with itchy and swelling sores that pioneers did not suffer lightly. Swarming, buzzing insects exacted a psychological toll, too, as they launched constant, unrelenting attacks, especially on heads and faces, where they got in eyes, nose, ears, mouth, and hair. Early settlers discovered that they could run, but could not always hide, from insect pests. Horace Greeley, after his very first visit to the Keweenaw in 1847, paid the local pests their due. He wrote that he encountered "denser and more ferocious clouds of mosquitoes and gnats than ever before or since presented me their bills. . . . I remember an instance in which several of us fled half a mile from their haunts to a hut, which we filled with a thick and pungent smoke, with very little abatement of their numbers or their appetite."[28]

In 1852 George McGill walked from Ontonagon to the Adventure mine. In his journal entry covering the trek, he discussed the hardships encountered while traversing a thick, tangled forest occupied by marauding insects:

> After obtaining directions . . . we started on an Indian trail. The walking alone was almost impassable. I never saw so dense a wood: it was perfectly wild; wild as the wild man ever was before a continent was discovered. The woods presented a continual mass of tall thick pines, huge cedars, and the most noble of maples. . . . There was a most rascaly set of galinippers which had an awful sting and most fearful bravery. In a short time my face was covered with bites.[29]

The diary of Cornelius Shaw, who was helping start a mine on Isle Royale in 1847, demonstrates just how far these little creatures could go in becoming bothersome, and how far they could insinuate themselves into a man's consciousness:

June 11:   "black flies troublesome"

June 13:   "face swelled from bite of sand flies"

June 16:   "went over to Bay exploring. Took canoes. . . . Sand flies outrageous.

June 18:   "black flies bad"

June 22:   "found a vein of copper . . . but was drove out of the woods by the black flies & almost blind when I got home by their bite."

June 25:   "got bit by flies so bad that I am almost blind & my face one complete sore. I would hardly be recognized by my most intimate acquaintances."

June 30:   "flies not so bad, [but] an increase of musketoes"

July 8:   "flies are leaving & musketoes take their place"[30]

The insect population declined in areas where the forest had been cleared for settlements. Still, the early mine villages were hardly bug-free. They had their complement of wild bugs, plus domestic ones, too, as Henry Hobart, the Cliff mine teacher, reported in 1863:

The mosquitoes are giving me fits . . . and when I retire the bedbugs will be more ravenous. I have killed nearly a pint of these sweet creatures before retiring. The ceiling, the bed ticks and everything in the room would be covered with them at times. O horrors, covered with the little biters, how can one sleep. This is a fine country for bedbugs, mosquitoes, black flies and Cornishmen.[31]

It was also a fine country for people fond of winter, because there was plenty of it. Charles Lanman, who in 1847 published a traveler's account of a trip to Lake Superior, noted that "the winters are very long, averaging about seven months, while spring, summer and autumn are compelled to fulfill their duties in the remaining five."[32] Lanman may have exaggerated a bit about the length of the winters—but not by much. A typical winter held tight for six months before letting go, and over that span settlers lived and worked in a very white world that was vastly different—more severe and physically and mentally more taxing—from the very green world of May through October.

Winter offered much beauty on the Keweenaw. Lake-effect snow might arrive daily, again and again blanketing everything in fresh, fluffy white. Glistening snow on a bright blue day, or large flakes gently descending on a moonlit night, offered picturesque scenes that inhabitants enjoyed. On April 1, 1872, Lucena Brockway wrote in her diary, "Sun shines today and the trees are lovely. Are loaded with ice and the sun shining on them makes them perfectly magnificent."[33] Winter presented its own amusements, too, such as skating, sledding, sleighing, snowshoeing, and snowballing. But settlers often endured too much of this good thing called winter.

The snowfall could exceed two hundred inches per year. Occasional blizzards brought life and work to a standstill. Temperatures dipped beneath freezing for months at a time, and sometimes nose-dived to far below zero. Only rarely did Lake Superior freeze over solid, but Superior's ice, plus the ice in lakes Huron, Michigan, and St. Clair and in the St. Mary's and Detroit rivers, brought water travel to and from the copper district to a total halt. Each year the Keweenaw's population was frozen out and separated from the world below for months at a time. So winter had a tremendous effect on everyday life in the copper district. It not only altered routines; it got into people's heads and drove their emotions.

Ruth Douglass enjoyed autumn on Isle Royale in 1848, but on December 8, she hardly looked forward to wintering on the island, due to the long months of cold, snow, and isolation that it promised: "It appears to me *now* that we are closely shut in for the winter. I endeavor to keep from thinking or even looking on the dark side of the picture. Did I allow myself to meditate on the situation in which we are now all placed and all the circumstances connected therewith I should be miserable enough."

Ruth surely felt this was a strange part of the world. On election day, November 7, the men on Isle Royale had not been able to vote, because the village "has not yet been incorporated" and no elections were held. Instead of casting ballots, the men "assembled in the Hall in the evening and had a little jollification. They drank to the candidates of both parties." Then Ruth ruminated: "I suppose in the region of the Magnetic Telegraph it is known ere this time who is President of these United States. I for one, think it quite doubtful whether the inhabitants of Isle Royale know who to hurrah for before next spring."

The onset of winter never went unnoticed. Lucena Brockway recorded the start of the 1866–67 winter this way in her diary: "Rained & snowed & the wind blowed & winter commenced in good earnest."[34] Ruth Douglass wrote, "I do not know but we shall be buried up in snow, I am sure we shall, if it continues in this way much longer. I never before saw the winter commence in any place as it has done here at this time." In December 1863, Henry Hobart at the Cliff mine echoed Ruth's imagery: "Everything looks snowy out: air, earth, building, forest, everything. It seems as if we should be buried up."[35]

Winter's closing of navigation was keenly felt. The population anxiously awaited the final boat of the season. Besides bringing the last supplies in, that boat would take the last people out. Cornelius Shaw, plagued by bugs on Isle Royale in the summer of 1847, had no intentions of staying on that island for the winter. He wanted off, and badly. So he watched and waited for a boat:

Oct. 7:   "finished all preparations to leave the Island"
Oct. 9:   "began [to] feel uneasy about S[team] Boat not coming. Finished up acounts with men"
Oct. 10:   "looked anxiously for boat but none came"
Oct. 11:   "no boat. No one can come here with this wind"
Oct. 12:   "commenced snowing"
Oct. 13:   "ground covered with snow. Thermometer stands at 30 at noon. . . . A dreary prospect to be on Isle Royale & no way to get off."

Oct. 15:   "no boat"

Oct. 16:   "all getting alarmed about a boat. Nearly out of Provisions & no means of getting any unless a boat arrives. I am about discouraged. Whorah, the Schooner Napolean is in."[36]

Sometimes the boat did not come in. Charlie Mott, a French Canadian, and his wife Angelique, a Chippewa Indian, were being paid to squat on a mining claim on Isle Royale in the summer of 1845. They were left off in July with short provisions—some flour, butter, and beans—and a promise that a boat would soon return with more supplies. Charlie and Angelique lost their canoe and fishing net and resorted to eating bark, roots, and berries. Their resupply boat never arrived, and a second promised boat—the one that was to take them off the island for the winter—also failed to appear.

Charlie died of starvation, and a famished Angelique later told how she was "tempted, O, how terribly I was tempted, to take Charlie and make soup of him."[37] Instead, she left his body frozen in their original shelter and kept her fire in a new primitive abode set up nearby. She survived the winter by learning how to snare rabbits, and a boat finally rescued her the next summer.

After being frozen out from the world below for so long, after enduring months of snow and cold, and after depleting their pantries, settlers eagerly anticipated spring and the reopening of navigation. They marked the progress of the long thaw that gradually unlocked the rivers and lakes, allowing ships once again to sail toward them, and they grew ever more anxious and restive until those ships came. (A local newspaper once advised, "Now don't go out and hang yourself, for navigation will open sometime this spring.")[38] Usually the earliest boats did not reach Keweenaw docks until the first or second week of May. On May 2, 1863, Henry Hobart recorded in his journal: "Yesterday was a day of great rejoicing with the people of our village. . . . We have been in a very starving condition or deprived of meat and almost everything else except bread and yesterday a boat came in at the [Eagle] River with cattle and many fresh articles from below."

Although the reopening of navigation was the most eagerly awaited sign of the end of winter and the start of spring or summer, it was not the only sign. Winter wore hard on people here, and as the snowfall diminished and the accumulated snow receded, they looked for springlike signs of rebirth and renewal. Lucena Brockway had good and bad days in the Aprils of the many years she resided on the Keweenaw. One time she wrote, "Oh! What a dismal morning for the 26th of April. The ground white with snow. Two or three inches of snow fell last night and still snowing moderately." The woman's spirits were clearly much higher on a very different April day in another year: "This is a lovely day. . . . I saw a butterfly today, the first of the season."[39]

All participants in the settling of Lake Superior—men, women, and children—took their own values, aspirations, and personalities with them. Some clambered over difficult terrain, longing to discover copper. Others searched blue skies, seeking the first butterflies of spring. Pioneers had many shared and yet many individual experiences. They did not all react the same way to the world they found on Lake Superior. Cornelius Shaw, for one, never made peace with the place called Isle Royale. He hated the bugs and was afraid of being stranded there over a long winter. On a particularly bad day in July 1847, even catching some fine trout did nothing to improve his spirits. He wrote that day in his diary: "Out of Tea, Sugar, & Molasses. Women ugly and mean."[40]

Ruth Douglass, on the other hand, did warm up to life on Lake Superior, even though she hadn't wanted to go there in the first place. Yes, it had its drawbacks, but all was not harsh or dreadful. On December 25, 1848, she recorded in her diary:

> Christmas has come with pleasant weather, and snow sufficient for good sleighing, but unfortunately for us we have neither roads nor teams. The contrast in the manner of our spending the day is quite different from last Christmas Day, then among our friends at Ann Arbor. Now, on a remote and lonely island, but I forbear to repine. We are happy here, even in this solitude.

Alexis de Tocqueville, that famous French traveler and keen observer of society, on his tour of America in 1831–32, made it out to the Great Lakes, but not quite as far as the Keweenaw Peninsula. Still, he saw some impressive "wild, open spaces" in this country, and he noted how Americans thought about them. Americans did not dwell on the wonders of nature. They did not give nature a lot of thought, or truly "see the marvelous forests surrounding them until they [began] to fall beneath the ax." He continued:

> The American people see themselves marching through wildernesses, drying up marshes, diverting rivers, peopling the wilds, and subduing nature. It is not just occasionally that their imagination catches a glimpse of this magnificent vision. It is something which plays a real part in the least, as in the most important, actions of every man, and it is always flitting before his mind.[41]

In the mid-nineteenth century, the Keweenaw Peninsula was one of many wildernesses that Americans marched through—accompanied, of course, by many new immigrants from other lands. They did not go out just to see the Keweenaw. They did not go out, after the fashion of trappers, hunters, fishermen, or explorers, just to use a tiny fraction of its bounty, while leaving the rest largely untouched. They went out to transform it, to people this wilderness for the purpose of mining copper.

Alfred Swineford captured this transformation when he wrote "then" and "now" descriptions of Portage Lake. He first saw that body of water in October 1846:

> The scenery bordering the lake was exceedingly beautiful. . . . Our cheerful Canadian boatmen, singing as they rowed, would often rest upon their oars in order to enjoy the quiet, brilliant panorama. The native forests in primitive grandeur, starting at the water's edge, slope up precipitously toward the sky, presenting a great variety of pleasing shades and colors.

Then he offered up this very different scene:

> Today—1875—the reverse of this picture is presented. . . . The busy, picturesquely situated villages of Houghton and Hancock . . . ; the giant stamp mills, which make the earth tremble with the heavy thud of ponderous hammers; the air dark with smoke, and the water discolored with rejected sand and slime . . . ; the fiery furnaces of the copper smelting works . . . ; the numerous manufactories, with their noisy rattling and banging; the fleet of steam and sail vessels . . . ; and latest innovation of all, there goes rushing up the hill-side a locomotive with a train of cars—all of these things . . . go to make up a picture characteristic of this age of progress.[42]

After the mine rush to the Keweenaw began in 1843, many newcomers to the place were taken by its beauty. But no romantic appreciation of nature checked or altered the work of industrialization. The wealthiest stockholders and the most humble miners thought that the copper existed to be exploited— to be wrested from the earth, milled, smelted, sold, often alloyed to form brass or bronze, and finally fabricated into pots and pans, machinery bearings, sheathing for ships' hulls, hardware, buttons, candlesticks, sheet roofing, or even cannon. And just like the copper, the rest of the Keweenaw's natural environment existed to be used. Swineford's "age of progress" demanded that settlers beat back the wilderness as best they could, without hesitation or reflection, wherever needed: drill and blast the earth; chop down forests and burn out the undergrowth; populate the shores of natural harbors; fill inland lakes with waste tailings and skies with wood and coal smoke.

The Keweenaw Peninsula and Isle Royale were, at midcentury, part of the American West—but they were an unusual part and made for an unusual frontier. This was not a frontier of free or highly accessible land taken up by common folk. Nor was it a frontier of farmers or cattlemen, of plows or barbed wire, of six-guns or rugged individuals. Instead, it was a frontier dominated by mining corporations, who bought up and dominated the land; of working-class men and women who did the hard work that needed doing; and of the merchants, professionals, and others who came to trade with and service the mining population.

Even under the assault of well-capitalized mining firms wielding hundreds, then thousands, of men wielding explosives and steam engines, the Keweenaw wilderness proved no easy place to settle or subdue.[43] Its remote location and its extremely long and harsh winters prolonged its frontier or pioneer era and slowed Lake Superior's transformation from an unsettled to a settled state.

Historically, the frontier can be interpreted as a place of transition between wilderness and full settlement. Through the first part of the nineteenth century, the American frontier could generally be drawn as a line representing the extent of the country's westward expansion. This frontier line had the wilderness to the west of it and settlement or civilization to the east—and not too far away. But in the 1840s, the settlement of the American frontier changed.[44] Pioneers started leapfrogging over places they didn't want to settle, in order to get to other places. That is what happened with the Keweenaw. Explorers, geologists, miners, entrepreneurs, and others jumped over hundreds of miles of upper Great Lakes wilderness to get there. The Keweenaw was not on any frontier line. It was not on the boundary between wilderness and civilization; it was *beyond the boundary*. It was a node of settlement surrounded by wilderness and water and, because of cold, icy winters, locked out from the world below for nearly half a year at a time.

It was a special place indeed—and no easy place to mine. No amount of human ambition, determination, capital, or technology guaranteed a winner in this "subterranean lottery" of copper mining. The copper was widely disseminated along the mineral range, and surface or shallow finds of copper ignited enthusiasm and optimism in location after location. But in relatively few spots was the copper sufficiently concentrated underground to support profitable mining. Consequently, even though the region quickly became the producer of 75 to even 90 percent of the nation's new copper, among its mining ventures the failures outnumbered the successes by a wide margin.

From the 1840s through the end of the Civil War, some ninety-four incorporated mining firms tried to exploit Keweenaw copper, and many firms attempted mining at more than one location. Two-thirds of these companies achieved little or no production at all, and only eight paid any dividends. A capital investment of $25 million in the mines yielded a return of only $5.6 million, so the nascent industry in the wilderness consumed over four times more money than it paid out.[45]

As money was being made and lost, men repeated essentially the same frontier experience of discovery, exploration, and settlement at place after place, decade after decade. They went, in small numbers, out into the woods to open mines. They cut primitive trails or roads and erected basic shelters. They swept away the forest, trenched the ground to crosscut lodes, dug test pits, then extended them as shafts blasted into solid rock. If the company ran short of copper and capital, the works shut down and the men left. But if they found a paying lode, a camp evolved into a community. More men came, then women and children, then churches, schools, shops, and other trappings of civilization.

After three decades of settlement and mining, some parts of the Keweenaw—those distant from the copper deposits—still appeared virtually unto-uched, save, perhaps, for a trail or primitive road passing through. The landscape in places remained a wild one of trees, rocky crags, swamps, or shorelines. In other places, nature busily reclaimed abandoned mine locations: shafts filled with water, cleared fields began to reforest, and empty shelters weathered and decayed, finally collapsing one winter under a heavy snow load. But along select stretches of shoreline, and in select pockets scattered along the mineral range, many well-established settlements (including several with populations of 1,000 to 3,000 persons) went about the business of commerce, industry, and life.

Only a few hundred Native Americans occupied the Keweenaw in the early 1840s. Then came Yankees, Cornishmen, Irishmen, French Canadians, and Germans to settle on an emergent frontier. By 1850, 1,100 pioneers lived on the Keweenaw and Isle Royale. The population rose quite steeply, reaching 14,000 by 1860, 21,000 by 1870, and 27,000 by 1874. This population increase followed the growth of the mining industry. Keweenaw copper production rose from 27,000 pounds in 1845 to nearly 6 million pounds in 1855, 15 million pounds in 1865, and 36 million pounds in 1875.[46]

In the course of exploiting copper and transforming a Lake Superior wil-derness into the home of a new, industrial society, settlers also transformed their individual lives. On moving to Lake Superior, they discovered that their lives first became more difficult, primitive, and fragile. Then, as wilderness conditions receded, human society became more secure and substantial. Life and landscape were transformed together by the arrival of mining towns, com-mercial villages, and women and children; by the arrival of houses, hotels, churches, schools, breweries, saloons, steam boilers, stores, hospitals, harbors, canals, lighthouses, wagon roads, and railroads. After providing the essentials of life on Lake Superior, society continued to march along by providing the frills, too, such as jewelry stores and millinery shops, and even carnivals and circuses.

The history of settling this frontier is a complex one of hard-fought change and adaptation. It is not easy to explain just when and why the pioneers' sense of living on the edge was replaced with a sense of greater well-being, comfort, and security.[47] Hundreds of little changes in everyday life on Lake Superior carried this transformation along, and the agents of change, the transformers of life and landscape, were many. Capitalists and mining companies played a key role. Government—federal, state, and local—played a role. American industrialization, which produced needed and desirable goods, and the new market economy, which distributed and delivered those goods, accelerated the winning of this frontier. So did the arrival of numerous professionals, small businessmen, and tradesmen. And, of course, "ordinary" settlers, men and women, did much for themselves, in terms of forming the familial and social institutions that encouraged civility and sustained, protected, and enhanced life along the copper range. After moving out to this new region and establishing a new life, many settlers reached back to retrieve the things and traditions they had known in the world below and had come to miss on Lake Superior.

TWO

HEAVING UP JONAH
The Travail of Travel

Several companies are this morning trying to organize to cut a road or path [from Copper Harbor] to the high lands. Small parties have tried to make the hills but have failed in consequence of the white-cedar swamps they had to encounter. . . . Not only the low lands, but the highest mountains are so densely covered with all the different species of pine, laurel, etc., that a single man cannot penetrate the country without a hatchet to cut the limbs from the trees.

H. Messersmith, letter,
June 24, 1843

People, possessions, provisions—all had to be transported up to the Keweenaw Peninsula and then distributed to the new settlements dedicated to copper mining. Besides the small stuff of life, early settlers moved in the tools of mining: explosives, sledgehammers, drill steels, wheelbarrows, wagons, and even steam engines and boilers. Then, of course, they also had to move out the object of their efforts: the copper.

At first, no portion of any journey was easy: not the water part and, especially, not the overland part. A region so laced with swamps and dense forests that it blocked the path of lone travelers on foot could not be expected to easily yield up tons and tons of copper to distant markets. Internal improvements to water and overland transportation—undertaken over several decades by various levels of government, by the mining companies themselves, and by other entrepreneurs—supported the growth of a new industry, while benefiting settlers in their everyday lives.

George Cannon was one of those who experienced the travail of early travel to and through the Keweenaw Peninsula. December 30, 1846—George's twentieth birthday—found him "frozen out" from the world below and squatting on a mining claim on the southern end of the mineral range, near the west branch of the Ontonagon River. As the "long and weary winter" wore on, four feet of snow on the ground and temperatures dipping to −27 degrees bound him tightly to his rude cabin in the woods. His winter surely contrasted sharply with his spring, summer, and fall, spent almost constantly on the move as an employee of the newly incorporated American Exploring and Mining Company.[1] This company, bigger and better capitalized than most participants in the copper rush, put about sixty men, divided into seven wide-ranging exploring parties, up on Lake Superior for the 1846 summer season.

Young George Cannon didn't suffer copper fever, and he didn't join the copper rush with any dreams of striking it rich. He simply needed a job, so he signed up with American Exploring. He'd go where they told him to go and do what they told him to do, all the while hoping they'd make good on his promised pay. The need for work that took him north in May kept him there throughout the winter, after all but a half dozen of his fellow explorers had returned south.

Like Ruth and C. C. Douglass's trip up to Isle Royale, George Cannon's voyage to Lake Superior started on a steamer at Detroit. On May 4 he boarded the *Ben Franklin*, and when it headed north, George watched with a "peculiar feeling" as the last vestiges of Detroit disappeared and "with it, Friends and Civilization." This young man was a novice explorer; so were most of the others in his party. They were "not much used to the woods, many having seldom, if ever, camped out or pitched a tent." Now they found themselves bound for the wilderness, where they would lead an uncertain life for months, "perhaps attended with peril and danger." George, apprehensive about his journey, took considerable comfort in knowing that Mr. Meriaw, a French Canadian, was aboard ship. This old voyageur had spent many years "in border life or in the wilderness," so he would show others how to cope with hardships and privation.

The two-day voyage from Detroit to Sault Ste. Marie was supposed to be the easy leg of the trip north and west to the copper fields, and it proved uneventful. The steamer passed up the Detroit River into Lake St. Clair, where George Cannon admired islands covered with green grass, "sporting immense numbers of Ducks and other wild fowl." Several schooners lay at anchor, while men in small boats skirted the islands, shooting game. It was foggy and rainy when the *Ben Franklin* steamed into Lake Huron; later, even when it cleared, George could see no land, because the boat was so far out.

The boat took on a load of wood to fire its steam boilers at Presque Isle, then continued on to the Montreal Channel. This passage—rock-strewn, narrow, dangerous, and dotted with small islands—was best navigated during the day. George leaned at the rail, studied the scattered wigwams on the island beaches, and watched "the Red Man in his bark Canoe . . . busily engaged with his seine and fish pole in securing the white fish for sustenance." Early in the afternoon, the *Ben Franklin* left the Montreal Channel and entered Mud Lake, which led to the entrance to the St. Mary's River. At 4:00 P.M., the boat docked at the Soo.

George Cannon and his exploring party stayed four days at Sault Ste. Marie. It was a busy place: "Hundreds of Persons were arriving in every Boat, destined for the Mineral Region." Thirty or forty tents were pitched at the head of the rapids, including several large ones that sheltered Cannon's party, and men constantly wheeled baggage across the portage. Cannon and his new friends slept on pallets of hemlock bows, cooked over open fires, ate sitting cross-legged on the ground, and enjoyed the local color of an outpost that still reflected its fur-trading heritage.

The Canadian side of the Soo had its British fort and the Hudson Bay Company's fur-trading station; the American side had its fort and the American Fur Company. Most dwellings were either log structures sided with broad strips of cedar bark or wigwams. The inhabitants were mostly French Canadians, American Indians, "half-breeds," and other "refugees of civilization," as Cannon called them. The Native Americans regularly fished the rapids, while woodsmen in nearby forests chopped wood for refueling boats. And voyageurs, who either still traded furs or now guided miners instead, "kept up a continual frolic of carousing and drinking."

Because of a dearth of large ships on Lake Superior, many travelers had to ship out of the Soo for the Keweenaw on Mackinaw boats or bateaux, or even in canoes. These small boats had already seen service in the fur trading and fishing industries. A Mackinaw boat was a small, two-masted sailing vessel, pointed both fore and aft, with a rounded hull, centerboard, and tiller. About thirty-five feet long and eight feet across at the beam, a Mackinaw boat was big enough to take out on Lake Superior with some confidence, yet small enough to run up on a beach when it came time to set camp for the night. The bateau was a heavier, flat-bottomed boat, about six feet across at the beam and forty feet long. Equipped with oars, setting poles, and sometimes a mast and sail, and crewed by four or five voyagers, a bateau could carry three to five tons of gear across Superior and up into the streams and rivers running into the great lake.[2]

For his first time out on Lake Superior, George Cannon was fortunate to gain passage on a bigger boat. The American Exploring Company chartered the schooner *Fur Trader* to carry its crew westward across Superior. The schooner left on May 10, but strong head winds beat it back toward the Soo, and the travelers spent a couple of blustery days in their tents again, as they were put ashore just six miles up from the rapids. They needed blazing fires to keep warm; on May 12 the water kept in camp froze at night.

The *Fur Trader* got underway again on the night of May 13 and enjoyed calm, pleasant sailing for a bit as it left Whitefish Bay and entered Superior. Then the great lake grew cantankerous and kicked up a storm at sundown on May 15. It "blew in a perfect gale and continued until near morning." The crew took in the sails, yet Cannon guessed the ship still "sped away at the rate of ten knots the hour, under bare poles." Earlier, the inexperienced explorer had fretted over what life would be like in the wilderness. Now life on the water gave him pause:

> A majority of the crew were sea-sick, and, as they expressed it, "heaving up Jonah" during the night. I went on Deck; the Schooner was pitching and rolling about at the mercy of the waves, and nearly every swell would wash over the deck. . . . Our Boat seemed to labor with the heavy swells, and her timbers writhed and cracked as she rode over and between them, and considerable water came into the hold.[3]

The *Fur Trader* weathered this storm and continued westward along Lake Superior's south shore. It dropped one exploring party off near the mouth of the Huron River, passed within sight of the "high knobs of Point Keweenaw," sailed south into Keweenaw Bay, and on May 17 anchored near the Methodist Mission at L'Anse. The missionaries had gotten to this part of the world even before the miners. At the bottom of Keweenaw Bay, the Catholic Mission, "with its numerous cabins and Chapel," stood on one side of the water, while the Methodists held the Protestant beachhead on the opposite shore. At L'Anse, Cannon went to listen to the resident minister, Reverend Pitezel, who was happy to address a white congregation for the first time in three years, "since he had left the scenes of civilization."

Going from the Soo to L'Anse, the *Fur Trader* had coasted almost three hundred miles of shoreline. At sundown on May 18, the schooner set sail for Point Keweenaw, almost one hundred miles distant. While heading north in Keweenaw Bay, the ship was sheltered by the rise of the peninsula on its port side. But as soon as it rounded Point Keweenaw, the schooner exposed itself to rough water and had to beat against another blast-in-the-face gale. Another schooner, running with the wind, shot by the *Fur Trader* with the "speed of an arrow." By the time Cannon's boat reached safety at Copper Harbor, nearly all its human cargo had "heaved up Jonah" once again.

For many during the early years of the mine rush, Copper Harbor was a favorite destination. But the American Exploring and Mining Company expedition had other destinations in mind, both on and off the Keweenaw. George Cannon's party, for instance, was bound first for the north shore of Lake Superior (in present-day Minnesota); later it would work its way back to the Keweenaw. So at sunset on May 20, the *Fur Trader* set out "again on the broad bosom of this inland see, plowing the water for Pigeon River." It sailed past Isle Royale, pulled along Superior's north shore, and started landing exploring parties, including George Cannon's. On May 23, his party landed about ten to fifteen miles southwest of the Pigeon, the boundary line between British America and the United States.

Cannon had seen his last sizable boat for some time. Over the next month, his exploring party coasted down the north shore of Superior to Fond du Lac, then came back eastward along the south shore until reaching the base of the Keweenaw and the mouth of the Ontonagon River. Along the way, they rowed and sailed their small bateau—later joined by a Mackinaw boat—from point to point along the shore, guided by voyageurs who helped pull the oars. Often, they spent a beautiful day out on the lake under blue skies, with warm temperatures and favorable winds. But occasional squalls and thunderstorms kicked up rough seas, threatened to swamp the explorers' boats, and chased them to shore.

Only really threatening weather kept the men on the beaches. If a long day's journey lay ahead, regardless of any fog or rain, they set off well before dawn and rowed eight to twelve miles before putting ashore for breakfast. Late in the afternoon or early in the evening, they went ashore again to set up camp, often choosing a spot that evidenced previous Native American occupation. Along this part of Superior, even the well-traveled voyageurs often found themselves at an island or river mouth with no name, so the crew provided one before heading off.

Ashore, they encounted a few Ojibwa and sometimes traded salt pork and flour for fresh fish and rabbit. George Cannon, so very new to these parts, initially feared the Ojibwa but soon realized they posed no threat. As he and his partners hiked up streams and rivers in search of valuable mineral deposits, their biggest enemy in the northern woods was no man, but the ubiquitous blackfly. Swarming insects, thick underbrush, fallen trees, steep ascents, strong May–June currents, and waterfalls made Cannon's exploratory hikes very damp and difficult adventures. Heading up the river valleys, the men fought for every mile of penetration. Rather than hacking their way through dense vegetation, they often walked right up the stream itself, in water one to four feet deep. In late May and early June this water was decidedly cold. Alongside the streams, in places of deep shade, the men still found crusted mounds of the last of winter's snow, and as late as June 12 they awoke to find the ground white with frost.

Setting off on these hard upstream marches, the men traveled as light as they could, leaving such niceties as tents behind. Still, they packed in their blankets, food for a half-dozen men for a week, and their camp kettle and utensils. Despite all the energy and effort expended, the men found nothing of note in their month of coasting and hiking. On June 25 they arrived at the mouth of the Ontonagon River, where they could expect better results, since this was the neighborhood of the famed Ontonagon Boulder. The voyageurs, having safely guided their party across open water for so long, celebrated their arrival at the Ontonagon by getting extremely drunk. The next morning, when the exploring party started rowing its bateau upriver, the voyageurs, still drunk and "totally unfit for duty," were "stowed away among the useless articles of the boat."

Because overland travel carrying packs was so arduous and slow, the explorers stuck with river travel as long as they could when pushing into the Keweenaw's interior. They rowed up to the first rapids, then started poling their supply-laden bateau. Where the river was too strewn with boulders, the men jumped overboard to lift the boat over obstacles. They encamped and beached their boat only after it had taken them as far upriver as possible.

Still they eschewed hiking. They went into the forest and collected wood and birch bark and spent two or three days making canoes. These smaller boats, with smaller loads, allowed them to negotiate rapids and boulders and paddle another eight or ten miles up the west branch of the Ontonagon. Cannon and others then set up base camps from which to launch overland explorations in different directions. Meanwhile, the voyageurs used the canoes to course up and down the river, resupplying the camps from a cache of provisions left downstream.

Traversing the Keweenaw's southern region on foot was hard going. At eight in the morning on July 15, George Cannon headed out on a not unusual trek:

> The route was difficult to travel, passing over clay hills, through deep ravines, and occasionally over many windfalls of fallen timber. On the sides of the clay hills were thick groves of the white birch, cedar, and balsam of fir. So dense they grew, and so close together, that we were frequently obliged to chop our way through them, which served to hinder our progress, encumbered as we were with packs and the various materials of the camp. Making but eight miles, we encamped for the night by the side of a ravine, that afforded water, an indispensible article in the wilderness on a warm day.[4]

Twelve days later, George Cannon embarked on a not-so-typical excursion through the woods:

> The sun shone warm, and the day was pleasant, which served to dispel, in part, the gloomy appearance of the thickets, ravines, and swamps through which the trail led. . . . I proceeded musingly and quietly along, and let my thoughts wander to the south [his home below] and to other scenes, proceeding thus slowly along when, crossing a ravine and climbing over a log, I was suddenly aroused from my reverie at the appearance of a large, brown-nosed bear, no more than one rod distant . . . , and she immediately came at me, jumping along sideways.[5]

Cannon whacked the female bear with his pack, and when she paused briefly to bite it, he scurried up a tree and prepared to defend his perch with a hatchet. But when her cub scuttled down from another tree, the mother bear rambled off with it, abandoning the field of battle, so that George could continue his journey.

The American Exploring and Mining Company's expedition to the Ontonagon River region collected some interesting specimens, including a piece of copper discovered on the surface that weighed over a hundred pounds. The men found outcropping lodes of possible interest and staked out five new mine locations. George Cannon and several other employees wanted to return home at the end of the summer exploration season, but they also wanted work. So they braved the elements, endured isolation, and squatted on the company's claims over the winter of 1846–47. After that winter, George Cannon didn't stick with copper mining. He left the Keweenaw and fashioned a fine career for himself as a surveyor elsewhere. In the 1850s, the American Exploring Company pressed ahead and developed the Norwich and other mines it first staked out in 1846.[6] But none of them ever proved profitable. They were among the many mines on the Keweenaw known for consuming wealth rather than producing it.

Other early travelers to the Keweenaw and Isle Royale related experiences much like those of George Cannon. They took a big lake boat from Detroit to Sault Ste. Marie, where the rapids forced a portage, a delay, and a reboarding, often onto a much smaller vessel, guided, sailed, or rowed by voyageurs. Once at the Keweenaw, travelers found many good natural harbors along the coast, but few navigable water routes leading into the hinterland toward the mineral range. So they left the water and took to land, where hills, forests, thickets, and swamps all conspired to slow forward progress to a crawl.

Charles Whittlesey got to the Keweenaw even before George Cannon. He recounted that in 1845, "the country was filled with explorers & speculators swarming through the woods along the mineral range." Whittlesey estimated that ten thousand went up to Lake Superior that season (and nearly all returned south again, before winter). Because there were "no steamboats & and but few sailing vessels . . . , a large portion arrived by canoes, skiffs & Mackinaw boats from the Sault Ste. Marys, coasting along the shore."[7] Because much of that shore was uncharted and unlighted, and because Lake Superior could storm suddenly and violently, waterborne travelers were advised to secure the services of voyageurs.

Voyageurs, who first learned their skills in the fur trading business, played key roles in the Keweenaw mine rush of the 1840s and remained important through the 1850s. They commanded the small watercraft that plied Lake Superior, and on reaching land they helped settlers find their way through the woods and packed provisions on their backs.

Yankees often denigrated the voyageurs' race or ethnicity. They described them as only partly civilized "half-breeds"—by birth often half French Canadian, "and half Indian, but in habit, manners and education, a full-blooded Indian." Observers of voyageurs' behavior frequently condemned their rude and unruly ways, their coarse language, and, especially, their penchant for getting roaring drunk while at rest in some port or camp. Yet at the same time, the voyageurs earned sincere respect.[8] They had "strong arms and backs." John Forster, an early settler, fondly remembered "Old Edward," once of the Hudson Bay Company, "who was the most muscular Frenchman I ever met. At the age of ninety he could lift from the ground a barrel of whiskey with ease. He could swallow the contents in detail with no greater effort."[9] Hard-working voyageurs were content with their lot. They loved to sing while rowing and stopped at regular intervals to pull on their pipes. They were unflappable in the face of danger: "it is a singular fact that when most troubled, or when enduring the severest hardships, they will joke, laugh, and sing their uncouth songs."[10] A visitor to Lake Superior in 1846 penned an enthusiastic endorsement of the voyageur and gave him high status in the folklore of settling Superior:

> In coasting, it is necessary to have at least one good "voyageur," ... who will most probably be a Frenchman or a half-breed, who understands the coast and weather-signs,—superintends the unloading and camping—interprets—knows where fish may be taken—the proper places for landing, and whose counsels—as to whatever implicates safety or convenience, must be followed. . . .
>
> You may go the whole voyage, even repeat it, without an occasion presenting itself for the Indian to exhibit what he really is; but if one should come, in which he is required to put forth his powers of judgment, skill, or endurance, to preserve the safety of one committed to his charge,—then, and only then, can the true character,—the endurance and self-devotion of those hardy and honest hearted *voyageurs* be truly known. Gay and mirthful by nature and habit,—patient and enduring at labor,—seeking neither care nor wealth . . . , such are the "voyageurs" of the lakes, a distinct and different people from all others upon the globe.[11]

The voyageurs continued to coast around the Keweenaw carrying passengers and provisions from point to point throughout the 1850s, but out on the long reach of Superior from Sault Ste. Marie to Copper Harbor and back again, the copper region's transportation demands quickly outstripped the voyageurs' bateaux, Mackinaw boats, and canoes. The region desperately needed to put large boats out on the large lake.

Prior to 1830, when the fur industry was in a more flourishing condition, at least five schooners of 20 to 100 tons burden sailed as traders on Lake Superior. That number dwindled to zero by the mid-1830s, but in 1835 the American Fur Company built and floated the 110-ton brig *John Jacob Astor* above the Soo rapids, and in 1840 the 50-ton schooner *Algonquin* started Lake Superior service. In May 1842, a year before the copper rush began, the *Algonquin* may have been the first American ship of real size to sail into Copper Harbor. Until then, that rocky stretch of Keweenaw shoreline had always been given a wide berth, because even the "hardiest sailors" looked upon it "with dread."[12]

This time, loaded with barrels of salted fish taken at Isle Royale, the *Algonquin* stopped at Copper Harbor to land a small crew, who were to summer there and test its waters as a commercial fishing site. The landing, undertaken in stormy seas, required a near act of faith—faith in the accuracy of a survey of the harbor made under the direction of Douglass Houghton in 1840. Faith in their ability to reconcile what they saw on the coast with what they saw on the published survey. Faith in their ability, despite crashing seas, to pass safely through an "unknown and narrow opening in the rocks." It was no time for timidity. The schooner "stood boldly in between the breakers to the west of the middle rocks." Then it passed the reef, and suddenly "the harbor opened out on each hand as by enchantment."[13]

A year later, in May 1843, the *Algonquin* entered Copper Harbor again, this time delivering its first party of mining adventurers. A month later, it brought in more miners, plus General Cunningham, who had orders to establish Fort Wilkins, and the federal land agent, who would handle mining claims. As the copper rush started, only two boats of any size—the *Algonquin* and the *John Jacob Astor*—worked the lake. In 1844, an officer at Fort Wilkins called these vessels "our sole dependencies"; his small garrison absolutely depended on them for supplies. The *Astor* first anchored at Copper Harbor in May 1844, and in September it broke up on the rocks there in a storm. The wreck caused anxious moments and provisioning problems for the new mining companies and for the Army: "The Brig was our main dependence and it is doubtful whether the Schooner can bring up our beef cattle. None of our winter's supply have yet arrived and we have but one ox on hand. It will also be observed that we are also deficient in flour, out of beans, and not sufficient pork to carry us through the winter."[14]

The successful establishment of permanent, year-round settlements along the mineral range demanded a greatly increased shipping capacity. A substantial number of new links were added to the Keweenaw's supply chain in 1845, when six schooners, with burdens of 20 to 90 tons, were sailed to the Soo, portaged around the rapids, and put onto Lake Superior. In 1846, the propeller *Independence* first plied the lake, as did a 240-ton side-wheeler steamboat, the *Julia Palmer*. More ships were portaged at Sault Ste. Marie, but in the early 1850s the waterborne lifeline to the Keweenaw copper district—and to the newly opened Marquette iron range in the Upper Peninsula—remained tenuous.[15]

For many sailing to and from the Keweenaw, the portage at Sault Ste. Marie had been a pleasant diversion. While getting their land legs back, visitors observed the behavior of the local Native Americans and the colorful voyageurs. During a two-day stopover in 1852, Edwin Henwood "saw about two hundred Indians decked in feathers and war-paint, doing a war-dance"—a scene he remembered for the rest of his long life. Some took the opportunity to fish, and many men and women felt duty bound to take a thrill ride down the rapids in a birch-bark canoe.[16]

But entertaining as they might be, the rapids blocked trade and travel. They slowed shipments down and drove the prices of provisions up, due to portage charges. Also, shipping charges on Lake Superior remained high, as long as the rapids limited competition by restricting the number of boats reaching that lake. Early in the 1850s, a short rail line built alongside the rapids sped up the portage business and helped alleviate the bottleneck. Still, a canal with locks was needed to bypass the rapids and allow ships, people, goods, and copper and iron to pass with little interruption between Superior and the other Great Lakes. Such a canal had been proposed as early as 1837—as soon as Michigan became a state. The St. Mary's Falls Ship Canal was finally built in the mid-1850s, with much support from state and federal governments.

Government had already done many things to facilitate the rise of a copper industry on Lake Superior. Both state and federal governments had sponsored explorations of the mineral range that collected and disseminated information regarding its copper. Under the guise of exploring military defenses or settling differences between Indian tribes, the federal government sponsored wide-ranging scientific explorations of this corner of the American West, which included geological surveys. In 1820 Michigan's territorial governor, Lewis Cass, headed an expedition to Lake Superior sponsored by John C. Calhoun, the secretary of war. Henry Rowe Schoolcraft—mineralogist, Indian expert, and author—accompanied Cass, and in 1831 and 1832, Schoolcraft returned to the copper range with his own explorations, again sponsored by the U.S. War Department.[17]

Douglass Houghton participated in the Schoolcraft expeditions and explored the Keweenaw in 1831 and 1832. In 1840, as Michigan's first state geologist, Houghton conducted his own state-sponsored survey of the copper district. Houghton's study of the copper deposits was cut short by his drowning in Lake Superior in 1845, but a few years later the federal government initiated a survey of the Keweenaw that resulted in an authoritative account of its geology authored by John W. Foster and Josiah D. Whitney.[18]

Besides sponsoring surveys and expeditions, the federal government concluded the Treaty of LaPointe with the Ojibwa in 1843, giving the United States possession of the mineral-rich lands. The federal government built Fort Wilkins, providing a military presence on the frontier, and gave Michigan a contract to conduct a linear survey of the region that subdivided the land into measured units. The federal government then established a land office that first leased and later sold mineral lands to those wishing to participate in the copper rush. In writing of the "pioneers of Lake Superior," Charles Whittlesey noted, "From 1843 to 1847 the government had an army of officers, agents & surveyors in the country to look after the rents & profits & to define the locations, which had now reached the number of about 800, none of them less than a mile square."[19]

The federal government also assisted those wanting smooth sailing into the copper district's new ports of call. In 1849 the U.S. Lighthouse Establishment, recognizing the importance of providing navigational aids to ships approaching and leaving the Keweenaw and Isle Royale, started erecting lighthouses in the region.[20] The first went up at Copper Harbor; by the end of the 1850s other lights shone their beacons to sailors at Eagle Harbor, Ontonagon, Eagle River, Manitou Island (off the Keweenaw's tip), and Isle Royale's Rock Harbor.

Government, then, was not an inactive, laissez-faire agent that merely watched events and industry unfold on Lake Superior. In some ways, government actively supported the region's settlement and industrial development. Especially at the federal level, however, this government support sometimes came after considerable delay and debate. The copper mines were launched during an era when politicians disputed the federal government's proper role in fostering "internal improvements" such as canals and roads. Fiscal conservatism, constitutional debates, and sectional rivalries turned needed public works projects into controversial issues. This was the case with the canal and locks at Sault Ste. Marie. After Michigan became a state, it took a decade and a half for the federal government to commit to this internal improvement.

Until the copper industry (and then an iron industry, too) was up and running on Lake Superior, a canal at Sault Ste. Marie was a hard sell in Washington. Henry Clay, generally a strong supporter of federally sponsored internal improvements—especially those that benefited the West—first balked at this one. In 1840 he described the proposed canal and locks as "a work beyond the remotest settlement of the United States, if not the moon."[21] By the early 1850s the project seemed more necessary and important, and the U.S. Congress passed "An Act Granting to the State of Michigan the Right of Way, and a Donation of Public Land for the Construction of a Ship Canal around the Falls of St. Mary's River." The federal land grant to the state, which the state later transferred to the canal's builder as payment for the work, amounted to 750,000 acres, or about 2 percent of Michigan's total land area.

In 1853 the Michigan legislature passed its own canal bill, which specified that the locks be 350 feet long and 70 feet wide and which set up a five-member commission to oversee construction of the waterway. The commissioners evaluated eight contract bids, and in the spring of 1853 awarded the project to the "St. Mary's Falls Ship Canal Company," a firm charted in New York expressly for the purpose of building the canal and "taking, holding, improving, selling, and conveying the . . . lands as granted."[22]

The company did not have an easy go of it in finishing this project. On-site supervision initially proved poor. Inadequate stone and timber in the immediate area necessitated acquiring supplies from distant sources, which had to be shipped to the site using twenty-five schooners, six barges, and four steam tugs. Cold, freezing weather shortened the construction season on both ends, in spring and in fall. A cholera epidemic broke out. Laborers made liberal use of alcohol; they also struck for higher wages. These problems resulted in a substantial cost overrun, and as the canal company was running out of capital, it petitioned Michigan for an early granting of lands that could be sold to fund completion of the work. After 320,595 man-days of labor and an expediture of nearly $900,000, the canal locked through its first ship on June 18, 1855.[23]

On the Keweenaw, mining firms usually did not rely on government to solve transportation problems; they eliminated many early bottlenecks themselves. On the northern end of the Keweenaw, mining companies shared an interest in a corporation that cut a deeper shipping channel from Keweenaw Bay into Lac La Belle, making that interior lake a better, more useful harbor. To the south, a new harbor was built at Ontonagon.[24] Most important, at the center of the Keweenaw, the mines and commercial interests there took measures to improve the navigability of Portage River running from Keweenaw Bay to Portage Lake.

Through the 1850s, the larger boats plying Lake Superior with cargo bound for Houghton or Hancock could not get there. At the juncture of Portage River and Keweenaw Bay, a sandbar and a meandering, shallow channel blocked their way. Machinery and provisions bound for the mines had to be taken off the lake boats and put on lighters to go up to Portage Lake. This transfer tacked on an additional shipping charge of about four dollars per ton for all goods docked at Houghton-Hancock.[25]

Sometimes lighters weren't available along Portage River. In 1854, the Albion Mining Company, erecting a stamp mill at Portage Lake, awaited receipt of two heavy steam boilers. The ship that brought them from the Soo to Keweenaw Bay could go no further, and no boat big enough to handle the boilers but small enough to negotiate Portage River was available. So men plugged all openings in the boilers, launched them overboard, roped them together, bolted planks across from one to the next, and raised a sail. In short, they created a "boiler catamaran," and with the help of a Mackinaw boat providing a tow, the strange iron "vessel" sailed fifteen miles up Portage River and Portage Lake to Houghton, where cattle-power dragged it ashore.[26]

The discovery of copper near Portage Lake encouraged mining companies and local merchants to organize the Portage River Improvement Company in 1859. That company (whose work was continued by a successor company formed in the early 1860s) removed the sandbar at the entrance to the river; improved the first three miles of the river by cutting a channel one hundred feet wide and twelve feet deep; dredged to an eleven-foot depth the rest of the waterway running to Houghton and Hancock; and collected tolls from ships using the channel, which were used to maintain and improve it.[27]

Late in the shipping season of 1860, the steamer *Illinois*, laden with four hundred tons of freight and drawing ten and a half feet of water, sailed up

Portage River into Portage Lake and docked at Houghton. This inaugurated a new era of water transportation, when all the large ships locking through at the Soo could sail into Portage Lake. The Portage waterway became a very busy place, visited by dozens of different lake boats and crisscrossed repeatedly by tugs and small ferries shuttling people and goods between Houghton and Hancock on their opposite shores.[28]

In the mid-1840s, the earliest pioneers had looked longingly, sometimes desperately, for the arrival of any of the scarce supply ships on Lake Superior. By 1859, during the peak months of July and August, seven ships per day used the canal, and in 1860, some eighty-two different ships (seventy sailing vessels and twelve steamers) passed through the Sault; many of them locked through repeatedly as the shipping season wore on. They carried an impressive array of cargo, much of it destined for the Keweenaw: 2,800 head of beef and 4,900 barrels of salt beef; 1,500 hogs and 5,700 barrels of salt pork. Ships brought up 4,050 barrels of salt fish, 50,250 barrels of flour, and 400,000 pounds of butter, plus 9,300 barrels of liquor, 74,000 pounds of tobacco, and 10,300 tons of general merchandise. In 1861, Houghton alone recorded 230 dockings of supply vessels of all descriptions.[29]

Other major improvements to water transport along the central part of the Keweenaw followed, some with government support, some done by the mining companies. After the channel from Portage Lake to Keweenaw Bay on the eastern side of the Keweenaw had been improved, it became desirable to cut a wholly new channel on the western side, uniting the waters of Superior and Portage Lake. Between 1868 and 1873, steam dredges operating on both water bodies moved closer and closer together as they ate away at the ground between them. Cutting this ship canal cost about $2.5 million; the canal company did the work in return for government land grants totaling 450,000 acres in the Upper Peninsula.[30] Completion of the canal resulted in a continuous, twenty-two-mile-long waterway that cut across the entire peninsula and in effect made its northern half an island. Now any boat sailing from Houghton to Ontonagon, or Wisconsin, or Minnesota, was spared the hundred miles of travel up the Keweenaw's eastern shore, around Keweenaw Point, and then back down the western shore.

Portage Lake "belonged" to the Quincy, Pewabic, Franklin, Huron and other neighboring mines; they sought its improvement to lessen the costs of shipping in goods and shipping out copper. They also lined its shores with stamp mills—which used vast quantities of water to separate copper from crushed rock—and transformed a beautiful, natural setting into a heavily industrialized one. Similarly, Torch Lake "belonged" to Calumet and Hecla and other mines operating in northern Houghton County. They put their stamp mills (and, later, smelters) on this interior lake, which initially had only a shallow, marshy connection with Portage Lake and thus with Lake Superior.

So Calumet and Hecla and its neighboring mines did in the mid-1870s what the Portage Lake mines had done earlier: they subscribed to a canal company; dredged out a new two-mile-long channel connecting Portage and Torch Lakes that accommodated all ships on Superior; and charged these ships tolls, which went toward maintaining the canal.[31]

The improvements to water transport were many, and they smoothed the flow of people and goods from the world below up to the Keweenaw's evolving commercial villages and mine locations. Travelers could board a ship in Cleveland, Detroit, or Buffalo and not get off until it docked at Houghton, Hancock, Eagle River, or Lake Linden. Instead of coasting in a small boat rowed by voyageurs, they enjoyed passage on a ship that offered greater security in its size, speed in its multiple masts or steam-power, and entertainment in the forms of card playing, on-board saloons, and musical bands and dancing.[32]

Of course, all these improvements were nullified by the hard winters, which drove the big boats off Superior from late November until the start of May. And even during the truncated shipping season, travelers and crew were well advised never to take safe passage across Superior for granted.

Storms, shoals, rocky shores, and equipment failures sometimes brought Keweenaw voyages to unexpected conclusions. Numerous ships ran aground or suffered collisions yet were saved. Others weren't so fortunate. Between 1844, when the 78-foot brig *John Jacob Astor* went down at Copper Harbor, and 1865, when the 199-foot sidewheeler *Traveller* went down near Eagle Harbor, a total of ten sizable vessels sank or were broken up in the immediate vicinity of the Keweenaw. Other boats sank in more distant waters while en route to or from the copper district. Fortunately, the Keweenaw shipwrecks claimed few lives. The tragic exception was the sinking of the 169-foot sidewheeler *Sunbeam* in 1863. This ship went down off Eagle Harbor, killing nearly thirty aboard, including the Methodist minister from the Cliff mine. Even the *Sunbeam*'s survivors did not fare well: "The waves dashed her to pieces, the steersman lashed himself to a door & was driven ashore in thirty-six hours & saved by a pleasure party down the Lake in a small boat. He was just alive & the waves had beaten the flesh from his limbs and body."[33]

The explorers and early settlers who sailed safely to the Keweenaw were not yet home free, if destined for the peninsula's interior. Hard by the shore, they encountered an obstacle-strewn landscape. George Cannon slashed away with his hatchet and pressed forward relentlessly, yet he could advance only eight miles per day. Cutting corridors through this wilderness—first trails, then roads—was an essential and difficult part of settling the region.

Many of the earliest overland routes connected interior settlements to the nearest harbors or ports; these pathways carried the essential items of life and commerce from the boats that delivered them to the people who consumed them. Next, a network of trails and roads, running across and along the Keweenaw, connected village to village and mine to mine. Later, routes would lead away from the Keweenaw and connect with other locations to the south, such as Green Bay, Wisconsin.

Road building did not progress rapidly in a far northern environment overgrown with vegetation in the summer and blanketed with snow in the winter. Early on, the mining companies hurriedly built the primitive roads they absolutely needed to get their people and goods in and their copper out. They routed them; they built them. Later, construction of a more extensive, complete network of roads lagged because of a lack of public funds and because of uncertainty as to who should "pave the way" in surveying routes, building roads, and paying for the work. Road building stagnated while various levels of government sorted out their obligations in the matter. On the whole, water transportation to, from, and across the peninsula improved far more quickly than overland transportation.

In the 1840s and 1850s, as new settlements sprang up along the mineral range, they were initially serviced and supplied by "mere trails, over which everything was carried to the mine by half-breed packers."[34] Footpaths linked far-flung settlements, and voyageurs tromped the hills and valleys, serving as guides and human mules. Father Frederic Baraga, the Catholic missionary who located at Keweenaw Bay in 1843, often availed himself of voyageurs while traversing trails through the 1850s.

Father Baraga was as well traveled as any explorer, miner, or geologist. He was almost constantly on the move, first tending to Native Americans and later adding the Catholics found in scattered mine locations. In the summer of 1855, Baraga hiked from Eagle River to L'Anse, accompanied by John Kohl, a German cartographer, and assisted by a voyageur. Kohl's good-natured account of the journey depicts how important a voyageur was and how bad overland travel remained, fully a dozen years after the initial mine rush to the north.

Father Baraga didn't need to transport mine equipment and supplies, but he did take from place to place his "liturgical objects," such as "crosses, crozier, vestments, chalice, silver vessels for the 3 oils, etc." Since these were quite heavy, Kohl and Baraga limited their other take-alongs to essentials and secured the services of a French Canadian voyageur, Du Roy, to carry them:

In order to make our good Du Roy's "paqueton"—thus the Voyageurs call their knapsack—as small and light as possible, we calculated every piece of paper, every pair of stockings we could possibly do without, and left the rest of our traps "en cache" with his squaw and half-breed children. . . . Du Roy thrust all our indespensible articles into his blue woolen "couverte," tied it round with his leathern "collier," and hung the whole on his back while fastening the broad band of the "paqueton" round his head, for the

Voyageurs carry with their foreheads and backs. . . . The weights these Voyageurs can carry are surprising; one hundred and fifty pounds is the ordinary and almost legal weight packed on every Voyageur in these lands.[35]

Freed of the burden of carrying their possessions, Kohl and Father Baraga nevertheless struggled to make their way down and across the Keweenaw: "At times we waded for whole hours through bottomless mud. Occasionally every vestige of any path disappears beneath the boughs. . . . We nevertheless crawled through and over this underbrush, not knowing, at times, whether to call this the most tiring or the most comical and entertaining experience that we underwent."[36] As the men pushed ahead through bogs and bramble, they improvised and created new trails for themselves whenever necessary. This is what the early mining companies had done, too. They'd jumped into the road-building business, blazing overland routes where most needed. Self-reliant and self-interested mining ventures did not wait for any arm of government to tackle needed "public works" like roads. They assumed that task themselves. They upgraded poorly marked or unmarked trails to footpaths; improved these to horse trails; and ended up with wagon roads. Not until the Civil War era— after nearly twenty years of settlement—did government act more vigorously, truly making public roads into public works.

The Lake Superior News reported in 1846 that mining companies had already constructed "over ten miles" of roads on the northern end of the mineral range. As each new company developed its location, it cut a road to the nearest commercial center on the coast. An 1849 map of the Northwest Mining Company showed a "pretty good common road" running some five miles from the mine to Eagle Harbor; it also showed "trails" running from mine and mill to nearby "meadows," no doubt used for agricultural purposes. An 1845 map of the Lake Superior Mining Company's holdings showed several internal improvements at the site: a dam; an 840-foot canal delivering water to a stamp mill; about 1,500 feet of local roads connecting mine, mill, and housing; and a road running a mile and a half to Lake Superior.[37]

After constructing primary roads leading to commercial villages on Lake Superior, companies worked on overland routes running from mine to mine to mine. In 1853, Copper Falls completed an "excellent road" from its mine to Eagle Harbor and boasted that it was "the best of its length in this region." The North American Mine contracted to have the road extended to its works, and Copper Falls figured that soon it would "be used by all of the companies" nearby. Also in 1853, the Lake Superior Journal reported that the Northwest, Connecticut, and Waterbury mining companies had shared the expense of cutting "a horse path . . . back of the [mineral] range, across Eagle River and Bay State locations . . . to the Cliff." That path then met another, providing "an opportunity for citizens and travellers to pass from Copper Harbor on horseback along under the bluff, from mine to mine . . . , a distance of 30 miles."[38]

Clusters of mines up and down the Keweenaw adhered to this same pattern of road building. They first connected to Lake Superior, saving their best road for this route, because it would see the heaviest traffic of supplies and equipment coming in and of mineral product going out. Then they connected with each other, often cooperating to share the costs and benefits of a new trail or road, albeit one that was often haphazardly cut. By 1855, a patched-together overland route of over one hundred miles of trails and roads extended down the mineral range from Copper Harbor to Ontonagon. But no wagons could roll this distance, end to end, and even travelers on horseback required good weather to complete the journey. Much of the route—which included only seven miles of wagon road—was "still impassable except to a man on foot."[39]

Even the best wagon roads of the 1840s and 1850s were quite terrible. John Forster had less than fond recollections of his pioneer travels over corduroy roads thrown over marshy, low-lying areas. Here, workers fashioned the ribbed roadbed from short lengths of small tree trunks, which they stripped of their limbs and laid side by side on the soft ground:

> Like all roads in the woods in a new country it is rough and crooked. The primitive corduroy so familiar to pioneers is one of its characteristic features. The terrible jolting one received while passing over it in a lumber wagon is not remembered with unalloyed satisfaction. But this was preferable to wallowing hub deep through mud and mire. The task of hauling supplies and machinery over such roads was herculean.[40]

The early roads were narrow, and in traversing forests they barely snaked through the trees bordering each side. Teamsters found poorly ditched and drained roads to be wheel-sucking quagmires in the spring and back-wrenching, head-snapping washboards in late summer. Horsemen and hikers alike needed to remain on guard for the rock outcroppings, boulders, and tree stumps that littered roadways.

A cluster of mines developing on the southern end of the mineral range in the early 1850s launched the region's most ambitious overland route of the era. The mines, located up to twelve miles inland from their commercial shipping port of Ontonagon, combined resources to build something smoother and faster than a common wagon road—a route that was less affected by bad weather and allowed draft animals to pull heavier loads. They organized the Ontonagon Plank Road Company, then built one: a roadbed formed of planks laid side by side and spiked across longitudinal stringers setting the road's course.

Between the plank road's termini at Ontonagon and the Minesota mine, it ran across or near eleven other mine locations. These mines had subscribed in the Plank Road Company principally to lessen the cost of transporting their copper to ships anchored at Ontonagon. The Toltec mine, for instance, paid over $12,000 as its share in the road—and was pleased with the investment, because the company's cost of shipping a barrel of mass copper to Ontonagon fell from $1.50 to just fifty cents between 1851 and 1855.[41]

Ordinary settlers also benefited from the plank road; they could ride over it to get to and from Ontonagon, rather than tramping this distance. About a decade after George Cannon had traversed this neck of the woods with great difficulty, Edwin Emmons was running "a daily line of stages from Ontonagon to the Minesota and National Mines, by way of the Plank Road, stopping for dinner at Maple Grove, and passing directly by or in the immediate vicinity of the Toltec, Adventure, Ridge, Evergreen Bluff, Mass, Nebraska, Flint Steel, Superior, and Rockland Mines." The stage departed on a set schedule and charged a one-way fare from end to end of $1.50, about equal to what a miner would make in a day.[42]

Up on Lake Superior, winter stopped all boats, freezing out water transportation. But winter wasn't all bad: frigid temperatures and snow often *improved* overland travel, especially the passage of horse-drawn vehicles over common roads. The snow roads of winter were smoother and firmer than the rutted, muddy, or stump-laden dirt roads of spring, summer, and fall. What residents hoped for was a quick transition into winter, one that skipped over a messy month of freeze then thaw, of snow then rain—a month when neither wagon wheels nor sleigh runners worked. On November 16, 1875, a Red Jacket correspondent reported in the *Mining Gazette* that just such a perfect, and rare, transition had occurred:

> Winter has set in upon us under very favorable auspices this year. We didn't have to go through the siege of mud, incident to this season, and which we so much dreaded. The transition from fall to winter has taken place very handsomely indeed. Sunday night we saw the bare bosom of mother earth, for the last time, possibly, in our lives, but certainly for the last time in six months. The ground was hard and dry when we went to bed, and the weather pleasant, and next morning we awoke to find six or eight inches of snow, with excellent sleighing. In this delectable climate of ours it seldom happens that the snow, "the beautiful snow," about which so much hath been said, and written and sung, comes and stays on nice, dry, hard ground, thereby making sleighing good and life pleasant, but it did this time and the resident population, or at least that portion of them who live on the surface of the earth, are jubilant thereat.

When winter arrived, teamsters swapped their wheels for runners and glided cargo from place to place over the seemingly frictionless snow. In the first decades, when common roads were so bad, many mining companies depended on snow roads to get much of their mine product to the nearest port. In 1849, the Northwest Mining Company described its road to Eagle Harbor, which traversed more than a mile of swamps with a corduroy surface: "It is a road that, for winter use, and perhaps three of the driest months, will permit two trips a day with a load of one ton each way for four miles." The Toltec Mining Company in 1855 noted that the "common roads in this country are impassable during the summer season," so companies shipped their heavy freight in winter, when "snow roads were good." Similarly, O. W. Robinson reported on copper shipped from the cluster of mines located by George Cannon and the American Exploring Company: "All the copper produced during the seven months of summer was stored at the mines until the snow roads were good. Then it was hauled to American Landing and the next summer was floated down the river on scows to Ontonagon."[43]

Besides improving travel over common wagon roads, winter worked like a civil engineer and built new overland routes where none existed in the summer. Actually, these were "overwater" routes, where the water had frozen to depths of several feet. By icing over rivers, lakes, and bays in December, winter created new roads and bridges that could be used, usually, into April.

Teams hauling mail, freight, or passengers cut straight across Keweenaw Bay, instead of going around it. Instead of following a summertime route up or down the Keweenaw, they ran just offshore on Superior's smoother ice. Instead of taking a boat across Portage Lake, they crossed between Houghton and Hancock on an ice bridge. By the mid-1860s, a commercial ice stage ferried passengers across Portage Lake in enclosed and heated coaches on runners.[44]

Frozen lakes provided much of the region's best recreational sleigh riding. In February 1866, the *Mining Gazette* in Houghton reported that "there would be great pleasure in driving on the [Portage] lake to-day, for it is hard and clean as a floor, and horses can be driven anywhere on it for a stretch of over 15 miles." Sleighing on Lake Superior was especially grand, but occasionally a bit foolhardy. Sarah Barr Christian long remembered one trip, when she and friends headed out from Isle Royale on a big, three-seated bobsleigh pulled by two horses:

> On April 29th . . . some one of the adventurous souls suggested a sleigh ride. . . . After arriving at the dock our driver . . . started across the ice and in spite of the protests of the two women, and the milder protests of two or three of the men, on we went, four miles straight out onto the ice of that great and terrible Lake Superior. Inasmuch as the first day of May, when we were supposed to pick May flowers, was only one day off, it seemed, to say the least, a little risky.[45]

Snow roads and ice bridges couldn't always be counted on to hasten horse-drawn travel. Sleigh riders and others couldn't go just anywhere, not after four or five feet of the white stuff had accumulated. An early settler recounted how "the deep snow rendered only well beaten and often-travelled roads at all useful." And even those roads were often pinched by winds and fresh snow. When one sleigh met another on a narrowed track, the drivers had to force the snow aside to make a turnout: "the common way to pass was for each teamster to plunge into the snow and break a road for his horse, leading him through the frozen flood."[46]

Occasionally, all signs of a well-beaten snow road disappeared under a blizzard that resculpted the landscape. Fierce winter storms first locked people in their cabins, then released them to the task of reopening buried roads. In January 1866, Lucena Brockway tracked the progress of such a storm in her diary:

Jan. 20:   "Still snowing & blowing fearfully. Have never seen a worse storm in my life."

Jan. 21:   "Still storming & nearly as bad as yesterday. The snow has drifted dreadfully & so hard one can walk on the drifts with ease."

Jan. 22:   "Is more mild and all have turned out to break roads. Find them hard & much worse than ever before."

Jan. 23:   "Has been pleasant today, and all have been breaking roads."

Henry Hobart, the Cliff mine schoolteacher, also wrote in his diary of roads clogged with snow. On December 15, 1863, he penned, "I went out and broke roads with my boys." Through the 1860s, communities had no plows to push snow from roads and no large rollers to pack snow down to make roads passable. Instead, they generally called on men, boys, and horse teams to reclaim roads by plunging through the snow and tromping it down, compacting it more with each footfall, each pass.[47]

Sarah Barr Christian had rightfully been afraid during her April sleigh ride on Lake Superior. Travel over ice roads and bridges always entailed risk, particularly early and late in the winter season. One of the first recorded deaths of a white settler in the Portage Lake region occurred during the winter of 1851–52. A fellow from the Wheal Kate mine, south of the Portage, tried to cross over the frozen lake for supplies but fell through the ice and drowned. In subsequent years, it was not uncommon for heavy horse teams to take a swim in the frigid Portage after breaking through its thin and, in places, unpredictable ice.[48]

Sometime around April, warmer breezes started blowing over the Keweenaw. These harbingers of spring promised release from the long winter. Everyone looked forward to this time, when the ice on Superior and local harbors disappeared, allowing precious supply boats to reappear. But while the spring thaw revived lake shipping, it mucked up overland transportation. A thick mat of hard, compacted snow made a nice winter road surface as long as temperatures stayed below freezing. But sunny days in the 40s and 50s turned this mat into a white, slushy bog; and beneath that, a brown, muddy bog waited to make its appearance. Animal hooves stabbed deep into the slush and mud, and for several weeks or a month teamsters cursed the roads where neither runners nor wheels worked. One way to cope a bit with the sloppy season was to put off hauling until night, when temperatures dropped and roadbeds froze again.[49]

Mine managers and merchants may have owned or had access to horse teams and sleighs, but most early settlers didn't, and these "common folk" kept closer to home during the winter than during the summer. With their feet bundled in shoe packs to protect them from the cold and frostbite, they trod over the packed snow in village lots and lanes and along well-traveled roads leading to neighboring settlements. Many laced on snowshoes, "the common thing for the foot passenger to do in winter," if traveling cross-country or through deep snow.[50] With snowshoes, a pioneer hunter could head into the woods for sport on a pretty February day and not sink up to his waist in chilly white.

Joseph Rawlings, an important master mechanic from Cornwall who settled at the Cliff mine, recalled a trek made on snowshoes from Ontonagon to Eagle Harbor in the mid-1850s. After a long march on the first day, his party made their bed that night "in a deep trench in the snow, in which we enjoyed a very refreshing sleep, rolled up in our blankets." On the second day, following in the tracks of another hard-traveling group, they found "miners' boots, hats, and other equipment" discarded in the snow, tossed off to lighten the burden. That night, Rawlings's party came to a small cabin kept by a man and wife, who graciously provided dinner and let the men put their blankets down on the floor. After two more days' tramping and camping, the men arrived in Eagle Harbor "cross and tired." Rawlings sat down to a surprise at the end of the journey: "Three of my toenails came off with the wrappings of my foot gear."[51]

Some who couldn't afford horses put together a different sort of team for winter service. In his diary entry for January 24, 1864, Henry Hobart wrote, "Bully for the dog teams of Clifton." Hobart noted that "every Cornishman is sure to have a number of dogs anyway" and that "a span of dogs make a smart team." Earlier that same winter he had observed: "It is fine sleighing and everyone is alive to have a sleigh ride. Dogs are harnessed to sleighs or small sleds. Men or women in the sled urge them along by a brisk application of the lash—very pleasant. . . . It is quite amusing and fine sport."[52]

For some, dogsledding was no mere sport, but a serious means of winter transport, essential to the conduct of business. This especially held true for mail carriers, who had contracts with the federal government to tote the mail to Keweenaw communities. In summer, lake boats brought up all the mail. In winter, dogsleds driven by Indians or "half-breeds" took two weeks or more to haul the mail along a circuitous route leading up from Green Bay.

Orrin Robinson encountered a dogsled mail runner in 1856, while he himself was traveling by dogsled from the Norwich mine to Marquette. Robinson had gone overland to L'Anse; he made the rest of the journey over lake ice. While being drawn by three dogs across Keweenaw Bay, Robinson spotted an Indian mail carrier who had stopped on the ice for his midday meal:

> He first built a fire with fagots brought along for the purpose. He then cut a hole through the ice to obtain water; then warming the mush for his dogs, brewing some tea for himself and thawing out his frozen bread and meat, the meal was ready and the dogs were soon devouring theirs. . . . This tall, untutored, dark man of the forest before partaking of a mouthful of his meagre repast knelt upon the ice, removed his hat and offered up a prayer of thanks to God.[53]

Many settlers also offered up prayers of thanks if and when they ever received winter mail. Many dogsled carriers met with condemnation for lightening their mail loads en route, either to put aboard different freight or just to make it easier to get through heavy snow. The *Ontonagon Miner* reported on January 12, 1856, that the first winter shipment of mail had just arrived (about sixty days late) and that three precious bags of mail had been thrown off at Chandler's shanty in Escanaba to make room for a barrel of salt pork. Another time, the same paper reported that "two Indian mail-carriers arrived at L'Anse with a small bag containing letters." Unfortunately, five other bags had been taken off the sled and hung up in some trees near the lakeshore. A. P. Swineford recounted how he had gone an entire winter without any mail, and then in June, after mail had been fetched from trees along the sled route, he received at least "half a bushel of letters."[54]

Starting in 1864, an improved road between Green Bay and the Keweenaw allowed mail contractors to abandon sled dogs in favor of horse-drawn stages, equipped with wheels or runners, as conditions demanded. In 1865, if all went well, it took three days and two nights to reach Houghton from Green Bay during the winter.[55] But it didn't always go well. On January 17, 1867, the *Mining Gazette* complained of "frozen and abraided mail matter" that arrived in "pitiful condition," because "in driving over the ice in Green Bay, the sleigh ran into a large crack, and team, sleigh, passengers, and mail 'went in.'" The paper also allowed as how overland mail delivery was "worse than useless" early in the winter, until the roads set up hard—and that mail that "ought to have gone clean and safe to the north shore of Siberia" was being damaged by sore-boned stage passengers who used bags of it as seat cushions.

In the mid-1860s, the retirement of dogsleds and the running of horse-drawn stages from Green Bay signaled the beginning of a new era of overland transportation for the Keweenaw. In the 1840s and 1850s, mining companies had led the way in building mine-to-harbor and mine-to-mine roads. These had been patched together with trails to form a primitive network of routes serving interior and coastal communities. Meanwhile, federal, state, and local government officials had done little, except to survey routes for roads left unbuilt due to a lack of funds.

The region dearly needed a good wagon road running the full length of the mineral range from Copper Harbor to Ontonagon; another road leading from the base of the Keweenaw south to Green Bay; and a third route passing around Keweenaw Bay and turning east toward Marquette. During the Civil War era, the U.S. Congress made land grants to Michigan and Wisconsin to be used in funding construction of a military road running down the mineral range and into Wisconsin. At nearly the same time, the Michigan legislature made land grants to support local road construction, and it also returned to the counties funds accruing from a specific tax on copper output. The counties applied these funds to needed internal improvements.[56]

A full two decades after the copper rush began, the region enjoyed a mid-1860s road-building rush. New and better roads ran to and through the Keweenaw, and these routes in turn encouraged private enterprise to spawn more commercial stage companies that served people in disparate, once very isolated communities. Stages that glided on runners in the winter ran up the Keweenaw, connecting the likes of Houghton, Eagle River, Clifton, Copper Falls, Eagle Harbor, and Copper Harbor. Crooks, Freeman & Brother, proprietors of the Marquette & Portage Lake Stage Line, advertised in 1870 that "their route is thoroughly equipped with teams, sleighs and stations, and that Passengers are taken regularly from Portage Lake to Negaunee in twenty-six hours, and connection with trains and stages guaranteed." The company promised patrons "Fast Teams, Comfortable Sleighs, Moderate Fare, and Two Good, Square Meals."[57]

Passengers in 1870 had to take the Crooks stage to Negaunee if they wanted to catch a train south, because no rail line as yet ran to the Keweenaw. Tracks running up to the copper mines had been drawn on many speculative maps since the 1850s, but none had ever been built—and none would be built until the Marquette, Houghton & Ontonagon Railroad finally reached Portage Lake in 1883. While waiting for this connecting service to extend up to the Keweenaw, enterprising groups had built a few short rail lines on the peninsula itself, north of the Portage. These lines primarily served the mining industry, which had to move vast tonnages of product from mine, to mill, to smelter, to shipping dock.

The first steam locomotive put into service on the Keweenaw arrived in 1864. At the jointly managed Pewabic and Franklin mines, it delivered rock from the shafts to the gravity inclines running downhill to stamp mills on Portage Lake. In 1867, the new Hecla and Torch Lake Railroad built a mine-to-mill line nearly five miles in length. Early in the 1870s, the Mineral Range Railroad Company constructed a line twelve and a half miles long connecting

Hancock with rapidly expanding Calumet, which was swelling due to the growth of the Osceola and, especially, the Calumet and Hecla mines.[18]

Formed by Hancock businessmen, the Mineral Range Railroad derived much of its revenue by carrying copper rock from the Osceola mine to its Portage Lake mill. But the Mineral Range Railroad also catered to and carried sustantial numbers of passengers. It enhanced everyday life on the Keweenaw by transporting people between two important copper-producing and population centers—Hancock and Calumet.

In its first full year of operation, 1874, the Mineral Range Railroad carried 25,600 tons of copper rock to the Osceola mill at Hancock. It also carried 70,824 passengers, collecting fares of five cents per mile. It started service with two cars that had a combined capacity of seventy-five passengers: a "smoking and baggage car" and a "ladies car." Brisk business prompted the railroad company to order a second set of cars, reputed to be "really very fine" in their outfitting. Roof monitors helped light and ventilate the cars, which were heated in winter by potbellied stoves. The Hancock to Calumet run, including a few stops, took about fifty minutes.[19] As always, snow could be counted on to delay things occasionally in the winter. The new railroad armed at least one of its locomotives with an iron plow, and when that was not enough, it dispatched a band of shovelers to clear the tracks.

In the early decades of settlement, getting up to the Keweenaw Peninsula was never particularly easy, and getting around *on* the Keweenaw was often even harder. The establishment of a large-scale mining industry in this remote wilderness demanded internal improvements to both overland and water transportation. Initially, the pioneering mining companies were the most active agents of transportation change. As the first important, capitalized institutions on the scene, they adopted the self-reliant attitude that "public works" were a corporate responsibility, so they built them. Driven by self-interest and a need to get their copper product out, they built the roads, dredged the rivers, dug the canals.

A bit later, federal, state, and local governments became more active participants in building an improved network of overland and water routes serving the Keweenaw. Entrepreneurs and big and small businessmen—sometimes aligned with the mining companies, sometimes independent—also joined in the mix, filling in transportation niches. They floated the lake boats, ran the ferries and tugs, contracted to deliver the mail on dogsleds, operated the stage lines, and put passenger cars on their early railroad from Portage Lake to Calumet.

Through the early 1860s, the most dramatic improvements in transportation involved water routes. While the Soo Locks were built and Portage River improved, overland improvements lagged behind. Finally, the mid-1860s saw the the pace of government-supported road building accelerate, and by the early 1870s, at least a few communities were served by local railroads moving both passengers and freight.

The improvements that helped move copper generally helped move people, too: roads, rails, ships. In many ways, the transport interests of the growing mining industry interlocked with and supported the needs of the general public. The people who came to settle on the mining frontier welcomed transportation improvements just as much as the mining companies. Settlers perhaps admired and made folk heroes of the hardy, skilled voyageurs of the 1840s and 1850s, but they didn't want to live and work like them. They preferred horse-drawn stage to snowshoe or dogsled, and steamer to canoe, bateau, or Mackinaw boat. They took a fancy to the just-arrived railroad, a sure sign that the wilderness and frontier eras had passed. The railway conductor was far less colorful than the voyageur, but the railroad offered far more comfortable travel.

THREE

SETTLING IN

Camps, Communities, Houses, and Hotels

We stopped, almost worn out, at the house of a dirty old bachelor [alongside the trail from Ontonagon to the Adventure Mine]. I am sure if any decent person of a bachelor could have seen this man's house he would have gotten himself a wife immediately. His bed looked just as if it had been made a month ago, and in one of the corners of this house there was a great pile of dirt. The plastering was of mud and his side board consisted of barrels with some boards upon them; and they were ornamented with some broken whiskey bottles.

George McGill's journal,
July 26, 1852

Not all pioneers on the Keweenaw lived as badly as George McGill's dirty old bachelor; some lived in even worse conditions, at least in terms of exposure to the elements. Early geologists, surveyors, and explorers who coasted along the Keweenaw shoreline in canoes or slogged their way through summer swamps or snowshoed through winter woods often had to improvise shelter at the end of an arduous day because they had no settlement in sight and no roof over their heads. Parties often left heavy, bulky tents behind—and if they brought a tent, they sometimes used it to shelter precious provisions, leaving the men to fend for themselves.

Sometimes that wasn't a bad thing at all. Many explorers and settlers romantically recalled perfect summer nights spent on a Keweenaw beach. A small boat rested peacefully on the shore or bobbed at anchor in shallow waters. Campfire smoke and a wafting breeze kept the bugs at bay. Men tapered off and enjoyed their pipes while watching a fiery sun set over Superior, or watching the northern lights burnish a nighttime sky. Weary travelers, wrapped in a blanket or two, fell asleep listening to repetitive waves run up on the shore. Often they arose early, while the stars were still out, and pushed off in their boats again just as the sun started to rise.

Of course, conditions were not always so ideal. Men also remembered miserable times when they came ashore wet and stayed that way all night long, under a constant deluge. Cross-country trekkers in midwinter slept bundled in blankets at the bottom of shallow trenches dug in the snow. Men in June, camping in the woods without benefit of tent or netting, got eaten alive by blackflies or mosquitoes. George Cannon, when he explored the Ontonagon region in 1846, was one of those men who had no tent, who slept under the stars when on the move and later, when it finally came time to occupy a mine claim, built himself a simple shelter.

When on the march, Cannon's exploring party would stop late in the afternoon to pitch camp near a stream so they'd have water for cooking, drinking, and washing. Beneath a large spruce or cedar tree, the men set up for the night by building a campfire. They cut evergreen boughs and fashioned them into pallets laid on the forest floor near the fire. Wrapped in blankets, using boots or a pack or a mossy log for a pillow, they fell asleep.

Sometimes they slept soundly and comfortably till morning; sometimes they arose "completely drenched," thanks to an unexpected, heavy shower. If they had warning of a storm, Cannon and his crew hunted out some natural waterproofing for their forest beds:

> A few sprinklings of rain showered upon us indicated that we might be washed before morning, which would probably be not very agreeable to a sound sleep. So, groping our way among the timber to find [cedar] trees of which the Bark would peel, after an hour's delay, we had succeeded in securing the required number of Bark, which was one for each person. . . . We gathered our blankets around us, crawled under them [the strips of cedar bark] and slept soundly, undisturbed by the rain.[1]

Late in the summer, to hold the claims for five promising mine sites they had found, Cannon's party set up squatters' cabins, which Cannon referred to as "shantees." On the first day of construction, Cannon chopped the needed logs. On the second day, they raised the cabin. On the third day, they covered the cabin with cedar bark, forming "a neat little canton of about ten feet long by eight."[2] The "shantee" lacked doors, windows, furniture, and a stove. Later, to seal out some frigid drafts, George Cannon probably fashioned a covering for his entrance and laid some mud in the chinks of the walls. Then he hunkered down with his cache of provisions to endure the winter of 1846–47.

The first squatters' huts at other mines were equally primitive: "A man was hired at twenty dollars a month and provisions, and sent far into the woods to hold possession of a claim. By the side of some brook he erected out of poles and cedar bark the rudest of huts." The squatter might have made his bed of hemlock boughs laid on the dirt floor, or fashioned one of poles and stakes driven into the ground, which he covered with moss, fragrant cedar, and blankets. As for heating and cooking, "some trap rocks rolled together in a circle, in the middle of the room, formed the fireplace, the smoke escaping through a hole in the roof, or spread itself throughout the hut as it listed, smoking the sole inmate a good bronze or ham color. In the ashes, like a light on a vestal alter, reposed a big iron pot, always holding a supply of simmering bean porridge." During the deep snows of winter, the isolated squatter's hut looked "like a white mound with smoke issuing from the top."[3]

Cedar bark, blanket wraps, tents, and smoky dirt-floored huts passed as shelter for the hardiest pioneers, but the opening of the mining district demanded that each new settlement—whether a waterfront commercial village or a hinterland mine—pay quick attention to building more comfortable and familiar accommodations. At the start of the mine rush in the mid-1840s, Copper Harbor was the prime destination for thousands of copper seekers washing up on the peninsula's shores, because it was the site of the federal office that leased and later sold mineral lands throughout the Keweenaw. Many of these transients put themselves up in a tent city hard by Superior during the summer, then retreated south for the winter. Some, however, ate and slept under real roofs, in log structures that had been erected by pioneering hotelkeepers or by the U.S. Army.

The words "frontier" and "hotel" hardly seem to go together, but up on Lake Superior the one brought about the other. Hotels quickly became important social fixtures in all the developing lakefront villages. Everybody used these commercial centers as jumping-off places: geologists, miners, shopkeepers, traveling salesmen, itinerant doctors and dentists, journalists, and (by the 1850s) growing numbers of tourists—men, women, and children who'd come up to take a Lake Superior cruise, see the mines and natural sights, and enjoy a beautiful summer. Many folks needed food and short-term lodging, and settlers of an entrepreneurial bent accommodated them.

The earliest commercial lodging establishments, such as the Astor at Copper Harbor, were small affairs. At the Astor, visitors in 1846 were welcomed by the host, Francois, "a cosmopolite" who spoke "all languages" and "was cook, waiter, porter, chambermaid and clerk." The hotel was none too fancy:· "a pine log structure, one and a half stories high, twenty-four feet long by sixteen wide . . . —having an addition that serves as a dining-room and kitchen, with a long table made by two boards laid upon horses;—each guest having a given space upon the main chamber floor to spread his mat and buffalo skin."[4]

Several early hotels were family operations, run out of a house that had extra rooms, with the wife cooking for family and guests alike. Daniel and Lucena Brockway set up a family-style hotel at Copper Harbor in 1846. They later moved to Eagle River and started another. In 1853, Robert Clarke visited the Keweenaw in preparation for writing an article about the copper region for *Harper's New Monthly Magazine*. Clarke stayed in small hotels in Eagle River and Eagle Harbor.[5] In Eagle Harbor, his considerate hosts lit smudge pots to drive away bugs and put him up nicely: "The first night of my arrival I was honored with a spare family room, which afforded a spice of home that was quite delightful." Then, the next day, a boat arrived carrying "ladies and gentlemen" from Pittsburgh. It was only proper that the ladies take the hotel's more private rooms, so the men lodged in the parlor, where Clarke slept on a couch.

In the mine rush season of 1844, dwellings and hotels along the mineral range from Copper Harbor to Ontonagon were few and far between, and explorations were just starting to result in the taking of copper. That summer, two small but well-financed companies initiated systematic copper mining: the Lake Superior Mining Company, working near Eagle River, and the Pittsburgh and Boston Mining Company, then operating at Copper Harbor. While these nascent firms employed and sheltered only a handful of men, another organization busily erected a settlement intended to house, feed, and otherwise sustain 120 persons year-round. That organization was the U.S. Army, builder of Copper Harbor's Fort Wilkins.

In March 1844, Michigan's congressmen petitioned the secretary of war to put a military outpost on the Keweenaw to protect the peace with the Ojibwa and generally help preserve law and order among the diverse adventurers scrabbling to find copper on Lake Superior. The War Department acquiesced and shipped two companies of troops from Detroit to Copper Harbor. Under the direction of Captain R. E. Clary, the army started building its stockaded fort in May and essentially completed it before hard winter set in.[6]

The frontier outpost included a powder magazine, stable, guard house, hospital, and blacksmith and carpenter shops. To keep, prepare, or distribute food and other precious provisions, the army erected a warehouse, icehouse, sutler's store, slaughterhouse, bakery, and two kitchens with mess rooms. The men lived out of tents while putting up the fort's permanent quarters. Seven officers' quarters and two barracks for single enlisted men faced the parade ground and defined that space. Some distance away, located outside the palisade, stood four dwellings for married enlisted men and their wives, some of whom served as army laundresses.

Soldiers detailed to fatigue duty gathered local stone to lay up in random courses for foundation walls; they went into the woods to fell timber for the fort's palisade and buildings. The troops handled rough construction and materials preparation. They squared logs with an adze and notched them at the ends so that, when put up into walls, the logs interlocked at a building's corners. At the fort's new blacksmith shop, army artisans forged wrought iron into door handles, hinges, and other hardware. Because nobody at Copper Harbor was equipped to do any extensive millwork, Capt. Clary ordered much-needed lumber and construction materials from Detroit, as well as furnishings. Small lake boats sailed into Copper Harbor laden with some 15,000 board feet of exterior weatherboard siding; 45,000 feet of tongue-and-groove flooring; studs, joists, and shingles; 57 doors and 138 windows, with frames and casings; lath, lime, and hair for plaster; 36 cast-iron stoves and 400 feet of stove pipe; and 12,000 bricks for chimneys.[7]

In September 1844, Capt. Clary wrote to a superior that "all the buildings erected, are made in a substantial and permanent manner, having regard both to the comfort and warmth, of the command."[8] The dwellings also had regard for the hierarchical nature of the army, which built different quarters for men of different rank and marital status. Enlisted men with washer-woman wives lived off the parade ground (indeed, outside the fort proper) in cabins constructed in a "rough manner." The walls, of undressed logs, carried no horizontal weatherboarding on the outside and no plaster on the inside.

The two large barracks for single enlisted men enjoyed a more prominent siting, and a long veranda overlooking the parade ground fronted each one. Their walls were of logs hewn square, covered on the outside with weatherboard siding, painted white. (To add a splash of color, exterior doors were green.) Inside, the walls were left as hewn logs, unplastered. Cast-iron stoves and fireplaces provided heat. The barracks offered little in the way of privacy: men bunked in common sleeping rooms and ate in common mess halls.

The army put up two side-by-side double houses and one three-unit structure to make up the fort's seven officers' quarters. These dwellings were less expensive to construct than individual, free-standing houses, and less exposed to winter's bitter cold, because they shared an interior stud wall. Also, the two- and three-unit officers' quarters, with verandas across their facades, closely matched the appearance and massing of the enlisted men's barracks, so together they provided the parade ground with a look of planned-for unity and balance.

The officers' quarters would have had a rough appearance and would have been below army standards had they been built solely of locally available materials, patched together by soldiers on the frontier. Capt. Clary's ordering of building products from the world below enhanced the structures' look and level of amenities and made them about the best-finished accommodations on the Keweenaw during the early mine rush.

Beneath the officers' quarters, shallow foundation walls of rubble masonry extended below grade toward the bedrock that was never far from the surface. If bedrock did not get in the way, under the back of the dwelling workers dug a small, six-foot-deep root cellar, lined with stone, perhaps floored with gravel, and reached by a short run of steps. Sawn or log joists running across the foundation supported flooring; hewn logs, weatherboarded on the outside, plastered on the inside, and painted on both sides, rose up to form the main walls. Rafters, sheathing boards, and wooden shingles provided a watertight roof, whose structure was hidden away behind a finished ceiling. To lay on the smooth interior wall and ceiling finish, the army called up skilled plasterers from Detroit.

One story tall, each officer's unit had a single room in front about twenty feet wide and twenty feet deep (inside dimensions), backed by a smaller kitchen and, behind that, by an even smaller storage area or pantry. A woodstove provided heat; a stovepipe leading to a brick chimney carried away the smoke. Each unit's entrance door off the parade ground was centered in the facade and flanked by a sash window on either side. Windows also pierced the side walls of the front room and kitchen, providing additional light and ventilation. A rear door led to a backyard, which in the original architectural plans, at least, was fenced, and at a back corner of each lot stood a privy. By no stretch of the imagination was the dwelling elaborate or plush, but at this frontier outpost, it provided an officer with considerable personal space, privacy, and comfort.[9]

In a sense, the army's Fort Wilkins served as a model for the mine villages soon to be erected. The fort was not just a military installation; it was a place where people of different rank and marital status lived, all of whom needed adequate shelter and food. Similarly, the new mining companies understood from the start that a new mine was not just an industrial installation; it, too, was a place where bosses, blacksmiths, miners, and teamsters lived under trying frontier conditions. The army took care of its troops; the companies served as community builders and tended to their employees.

In another sense, Fort Wilkins served as no model at all for the mine villages. While the fort went up all at once in accordance with a preset plan, the new mines and their attendant villages passed through evolutionary stages. The army built Fort Wilkins over a single summer, then decided just two years later that it really served no purpose, so they abandoned it. (Almost inexplicably, the army regarrisoned the fort in 1867, before closing it permanently in 1870.)[10] Smart mining companies didn't work that way. They knew they were engaged in a "subterranean lottery," where the odds were against success, so most did not lavish precious investment capital on surface improvements like housing, then go out and seek copper. Instead, they spent the bulk of their money opening up the underground and added more to the surface plant—including housing—only as copper returns justified optimism and expansion. In the meantime, the mine camp "remained in the rough, with no effort at embellishment, and presented about as forbidding an aspect as could well be."[11]

Finding and opening a fissure vein charged with mass copper, or a rich lode of more finely disseminated amygdaloid or conglomerate copper, was no simple task. Some of the earliest mines had as many as nine square miles of leased mineral land to explore; later ones, able to purchase their land outright from the government, usually had a square mile to search.[12] Some claims included rough, ragged bluffs or cliffs; some were swamps; most were densely wooded. Companies usually started their site explorations by hiring five to thirty men who slashed and burned away vegetation, dug trenches hoping to expose the tops of outcropping lodes, and then sank test pits into the most promising finds.

The men who came up to Lake Superior to perform this arduous labor and live in primitive and isolated mine camps were almost all in their twenties and thirties and single. They lived in company boardinghouses, in a fashion not unlike the single enlisted men at Fort Wilkins, who resided in barracks. As many as eighteen to twenty men bunked together in one- or one-and-a-half-story structures, usually about twenty to twenty-eight feet wide and thirty to forty feet long. The men slept stacked up in hard, tiered bunks—each furnished, in winter, with several heavy Mackinaw blankets—that ringed the walls and perhaps filled a loft under the roof.[13] Inside, the men enjoyed almost no private space. Their personal stuff of life was minimal and maybe just filled a satchel or trunk, tucked away under a bunk. Boarders had little say over important matters, such as who they'd be spending time with, or what they'd have for supper, and when. A man's peace and quiet, and his personal security, were constantly at the mercy of the others he boarded with.

The earliest boardinghouses were built of logs cut and dressed at the site; by the late 1850s, wood-frame construction and clapboard siding became fairly common. Unlike a squatter's hut, a company boardinghouse usually had wooden doors, sash windows, flooring, and a cast-iron stove for heat. Some boardinghouses had an attached kitchen and dining area with a long planked table and benches, where the men took communal meals served up by a company cook. At other places, like the Isle Royale mine near Portage Lake in the early 1850s, the men bunked in one place and ate in another: "At this mine a large dining room with a kitchen was built of logs, in which the men were never allowed, except for meals. Two log houses were built for sleeping and living rooms, one being occupied by the Americans and Englishmen, and the other by French-Canadians and Irishmen."[14]

In 1849, John W. Foster and Josiah D. Whitney examined about twenty mine camps as part of a federally sponsored survey of the Lake Superior copper district. Foster and Whitney reported on at least fifteen companies still in their exploratory stage of evolution. At ten of these, the prospecting had gone so poorly that companies had temporarily suspended operations, perhaps leaving only a caretaker or two on site. Five other mines still actively looking for copper employed only eight to twenty-four men each. By contrast, four companies had clearly advanced to a a higher level of operations: the Minesota mine employed 84 workers; the Northwest, 95; the North American, 105; and the Cliff, 160.[15]

Many companies never found substantial deposits of copper, so they lived and died in fits and starts. Maybe a company hired a boardinghouseful of men one summer; then laid them off over the winter; then hired only a half-dozen men the next summer; then just a caretaker or squatter; then, in a last-ditch effort, another boardinghouseful; then nobody at all. On the other hand, if the trenches and test pits exposed enough copper to energize investors' enthusiasm, then a company entered its developmental stage. Instead of looking far and wide for copper, it singled out a promising lode for development, opened it up, and tested it. Men drove shot-holes into the rock using sledgehammers and hand-held drill steels. They charged the holes with black powder, fired them, removed the debris, then did it all over again. They sank shafts into the lode or vein, often going down several hundred feet, and at a set distance, usually every ten fathoms (sixty feet), they drove a horizontal drift or tunnel along the lode and through the copper rock.

To push this development work, a company hired, sheltered, and fed more than a hundred men. Still, all this effort was only a test, with no guarantee that the lode or vein would prove valuable, no guarantee that the miners, trammers, windlassmen, blacksmiths, carpenters, and cooks would be staying long. The mine settlement still resembled a camp more than a community. The new men joining the mining ranks remained overwhelmingly young and single. They lodged and ate in more company boardinghouses, and in return for providing room and board, a company usually held back about one-fourth or one-third of a man's pay. In the early 1850s, skilled miners earned about $35 per month and paid $9 for the privilege of stretching out on a boarding-house bunk and eating a steady stream of salt pork, beans, and coarse bread. By 1860, when a miner earned $45 to $50 for working twenty-six days a month and an unskilled worker earned only $30, companies withheld a monthly boardinghouse charge of $11 or $12.[16]

At each location, the men at the bottom of the mine sooner or later had to find copper deposited in commercial quantities. If not, company officers ran out of optimism, investment capital, or both, and shut the operations down. Then boardinghouses fell empty and silent, and grasses, wildflowers, and new timber started growing in once-worn trails and clearings. Charles Whittlesey traveled the Keweenaw in the late 1840s, after "the season of fictions had passed," when every adventurer had expected to strike it rich. In traversing the mineral range he "found an abundance of deserted cabins, gardens, trails where a short time before there were throngs of laborers & explorers. The forests had become again solitary."[17]

At more fortunate camps, pioneering shafts and drifts exposed enough cop-per to prompt a company to advance into full production and transform its mine site in important and expensive ways. Typically, it sank more shafts; built more substantial warehouses and blacksmith and carpenter shops; put up shaft-houses, sortinghouses, and kilnhouses; and installed boilerhouses, steam hoists, and stamp mills.

As facilities expanded, so did jobs. Many companies, as their labor rolls doubled and tripled, hired still more single men, putting them up in more boardinghouses. When the Minesota mine started taking great quantities of mass copper in the late 1850s, it put up five boardinghouses in a single year to handle more than a hundred new men. Fifty miles north of the Minesota, on the brow of the hill overlooking Portage Lake, the Quincy and Pewabic mines followed suit. As they energetically exploited the newly discovered Pewabic lode of amygdaloid copper, each company's labor force quickly jumped to more than two hundred men and kept climbing. To keep pace with hiring, Quincy built four large boardinghouses, each for as many as forty or fifty men. Pewabic erected eleven smaller boardinghouses, equipping each one with stoves, furniture, and bedding for eighteen workers.[18]

But after an intensive flurry of boardinghouse construction, a different pattern of growth and settlement usually emerged. A mining company engaged in production—seeking profits through the employment of several hundreds of men and the operation of a large, expensive physical plant—stopped acting like a speculative, high-risk venture operating on the brink of oblivion. As it worked to become a rooted fixture on the mining frontier, it took measures to transform a camp into a community. At the same time, however, it usually put some interesting limits on community-building efforts.

A company sometimes put up and operated a store near its mine office. Sometimes it leased out a building to a butcher, cobbler, or doctor.[19] But generally, while it might encourage a small number of commercial or professional tenants to operate on its property, it had no desire whatsoever to erect a full-fledged company town and serve as everybody's landlord.

A company did not lay out, build, and operate an extensive street of stores and shops right at its mine location. However, it might encourage others to develop a well-rounded commercial and service community on the *margin* of the mine. While a mining company held on tenaciously to all property needed for extracting and processing copper and for housing select employees, it could dedicate some copper-poor land next to its mine for independent development. It could plat the land, sell it off, and watch the purchasers put up stores, stables, blacksmith shops, houses, hotels, or saloons.

Thus the Northwest Copper Company laid out and sold lots in the new village of Wyoming, while the Mendota Mining Company platted the village of Mendota. The National mine created Webster, and the Minesota mine, Rosendale. On the south shore of Portage Lake, Ransom Shelden reserved the eastern end of his land holdings for developing mines and mills; he platted the village of Houghton on the western end. Opposite Houghton, on the other side of the Portage, while the Quincy Mining Company developed its works on the Pewabic lode, it sold off platted land to encourage and sustain the growth of the village of Hancock.[20]

Firms eschewed building complete company towns but did develop residential neighborhoods right at the mines, where favored workers rented company-owned dwellings at low cost. These favored workers weren't the same unmarried roustabouts who had been willing, a few years earlier, to camp out in a wilderness and help the company hunt for copper. Instead, they were skilled workers who had come up to Lake Superior with their families.

The mining industry always needed thousands of young, single, unskilled men—men with strong backs to wheel rock, raise timbers, chase supplies, load wagons, and stack cordwood. But while companies needed such men, they held them in low esteem and saw them as replaceable transients, as well as likely sources of labor trouble, ranging from wildcat strikes to drunken brawls. Maturing companies started seeing their own boardinghouses, filled with young, single men, as incubators of unrest. So they stopped building new ones, converted several old ones to new uses, and maybe kept only one or two open if absolutely necessary.[21]

As they halted boardinghouse construction, companies started building single-family dwellings to lure and keep the married men they deemed more likely to show up for work sober on any given day, and more likely to put down roots and put in years of steady, dependable service. They built houses for the families of skilled miners, mechanics, bosses, engineers, clerks, doctors, and managers. They also made it possible for married employees of sufficient rank and worth to build their own houses on company-owned lots, leased for next to nothing. As for the single men still employed, companies drove them away or split them up. They could either board off mine property at a nearby commercial village or board individually with families at the mine. The latter arrangement brought working-class families additional income, and the families, companies hoped, would have a moderating influence on the behavior of young men.

Between 1850 and 1870, the faces of the commercial and mining villages on the Keweenaw changed a great deal as copper industry employment rose from 800 to 4,200 and the peninsula's total population climbed from about 1,100 to 21,000. By 1870, nearly 4,000 families lived on the Keweenaw, in almost as many dwellings.[22] Many of these dwellings were company-built and stood in the various mine villages, ranging from "old" Clifton, established in the 1840s, to "new" Calumet, which started twenty years later.

These mine villages showed little obeisance to some envisioned model community or long-range plan. Rarely did companies lay an extensive, continuous rectangular grid over a mine site and then construct a full array of streets and housing blocks. Instead, they often scattered first-generation houses among other mine structures, putting them alongside preexisting roads or trails that maybe meandered a bit as they ran from the office to the boardinghouses to the shafts, or from mine to lake, or from mine to neighboring mine. The early working-class families that settled into company houses on the Keweenaw often found that their closest neighbors were not fellow countrymen from Ireland or Cornwall but a poor-rock pile and a mine shaft. They also found their quarters small and primitive.

At some mines, the first company houses were one-room cabins, maybe with a cramped sleeping loft tucked overhead, constructed of unhewn, round logs. This house type was nothing new. Pioneers in need of shelter in wooded territories had built such cabins in many spots along America's westward-roaming frontier line. Companies adopted this folk-style dwelling for the same reasons other pioneers had: it was cheaply and easily built. The crudest log cabins at the mines were founded not on a masonry wall but on a timber sill, laid right on the ground. They had no root cellar, no joists or floors (save, perhaps, for flat stones or boards put over the dirt). A single door and very few windows pierced the walls. A simple stovepipe, not a brick chimney, rose from the cast-iron stove up through the roof, which was merely planked, rather than shingled. Such cabins were a distinct cut above the squatter's shanty but still left much room for improvement.[23]

When their fortunes and futures looked good, companies improved their family housing. Hewn log houses soon became more numerous than earlier log cabins. The chinks between hewn logs could be more tightly sealed against bad weather, and the walls might even be weatherboarded on the exterior and plastered on the interior. Second-generation log houses usually exhibited more refinement and solidity: root cellars, masonry foundations, wooden floors, brick chimneys, more windows, and wood-shingled roofs became commonplace.

Company-built log houses also became larger, expanding to up to three or four rooms in size. By raising the walls and roofs higher, primitive sleeping lofts expanded to become sleeping rooms. Many companies added a framed kitchen off the back of the dwelling. Moving the kitchen outside the main house rectangle made the kitchen more workable and the front room more livable.[24]

By the 1860s or early 1870s, most established companies abandoned log houses for workers' families and adopted clapboarded, frame dwellings one and a half or two stories tall. Several factors encouraged the change. With a larger fleet of lake boats and with the canal and locks open at Sault Ste. Marie, companies received a wider range of lumber and other building products at competitive prices. They also turned to new, local mills on the Keweenaw (some of which were mining-company operated) that produced sawn studs, joists, sheathing boards, and the like. Compared to working with walls of hewn logs, whose stability depended on strong, notched corners and a minimum number of midwall openings, carpenters had more freedom working with framed dwellings.[25] This building technology readily allowed for more diverse forms—more wings, extensions, doors, and windows. Also, the framed dwelling simply looked more modern and finished.

At each mine location, the adoption of frame construction for ordinary housing symbolized that the hardest, roughest pioneer days had passed.

The early frame dwellings were small and plain. The ordinary worker's
house never carried a porch or shutters. It had a flat front and an entrance
bearing no gingerbread, turned columns, or railings. Usually, these sound but
modest houses provided a miner and his family with four or five small rooms.
Living, work, and kitchen spaces occupied the ground floor, with sleeping
rooms above, where a slanting roof was sure to take away much headroom
around the perimeter. Companies built their framed houses in different forms.
The T-shaped plan, with the kitchen extending off the rear of the main structure, was common, as was the saltbox house, which borrowed its shape from
an old New England house type.[26]

As labor forces continued to expand and companies became more experienced as community builders, they started laying out new roads for the express
purpose of accommodating orderly rows of houses. That was how the mine
villages generally evolved and matured: one batch of new houses at a time.
Companies put up a neighborhood over here, then a neighborhood over there,
usually tucking them in close to the shafts and shops. At a mine, there was
rarely much physical separation between where a family man lived and where
he worked.

Companies set their dwellings on lots of good size, often fifty by one hundred feet, or even greater. Ample lots allowed room for a privy, a well, maybe
a small outbuilding, a chicken coop or animal pen, and a vegetable garden.
As they put up their houses during a particular boom on a particular block,
the mining companies imprinted a sense of order and regularity on life at Lake
Superior. The houses were usually identical in size, shape, and trim. Most
expressed a strong appreciation of symmetry: the front door stood in the middle
of the facade and was flanked on either side by a single window. Houses were
set back an equal distance from the road on identical lots, which sometimes
were fenced. Maybe burned stumps still filled the yards and pigs roamed the
streets, but the little log houses stood all in a row.[27]

Besides according a spatial sense of order to the mine villages, housing
reinforced a social order. At Fort Wilkins, the army built different quarters
for officers, single enlisted men, and married enlisted men. In the military, a
man had his place and his rank, and they were made clear to him in many
ways. The mine villages were a lot like that. In fact, an early settler and
longtime mine superintendent wrote, "Social life at the mines partakes somewhat of the characteristics . . . of an army post."[28] Mine villages had a social
hierarchy, where occupation, ethnicity, and marital status counted a great deal.
A company's housing stock reflected and reinforced its social pecking order.

A single, unskilled worker—the man at the bottom of the social hierarchy—
maybe landed a job, but he had to secure his own housing. (In 1861, for

instance, 350 Quincy employees without families boarded at eighty-two different places scattered atop Quincy Hill or down in Hancock.)[29] The married man who barely cracked the skilled-worker barrier, and perhaps was a new employee, might find himself domiciled in one of the mine's smallest, oldest dwellings—a structure built for a hundred dollars or less that rented for only one dollar per month. The next step up was one of the newer, larger, hewn-log houses, built for maybe two or three hundred dollars. Above that was the small, wood-frame house of four or five rooms. This house was still intended for "ordinary workers"—but ordinary workers of the best kind: men who had proven themselves skilled, diligent, and loyal employees. Companies erected these frame houses for four or five hundred dollars each and rented them out at a charge not exceeding one dollar per month per room.[30]

Next came a mine village's "better class" of houses for bosses, doctors, chief clerks, mine captains, and superintendents. These often had eight or more rooms; cost from one thousand to several thousand dollars to build; were more distinctive in appearance; and sometimes came furnished. The top men at the mine—who received the highest salaries—also received the best houses, for which they often paid nothing. Free company housing was a perquisite granted to high-ranking Americans, Cornishmen, and other elites, who needed enticements to come and stay on Lake Superior.

Social conditions changed rapidly along the mining frontier. People picked up and moved from place to place as the fortunes of different mines rose or fell. While some mines were just getting started, others, having seen their best days, were shutting down. New towns and ghost towns both had their place.

A substantial reordering of copper production and population occurred between 1860 and 1870. During this decade the two most important and profitable mines of the 1850s—the Cliff mine in northernmost Keweenaw County and the Minesota mine in southernmost Ontonagon County—faltered as the mass copper yield coming from their fissure veins fell off precipitously. Not only did these mine villages decline; so did the commercial villages in their vicinity, such as Eagle River, Eagle Harbor, and Ontonagon. But these losses of production and population were more than offset by greater gains made in Houghton County, the Keweenaw's middle.[31]

In the late 1850s and first half of the 1860s, the Portage Lake mines—working lodes of amygdaloid copper deposited in volcanic rock—experienced tremendous growth. Then, in the late 1860s and early 1870s, the Calumet conglomerate lode—copper deposited in a sedimentary rock matrix of sand, pebbles, stones, and boulders—proved so rich that the Calumet and Hecla Mining Company soon outproduced all other Keweenaw mines put together. So as the frontier era was drawing to a close, the most bustling, rapidly developing Keweenaw communities were Houghton and Hancock on opposite sides of Portage Lake, and the new village of Calumet, just a dozen miles to the north.

While American companies launched the Keweenaw's copper industry, thousands of miles away on another peninsula in the extreme southwest corner of England, Cornish copper and tin mines suffered a steep decline. Social conditions there, too, were changing. In order to make a living at his trade, many a skilled Cornish miner had to give up on the depressed economy of his homeland and book passage to a distant mining district. Some sailed to Australia, Cuba, or Canada, some to the Keweenaw.

In the late 1860s, if an emigrating Cornishman—say, a young fellow named Josiah Penhallow—just happened to end up on the deck of a steamer sailing into Portage Lake from Keweenaw Bay, up on top of the valley, on both sides, he saw mines dominating the crest.[32] Along the shoreline his vessel slipped past several stamp mills, each rumbling as powerful machines pulverized copper-bearing rock, each spilling smoke into the sky and waste tailings into the water. Inside, men and boys tended the machines.

Our Cornishman steamed by the Detroit and Lake Superior Copper Company's smelter. Coal for firing its reverberatory furnaces filled one yard; stockpiled copper ingots filled another. Lake boats at the dock were just receiving their red-metal cargo to carry south, while a couple of smaller boats shuttled passengers and freight across the Portage from Houghton to Hancock.

Just after passing Quincy's stamp mill, maybe the lake boat put Josiah Penhallow off at Hancock, now a village of about two thousand inhabitants. From the waterfront dock, lined with warehouses, he followed a board sidewalk that aimed uphill toward the heart of town. After carrying his satchel up a half-dozen flights of steps, he took a breather in front of the Leopold, Austrian & Bro. general store, one of the village's earliest and largest mercantile establishments, which showcased kitchen utensils and foodstuffs in one display window, and clothes and toiletries in another. After making an inquiry or two, he found his way over to Hancock's "first-class Cornish Hotel," a former general store just converted into a commercial boardinghouse for up to 150 men.[33]

With his gear stowed away, the Cornishman took a little walk around the town, whose dirt streets ran about three blocks in one direction and four in the other. Within this core, the buildings had a fairly orderly appearance, but along its fringes the settlement still appeared ragged.

Hancock wasn't a particularly attractive place. Settlers had left only a few trees standing on the eastern end, and the architecture was hardly distinguished. Landscaping was mostly done in dirt and rock, while the buildings—stores, hotels, and houses alike—were constructed in a solid yet plain manner. Traces of America's stylish architecture of the day—Italianate villas, Greek temples, and Gothic Revival houses—could hardly be found yet in Hancock, or any-where else on the Keweenaw. Hancock's tallest buildings stood three stories high, but for the most part it was a two-story town, with almost every structure made of wood, and almost every structure painted white. Any red or gray building stood out, as did a couple of Hancock's churches, because of their steeples.[34]

As Penhallow ambled around town, a few carriages and heavy dray wagons moved about, but most traffic was pedestrian. A number of dogs ran loose in the streets. At a couple of corners, hucksters sold vegetables out of carts. The new arrival noted that a number of artisans had set up shop in Hancock: a cobbler, several tailors and milliners, a tinsmith, and even a photographer. He passed a bakery, a carriage dealer, a couple of hardware stores, and a clothier. He also saw signs advertising the services of a doctor and druggist. He walked by a half-dozen general stores, where the people inside always seemed to be congregating at the counter talking, and about as many saloons.[35]

The Cornishman decided to take a closer look at the mines above Hancock that he'd seen from the boat. To get to the Quincy mine, Penhallow hiked about a mile up a hillside, gaining about five hundred feet of elevation along the way. He started the climb on Reservation Street, the extreme eastern boundary of the town. Just off to his right, on a steep tramroad paralleling the street, trains of cars delivered copper rock down Quincy Hill to the com-pany's waterfront stamp mill. To the hiker's left, the houses on Reservation Street were interspersed with small barns, warehouses, outhouses, and slapdash fences erected around barren, rocky, canted yards.

Reservation Street ran straight up the hill for only a few blocks, then turned into a rutted wagon road that wound toward the top of Quincy Hill. Until the late 1840s, the land traversed had been dense, verdant forest. Now, hardly a living tree stood among the thousands of dead stumps, two feet tall, left slowly to rot. A decade of Quincy prospecting, followed by nearly a decade of mining, had put a pox on the hillside. Penhallow walked by cuts and trenches and adits and test pits, by little hillocks and large dumps of dark gray rubble rock from the mine, spilled out over the land because it contained scant or no copper.

As the Cornishman approached the crest of the hill, company-sponsored desolation started to recede in the face of company-sponsored civilization. He had passed a few dwellings scattered on the hill between Hancock and Quincy; now he passed a straight row of small houses, probably some of the initial twenty-seven log houses built by Quincy just as it started expanding in the late 1850s.[36] Then he joined the main road on the brow of the hill that cut right through the Quincy, Pewabic, and Franklin mines, as it ran northeast-wardly toward the new Calumet and Hecla mines.

Even at a glance, Quincy looked unlike any mine village Penhallow had seen in Cornwall. The Cornish brought much cultural baggage with them that influenced life and work on Lake Superior. They brought their knowledge, their jargon, their skills, and even their employment system, which had mining teams work under contracts, not for daily wages. But they hadn't been able to replicate their architecture or neighborhoods on the Keweenaw. On Quincy Hill, Penhallow saw many fellow Cornishmen, or "Cousin Jacks." But he saw no distinctive Cornish engine houses of stone, driving hoists or pumps. No stone cottages or row houses. No stone walls boxing in small yards. As in Hancock, almost everything at Quincy was built of wood: the shafthouses, hoisthouses, and other mine buildings lining one side of the main road, and the houses on the other side.

After walking by a half-dozen company houses fronting the road, the Cornishman came to the settlement's largest single-family house, the mine agent's. Samuel Robinson, a Yankee from New Hampshire, occupied the house and superintended Quincy's operations. Robinson's two-story house stood on a very large fenced lot; on one side of the house, paths outlined several formal, elliptical gardens.

A bit farther on, just past the company office and company store, the Cornishman walked past two other large, wood-frame houses on fenced lots, each different in plan and appearance. Thomas Flanner, the company doctor, occupied one; James North Wright, the other. Wright, from Connecticut, served as company clerk and ran Quincy's supply orders, payrolls, and other business affairs.

Our visitor walked up onto a skull of outcropping rock marking high ground at the mine and got a good panoramic view of the operation. Across the road to the south, Quincy's six shafthouses stood in a row along the top of the Pewabic Lode. Some immense stulls—sections of tree trunks—lay near the shafts. Timbermen would take them underground, as needed, to prop up loose parts of the hanging wall over miners' heads. A tall wrought-iron smokestack and an impressive stockpile of cordwood marked each boilerhouse and hoist-engine house. These wooden structures sheltered the mine's most expensive equipment, so Quincy took some extra precautions against fire. A permanent ladder ran up to each roof peak, where a line of water-filled barrels stood perched on a catwalk, ready to provide an emergency dousing.

(Fire on the mining frontier, when almost everything was built of wood, and before water mains and hydrants were in place, was no small threat. Several Keweenaw villages suffered catastrophic fires, including Eagle River in 1867, and Hancock two years later. The original Hancock toured by Penhallow did not last much beyond his visit. On April 11, 1869, over the span of six hours, fire destroyed the business part of town and about 120 dwellings, leaving nearly two hundred families homeless.)[37]

The Cornishman perused the mine location on the north side of the road.

Nearby he spied Quincy's two remaining boardinghouses and a cluster of dwellings occupied by Cornishmen like himself, who served as mine captains and supervised underground operations. He noted the only two buildings constructed not of wood but of dark gray poor rock taken from the mine. Smoke from a forge fire rose from one of them. Inside, blacksmiths hammered and sharpened the chisel points on the drill steels used for driving shot-holes. A trail of weary men wearing coarse, grime-covered mine gear trod in hobnailed boots along a footpath leading to the other stone building. Inside this dryhouse (also called simply "the dry") or change house, they'd wash up, getting the worst of the dirt off their hands, arms, and faces, and then put on their going-home clothes, leaving their work clothes behind.

The Cornishman stepped down from the outcropping and followed a trail leading away from the road and toward the back side of the mine location. Some draft animals and carriage horses loitered by company barns, while a number of milk cows roamed a "pasture" (if that word could properly be applied to the rockiest of soils and the coarsest of weeds). Penhallow saw a nearly new, two-story, clapboarded building he assumed was the school; because this was summer, though, it was unoccupied.

The Cornishman walked past another smattering of small cabins; then, a quarter mile back from the main road his meandering lane straightened out and ran to Quincy's Hardscrabble neighborhood, named for the poor, rocky ground it stood on. Here, forty-four small frame houses stood in four tidy rows of eleven each. Like the school, the houses all looked nearly new, and they were absolutely identical in their T-plan with a small kitchen extending off the back. Outside many of them, the big tubs women and girls had used earlier in the day to do the washing still sat around, while the clothes fluttered on strung-up lines. Beneath the lines, chickens and ducks idly pecked away at the dirt.

In front of one house, a man knelt down in a circle of boys for a game of marbles. Out back behind the neighborhood, another group of boys played catch with a rag ball. Once in a while they'd toss it up and whack it with a broken sledgehammer handle, used as a bat. The women were now all out of sight, presumably preparing supper, while their husbands, sons, and boarders trickled home from the dry.

Penhallow turned back toward the main road. Just before getting there, he encountered another cluster of small houses, just like those in Hardscrabble, and just as new. Limerick was a smaller neighborhood, though: about thirty houses on three straight lanes. Interesting that Quincy divided over seventy identical houses, built at the same time, into two separate and distinct neighborhoods. Penhallow walked past a group of men returning home to Limerick from the dryhouse, and heard them speak in their distinct Irish brogue. Not a bad idea, the Cornishman thought, segregating the troublesome Irish from the others by putting them up in their own neighborhood.

(Our Cornishman had no way of knowing it, but in 1864, while putting up Hardscrabble and Limerick, Quincy had built a third neighborhood that wasn't visible at all from the main road. Quincy hid it away in an isolated spot a mile from the mine. Its thirty-seven dwellings were inferior to those of Limerick and Hardscrabble: they were smaller and of log, rather than frame, construction. This neighborhood, too, had an ethnic presumption: its name was Swedetown.)[38]

Passing Limerick, Penhallow rejoined the main road, where a heavy wagon drawn by a pair of methodical work oxen creaked by. Some large pieces of mass copper lay in the bed; the wagon also carried several barrels full of fist-sized pieces of mass copper. This cargo was headed down the hill and straight to the smelter. Penhallow soon left Quincy property and crossed onto the Pewabic mine location, where he encountered more housing. Some Pewabic neighborhoods were atop the hill, just above the heart of the mineworks; some were below, on the hillside running to Portage Lake.

The shells of Pewabic's early boardinghouses still stood, but most didn't serve as boardinghouses anymore. Company carpenters had divided them into two or three "tenements" each, and families now resided there. Pewabic's officers and bosses who happened to be single still boarded at the mine, in rooms attached to the main mine office. And the engineers, who operated the hoists, boarded together in a frame dwelling "of the better class" located right near the engine house.[39]

The mine agent and other married company employees of high rank had their individual houses, more distinctive in style and larger than the rest. They were certainly larger than the two dozen original log houses that still dotted the location. The Cornishman ruminated that Pewabic, unlike Quincy, had adopted the small, wood-frame, side-by-side duplex as its standard form of dwelling; he must have seen seventy or eighty of these double houses. Given that most company housing was so alike, one neighborhood in particular caught the stroller's eye, precisely because the houses were not uniform. On half-acre lots laid out in a regular manner, over twenty families lived in houses they'd built themselves, on leased company land.

Penhallow decided he'd come back early the next day and see the mine captains about work. Before leaving the hilltop, he looked down over the industrialized valley, then across at the forest that still stood on part of the opposite crest. In Cornwall, he'd never seen stands of trees like those along Superior. He'd never seen mines that looked just like these, either. He figured he might be in more familiar surroundings underground, once he got a job.

Instead of retracing his steps, Penhallow took a different route back to

Hancock. He followed a road running from Pewabic's mine down to its mill on Portage Lake. He expected that once back in Hancock, he was bound to run into somebody he knew from the mines back home near Cambourne. Fellow countrymen could fill him in on the best places to look for work and permanent lodging.

FOUR

A LAPFUL OF APPLES

Foodways in the Far North

As the number of boats [on Lake Superior] increased so did the comforts of the people. Fresh meats and apples were among the luxuries that found their way into the home of the pioneer. In autumn, when cold enough to carry meat without too great danger of spoiling, it was an amusing sight to see steamers come into port with the carcasses of sheep and sides of beef hanging from upper and lower decks. These were sold in halves or quarters, cut into suitable shape for cooking and carefully packed in snow to be used as occasion demanded.

Mrs. W. A. [Susie] Childs,
"Reminiscences of 'Old Keweenaw' "

Horace Greeley, remembering the 1840s, recalled that Lake Superior was not "calculated to attract a . . . gourmand."[1] Food was frequently scarce, sometimes rotten, and often monotonous and boring. Pioneers could not eat a year-round diet of nourishing, varied, and appetizing food. But two or three decades of occupation brought a great deal of change to the Keweenaw diet. In the mid-1840s, a hungry man with a shotgun might walk into the forest, ready to target as food virtually anything that moved; by 1870, he could stroll into a church social and sit down to a dish of strawberries and ice cream.[2]

Local forests, meadows, lakes, and streams continued to offer up food. Gardens and farms cultivated by settlers yielded a modest amount of fruits and vegetables, and some meat and dairy production was undertaken. More and larger supply ships plying the waters of Superior delivered not only a wider array of fresh and preserved foodstuffs to Keweenaw stores but also the cookstoves, kitchenware, and tableware used to prepare and eat meals. Importantly, as more women settled on the Keweenaw, they assumed the lion's share of the essential task of feeding the population.

As a result of these factors, over time settlers felt more secure about having adequate quantities of food. Their lives became more comfortable when they were able, first, to reestablish a familiar diet, consumed in a traditional manner, and, later, to expand on that diet by adding greater and healthier variety to their meals. Nevertheless, even through the 1870s the copper district's food supply remained more restricted and tenuous than that found in many other parts of the country. The region's short, cool summers discouraged intensive agricultural pursuits and made the population highly dependent on foodstuffs shipped up from the world below. Because the Keweenaw lacked direct rail connections with that world, its two main supply routes remained the overland roads running up from Wisconsin and, of course, the shipping lanes of Lake Superior. Every year, winter's cold, snow, and ice rendered the land route difficult and the water route impossible. So larders continued to run low as each winter dragged on.

Few members of the earliest geological and mine exploration parties were veteran frontiersmen, capable of living wholly off the land, and few men came to the Keweenaw carrying a rifle or shotgun. Nevertheless, the well-equipped party brought along at least one skilled hunter and fisherman, plus a couple of firearms and fishing tackle.[3] Because the parties coasted in small boats and then trekked through dense woods, they packed in limited provisions and acquired food as they went along. They hunted, fished, and expanded their palates, eating an array of local creatures taken from the air, land, and water. Some, like the fish pulled from Superior and inland lakes and streams, remained important parts of the Keweenaw diet. Other species of small game and fowl found themselves safe again from hunters as soon as more traditional foods became available.

Early on, the Keweenaw forests were absolutely thick with passenger pigeons, a bird later to become extinct. On the day after the Cass expedition visited the Ontonagon Boulder in 1820, David Bates Douglass recorded in his journal: "The pigeons are so numerous . . . that a great many have been killed with clubs. Forsyth killed several in the morning . . . as they flew past the tent and Riley, the interpreter, killed two with his fist." Twenty years later, Bela Hubbard, on Douglass Houghton's geological exploration of 1840, reported that "pigeons have been found in plenty & liberally supplied our table."[4] Early explorers also ate partridges, ducks, geese—and seagulls. For eggs, they raided nests of gulls and wild geese. George Cannon reported that in 1846, the residents of Copper Harbor rowed out to Manitou Island, a "general rendezvous" for gulls and geese, to collect eggs in any quantities they wanted.[5]

The earliest settlers did not kill many large game animals for food. On occasion, they took a moose or bear; even more rarely, a deer. The dense Keweenaw forest originally constituted very poor deer habitat. Deer migrated into the region later, after much of the native forest had been cleared. In 1870, the *Portage Lake Mining Gazette* ran a short blurb on the arrival of a 160-pound deer at Houghton. It had not walked into town, nor had a local hunter brought it in. Instead, the stage from Negaunee delivered it, and shortly thereafter Alex Gutsch's restaurant started serving up venison steaks.[6]

Small game was more plentiful and diverse. In the 1840s, Charles Whittlesey wrote that "most of the disagreeable effects of a short allowance [of food] were avoided by the capture of a porcupine, of which we made by long boiling in the camp-kettle, a very palatable soup." Charles Penny's geological expedition "caught an enormous turtle, of some twenty pounds weight," and the next day they "dined at ½ past five on turtle—boiled, fried and souped—quite a feast." Penny, a hard-working, hungry man out in the woods, ate whatever the air, water, or woods provided: "I have made acquaintance with several new dishes . . . ; speckled trout, sea gull, porcupine, muskrat and river turtle all in their place. . . . I have nothing, however, to complain of, on the score of eating. My appetite gives relish to everything."[7]

Penny saved his greatest praise for local fish: "We have a good supply of the finest fish. Night before last we caught three whitefish and one trout; last night two large whitefish. One can never get tired of them in this latitude. The meat is so fine, hard and white, and so sweet, that all other fish seem 'flat, stale and unprofitable' when compared with them." Horace Greeley was none too enchanted, overall, with the pioneer's standard fare of salt pork, bread, beans, and potatoes. But he, too, admired the whitefish and large lake trout taken from Superior, and the speckled trout from streams.[8] Local waters also yielded plenty of brook trout, pike, and pickerel.

Expedition parties carried few kettles, pots, and pans, and no stove. They cooked over an open fire and ate sitting cross-legged on the ground. At its simplest, a mid-1840s meal of bread and meat could be cooked on sticks, as described by George Cannon:

> We were obliged to make some bread. . . . If you have no cup, the water can be dipped into the flour with the hand and made of the usual tenacity for bread. It is then wound around several sticks separately, and these are placed erect in the ground before the fire. They are to be occasionally turned around, until the bread is thoroughly baked, which serves to form, with some meat fried in the fire by means of a stick, a most delicious meal.[9]

If Cannon's was one of the simplest camp meals, Bela Hubbard enjoyed one of the most bountiful ones, taken at Copper Harbor on Independence Day in 1840:

> Several blasts were got ready for the great national jubilee, which we commemorated in the noisy manner usual with Americans, by a grand discharge from the rocks. . . . Later in the day we retired to our camp and partook of an equally grand dinner. It consisted of pigeons, fried and stewed, corn and bean soup, short-cake and hard-tack, pork, and— last but not least—a can of fine oysters. . . . Truly a sumptious repast for a party of wilderness vagrants![10]

The era of "wilderness vagrants," who cooked bread on sticks and happily feasted on pigeons, turtles, or porcupines, was short-lived. In the late 1840s and 1850s pioneers who settled the Keweenaw had no desire to live off the forest. These settlers didn't want to worry about where their next meal was coming from, or what it might be. They didn't want to hunt their supper. They wanted the ordinary foods they were used to *before* moving up to Superior, such as the flesh of domestic cattle. They wanted fresh foods, not always salted, or smoked, or dried. And they wanted variety and choice. Of course, what they wanted and what they got were often different things.

In 1846–47, John Forster, wintering at a small mine camp, hungered for fresh meat, but he partook of only "one dish of fresh beef, and that came to us through the accidental death of a work ox of a neighboring mine." The larder was too full of some things, too depleted of others: "We had plenty of potatoes, salt white fish, a little flour, but only one barrel of pork to last seven months. To live on salt white fish for several months, without grumbling, is assuming the possession of saintly qualities which few men possess." A French Canadian woman cooked for the small band of miners, and Forster allowed as how "she displayed a real genius in handling her materials." Still, one could tire of salt fish, no matter how adroitly disguised or used: "Allow me to enumerate some of her dishes—namely: chowder, fish balls, fish stews with potatoes and without, mashed potatoes and fish, boiled fish, broiled fish; but the *chef d'oeuvre* of all . . . was the salt fish pie, with delicate crust, baked in a large tin pan."[11]

Occasionally, men threw off their saintly qualities in the face of too much repetition at the table. At a boardinghouse at the Cliff mine in the late 1840s, there was "very little variety in the food served. . . . About mid-winter, when supplies of potatoes, turnips and cabbage began to run low there was an unending round of dried beans, salt-pork and beef, with bread." The boarders noted that the same ham bone was being served up time after time. They eliminated that morsel by bringing home a touch of blasting powder, laying a charge where marrow once had been, and blowing the bone up.[12]

Acquiring food was an activity that sometimes brought early white settlers into contact with the small band of Ojibwa resident on the Keweenaw and Isle Royale. A woman recalled how at Copper Harbor, "Indians come to the door, and without knocking, open it and walk in." The men "are sure to be smoking," and for a time "it is puff and spit." Usually, she interpreted such a visit as an appeal for a handout of pork or bread, and "in sympathy with the hungry, and sometimes fearing for her life, she gives them what may be left from the last baking." One time the tables were turned. The woman, "having grown tired of salt pork—the only meat she had eaten for months," asked her visitors if they "could not bring her something from the forest." A few days later they returned, presenting her with a beaver's tail.[13]

Many newcomers initially feared the Ojibwa. Jane Masters recalled how in the early 1850s, after receiving reports "of an Indian massacre in Minnesota," every woman and child at the Delaware mine was "in constant fear of Indians."[14] But no violent confrontations occurred during the establishment of the mining industry, and in several of the early white settlements the Ojibwa sold their catch of fish or their harvest of wild berries door-to-door. They worked as boatmen, transporting food and other supplies from lake ships to shore. Down at Ontonagon, they poled and paddled supplies ten miles up the Ontonagon River to the rapids at American Landing, where roads then led off to the hinterland mines. They showed settlers "their process of making maple sugar" and passed along their recipe for a "peculiar forest drink . . . , spruce beer," which started out as "freshly-cut twigs pickled in a brown sauce."[15]

For a brief period, white settlers happily drank an unusual concoction like "spruce beer," just as they hungrily ate a little turtle or seagull. For a much longer period, they enjoyed making maple sugar or foraging for wild pears, cherries, whortleberries, blueberries, raspberries, thimbleberries, mulberries, and strawberries. Berry picking supplemented the diet while serving as a pleasant pastime. But for the most part, settlers did not want their diet to rely heavily on foodstuffs found in the local environment.

The men were miners, managers, mechanics, or merchants, not savvy woodsmen. To the extent that they hunted and fished at all (and many did neither), they often participated not out of necessity but as sportsmen enjoying outdoor recreation. Agriculture and commerce, not rifles and shotguns, were supposed to put food on the table.

Michigan's legislature acknowledged this fact by the 1860s, when it started putting constraints on both hunting and fishing. By 1863, for the Lower Peninsula, and 1869, for the Upper Peninsula, state game laws set up limited hunting seasons for the likes of deer, elk, pheasant, partridge, woodcock, grouse, ducks, geese, and wild turkeys. The state protected some species from hunting altogether; forbade raiding the nests of fowl for eggs; and outlawed the use of select types of guns, snares, traps, and nets. The passage of fish and game laws was a clear indication that Michigan's frontier era was passing, even on the Keweenaw.[16]

An important part of settling Lake Superior was the cultivating of land and the raising of crops, poultry, and livestock, albeit on a rather modest scale. Nobody ever mistook the Keweenaw for an agricultural paradise, because the growing season was short, summer temperatures low, and the soil in many places poor. In May 1842, before the mine rush even began, the schooner *Algonquin* landed a fishing party at Copper Harbor. While testing the harbor as a commercial fishing site, the men were supposed to raise some crops to help feed themselves. Neither endeavor went well. When the *Algonquin* returned in September, the men had put up and salted "only thirty barrels of trout and siscowit." As for raising potatoes, corn, and beans, they hadn't even tried. They reported "that they could find no ground which in their opinion offered any encouragement, and that they had therefore omitted planting."[17]

Two years later, in 1844, due to Copper Harbor's limited potential for agriculture, an officer at Fort Wilkins requested more supplies for his troops: "I beg leave to state that in this sterile region around us there is no provability of obtaining by cultivation such vegetables as the health of the Troops in their isolated position may absolutely require."[18] But while less-than-ideal conditions surely limited the practice of agriculture, they did not dissuade early settlers from producing a portion of their needed food on the margins of the mines.

The paternalistic mining companies encouraged local food production in several ways. They created tillable land as a by-product of opening mines and erecting villages. Mine locations needed building materials, fuel, and underground mine supports. The wood found in adjacent forests nicely filled the bill, so companies cleared away the trees, which left them with improved land to put into pasturage or production. Some companies, like the Cliff mine, employed their own boss and hands, farmed their own land, and sold vegetables, grains, and animal feeds. Others, like the Minesota mine, leased large tracts to others to work, and the contract farmers supplied company employees "with the produce, at reasonable rates." The Minesota mine contracted to have about two hundred acres of land cultivated in 1855; three hundred acres in 1858; and seven hundred acres in 1861.[19]

The mining companies established commercial farming on Lake Superior; they also set aside land for employees' personal use. The Minesota Mining Company reported in 1858 that "many families and others in the employ of the company have cultivated small patches of ground from which timber had been removed." In 1863 the Pewabic Mining Company opened another seventy acres "to our people for planting." In addition to providing gardens, where families staked out individual plots, companies put dwellings on lots big enough to accommodate many rows of vegetables. And finally, if nothing else was available, a man or woman could just go off and make a clearing somewhere, as Henry Hobart, the teacher at the Cliff mine, did in 1863: "I went last night to clear out little potato patch. It has all been burnt over but we have cleared it of brush, roots, blackened logs, etc. It is quite amusing to see men up here in all directions preparing a small patch of potatoes."[20]

The Michigan census counted about 2,200 improved acres of farmland on the Keweenaw by 1854. This doubled to 4,400 acres in 1860 and rose to 9,900 acres by 1870. By the last date, only 400 of these acres were in northernmost Keweenaw County; 2,100 were in central Houghton County; and 7,400 were in southernmost Ontonagon County, where mining activity had slowed and the climate and soil had proved most supportive of farming.

Local farms largely restricted themselves to growing root vegetables, grains, and grasses that could thrive in this northern clime. Here, the potato ruled. The region produced over 25,000 bushels per year from the mid-1850s onward. The turnip and rutabaga also grew well. (In 1855, Mr. Little of the Forest mine produced "superb samples" of potatoes, carrots, and turnips. His prize turnip, measuring forty inches around, weighed twenty-one and a half pounds.) Farms also produced considerable hay, timothy, and oats for animal consumption. But farmers planted very little wheat and virtually no corn.[21]

Small-scale gardeners, who didn't need a dependable cash crop but wanted some tasty additions to their diet, attempted a more diverse harvest. Besides the potato and turnip, families tried a bit of corn; planted onions, cucumbers, cabbages, squash, tomatoes, and melons; and picked the yield of an imported fruit tree, planted next to the house.[22]

Very few commercial farms in the first decades of settlement engaged in significant beef, swine, poultry, or dairy production. However, select families in the mining and commercial villages kept their own milk cow or raised an occasional hog. On a dismal "spring" day in April 1863, the acerbic Henry Hobart surveyed his world at the Cliff mine and found it full of water, mud, stumps, and a few snowdrifts, "and in the streets may be seen the very smart intellectual-looking animal, the 'Hog.' " By the 1860s the village of Houghton passed ordinances prohibiting owners from letting their hogs or cattle run at large in the public streets. Still, the prohibition could be ignored. In 1870, a cow belonging to Alex Gutsch walked into the First National Bank twice in one day.[23]

Even more families kept ducks, geese, or turkeys, which, throughout a long winter, could be dispatched one after the other to put fresh food on the table. This food did not always go to the proper owner. On October 25, 1862, Houghton's *Mining Gazette* reported numerous complaints of thievery: "In one night a hog and thirteen chickens were taken out of one man's yard. . . . Ducks, geese, and chickens stand a poor chance, when left on the street these cold nights, especially if they have fallen under the observation of some hungry loafer."

While cows, swine, and domestic fowl contributed substantially to the local diet, by the 1860s and 1870s they also contributed to village blight and to public health problems, which residents could most noticeably see—and smell—late in the spring. Winter's freezing cold canceled out stenches, and snow regularly hid filth under a white blanket. People grew careless with their garbage. Months of animal slop and offal piled up in yards, as did manure and droppings. Then came warmer temperatures and the melting and puddling of winter's debris, which assaulted the eyes and the nose. In Houghton, village ordinances regarding dead animals, putrid meat, spoiled fish, and decayed vegetables and all "substances emitting a disagreeable, nauseous or unwholesome odor"—coupled with regular newspaper diatribes against winter's accumulated rubbish and filth—were intended to stimulate a brisk spring cleanup in "every street, alley and back yard."[24] If a civilized community kept animals, it had to clean up after them, too.

To fill their plates, pioneers on the Keweenaw took a bit from the local forest, lake, or meadow. They gathered vegetables from their own garden. They caught and killed their backyard goose. But most important, they went to the store and bought provisions shipped up from the world below. The store was a place that helped "erase differences between here and there, between now and then"—a place where settlers could buy a life more like the one they had left behind, or more like the one lived by residents of more populated, less remote regions.[25]

Small acts, when repeated endlessly by individuals living in numerous, disparate locales, collectively add up over time to become national trends. National trends very much reflect—and affect—private lives. Edwin Henwood, reminiscing about his childhood spent on the Keweenaw in the 1850s, recalled his father's trips to Copper Harbor. Every time he went there, father Henwood shopped at the store and then "brought something home that would be a great treat in those days."[26] The treats included canned goods: sardines, oysters, and strawberries.

When he purchased family treats in Copper Harbor, Edwin Henwood's father was an active participant (today we'd call him a "consumer") in what amounted to a fundamental restructuring of the American economy. This restructuring, this creation of a new, national market economy, made it possible for a Lake Superior pioneer to walk into a store and buy cove oysters, taken from the Chesapeake and cooked and canned in Baltimore, about twelve hundred miles away. Or fresh apples picked from a New York tree. Or salt pork—the flesh of a hog slaughtered, butchered, pickled in brine, and barreled in Cincinnati.

This market economy, as it evolved in the middle decades of the nineteenth century, had a profound effect on how settlers acquired and prepared their foods and on their overall diet. Several interconnected social and technological phenomena combined to support the market economy, not the least of which was the transportation revolution. Improved roads and turnpikes, canals, steamboats, and railroads forged better links between east and west, between north and south, between agricultural and urban areas. The cost of shipping raw materials and finished goods—of shipping the products of farm and factory—decreased substantially.

Reduced transportation costs encouraged farmers to produce more. Instead of limiting production to what their local market could use, they increased production and shipped corn, wheat, and other farm produce off to distant, larger markets. The market economy also encouraged regional specialization of agriculture. Farmers in the various parts of the country no longer had to be "jacks of all trades" who planted or raised a little of everything in order to provide for their local markets' diverse needs for dairy products, meat, grains, fruits, and vegetables. Since people could buy needed foodstuffs from faraway sources, farmers could specialize in the animal husbandry or crops best suited to their particular place.[27]

Select regions of the South dominated rice and sugar production. The new midwestern prairie states became centers of wheat and corn production. Older agricultural areas in the East, surrendering wheat and corn production to their western neighbors, intensified their production of fruits and vegetables. Specialization, because it encouraged the garden farming of vegetables and the establishment of extensive nurseries, orchards, and vineyards, made a more healthy diet available to the population. In the mid-nineteenth century, proper nutrition was little understood. Food was food. People wanted to be full and content, and they knew little (or, in some instances, absolutely nothing) about the importance of "food groups," protein, carbohydrates, vitamins, and minerals. They didn't eat in a "heart smart" manner, skimp on fats, or worry about cholesterol. But they did worry about consuming a monotonous diet. So a market economy that allowed for a special treat—be it a peach or a plum, a string bean or a sardine—was a welcome addition to life.[28]

The industrialization of food processing, preserving, and packing was another key component of the market economy. Commodities once produced in small local establishments, like butcher shops and little water-powered gristmills, or once produced at home, like butter and cheese, now came out of large mills, factories, or packinghouses. Baltimore became an early grain milling center, producing and shipping a half-million large barrels of flour per year by 1850. Richmond, Virginia; Rochester, New York; and, by 1870, St. Louis, Chicago, Milwaukee, and Minneapolis joined Baltimore as major flour-milling centers. Factories in New York, Ohio, and Pennsylvania literally churned out half the nation's butter by 1860; and after 1850, cheese factories had started up in New York and other dairy states.[29]

In the Midwest, meatpacking—especially of pork—became a major new industry. Hogs were easy to raise, they multiplied quickly, and their meat could be preserved in a variety of tasty ways, such as cured hams and bacon. By 1850, no fewer than a hundred towns in Ohio, Illinois, and Indiana had meatpacking plants, and Cincinnati then led the way, packing a half-million butchered hogs a year into barrels.[30] (An Ohio Valley hog, once killed, cut up, salted, and packed in Cincinnati, could reach the Keweenaw by riding the rails or taking the Miami & Erie Canal up to Toledo. From Toledo, schooners or steamers would have carried it on Lake Erie, up the Detroit River, across Lake St. Clair, up Lake Huron, into the St. Mary's River, past Sault Ste. Marie, and then westward over Superior.) By 1860, Chicago was well on its way to packing more meat than Cincinnati and to becoming the premier "Hog Butcher for the World." From May through November, Lake Michigan and other waterways carried preserved meats from Chicago northward to the copper towns.

Numerous foods needed to be preserved in one way or another—not only to enable them to survive long-distance shipping but also to give them an extended shelf life once they reached their destination. The preservation technologies of drying, smoking, and salting, around for centuries, had been applied successfully to meats, fish, and relatively few fruits. By the time Lake Superior was settled, a new preservation technology—canning—allowed settlers to enjoy a healthier and more varied diet.

In canning, food is sterilized by heat and then sealed in an airtight container. This technology originated in France, where in 1809, after fifteen years of experimenting with food preservation, Nicholas Appert won a prize offered by Napolean for devising a method of providing the French navy with a better diet that protected them from scurvy. Appert did his original "canning" in glass jars. By 1820 the technology had diffused to several nations—including the United States, where seafood and fruit were already being put up, and the tin can, rather than the glass jar, was becoming the container of choice, one that proved well suited for use along westward-leading trails, remote settlements, and boomtowns.[31]

Early tin cans were made, packed, and sealed by hand. Prior to 1860, when the canning industry was still centered on the east coast, the nation's maximum output amounted to about five million cans of preserved food per year. Those cans contained meat, fish, shellfish, berries, fruits, vegetables, and even Gail Borden's new product, condensed milk.[32] Canned-good production rapidly escalated in the next decade or so, as the Civil War put a premium on food that could be taken on the road from camp to camp, and as additional canneries opened in the Midwest and along the Pacific coast.

Once foodstuffs were landed at Keweenaw docks, they went to merchandisers for sale to settlers. General stores—selling food, clothes and cloth, hardware, furniture, and many other goods—dominated local merchandising from the mid-1840s until after the Civil War. Some operated right at the mine locations, but most general stores conducted their trade in nearby commercial villages. Men like Ransom Shelden and John Senter, and others like them who came to Superior from New York and New England, were important pioneers who formed a merchant class on the mining frontier and brought the earliest stores to the likes of Copper Harbor, Eagle River, and Houghton.[33]

The account book from John Senter's Eagle River store survives from 1849–50, as does the 1859–60 book from Ransom Shelden's Houghton store. Six other account books from local stores, including one from the Minesota mine company store, cover the years from 1862 to 1870. These eight store account books present a detailed picture of the fixings that went into early settlers' meals.[34]

The stores sold beef and especially pork, most commonly in the form of "barrel" meat, which had been salted and preserved down below and shipped up to Superior. In addition to salt pork, the stores sold smaller quantities of smoked and pickled hams, and they also dealt to a limited extent with freshly butchered hogs. They sold the occasional fresh ham or shoulder, hog's head, and pig's feet.

In addition to barreled beef, the stores sold smoked, canned, and corned beef. It was easy to tell when cattle had recently been slaughtered for a store. Suddenly, large sides of beef went out the door, as did many of the smaller parts: heads or head cheese, tongue, tripe, hearts, liver, and hooves. In the case of both fresh pork and beef, consumers usually purchased large cuts, weighing twenty-five to over a hundred pounds. Home butchering later reduced these to meal-sized portions. Only rarely did a customer go home with a processed food, such as pork sausage, or with a specified small cut of meat, such as the few "rump roasts" or "steaks" sold out of Ransom Shelden's store in 1860.

Fish was another staple in the diet, but general stores traded almost not at all in fresh whitefish or lake trout. In addition to the Ojibwa who peddled fish, only a few commercial fishermen made the Keweenaw their base of operations.[35] During the four or five months they fished each summer, they took their catch directly to consumers, without passing it through the general stores. The stores, however, did a brisk trade in a variety of preserved seafoods taken from the Atlantic. They sold large quantities of salted cod, halibut, and mackerel out of the barrel. Pickled herring was usually available, and thanks to the tin can, settlers even in the 1840s occasionally enjoyed sardines, oysters, and lobster.

In 1860, some 1,050 sheep were locked through at Sault Ste. Marie and taken up to Lake Superior, yet mutton was very rarely sold in the stores. Apparently, those who wanted it must have raised it for themselves. The same was true of poultry. Diaries record that people ate a considerable amount of chicken, turkey, duck, and goose—but these were not sold, alive or freshly killed, in the stores. Similarly, general stores sold very few eggs. And although they sold a great deal of butter and considerable cheese, they carried extremely little fresh milk, and just a tiny bit of canned or condensed milk, by the mid-1860s.

Mutton, poultry, eggs, milk: the early settlers who wanted these foods kept their own animals or fowl, or perhaps obtained them from a friend, neighbor, or peddler. Baked goods formed another important food type little found in general stores. Stores sold soda crackers in the 1840s and 1850s. In the 1860s they started selling sweet, rice, and butter crackers; soda biscuits; and ginger-snaps, which must have been the first mass-produced cookies tough enough to endure transit packed in barrels. That was about it. Customers found little bread and no doughnuts, pastries, pies, or cakes on the shelves of general stores and groceries. In addition, specialty bakery shops were few and far between. Through the early 1870s, census reports showed no bakers in Keweenaw and Ontonagon Counties. And while Houghton County boasted seventy-six blacksmiths, it had but three bakers, all German immigrants: Conrad Eisenhart in Houghton, William Hoffenbecker in Hancock, and Joseph Jacob Merz of Calumet.[36] Residents produced baked goods at home or consumed them at hotel dining rooms or saloon-restaurants.

General stores did peddle the raw materials for baked goods and other foods. They regularly sold baking powder and soda, starches and yeast, sago and saleratus. They mainly carried whole wheat flour but also traded a bit in fine or "best" white flour, plus buckwheat and rye flours. They sold cornmeal and oatmeal; corn, rice and, to a lesser extent, oats, barley, and hops; and, rarely, hominy and farina.

For residents who did not cultivate their own root vegetables, merchants offered Irish potatoes, rutabagas, turnips, carrots, onions, and beets. They also supplied the local diet with peas, beans, and tomatoes, sometimes selling fresh varieties by the bushelful, and often selling them by the can. Many children helped their parents trek home from the store by toting a pail filled with pickles or sauerkraut. Only very rarely did anyone take home a cabbage, yam, sweet potato, pepper, or pumpkin.

In diaries and reminiscences, settlers complained about eating too many potatoes, and they never seemed too enthusiastic about split peas or turnips. Not so with fruit—especially fresh fruit recently arrived from the world below. The occasional apple or lemon was a real treat, sometimes a memorable one. Clarence Bennetts always associated his childhood Independence Days, spent at the Central mine in the 1860s, with lemons and other delectables:

> [On] Fourth of July [we] had our Sunday School picnic out in the woods. A box of lemons, would be sent to our cellar the night before. . . . The Committee would squeeze out that box of lemons . . . add sugar and water and make the three barrels of good lemonade. The Women of the church would supply a bountiful supply of saffron and other delicious cakes. Each teacher would take care of his or her Sunday school class in supplying them with cake and lemonade. . . . After the repast we would play kissing ring or happy is the miller.[37]

Susie Childs remembered an embarrassing moment that occurred about 1850, when, as a little girl, she got a bit carried away by the sight of apples:

> Apples were so rare that they could only be indulged in by the few who were considered affluent. I recall that one particular barrel found its way into a house at Copper Harbor. One evening quite a number of friends had gathered . . . and as a treat a large plate of

apples was brought out. One little girl [surely the author herself] sat quietly by and saw the apples passed to one and another of the old people. . . . Finally the looked for moment arrived and she was invited to take one. . . . She was then asked to take another. . . . Then asked to take another, and another till her little lap was full, her eyes dancing with pleasure, and cheeks outshining those of the apples. Finally she heard a snicker go around the room and realized she had been made the butt of the company. Burning with shame she settled back into the corner of the old lounge on which she sat, and the apples one by one rolled to the floor.[18]

By the late 1840s, fresh apples, peaches, lemons and oranges occasionally arrived at Lake Superior stores, and a bit later came some citrons, limes, and plums. All were available in limited quantities. Tagged with a substantial price, fresh fruit typically sold out within a day or two of arrival—and sometimes another shipment wouldn't be seen until the next summer or fall. When the fresh article was unavailable, settlers bought fruits and berries dried, canned, or processed into a syrup, jelly, or jam. In these forms, they traveled better, had a longer shelf life, and could be enjoyed throughout the year.

Dried fruit—especially apples, raisins, and currants—was an important part of the local diet. Settlers commonly found dried peaches and prunes at the stores, but figs and dates remained scarce. The most important canned fruit was the peach, carried at several early stores, while canned pineapple, blackberries, and strawberries remained extremely rare. Consumers regularly purchased bottles of lemon extract or syrup; far less frequently they obtained blackberry or strawberry syrups or jams and the likes of peach and orange marmalade or guava jelly. Since local berries were plentiful, and berry picking was a popular endeavor for some and a commercial endeavor for others, many residents put up their own jellies and jams. In August 1874, Lucena Brockway purchased fifty quarts of whortleberries one day; she worked long and hard the next day to put forty of them up.[39]

Merchants offered customers a considerable range of sweeteners and flavors. They all stocked sugar of various types (white, brown, and maple sugars) and various forms (loaf, lump, crushed, pulverized, powdered, and granulated). They stocked and sold lots of molasses and corn syrup and some honey. Of spices and flavors, salt and pepper were ubiquitous. Nutmeg, cinnamon, allspice, and mustard powder were regularly stocked and sold, as were, to a somewhat lesser extent, cream of tartar, peppermint, cloves, ginger, and caraway seed. Consumers made relatively few purchases of vanilla, almond extract, saffron, pimiento, and alum. They also flavored foods with the common condiments of ketchup and vinegar; with the less widely used pepper sauce and horseradish; and with the rare "Worcester" sauce, available in Hancock by the mid-1860s.

The general stores sold small amounts of nuts (almonds, with rare sales of pecans, peanuts, filberts, chestnuts, and walnuts) and of candies (licorice, gumdrops, lemon drops, and other hard or rock candies—and, by the late 1860s, even some chocolates). In terms of beverages (or the fixings for beverages) they did a small business in cider, sarsaparilla, and cocoa, but a brisk business in black and green teas and in Java, Rio, and other coffees. Most stores also conducted a lively trade in alcoholic beverages.

Hardware stores and some general stores sold the wood-fired, cast-iron stoves used for frying, boiling, roasting and baking—and for heating the miner's small house during cold winter months. Many stores carried mass-produced, utilitarian kitchenware items fabricated of tin, cast iron, glass, wood, and brass. These included a wide variety of containers: teapots and coffee boilers, milk and molasses pitchers, jugs, tubs, bowls, and crocks. Even a modest household needed an array of sharp-edged kitchen tools, including butcher, chopping, carving, and paring knives; peelers; and perhaps a meat saw, small ax, or hatchet for splitting carcasses.[40]

Stores sold an occasional churn, indicating that some families still produced butter at home rather than buying butter made hundreds of miles away in New York or Ohio. Few kitchens were without whips or whisks, rolling pins, potato mashers, meat pounders, skimmers, dippers, sieves or strainers, ladles, and large spoons. Graters reduced spices like nutmeg to useable form, while hand-cranked mills ground coffee beans. Food was cooked on the stove in a wide variety of kettles, saucepans, stew pans, or "spiders" (cast-iron frying pans). To help take care of those with a sweet tooth, stores sold cake tins, pie plates, muffin pans, and jelly glasses.

Besides trading in kitchenware, merchants offered a range of tableware suited to the incomes and tastes of customers ranging from woodchoppers, trammers, and other unskilled laborers to mine managers and professionals. Not all knives and forks and cups and saucers were equal. Some were of a higher order, based on their specialization, decoration, and materials.

Many working-class families made do with a minimum amount of tableware of the ordinary, inexpensive kind. In November, 1859, the South Side Mining Company purchased $40.77 worth of goods to get some household up and running. Besides blankets, quilts, and mattress material, the purchase included a dozen plates, a set of cups, one pitcher, two bowls, one salt cellar, a set of knives and forks, a set each of teaspoons and tablespoons, one butcher knife, and a broom. In 1867, Francis Kitto pinched pennies while setting up his household in Keweenaw County. Still, it cost him $80—about a month and a half's pay for a miner—to get the essentials: bed, broom, ax, scrub brush, washbasin, washboard, clothespins, groceries, plus kitchen- and tableware. To supplement whatever he might have already had, Kitto acquired a pan, a pitcher, one knife and a knife and fork set, one cup and saucer, one dipper, two bowls, two bottles, two gallon crocks, two tumblers, and nine plates.[41]

Many settlers, like Francis Kitto, used common glass tumblers; iron spoons, knives, and forks; tin cups; and tin or earthenware plates. At the same time, others set more elaborate tables, virtually indistinguishable from those they would have set if living in lower Michigan, New York, or New England. Not everybody roughed it, and stores catered to those who sliced their roast turkey with a fancy carving knive and fork; who ate off sets of china with matching platters, vegetable dishes, gravy boats, and soup tureens; who perhaps took their dessert on glass dishes; who ate with silver or silver-plated knives, forks, and spoons; who dispensed spirits from a stoppered decanter and drank from goblets, wineglasses, and champagne glasses.

Within settlers' houses, and particularly within a mining company's board-inghouse, the kitchen was a serious place of repetitive, often arduous work, most of which fell on the shoulders of women and girls—girls who helped their own mothers or who hired out to women of greater means. No public utilities and very few mechanical devices served the kitchen workspace, so preparing and cooking foods and providing water and heat were onerous daily chores. In kitchens lacking fixed sinks, running water, and drains, women and children hauled in the water used for cooking and cleaning up, then hauled the wastewater back out, getting at least a pace or two beyond the door before letting fly with the dirty contents of basin or bucket. Aside from coffee grinders, prior to 1870 women on Lake Superior were armed with almost no hand-cranked machines or gadgets—no "kitchen magicians" such as mechanical parers, pitters, meat grinders, or even eggbeaters. And although industrialization and the market economy managed to deliver canned goods to the copper frontier, women could find no accompanying can openers in the local stores. They must have muscled their way in, gashing the containers open with the tip of a stout knife.

The cook and her helpers tended the woodpile and started, fed, and banked the fire in the cookstove, adjusting it to the time of day and the task at hand. Tending the cast-iron stove was something a woman did from first thing in the morning until just before bed. That stove, one historian has noted, was "the single most important domestic symbol of the nineteenth century."[42] As the Keweenaw was being settled in the 1840s and thereafter, the cookstove was rendering fireplace cooking obsolete and, at the same time, changing a woman's work routine and her family's meals.

The cast-iron stove began supplanting the open fireplace hearth in the 1830s. This new technology caught on rapidly. By midcentury, numerous stove makers plied their trade in different regions of the country, and the stoves themselves—at least the higher-priced ones—were becoming more elaborate. The firebox heated the top surface of the stove, which, depending on its size and cost, might contain just one or two or as many as eight cooking holes with removable covers or plates. With the holes covered, the flat stovetop slow-cooked, simmered, or kept foods warm. Uncovered, the holes nestled the bottoms of pans, pots, and kettles while exposing them to greater heat. In addition, stoves housed one to three ovens, and some included a reservoir for holding and dispensing hot water.[43]

The new stoves offered several advantages over the old fireplace. They were portable and could move with a family from place to place. Along with their stovepipes, they were cheaper and easier to install than masonry hearths and chimneys (an important factor that encouraged mining companies to install stoves in their boardinghouses and single-family dwellings). They burned far less fuel (wood or, later, coal). By boxing in the fire and cutting down on spitting sparks, stoves were less likely to set the cook or her house on fire.

The cook at her stove did less stooping and awkward reaching, because its top was at a more comfortable, convenient height. Instead of being squeezed against a wall, the stove could sit out in more open space—important not only in terms of access to its various features and parts but also in terms of its ability to heat the surrounding space in the wintertime. The stove also offered versatility. It would "enable the housewife to wash, stew, boil, bake and heat her irons at the same time, and if necessary, she may cook for a dozen of people without inconvenience."[44] (This according to a *male* booster of the new technology.)

Many interpreted the cast-iron cookstove as a sign of progress, as a great labor-saving device for women everywhere—including those preparing meals in remote mine villages hard by Lake Superior. But its benefits came with some costs. Women had to learn how to cook on the new devices. (Cookbooks helped; before the Civil War, many gave instruction in both fireplace and stove cooking.) Those seated at the supper table had to learn to accept new tastes. Meat, for instance, tasted quite different when roasted in a stove oven instead of over open coals. Women needed to learn how to light and keep a different kind of fire, how to adjust dampers and grates to reach and sustain the desired level of heat. They still hauled in fuel and hauled out ashes, and now had the added task of regularly cleaning the stove and brushing on waxy stove black to keep it from rusting. Although family members were now safer from fire, they were still exposed to severe skin burns if they touched the hot stove. And its metal could seem unbearably hot in summer. Due to its black polish, its appetite for fuel and production of ashes, and its sweating heat, the stove often soiled the chef, and as one woman wrote in 1848, it produced "roasted lady" along with roasted meat.[45]

Industrialization and the growing market economy produced versatile cast-iron stoves, a proliferation of cooking utensils, and new foods and ingredients. Taken together, these changes had the effect of raising dietary standards in this country—including on Lake Superior by the Civil War era. The burden of meeting these new standards fell on the housewife and "probably increased the time that women spent in preparing foodstuffs for cooking." For instance, as finely milled wheat flour became more available, women found themselves preparing more time-consuming breads and cakes and using less cornmeal. And because the stove could cook a variety of things simultaneously, the one-dish meal, such as a stew bubbling in a single pot, was starting to give way to multiple-dish meals. Women did the extra work that this menu required and juggled the production of several foods at once to complete a dinner or supper.[46]

If a family kept domestic fowl, or swine, or a milk cow, this put more food on the table, but at the cost of adding still more work to a woman's routine. Partridges and wild ducks and geese belonged to men, who hunted them as sport. But backyard ducks, geese, chickens, and turkeys belonged to the women, who fed them, collected their eggs, caught them, lopped off their heads, scalded and plucked them, and dressed and cooked them. At Clifton, Henry Hobart described a butchering day in 1863: "Mrs. Rawlings had six geese to kill which she done herself, holding them while she cut their necks with a knife." A decade later at the Cliff, Lucena Brockway, not husband Daniel, counted and collected all the eggs and kept and killed the roosters and hens. She once wrote in her diary, "Mrs. Lytle had her ducks killed by a skunk last night. I hope nothing will happen to mine."[47] She meant exactly what she wrote; the ducks were *hers*, and they were not an inconsequential part of her life. In 1873, she succinctly reported on the important events of four sequential days, giving equal weight to life and death, to chickens and turkeys:

Aug. 15:   "Mr. Olds was killed this morning."
Aug. 16:   "10 chickens hatched today."
Aug. 17:   "Charlotte's little baby girl was born."
Aug. 18:   "Young turkeys hatched today."[48]

Keeping large animals also added to a woman's burden. At the least, she slopped the family hog with kitchen refuse and skimmed and prepared the milk of the family cow. Generally, the chore of butchering cattle or swine fell to men, but not always. Hobart recorded another butchering scene in 1863, when a French Canadian woman was helped by some male friends:

They were looking at a fine pig who was nearby, unconscious of anything wrong. Soon they caught Master pig and by dint of some swearing and tumbling succeeded in bringing his huge body low upon the ground. By getting onto him they were able to hold him until the little short dirty woman of the house came in time of need with an exceedingly long butcher knife and stuck it . . . into the neck which soon caused Master pig to die. . . . The dirty woman brought out a bedtick full of straw. . . . The straw was emptied on piggy & set on fire. Piggy's bristles were soon gone & he as black as a darky.[49]

A dead hog in the dirt needed much home butchering before making it to the table. So did the large cuts of meat obtained at stores. Much of what was bought, meat and otherwise, was bought in bulk, and merchants sold few prepared foods that quickly passed from shelf to stomach. True, most women no longer churned butter or made cheese. If they had money, they could buy ready-to-eat sauerkraut, pickles, jellies, and jams, instead of making them. By 1876, an advertisement in the *Portage Lake Mining Gazette* even announced that there was "no need of housewives suffering this summer over hot fires cooking dinner"—because Smith & Harris was selling "delicious canned roast chicken . . . , all ready for the table."[50]

But few families could afford to eat main courses from a can, and women bore the responsibility for knowing how to make food "from scratch," whether breads and pastries, sausage or stews, sauces or soups, or desserts. They also bore the responsibility, by relying on cookbooks or memory, for turning home-raised and store-bought ingredients into *familiar* foods, like those consumed in the old country. Ethnic favorites, like the meaty Cornish pasty, or eggs and milk, or saffron cakes, were made in local kitchens, not bought in local stores. Traditional foods made life on the Keweenaw a bit less strange and a bit more comfortable, as Jinny Penhale expressed in a poem sent back to Cornwall:

> We're livven at the 'North West Mine.'
>   And eer we found ould Stephen Vine
> and Joey Blewett, and lots more
>   We wor acquainted weth before;
> and they wor glad to see us too,
>   and gav us hall a tatie stew;
> and cook'd a oggen and a caake,
>   and put a pasty in to baake,
> and gav us coffee and good tay,
>   and mad us appy right away.[51]

Of course, the food that made some "appy" caused others to lose their appetites. Henry Hobart, the staunch Yankee from Vermont, was a fastidious man and finicky eater who seemingly condemned every mouthful of food he ate at the Cliff mine. Like many single men, Hobart did not keep house for himself or prepare meals. Instead, he boarded with the Rawlings, who fed and sheltered him in order to supplement the family income. His hosts were hardly poor. Mr. Rawlings was a highly skilled Cornish mechanic; Mrs. Rawlings regularly employed girl servants in her house; and the family kept a sixty-dollar milk cow. Nevertheless, Hobart felt he "could never enjoy Cornish living," and he was very unhappy being at the mercy of Mrs. Rawlings's kitchen.[52]

He thought her kitchen was a slovenly place. She dumped fresh bread from the oven out of pans and straight onto the floor to cool. The lone kitchen towel wiped up whatever needed wiping: now a dirty, unwashed fork, then hands, then a washed plate or glass. Mrs. Rawlings would sometimes "wash the plates in the wash dish & perhaps in the same water that some nasty little urchin had used." Beyond matters of cleanliness, Hobart hated the Cornish woman's customary cooking. The meaty pasty, the bachelor thought, produced unattractive, meaty, 180-pound Cornish girls. After Mrs. Rawlings had butchered six geese, instead of enjoying a feast, Hobart said "no thanks" to the meal: "Giblets for dinner of the feet of the geese. One head of same, etc. in a thick kind of gravy. O, Horrors, how was I to eat the feet and head of a goose. I could not." A slain cow promised him nothing any better, because Mrs. Rawlings "was talking about the guts of the cow for to be used to stuff with sausage—calling them 'pudding skins.' Sweet pudding, I should think."[53]

Hobart dreaded eating animal parts on Lake Superior that would have been thrown away in Vermont; he abhorred the boring sameness of Mrs. Rawlings's meals and the lack of special treats and sweets. He yearned for a piece of pie or cake. He filled his diary with food fantasies: "Oh, when shall I see a meal at home [in Vermont]?"—"My anxiety for supper is so great that I will close for fear I shall be writing about Yankee pies and suppers—which look like Gold in my eyes when I think of my present style."[54]

Hobart noted that some mine doctors and clerks, by paying $20 to $25 per month for board, could enjoy "the Yankee style of living," with more varied dishes, including desserts. But because they paid so much board, they "made nothing," and Hobart couldn't afford it. In desperation he obtained a small stove for himself, so he could occasionally make and enjoy a treat like an apple pie.[55]

At early houses, a cellar often served as an important addendum to the kitchen. This storage space relieved a kitchen's cramped quarters. Its below-grade environment also helped preserve fruits, vegetables, and other foods by keeping them cool in the summer, but warmer than freezing in the winter. If early settlers purposefully wanted to freeze a food to preserve it, they turned to the great outdoors. They divided a side of freshly killed beef into manageable portions, which they then packed in snow. As the winter wore on, they periodically fetched and thawed their meat.

By the late 1860s, the Keweenaw's well-to-do families kept select foods cold in their kitchens year-round, thanks to new refrigerators (or ice chests) and to the rise, locally, of a commercial ice industry.[56] That ice industry did not use compressors to produce below-freezing temperatures because the technology of mechanical refrigeration had not yet been developed. Instead, men went out on Portage Lake with large saws and harvested hundreds of tons of ice in the form of blocks two feet wide, three feet long, and from eight to thirty-three inches thick. Nearby icehouses kept this frozen harvest under sawdust and other insulating materials, then sold and distributed it in the spring, summer, and fall months. In July, when a church social in Houghton offered fresh strawberries atop vanilla ice cream, smiling consumers owed their summer treat to the icy Portage Lake of January and February.

For only a brief time did new inhabitants on Lake Superior have to knock passenger pigeons out of the sky for supper, or eat seagulls or turtles, or row out to islands to collect goose eggs. Commerce and agriculture came quickly on the heels of the mine rush, and for most, hunting birds and game, fishing lakes and streams, and gathering berries soon became pastimes, not essential activities, when it came to putting food on the table.

Mining companies cleared away forests and encouraged farming on this northern frontier. Settlers pitched in and helped feed themselves by planting vegetable gardens and keeping domestic fowl and animals. But many bought what they needed, taking advantage of the rise of a merchant class on the Keweenaw, men who came to Lake Superior not to mine copper but to run stores. These merchants peddled goods provided by a developing market economy that included an expanding food industry in the world below, one that produced an increasingly broad array of provisions. Settlers ate better because of innovations like the tin can, which preserved the likes of peaches and pineapples. They ate better because of the construction of the Soo Locks, which locked through more and faster boats laden with supplies. By the mid- to late 1860s, a steamer could leave the Keweenaw, resupply at Detroit, and return to Houghton in less than seven full days.[57]

In the mid-1840s, soldiers at Fort Wilkins happily received a late November shipment of food, then unhappily discovered that of 632 bushels of potatoes, only 25 weren't spoiled—and of 40 barrels of pork, 23 were bad and the remaining 17 had to be eaten immediately, for fear they wouldn't keep much longer.[58] That was a disheartening way for a garrison to enter into a long Keweenaw winter.

A decade later, men at the Norwich mine found themselves running out of provisions in winter. The company was short on beef and flour but did have some cornmeal intended as animal feed, and three yoke of work oxen. To get by, the company killed two yoke of oxen, which provided fresh meat and allowed more cornmeal to be rationed to the men. Still, this wasn't enough. Due to a lack of food, the Norwich mine and others discharged many single workers, who figured that the best way to survive the Keweenaw winter was to leave it. They "took the trail through the woods to Green Bay."[59]

Such incidents became rarer with each passing year. Between the 1840s and 1870, the food supply to the Keweenaw became more reliable in its delivery and more varied in its content. Sarah Barr Christian, wife of a man who was second-in-command at a mine on Isle Royale in the early 1870s, found she had nothing to complain about in the food line. Their company store was "abundantly stocked with all in the way of salt meats, fish, and such canned vegetables as were available." Plus, her family had its personal larder: "We had our own smoked hams, barrels of corned beef, kegs of mackerel, dried beef, sardines, and all canned fish available, canned tomatoes, corn, peas and beans."[60]

Still, as the food supply evolved and changed from the 1840s onward, not all was perfect. Some people clearly ate better than others because they could afford to or because they lived and worked at a successful mine or village, not at a less-developed, struggling one. The fare provided to single men who boarded was often monotonous and not always to their liking. And especially near the end of winter, residents complained of short rations, a lack of choice, and some food that was literally rotten. Henry Hobart complained, "We have had no good butter this winter. It is stinking stuff from old warehouses & would make a good soap grease." And late one April, while waiting for the reopening of navigation, he noted in his diary that "the warehouse pork would do for one to eat who had lost the sense of smell."[61]

Others echoed Hobart. Dr. A. I. Lawbaugh recalled how Keweenaw cattle were slaughtered late in the fall or early in the winter, when it was expected that ice, snow, and cold temperatures would keep them frozen solid for up to five or six months. But a January thaw occasionally came up that ruined those plans and spoiled the beef. John Forster allowed as how the beef wasn't that good even if it *did* stay frozen: "Before spring—frozen beef carcasses were about as choice eating as the frozen elephants found in the ice drifts of northern Siberia."[62]

From the diaries and reminiscences of men, it seems that a lack of fresh meat—especially beef—was a hardship particularly felt. Lake boats brought up beef on the hoof during the navigation season. At Ontonagon in late autumn, while that village still lacked a proper harbor and pier, they'd drive cattle right through the gangway of an anchored boat, making them swim the cold water to shore. On the other end of the Keweenaw, the first boat of the season, carrying a precious cargo of cattle, once arrived on May 7, but ice still blocked all the established harbors. Finally, the steamer landed its cargo on the ice extending out from the shore, three miles above Eagle River. It "made a good dock." They immediately drove the cattle to meet the hungry population waiting for them at the Cliff mine.[63]

Despite such efforts, the boats seemingly never delivered enough fresh beef to the Keweenaw. By the mid-1860s, a new supply line opened in the winter, when upper Great Lakes cowpunchers drove cattle up from Wisconsin, through the snow, and onto the Keweenaw, thirty to 120 at a time. In a place where getting any winter beef was hard—and getting *good* beef was even harder—it was easy to understand how in 1869 the *Mining Gazette*, in a short article headed "Christmas Beef," could work up so much genuine enthusiasm for a single dead animal:

> On Monday last Baer & Bro. killed, at their market in Hancock, the finest heifer we ever saw. It was but three years old, and weighed 2,160 lbs. on the foot. . . . The meat has been on exhibition at their market since Monday, and is now for sale to those who like a choice piece of meat for their Christmas dinner, and are willing to pay a fair price for it. As we saw it, hanging up, it was worth a dollar just to look at the morsels of fat and lean, the only disagreeable sensation being that we got hungry very fast.[64]

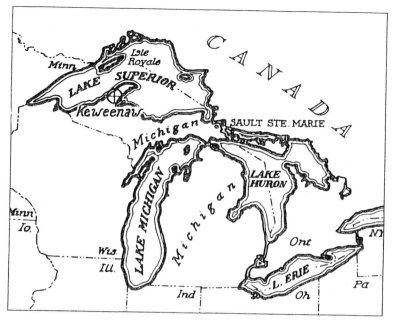

Early pioneers taking the water route to the Keweenaw Peninsula or Isle Royale traveled north on Lake Huron, past the rapids at Sault Ste. Marie, and then west across Lake Superior. *(Historic American Engineering Record)*

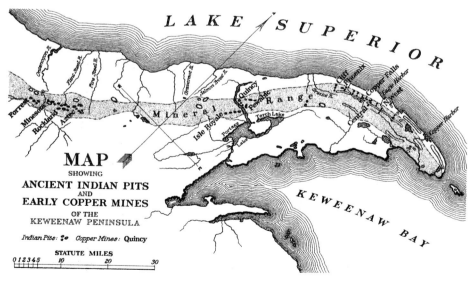

The mineral range ran along the Keweenaw's central spine. The copper mines concentrated along the tip of the peninsula in the 1840s, at the base of the Keweenaw in the 1850s, and near Portage Lake in the 1860s. *(Quincy Mine Hoist Association)*

For many, the trip to Lake Superior began at the Detroit waterfront, depicted here in 1837. The steamer *Michigan*, shown in the foreground, carried Ruth and C. C. Douglass up to Sault Ste. Marie in 1848. *(State of Michigan Archives)*

Travelers en route to the mines, when their passage was blocked by rapids on the St. Mary's River, often spent several days at Sault Ste. Marie amid Native Americans and voyageurs. This view dates from 1839. *(State of Michigan Archives)*

Several types of small watercraft transported exploring parties as they coasted the shores of the Keweenaw and Isle Royale. These men are at Isle Royale in the late 1860s. *(Michigan Technological University Archives and Copper Country Historical Collections)*

The locks at Sault Ste. Marie, shown here about a decade after they opened in 1855, allowed large boats to enter Lake Superior and thus speeded the transport of passengers and freight to and from the Keweenaw. *(State of Michigan Archives)*

Foster and Whitney's government-sponsored *Report on the Geology and Topography* of the copper lands, published in 1850, included this view of an unsullied landscape at Carp Lake, now called Lake of the Clouds, near the extreme southern end of the mineral district. *(Michigan Technological University Archives and Copper Country Historical Collections)*

BIRDS EYE VIEW OF COPPER HARBOUR.

Water and woods serve as dominant elements of many early illustrations of the Keweenaw. They help convey the remote, wilderness setting of frontier communities, such as Copper Harbor, shown in this 1849 view published as part of Charles T. Jackson's geological survey of mineral lands in Michigan. *(Michigan Technological University Archives and Copper Country Historical Collections)*

Harper's New Monthly Magazine, in 1853, depicted civilization as having gained a picturesque toehold where water and woods met at the commercial village of Eagle Harbor. The place could be beautiful, but was not always secure or serene, as evidenced by threatening lightning strikes over Lake Superior. *(Michigan Technological University Archives and Copper Country Historical Collections)*

SOUTH·VIEW·TOWN·ONTONAGON
LAKE SUPERIOR MICH

In the mid-1850s, Ontonagon, on the southern end of the mineral range, was the Keweenaw's largest commercial village. It already boasted several churches, a large hotel, numerous mercantile establishments, and a lighthouse. *(Clarke Historical Library)*

The Grand Portage Copper Company included this view in its 1863 report to stockholders. Depicting an idyllic Houghton village in harmony with water and land, the sketch minimizes the environmental changes wrought by hilltop mines and lakefront stamp mills. *(Michigan Technological University Archives and Copper Country Historical Collections)*

The frontispiece of the New York and Michigan Mining Company's report of 1847 presented cabins and exploratory mine works as minor parts of a landscape still dominated by natural elements—a stream and a tree. *(Michigan Technological University Archives and Copper Country Historical Collections)*

Foster and Whitney's 1850 report on the copper lands depicted Fort Wilkins as nestled, very peacefully, in an attractive setting of woods, water, and hills. *(Michigan Technological University Archives and Copper Country Historical Collections)*

Settlers fished, hunted, picnicked, and took "rambles" in the Keweenaw's abundant woods. A party of eleven men, several carrying firearms, poses at a waterfall, perhaps as part of a Fourth of July holiday expedition into the hinterland. *(Houghton County Historical Society)*

The underground world offered strong contrast to the aboveground environment. In dim and eerie light, a miner stands next to a large piece of mass copper nearly blasted free from the rock. *(Quincy Mining Company)*

In 1850, at the base of a rugged, forest-covered bluff, the Cliff mine's works included horse-powered whims (or winding drums) and rock stamps powered by a steam engine. One flatbed wagon, loaded with large masses of native copper, and a second wagon, carrying smaller pieces of copper packed in barrels, are shown ready to head out on company-built roads toward the Lake Superior shore. *(Michigan Technological University Archives and Copper Country Historical Collections)*

In the 1850s, large pieces of mass copper sit on the dock in Ontonagon, awaiting shipment to a distant smelter. *(Michigan Technological University Archives and Copper Country Historical Collections)*

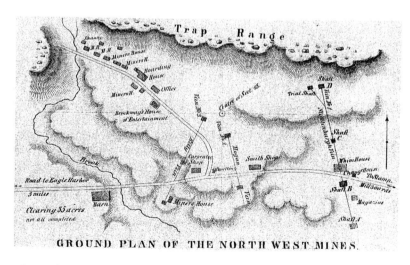

The Northwest Mining Company published this map of its location near Eagle Harbor in 1849. Daniel D. Brockway served as the mine's agent at the time and also operated "Brockway's House of Entertainment," shown standing in the middle of the mine works, agricultural clearings, and company houses. *(Michigan Technological University Archives and Copper Country Historical Collections)*

An illustration from Foster and Whitney's 1850 geological report shows workers' log houses standing near the horse-whims and stamps at the North American mine. Tree stumps mark the old wilderness; new houses and fences indicate the coming of a new order on the frontier. *(Michigan Technological University Archives and Copper Country Historical Collections)*

Illustrators and artists sanitized their views of early mines and settlements; they almost always made them look very tidy. This photographic view, ca. 1880, presents a very different mining landscape. It is littered with stumps, poor rock, and discarded tools and materials—and the workers' houses are little more than shanties. *(Houghton County Historical Society)*

Log and frame houses stand in a mine location's clearing, an island of settlement surrounded by forest, fields of tall stumps, and immense stacks of cordwood. *(Houghton County Historical Society)*

Amid the houses and fields of Clifton stood an Episcopal church (*left center*) and a Methodist church (*right center*). *(Houghton County Historical Society)*

Nearly forty years after Henry Hobart lived at Clifton during the Civil War, the village and mine stood abandoned and in ruins. *(Michigan Technological University Archives and Copper Country Historical Collections)*

The Central, shown here in 1921, was another early mine that settled in a basin carved out of the wilderness and had its heyday, then left behind poor-rock piles *(left center)*, mine structures, and abandoned neighborhoods. *(Michigan Technological University Archives and Copper Country Historical Collections)*

In the 1840s, pioneers extolled the beauty of Portage Lake, especially that stretch where heavily wooded hills ran down to water on both sides. By the early to mid-1860s, an expanding Houghton village had displaced considerable virgin forest on its side of the lake, while mill tailings dumped into the opposite side of the Portage were altering the shoreline there. *(Michigan Technological University Archives and Copper Country Historical Collections)*

This bird's-eye view of Houghton shows the extent of growth and development there by 1872. Dominant features of the landscape included a four- or five-block-long commercial district, three churches, the county courthouse and jail, Houghton's graded school, the Douglass House hotel, and a tramroad leading from the Shelden-Columbian mine down to its waterfront stamp mill *(far left)*. *(Michigan Technological University Archives and Copper Country Historical Collections)*

At Hancock in the mid-1860s, warehouses, docks, and the Quincy stamp mill *(far right)* lined the waterfront. Steps led up to the commercial, residential part of town—then a desolate, stump- and rock-strewn hill climbed steeply toward the Quincy mine. *(Michigan Technological University Archives and Copper Country Historical Collections)*

After suffering a catastrophic fire in 1869, Hancock rebuilt, as evidenced by this detail taken from an 1873 bird's-eye view. The village, sited between a heavily industrialized waterfront and a hilltop laid out with mines, had found enough fairly level ground to lay out a baseball diamond. *(Houghton County Historical Society)*

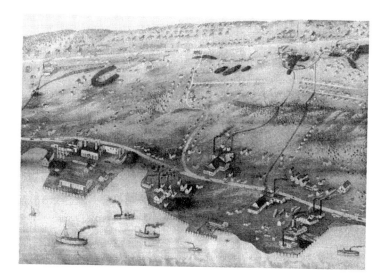

Voyageurs and explorers in the 1840s had pulled up their paddles to rest, relax, and enjoy the beautiful scenery while coasting along Portage Lake. Later travelers looked up at a hillcrest lined with several mines and coasted along a shoreline filled with smelters and stamp mills. *(Houghton County Historical Society)*

A dozen miles north of Portage Lake, the discovery of a copper-rich conglomerate lode spurred the post-Civil War development of the Calumet and Hecla mines and of the village of Red Jacket (later called Calumet). By 1872, the company and community had achieved rapid growth, as depicted in this bird's-eye view. *(Michigan Technological University Archives and Copper Country Historical Collections)*

In addition to erecting its mine location, Calumet and Hecla sited another community on Torch Lake, one dedicated to milling and concentrating copper rock, which traveled from mine to mill on the company's railroad. The lake provided water to wash the mineral concentrate and also served as a dump for tailings. This 1873 bird's-eye view suggests how local forests will fall to feed the mills' boilers—but it does not even hint at how the dumping of tailings will drastically alter the lakeshore and bottom. (*Houghton County Historical Society*)

Quincy's underground workers posed near a hoist-house, ca. 1875–80. The low board-and-batten structure is a snowshed built over a tram-road. About eight to ten boys sit atop the snowshed on the far left. (*Quincy Mining Company*)

When Houghton's graded school opened in 1866, it was one of the finest schools in the region. Many of its graduates went on to teach in other Keweenaw communities. *(Houghton County Historical Society)*

In winter months, Antoine LeDuc delivered the mail by dogsled. *(Michigan Technological University Archives and Copper Country Historical Collections)*

Starting in the late 1860s, baseball became the first popular team sport on the Keweenaw. Hancock's First National Bank team played its first game against the Houghton Baseball Club in 1870 and lost in a squeaker, 36 to 35. *(Michigan Technological University Archives and Copper Country Historical Collections)*

At successful, long-lived mines, workers in the early twentieth century sometimes still occupied small, pioneer-era log houses built half a century earlier. *(Michigan Technological University Archives and Copper Country Historical Collections)*

Decade after decade, the pioneer experience was recycled on the Keweenaw and on Isle Royale as companies struggled to open new mines in isolated forest locations. Isle Royale saw three eras of failed mining attempts: 1843 to 1855, 1873 to 1881, and 1889 to 1893. Even in the last era, around 1890, workers' families at Wendigo resided in small primitive log houses with timber sills, plank roofs, few rooms, and stovepipe chimneys. *(Michigan Technological University Archives and Copper Country Historical Collections)*

Daniel D. Brockway, with beard and walking stick, and his wife, Lucena, in wheelchair, passed their retirement years in Lake Linden, before both of them died in 1899 after sixty-three years of marriage. One of the earliest white families to settle on Lake Superior, they migrated north in 1843. In the course of running several mines and hotels, the Brockways knew everybody who was anybody on the Keweenaw for half a century. *(Michigan Technological University Archives and Copper Country Historical Collections)*

KEEPING HOUSE
All the Work of the Family

Another of the hard-working, uncomplaining pioneer women of Lake Superior has passed away. Though not conspicuously placed, hers was none the lighter burden nor sacrifice. Her mildest praise is that she knew her duty and did it well. . . . Mrs. Mulock was the mother of seven children, four boys and three girls, the youngest being but two years old. Like her husband, she was (until the past few months) a strong, healthy and exceedingly industrious person, performing all the work of the family without assistance, and with every prospect of a prolonged life and comfortable close. But the end was nearer than expected, and she passed away [at age forty-two] while yet in her prime and usefulness."

Portage Lake Mining Gazette, obituary for
Mary Ann Mulock, who settled at Lake Superior
in 1852 and died in 1870

In the beginning, it was a man's world. The explorers and geologists were men. The voyageurs were men. Those who cut and burned off the forest and sank the exploratory shafts were men. But where explorations uncovered rich deposits of copper, and where good natural harbors spawned commercial establishments, tent cities and mine camps evolved into communities where men shared the northern frontier with women and children.

When twenty-four-year-old Mary Ann Mulock arrived on the Keweenaw in the early 1850s, she discovered that it was still pretty much a man's world. The copper industry absolutely depended on the strong arms and backs of vigorous men, and in 1854 men aged twenty-one to forty-five comprised a full 55 percent of the Keweenaw's total population. That year, adult males outnumbered females by a ratio of 3.5 to 1. Right at the mines, women sometimes proved even scarcer. In 1857, men outnumbered women by about 6 to 1 at the Minesota and Rockland mine locations.[1]

As frontier conditions receded and a speculative mining industry matured into a productive, profitable one, the gender imbalance leveled off. By the first half of the 1870s, men still outnumbered women on the Keweenaw, but the ratio had fallen to 1.5 or 1.8 to 1, and men over the age of twenty-one made up just 25 to 30 percent of the total population.[2]

Few older men and women migrated to Lake Superior, so the Keweenaw became home to a young, marrying, child-bearing society. The men the companies needed and recruited were of the age to start or maintain families, and correspondingly, young women did not have to look long or hard for mates. In 1874, 90 percent of all Keweenaw women aged eighteen or over were wives (or widows)—and one of every three residents in the copper district was a child aged ten or younger.[3]

As the population became larger and more diverse, family housing, stores, churches, and schools became essential elements of the Keweenaw landscape. Satellite businesses and industries—ranging from barber and jewelry shops to iron foundries—migrated north to trade with the mining companies, their workers, and workers' families. Residents moved and interacted in a social setting that became more complete and varied with each passing decade. That setting offered residents more opportunities for work, education, and worship; more comfort and service; and a life seemingly less isolated and estranged from that lived in the world below.

A society is one people and many peoples, all at the same time. Lake Superior society was a collection of individuals possessing various skills, interests, and aptitudes; a collection of ethnic groups; a collection of social and economic classes. It was also a collection of men, women, and children, and gender and age were key variables in shaping everyday life. Even if they were part of the same family, even if they were domiciled under the same roof, even if they shared the same table, and language, and religion, and material comforts, and social status—even with all that, men, women, and children experienced different lives on the evolving frontier.

For instance, the expanding copper industry and proliferating commercial and professional establishments created many new employment opportunities for men. But most women still toiled in and around their homes, performing a multitude of essential, albeit unheralded, chores. Few women ever received much public attention or acclaim for their efforts as mothers or homemakers on the mining frontier. The praise the *Portage Lake Mining Gazette* heaped on Mary Ann Mulock on her death in 1870 was especially noteworthy because the paper rarely ran obituaries at the time, even for more public figures. Mrs. Mulock, praised for her hard work, industriousness, and dutiful service to family, received about the highest accolades an early woman settler on the Keweenaw could ever expect to get.

Certainly, George Buehler's mother didn't fare as well. She lived out her life in unremarkable obscurity. Even her son paid scant attention to her life and lineage. In 1917, George wrote a family history as an assignment while a student at Houghton High School. The young scholar knew that his father's side of the family was important, so he wrote several pages on that subject. In fact, George traced his father's lineage back for more than two centuries— back across the Atlantic, all the way back to the birth of Alfred Buehler in Switzerland in 1698. Then he summed up his mother's side in a few dismissive lines: "My mother was born in 1871 in Hancock. As the women were but a minor part in the world till today no records are kept hence I can not relate anything about them. So endeth our family history."[4]

Men on Lake Superior often treated women—and the domestic labor they performed—as if they were "but a minor part in the world," a part that could be taken for granted or even made sport of. On December 24, 1870, the *Mining Gazette* advised that "a good housewife's motto" was "whatever thou dost, dust with all thy might." In this era (when, of course, women did not have the right to vote), a nascent women's rights movement had been launched at a convention held in Seneca Falls, New York, in 1848. Because of the Seneca Falls meeting and subsequent pushes for political and social reform, "women's rights" came to be talked and written about on Lake Superior, but often in jest. The *Mining Gazette* informed women that they could get their rights— and their lefts, too—at the local shoeshop. And an advertisement selling Hall's Balsam lung remedy (published twenty-eight years after the Seneca Falls convention) started by taking a swipe at women's rights: "We do not hear much said about women's rights now-a-days. The majority of the ladies seem quite content to keep within their old-time sphere of usefulness. This seems to us to be very sensible."[5] The patent medicine company's self-interests were clearly tied to the notion that a woman's proper "sphere of usefulness" was not the world at large, but house and home. If she stayed there and performed all her domestic chores assiduously, *including* the chore of nursing the sick, then surely she'd notice all the family's aches and pains and coughs and wheezes and go down to the drugstore to buy more pills and potions.

During the time the Keweenaw was being settled, industrialization and the growing market economy were having profound effects on the division of labor practiced by families. Industrialization undergirded the rising social doctrine of "separate spheres" for men and women.[6] As industry grew, more and more men who had once labored in and around the home to support their families left home to go to work for wages. Instead of raising the crops, butchering the animals, and cutting and splitting the firewood, men went off to mine or mill, then used their wages to buy from others the goods and services that they themselves had once provided. At the mine villages, many men were even freed of the chores associated with normal house maintenance. If domiciled in a company house, a man didn't have to fret about repointing a chimney, replacing a window glass, or painting; those were his company's responsibilities.

As the outside workplace became the man's sphere, the inside jobs at home became the woman's sphere. She took care of domestic chores with less help from her mate and, as public education become more popular, with less help from her children. While the home remained a busy place of production, it also became a place of consumption, where more store-bought goods came to be used. The market economy affected a woman's work not only by changing how and what she cooked but also by providing new lighting devices, textiles, soaps, and other products.

In a sense, a woman's work during this era became harder and easier at the same time. She had less help with many tasks, but the market economy sometimes helped redefine and shortcut select tasks. The housewife still had to do the laundry but perhaps escaped having to make her own soaps. She still sewed much of the family's clothes but now started with store-bought dry goods and thus escaped spinning and weaving.

Up on Lake Superior, women settlers had the responsibility of trying to obliterate frontier conditions within the home. They disguised or eliminated deprivations and primitive conditions and replicated, as best and as soon as they could, households in the world below. Susie Childs, married to Will Childs (a mine manager and hotelkeeper), had a keen understanding of how hard women worked in a strange, new place to create an acceptable and familiar home life. Also, she well understood how her world of work differed from her husband's, because of the way she had to shuttle from task to task as the day wore on and family activities moved through their rhythm. There would be no rest for her even at the end of the day, although she could then at least sit down as she stitched her family's clothes:

> Her domestic cares are onerous and trying, and if everything else differs about her, she must have her home regulated as much as possible after the old sort. She is expected to be nurse, cook, housekeeper, seamstress and governess, while a man thinks he does well if he is a specialist in one line. After everything is in order she takes up knitting or sewing as a respite from more active toil.[7]

Within their houses, settlers sought a decent measure of comfort and security. They created heat to drive off the cold and light to drive out the darkness. They prepared and ate meals; performed domestic tasks; produced, repaired, and stored personal items. They slept, rested, relaxed, and amused themselves. They washed, dressed, undressed, and tended to matters of personal hygiene and adornment. They had sex, birthed babies, raised children, nursed the sick, kept watch over family members who died, and then held their funerals. They socialized with visitors, and many brought outsiders in to live with the family. They put up boarders (if they needed more income) or servants (if they could afford them). There was much to do, especially for the wives and mothers who kept house, and usually little space and few rooms in which to do it.

Not all families were equally hard-pressed when it came to setting up house and getting secure and comfortable. Ruth and C. C. Douglass, a childless couple of the managerial class, enjoyed a bounty of space and other amenities on the early frontier. When Ruth arrived on Isle Royale in August 1848, her husband's employer provided living accommodations that surprised and pleased her: "Very busy today house cleaning, and making an effort to get settled in our new log cabin, which I find more pleasantly situated and comfortable than I anticipated."[8]

Ruth had sailed north to Superior with great trepidation, uncertain of the hardships and dangers she might face. But her mining company house, located in its picturesque setting, quickly reassured her, providing immediate security and contentment. So the energetic woman cheerfully shouldered her house-cleaning and homemaking responsibilities, while her husband went about the business of trying to set up one of the region's first copper smelters.

Working-class families were less privileged than the Douglasses. They lived in small houses, which they typically shared with three to a half-dozen or more children. The combination of small houses, large families, working-class wages, and limited household technologies (especially for providing heat, light, and water) affected day-to-day home life at every turn.

A house not only provides shelter from rain and snow. It also encloses family members and shelters them from other people, from the rest of society. A house physically separates space. It has an inside and an outside. If not always a protective haven, it nevertheless helps residents separate "our life" from "their life" and defines "us" as different from "them." It provides an environment that belongs to the smaller group living within it, not to everybody.

If a house is large and elaborate enough, it may include a place such as a front porch or parlor—a place where public and private worlds can merge and meet, where "insiders" and "outsiders" can comfortably interact, without worry that the visitor is infringing unduly on the personal life of the visited. Working-class houses on the Keweenaw almost never featured a front porch. They had only a front wall and simple doorway separating living quarters from outside environment. Also, most did not include a formal front parlor or hall in their plan. That additional room and space—showcasing a family's furniture and taste and largely reserved for welcoming and entertaining guests—was a luxury enjoyed by very few on the Keweenaw. Consequently, the plan of the small house offered no transition space between inside and outside and did little to separate or protect the privacy of the family from the world at large. When visitors stepped through the door, they stepped right into the middle of whatever was going on inside.[9]

The early houses—many of which had only three to five rooms—limited personal privacy as well. They offered more shared space than private space and, by twentieth-century standards, encouraged "togetherness" to a fault. Second-story bed chambers were typically in short supply and therefore crowded. Mother and father were lucky if they didn't have to set aside a corner of their own bed chamber to serve as a nursery for an infant or young child. Parents would have scoffed at the fanciful, impractical notion that each child needed his or her private room. An older, mature son—working full-time, unmarried, living at home, and contributing to the family income—might have hoped to receive an adult's privilege and occupy a private chamber, but that wish could not always be obliged.

Besides sharing a room, many children shared a bed with siblings. During the Civil War era, when Clarence Bennetts was a young boy, his family lived in a larger-than-average house on the Keweenaw; it had four rooms downstairs and three second-story bed chambers. But Clarence's family was also larger than average: he shared space with two parents, five sisters, and three brothers. The family of eleven squeezed out a sleeping spot for everyone and shuffled children from bed to bed as they got older and some moved out: "In the large front room we had 3 beds. E. Ann and Jennie in one bed, Kate and Annie in the other and Grace and I in the third. Grace and I were bed partners up to the time W. Henry left home [to get married at age twenty-one]. Then I went in Frank's little bed and Frank with Sam."[10]

The need to stay warm over long, cold winters also encouraged togetherness. Houses were not insulated (unless one counted as insulation the deep snow piled up on roofs or purposefully banked against foundations and walls). A cast-iron stove in the kitchen, with perhaps a second parlor stove in the main living space downstairs, provided heat for the entire house, and that heat was unevenly distributed. Near a well-fired stove, it was not just warm; it was hot, with a glorious kind of heat. A person just in from a January blizzard, chilled to the bone, with aching hands, feet, and face, could find quick, blessed relief right next to a stove. But the farther you moved from a stove, the colder it got, and the more chilly drafts you felt. Portions of the downstairs could be unpleasantly cool, while upstairs rooms stayed frigid for months on end (making bed sharing a more appealing proposition). As a result, in winter the house "shrank" as people moved in toward the heat of the stove, instead of spreading throughout the dwelling.[11]

People also moved in toward the light, especially in winter. In the summer, the Keweenaw enjoyed very long summer days, which were often clear and bright. Dawn to dark stretched for sixteen hours in July, including several hours after supper, when many tasks and activities could be completed before the sun finally set. Winter presented a much darker, even gloomier picture, as daylight hours diminished to eight or nine, and cloudy, wintry skies dulled the sun. A family would breakfast before dawn; live and work through a short, gray day; and then sup after sunset.

To peel vegetables, wash dishes, write, read, sew, play cards, or just sit and talk, people needed light—either natural light coming through windows or artificial light produced by burning candles or lamps. When the Keweenaw was being settled, the production of artificial lighting was another domestic technology—another part of women's work—being altered by industrialization and the market economy.

From the colonial era into the nineteenth century, homemade candles were a mainstay of domestic lighting. Women produced candles either in molds or by repeatedly dipping wicks into hot tallow or beeswax, building up their tapers layer by layer. Up on the Keweenaw, some pioneer women no doubt still made their own candles; early stores traded a bit in candle wicking, beeswax, and tallow. But most women bought their candles rather than making them, and stores from the late 1840s on did a brisk trade in factory-produced candles. The Keweenaw, in fact, was a prime market for such candles, because they were used not only in homes but also underground, to light the mines. Indeed, by the Civil War era, businessmen were setting up candle factories right on Portage Lake.[12]

In lieu of candles, some settlers lighted their rooms with lamps fueled by various oils, such as the sperm oil produced by the whaling industry. In the 1840s, sperm oil was lauded as producing the best, brightest, and cleanest light, but it was becoming expensive. Other lamp fuels included lard, castor and cottonseed oil, turpentine, and camphene. By the late 1850s and 1860s, a new lighting device—the kerosene lamp, which produced more light and burned an inexpensive fuel—started taking over the home market. Keweenaw stores stocked the new petroleum-based kerosene, as well as the lamps, wicks, burners, chimneys, and globes that went with it.

Even if they no longer had to render their own tallow or make their own candles, women still had the task of tending to the store-bought paraphernalia that went with domestic lighting, whether candlesticks and candlesnuffers, matches, lamp burners, chimneys, cans of kerosene, or fancy globes. They had to fuel the fonts, then be vigilant against the danger of an overturned or unattended lamp setting the whole house afire. They carried lamps from room to room as they moved about doing chores or saying good night. To reap the benefits of artificial light while minimizing the odor and smoke produced as by-products, women learned to keep burners properly maintained and wicks properly trimmed. Still, since all artificial lighting involved combustion, sooner or later, by washing glass chimneys almost daily or by periodically scrubbing ceilings, housekeepers had to remove the layer of soot that candles and lamps left behind.[13]

To save on the expense, mess, and hazards of burning candles or oil or kerosene lamps, people relied as much as possible on natural light. Most houses had few windows, and these were often small and set in thick log walls that blocked out some of the sunlight trying to angle in to the interior. The wood-frame dwellings built after the era of log construction usually carried more glass; that was one of their principal amenities. But even on a bright summer day, much of a house's interior remained dim, so people gravitated toward the window admitting the most natural light into the room. At night, in parallel fashion, they huddled in that small portion of the house made bright by candle or lamp and made warm by a nearby stove.[14]

In the nineteenth century, the larger houses of the more well-to-do had rooms set aside for special purposes: a kitchen for food preparation and cooking; a dining room for taking meals; one or more parlors for entertaining and family activities; maybe a study for the businessman and a sewing room for his wife; a nursery for their newborn child; and servant's quarters for a maid or "domestic." But ordinary houses on the Keweenaw didn't allow for such specialization. When large families carried on all of life's domestic activities within small houses, they had to tolerate inconveniences and bothers. They lived in a world of flux and makeovers, where the housewife and other family members, as they moved from one activity to the next, changed a room's function by putting just-used things away and by getting now-needed things out. The area right around the kitchen stove, at different times, was used for cooking, refueling and polishing the stove, washing dishes, bathing babies, getting dressed on a cold morning, doing the laundry, and ironing clothes. Orchestrating these spatial/functional makeovers and keeping the house in order significantly added to the woman's burden of chores.

Men, women, and children on the mining frontier cleaned and groomed themselves and eliminated human wastes without benefit of one specialized room: the bathroom. Their unplumbed houses had no toilets, fixed tubs, or washbasins with running water. Instead of a toilet, people used a wooden privy, set out in the backyard over a dug-out waste chamber. Locating the privy near the rear of a lot put foul, smelly wastes away from the house but also made people walk farther to use it, which was particularly bothersome in winter. (Some larger establishments, such as schools or hotels, sometimes had privies attached to the back of the building, or connected via covered corridors, so that users didn't have to go outside.) In lieu of walking out to the privy in the middle of a blizzard, or just before bed, or in the dead of the night, those in need had two choices. One, they could ignore the need, endure discomfort, and suffer through a bout of self-inflicted constipation. (In the nineteenth century, overly modest or fastidious persons might stay out of the offensive privy as much as possible and therefore pass stools very infrequently.) Or they could relieve themselves into a ceramic "piss pot," more politely known as a chamberpot, which came with a much-appreciated lid. "Women's work" included the disagreeable, yet necessary, task of carrying chamberpots out in the morning, dumping their "night soil" down the privy, and tidying them up for the next night's use.[15]

The lack of indoor plumbing affected women's work and home life seemingly at every turn, from filling cooking pots to emptying chamberpots, from washing the laundry to bathing the baby. Water was not available at the turn of a tap for early settlers. It came from a stream, or was drawn from a well, or was captured in a cistern as it cascaded off roofs, or it fell as snow, to be melted on the stove.

In the second half of the nineteenth century, modernizing communities across the nation provided new utilities—especially water and sewer service—for industrial, commercial, and residential users. Often, satisfactory water supply systems came to cities, towns, and villages only after their citizenry had first suffered through catastrophic fires, deadly epidemics, and years of insufficient and impure water. The largest communities on Lake Superior, such as Houghton, Hancock, and Calumet, were still quite new when they built their water distribution systems, yet they, too, incurred a decade or two of water problems before moving to solve them. The *Portage Lake Mining Gazette*, in the early 1880s, faulted Houghton's common council for not addressing the village's water problem. The paper noted that Houghton's wells did not provide enough water for household purposes and that "the drinking water facilities . . . are a hollow mockery" and "pathetic."[16]

Even the region's largest and most progressive communities did little to modernize their water supply systems until the late 1880s and 1890s. Prior to that, water remained a heavy, sloshing load that had to be lugged about, bucketful after bucketful, day after day. The time and work involved in fetching pailsful of water encouraged conservation; water was to be rationed and reused, not wasted. This meant that men, women, and children living in unplumbed houses were well advised not to be overly fastidious when it came to inspecting their plates, knives, and forks for evidence of prior meals, or when it came to inspecting each other—especially their scalps, which not infrequently hosted lice. Henry Hobart, in his role as teacher at the Cliff mine, encountered many of the village's children. Many were "quite filthy," with "smutty faces." (Dirty-faced children, Hobart thought, surely sprang from dirty mothers at home.) But lousy heads were an even better indicator of poor home hygiene: "Black hair white with the eggs of the sweet animal. There are lice enough in the head of most any child to make a cornish pasty."[17]

Standards of personal hygiene were lower when families lacked indoor plumbing. Settlers rarely stripped down naked to sit or squat in large tubs and take head-to-toe baths in water that had been heated on the stove. If and when they engaged in this luxury, no doubt a small parade of bathers used the same water before ever changing it. The occasional addition of a bit more water from the stove freshened the bath, while reheating it some.

In 1866, the *Portage Lake Mining Gazette* editorialized, "Frequent bathing is an important auxiliary of health, and one of the necessities, as well as luxuries, of a civilized people." The paper noted that, unfortunately, "facilities for bathing seem to be left out of account in the arrangements of our hotels, as well as private houses." The paper urged some enterprising individual to open up a good bathing establishment in Houghton; people in the world down below enjoyed such facilities, and it was time people on the Keweenaw did, too.[18]

Soon, the Richey Bros. commercial bathhouse opened in Houghton.[19] Still, up and down the Keweenaw, most people continued to wash standing at a basin: they'd wipe down a part of the body; towel it off; wash another part; towel it off. Some took their towel baths in the privacy of a bed chamber, using the washstand and a large, decorated ceramic wash pitcher (or "ewer") and basin.[20] Others of lesser means used any convenient water pitcher and basin found in the kitchen. In the summer, residents could take themselves out to the water instead of carrying the water into the house. If they braved chilly waters, they could bathe in a local stream or lake. And underground mine workers could lessen the amount of wash water that had to be fetched at home by cleaning up at work. As their shifts ended, they walked from shaft to company dryhouse, where they changed clothes and washed off the worst of the grime before heading home.

Putting a family of two adults and four to eight children in a house of four to six small rooms left little space for bric-a-brac and furniture, and local store records suggest that most homes were sparsely furnished. To be sure, mothers and fathers must have hand-fashioned some furniture, toys, and dolls for their offspring. But through the 1860s, settlers bought extremely few high chairs, cradles, and cribs, and almost no rattles, games, or toys.[21] In 1870, "Mrs. Enderich's Bazaar," a ladies' shop in Houghton, was among the first to advertise the sale of "Children's Toys."[22] In this society, consumerism, parenting, and childhood were not yet linked, and parents did not lavish financial resources and precious interior space on their children.

Stores traded with well-to-do adults in armchairs, sofas, chests of drawers, pianos, and parlor furniture, but working-class families generally weren't in the market for expensive, heavy, and specialized furnishings. Instead, they bought or fabricated more inexpensive, lighter furniture that could be moved easily from room to room as needed, or from house to house, if the family moved.

Working-class families did not have extensive wardrobes, so they didn't need extensive chests of drawers to keep their clothes, just as they didn't require multiple cupboards and sideboards to store their modest tableware.

Small houses and limited wages discouraged householders from acquiring a host of tables for various uses. (The top of a trunk filled with blankets served nicely as a table, and a wooden barrel standing on end presented a fine perch for a candlestick or kerosene lamp.) Probably the most common piece of furniture in the working-class home was the light, inexpensive, and mass-produced wooden chair: a side chair or armchair, maybe caned, maybe a Windsor chair, maybe a rocker.[23]

The bed—as close as there was to an essential item of furniture—was a smaller, more portable item in the mid-nineteenth century. The head, foot, and side rails broke down, and instead of sitting on a box spring, the mattress lay on a web of bed cord strung across the frame. The mattress itself was usually a homemade affair intended for regular replacement—basically, a large sack of sewn-up bed-ticking, stuffed with straw, corn husks, or feathers. Lucena Brockway tended to mattresses in October, just before winter. Since she kept many fowl, she filled her mattresses with feathers, which she deemed a "dreaded job." Clarence Bennetts, on the other hand, recalled the annual changing of the mattresses with fond humor: "Our boys' mattresses each spring were opened and the old husk taken out and a fresh bale of husk from the stores to stuff for another year. It was amusing on going to bed the first night after the mattresses were newly replenished with fresh husk. It almost required a step ladder to get up to the first night."[24]

Houses on the mining frontier could be short of many things: rooms, space, furniture, privacy, and convenience. Other things they had too much of: grime, bugs, and small critters. At the Cliff mine, Henry Hobart recorded in his diary that his rented lodgings were "infested with vermin of many kinds." Local stores confirmed Hobart's observation and offered a fatal solution: mouse and rat traps. Hobart also railed against the hoards of bedbugs that plagued his night hours. Changing mattress stuffing not only provided recumbent settlers with a loftier perch; for a while, at least, it also eliminated bug infestations.[25]

Restuffing mattresses was part of a larger ritual—spring and/or fall cleaning—that many women dreaded because of the solid week or more of arduous work it entailed.[26] Wood-burning stoves, candles, and lamps generated soot that lay on all interior surfaces. The debris fallen from load after load of fuel lay on the floor. A half-dozen or more people tromped through a worn, grass-less yard, once dusty, then muddy, then snowy, and then tromped though the house. Because water was hard to get, and mother had other daily chores to tend to, a lot of small cleanup jobs went undone until they could all be done at once.

In the spring, after the house had been shut up for months over winter, it was time to throw open the windows, air out the house, and wield corn broom, rag mop, scrub brush, pail and soap, and elbow grease against winter's accumulated grime. Psychologically, at least spring cleaning came at a time when the world was opening up, summer was coming, the lake boats were coming, and many outdoor pastimes could be resumed. The season no doubt helped many weary women get through all the scrubbing, washing, mopping, sweeping, polishing, and shaking out that came with it. In fall, the feeling was probably quite the reverse. As women cast out the dirt of summer, they knew they were preparing to live again in a small, shut-up house over a half-year-long winter.

Through 1870, the stores up on Lake Superior did little trade in decorative items to embellish and brighten the home. Merchants sold small looking glasses, but no large hall mirrors; some watches, but almost no mantel clocks. By the 1860s, photographers had set up shop in a few towns, and portrait photographs of relatives near and far graced many homes. But stores didn't stock prints, illustrations, statuettes, busts, or other objets d'art. Design and color did get into houses in other ways, however, especially in the form of wallpapers and textiles.

From the late 1840s onward, stores on the Keweenaw sold wallpapers that added color and interest to interiors. Window curtains and drapes also decorated walls. Women sewed them of suitable fabrics or, by the 1860s, bought ready-made curtains. Some householders covered their wooden floors with canvas. Others chose more elaborate carpets, floor rugs, or mats. Clarence Bennetts described his home furnishings as "crude but neat"—"a fancy carpet in the Parlor tacked down. All the rest home made rag carpets and mats."[27] Upstairs, in settlers' bed chambers, quilts and coverlets provided both warmth and decoration.

The work that women put into curtains and quilts was but a small part of their sewing. Their greater sewing burden entailed making clothes for themselves and other family members. When it came to clothes, the man's world and the woman's world sharply diverged. A man was expected, perhaps, to be proficient enough with needle and thread to repair his togs. On a July Sunday in 1847 on Isle Royale, Cornelius Shaw's band of miners took their first day off work in six weeks to stay in camp and mend their clothes and boots.[28] But a man's rugged individualism and self-sufficiency—and sewing skills—did not extend to making his own pants. For that he needed a woman, and if he lacked a woman, he needed a store.

Samuel Worth Hill was a single New Englander who arrived on Lake Superior in 1845 at age thirty.[29] Hill worked on state-sponsored and then federally sponsored geological surveys. Thereafter, he slid from geology into mining and had a hand in the operations of several key, early companies. Hill apparently had a coarseness about him. Local folklore has it that he cursed with consummate skill, and hence "What the Sam Hill!?" became a substitute, on the mining frontier, for "What the hell!?"

When Hill settled on the Keweenaw, it was still very much a wilderness, devoid of creature comforts and nearly uninhabited by white women. Fashion, supposedly, was not much thought of. Mine workers spent much of their time wearing flannel drawers, coarse pants made of duck or bagging material, a flannel shirt, and a sack coat. On their feet they wore hobnailed boots while at work, and often moccasins at other times. When it got colder, they might wrap their feet in "nepes," squares of blanket material, before putting on their moccasins. In truly wintry weather, they slipped a Mackinaw coat onto their backs and heavy, well-oiled, rawhide shoepacks (with felt or wool liners) onto their well-socked feet. On a Sunday, a man in his finest wore " 'pepper and salt' pants, high boots or moccasins, and a red or blue flannel shirt with a silk sash or scarf twisted around the body a few times instead of suspenders."[30]

Only five years after landing on the Keweenaw, Sam Hill, the rugged, hard-swearing pioneer, walked into John Senter's general store in Eagle River and purchased, of all things, a "Splendid black hat" and a black satin vest. Whether a man wanted a satin vest or a flannel shirt, as early as 1849–50 he could walk into a frontier store and buy it. He could literally clothe and adorn himself from head to toe with store-bought goods.

In 1849–50, John Senter's Eagle River store sold a wide range of ready-made clothes for men, both coarse goods and fine ones. Senter sold drawers, undershirts, socks, pants, overalls, shirts, vests, jackets, and overcoats. He also traded in men's slippers, shoes, boots, and gaiters; in gloves and mittens; in suspenders, cravats, caps, and hats. In the 1860s, stores added other merchandise: shirt collars, neckties, rubbers, hip boots and rubberized coats, leather belts, and suits. In the realm of personal items, the man could purchase shaving kits and soap, handkerchiefs, hair oil and pocket combs, and wallets and pocketknives.

Women and children did not enjoy such a wide selection of clothes or personal items. Instead of stocking clothes for them, merchants traded briskly in diverse dry goods and sewing notions. Store tables and shelves loaded with bolts of cloth told a woman that she was supposed to make most of her own clothes—and, if she was married, clothes for the rest of her family, too.

Extant store records indicate that through the 1860s, women rarely purchased finished blouses, skirts, dresses, or jackets. More hoops were sold than ready-to-wear hoop skirts. The Minesota mine store sold a pair of silk panties in the mid-1860s, but women generally made scant purchases of underclothes, slips, and whale-boned corsets, and trade was far from brisk even in such items as capes, cloaks, shawls, veils, and scarves.

The "ladies' goods" most often sold were worn on legs, feet, hands, and heads—items of clothing whose production called for more than the sewing of light fabric. The general stores carried stockings and hose, boots and shoes, gaiters and gloves, and bonnets or "head-dresses." They also traded some in personal items for women: looking glasses, perfumes or "essence," shawl pins, hair nets, shell and side combs, hair brushes and hairpins, and silk sunshades.

Drugstores (in the 1850s) and millineries (in the 1860s) opened on the Keweenaw and started competing with general stores for part of the ladies' trade. Drugstores sold "fancy soaps" and "perfumeries and toilet preparations." The arrival of millineries underscored how women had become more numerous and important in this industrial society. These specialty shops sold accessories and embellishments to more well-to-do and fashion-conscious women. In Hancock, Hocking's millinery advertised in 1867 that it was "filled with fresh goods of all kinds, of the latest styles and best materials, which will be made up to order in a superior and tasty manner. There is an endless variety of feathers, flowers, ribbons, parasols, etc., and also a fine assortment of the latest styles of bonnets and hats."[31]

By advertising and selling "fresh" goods done up in a "tasty manner," millineries raised the standards of female adornment and dress on Lake Superior. By doing so, they perhaps even increased the home sewing burden on women, who had to do more needlework to "keep up" with trends. In 1857, the *Lake Superior Miner*, in support of more salt-of-the-earth women, had inveighed against girls who did little work and sat on sofas looking like wasp-waisted, rosy cheeked, full-breasted, putty-faced daughters of fashion. By 1870, daughters of fashion were less vilified and more in vogue. The *Portage Lake Mining Gazette* that year informed its readers of various fashion facts: velvet scarves are becoming very popular for evening wear; black is becoming very fashionable among the ladies; and "black lace veils are just the thing, now-a-days, provided they are pointed and long, set off with fringe or wide lace, and are worn over the face."[32] By the mid-1870s, the *Ontonagon Miner* encouraged hard-sewing, fashion-conscious women of all classes—"the wealthiest and the least wealthy"—to subscribe to *Ehrichs' Fashion Quarterly*: "A magazine which supplies information on every article a lady or child can wish to wear, from the sole of her foot to the top of her head. Every article is richly illustrated; underneath stands the description, with the number of yards it takes to make it; and then comes the price at which you can purchase [the material]."[33]

Early Keweenaw stores stocked even fewer clothes for children than for women. Besides diaper cloth and pins, they sold only a small number of frocks, booties, hats, or hoods for infants. For "boys" or "misses," stores carried almost no finished undergarments, pants, shirts, skirts, dresses, or coats. They traded some in hose, gloves and mittens, and hats and caps. The store-bought item most likely worn by a young boy or girl was a pair of shoes or boots.

Many a woman sewed clothes for everyone in her family. Thanks to textile factories and the market economy, she could skip over the once-common practice of home spinning and weaving and start out by shopping at the store for her dry goods, as well as sewing notions and tools of the seamstress's trade: scissors and sewing baskets; thimbles, needles, pins, and patterns; thread and yarn; ribbons and beads, buttons and bows; hooks and eyes and colorful dyes; lace, tassels, fringes, borders, and braid; tape, trimming, edging, and elastic; bonnet flowers and flounce.

As soon as stores opened on the frontier, a wide range of cotton, linen, woolen, silk, and satin fabrics became available. In 1855, S. A. Parker's Dry Goods Emporium at Ontonagon advertised the "Magnificent Arrival" of twenty-five fabrics, ranging from silks, satins, and dress goods down to domestics; from mohair and cashmere down to calico, denim, and plain linen.[34] Other stores from the late 1840s through the 1870s were equally well or better stocked. Some fabrics came in solid colors; some bleached white; some as prints, plaids, checks, or stripes. Among the most frequently sold fabrics were cambric and other linens, muslin, shirting, drill, flannel, delaine, denim, and calico.

Sewing for herself and her family was work that even well-to-do women, such as Lucena Brockway, had to tackle. She sewed or knitted socks, mittens, cloaks, shirts, chemises, and other clothes, plus quilts, coverlets, bed-ticks, and sheets.[35] Diary entries penned early in 1874 documented that sewing was an important part of her work routine:

Feb. 4:   "Today I made me a pair of drawers and Pa a pair of drawers too."
Feb. 5:   "I went to work on my dresses today and have made & trimmed one skirt."
Feb. 6:   "Have worked on my dress again today but I have a sore finger & hinders very much."
Feb. 7:   "I am trying to sew but my finger is so painful I can do but little."
Feb. 16:   "Today I made Mr. Brockway three pairs of drawers—were canton flannel and made them good."
Feb. 28:   "Have finished Sophie's white dress."

Making new clothes was not the end of it. Women mended clothes and laundered and ironed them. Wash day—often a Monday, with some of the work spilling over to Sunday and Tuesday, or even Wednesday—was a hard way to start a week. Many women dreaded this chore, which was never finished but kept coming back, week after week. It entailed carrying and lifting many heavy loads of water and hauling the wood needed to boil that water. Stooping and standing. Kneading and scrubbing clothes. Wringing them out. (Even if a woman owned one of the newfangled, hand-cranked, patented clothes-wringers being sold on the Keweenaw by the late 1860s, wringing out the laundry remained tiresome work.)[36] In the process, hands chapped. Fingers and wrists grew sore, as did neck, back, and arm muscles.

Girls learned laundry (and ironing) lessons from their mothers, or women instructed themselves by reading domestic manuals, such as Catharine Beecher's *A Treatise on Domestic Economy*, published in 1842, or the book she coauthored with her sister, Harriet Beecher Stowe, in 1869, *The American Woman's Home*. Catharine Beecher called getting the laundry done "the American housekeeper's hardest problem." Doing laundry was the first job a woman would pay another woman to do for her, if she had the money.[37]

To ease her burden a bit on laundry day, a woman started the night before by collecting and sorting what was to be washed, separating it by color, fabric, and degree of dirtiness. She'd get out her tubs, fill several with warm water, and set many stained and soiled items to soaking overnight. She could ready her homemade or store-bought soap. Whittling at bar soap with a knife produced shavings that sudsed up faster in the washtub.

In the morning, all the sheets, shirts, skirts, tablecloths, curtains, pants, and drawers came out of the soaking tubs and were wrung out. A woman put a load of some of the family's finer things into a tub, poured hot, soapy water over them, and stirred them up. Then she drew each item out and rubbed it up and down against a ribbed washboard. If she noted a stubborn stain, she worked soap into it and vigorously worked that particular spot with her hands. The first load then went into a boilerful of soapy water sitting on the stove, while a second load went into the tub of wash water.

From the boiler, the wrung-out laundry went to its first rinse. After being wrung out again, finer whites, at least, went into a second rinse, which had store-bought bluing in the water to keep the whites white and dingy yellow at bay. The housekeeper wrung out the load another time, then dipped items in need of ironing in starch before hanging them to dry on a clothesline. The next day, she dampened the items in need of ironing, then pressed them with irons weighing about eight pounds each, which she reheated after each use by putting them back on top of the stove. Finally, she folded the laundry and put it away.

In the summer, a woman might move some of her laundry tasks outside in order to get away from the hot stove; in the winter, a chilled housekeeper might watch her laundry freeze on the line, as well as dry there. At any time of the year, she might cut down on the number of rinses used, eliminate a boiling, or reuse a wash. The laundry might not get as clean—especially the coarsest, dirtiest items, which were done at the end. But shortcuts saved time and work, including the work of fetching and dumping water. Given that it took about fifty gallons (or four hundred pounds) of water to fill a washtub, boiler, and rinse tub just once, a woman had a strong incentive not to change the water too frequently.[38]

The work of keeping house had a predictable rhythm to it. It had daily tasks, such as getting water, fueling the stove, tending the lamps, fixing the meals, and washing dishes. It had weekly tasks, especially the dreaded laundry; and seasonal or annual tasks, such as the wholesale cleaning of the house and its contents in spring, fall, or both. A woman was most hard-pressed to keep up with her daily chores when the weekly or seasonal ones rolled around.

Children helped with chores, but they also made chores bigger. Children presented more mouths to feed, more clothes to sew, more laundry and dishes to do, and more tracked-in dirt to sweep off the floor. In any small house, a half-dozen children invariably got underfoot and created enough noise and mayhem to occasionally drive a mother to utter distraction, if not despair. And in their first five to ten years of life, children also fell sick time after time, till they either passed through all the various childhood diseases or died from one of them. As the family's chief nurse, a mother scrambled to keep on top of her regular tasks, while tending to everyone's ailments.

And much of the time she did all this work, a mother herself was either pregnant, or recovering from a birth, or breast-feeding an infant. During this era, women not uncommonly spent half their years between ages twenty and forty either pregnant or suckling infants. To free themselves a bit from the demands of motherhood, some women started turning to another new store-bought device: the baby bottle. A male writer for the *Portage Lake Mining Gazette* uncovered about fifty rubber-nippled baby bottles for sale in Houghton in 1869 and reported that "our druggists feel confident of selling their entire stock of patent lacteal reservoirs."

For women, the baby bottle filled with cow's milk offered some relief and freedom from the demands of raising an infant. While the bottle quieted the fuss and nourished the baby, a mother could do other things. But the *Mining Gazette* reporter, unsympathetic about the wide-ranging domestic demands put upon women, wasn't so sure of the social benefits of this innovation. He made his opinion perfectly clear in a satirical article:

> Think of it! Fifty infants drawing their sustenance from other sources than the maternal fount—dependent on the whims and caprices of animals instead of the beauty and tenderness of a mother. If the bovine supplier wanders off, or comes home late, will baby go supperless to bed, or chew a tasteless quid of rubber till all signs of intelligence are erased? Is this the beginning of another "great improvement of the human race"? Will the sulphurized tubes and rude bottles give way to deliciously perfumed ducts, pendant to delicately tinted spheres, having palpitator attachments, with chemical self-regulating and supplying reservoirs? Will babies finally have a being and live by virtue of a series of patents and re-issues? And are these to be the issues of marriage? Are babies to be exhibited with "patent applied for" conspicuously stitched or embroidered on their pinafore? Are—but we refrain. If we, as a people, are opposed to the bottle as a means of sustenance for adults, how can we allow it to become a source of comfort and "milk for babes"?[39]

The writer, in a sense, paid mothers a backhanded compliment. Within the domestic sphere of activity—as opposed to commerce or industry—science, technology, and new marketplace products were no substitutes for caring, hard-working women.

TASKS AT HAND

Making a Living:
Men and Women, Boys and Girls

Let a contract to a party of 4 miners to drift So. of No. 3 Shaft at 2nd level. . . . A drift 5' × 7' at $10 per foot. Measurement to commence 2 feet so. of mark back of drift.

		Contracted by	John Lynch		
			Jerry Lynch		
			Dennis C. Holland		
			Wm. Downy		
Credit	25	feet 6 in. @	$10,	$255.00
Debit	8	kegs Powder	$40.00	
	600	feet fuse	$7.50	
	1	pick handle	$ .25	
	1	Box Candles	$11.40	
	47#	steel	$11.75	
			$70.90	

Pewabic Mine contract book,
December 6, 1859

The Keweenaw mining frontier was in the business of making itself over, of making itself into a more habitable and hospitable place. If it didn't take all kinds, it surely took many kinds of people to transform a wilderness into a frontier and then into a suitable home for an industrial society dedicated to copper mining. Frontier society had many niches that needed filling as it matured, and diverse peoples came to fill those niches and round the place out.

As society rooted in, a growing force of workers—first nearly all men, but then women and children, too—toiled at different tasks in many different environments. They worked in the woods or under the ground. They labored in stamp mills or stores, in offices or houses. They harvested ice off frozen lakes or ladled molten copper through furnace doors. They sold their time or skill to earn the money needed to pay for food, shelter, clothing, and other essentials. The money needed to go, in some cases, into the church collection plate, or in other cases, into the till at a nearby "scrub tavern."

Settling Lake Superior took the voyageurs who paddled the boats and carried the packs; the rugged explorers, geologists, and surveyors who tramped the woods and swamps, studied the copper, and mapped the land. It took skilled miners who blasted rock, and unskilled workers who lifted the broken rock and hauled it around. It took woodchoppers and building tradesmen who turned forests into critically needed fuel, or buildings, or mine supports; skilled mechanics; merchants who shipped in and sold needed supplies; custodians who mopped up the courthouse and jail; domestics who cooked and cleaned; and teachers, preachers, and professionals, including doctors, dentists, and an occasional lawyer or newspaper editor.

As local society became more mature, diverse, and complete, one thing never changed: copper mining was the engine that drove all the rest. The economic and social development of Keweenaw society depended on the fortunes of the copper industry, and that industry, in turn, absolutely depended on having several thousand young, strong men around to tend to all the tasks involved in making copper: mining it, milling it, and smelting it.

For a while, Josiah Penhallow, our fictive yet representative Cornish miner, figured that all the luck he had was bad. He'd fled Cornwall because of its depressed mining economy, only to arrive in Hancock in 1867—just as the Keweenaw's copper industry was falling into a deep recession lasting half a decade.[1] Penhallow escaped the adventures and misfortunes of the pioneers who'd beaten back the wilderness to settle the first mines. Instead, he and his contemporaries coped with an industry, over two decades old, that was maturing and struggling at the same time.

During America's Civil War, the demand for copper had risen, taking the price of the red metal along with it. Copper, which sold at twenty cents per pound in 1861, peaked at forty-six cents in 1864. Laboring men who stayed out of the Union army had their pick of jobs because every mining company tried to push production and take advantage of the wartime price increase. The number of active operations rose. Many mines which had failed in the past reopened as companies hoped finally to earn a return on their investment.[2]

Then the war ended, the price of copper fell, and only a handful of companies remained profitable. A dozen or so mines closed all over again. Others, including the Quincy mine above Hancock, trimmed back operations and wages. Fewer men worked, and they worked for less. The only bright spot in the district emanated from ten miles northeast of Quincy. There, two new companies, the Calumet and the Hecla, after stumbling, mismanaged starts, opened up the Calumet conglomerate lode.[3] So far, everything had gone wrong. But new investors and managers had come in, and folks figured it was just a matter of time before this lode proved the richest in the district.

Josiah kicked around Portage Lake for several weeks trying to land a job. Almost daily he walked up to the several mines above Hancock, stopping at the shafts and at the head mine captains' offices, inquiring about work. There was nothing to be had, at least nothing that he wanted. Penhallow was a skilled miner, just as his father and his father's father had been. He didn't want a surface job, and he wouldn't work as an unskilled laborer underground who just loaded and pushed rock—unless he absolutely had to.

Once or twice Josiah took the ferry across Portage Lake to inquire at the mines above Houghton. They, too, had no work. Just as he was about ready to hike the road to the new mines at Calumet, he ran into fellow Cornishmen he knew from the South Crofty mine back in Cambourne. These Cornish "Cousin Jacks," John Roberts and Samuel Ley, had worked as contract miners at the Quincy mine for several years now.[4] A member of their contract team was quitting, and Roberts and Ley invited Josiah to take his place when the crew started on the next month's contract. They figured they'd likely keep working in about the same place—stoping out copper rock on the 110-fathom level, between shafts 2 and 3.

Penhallow was fortunate to link up with a hard-working contract team— men Quincy wanted to keep even in a bad year, when it was letting go a couple hundred workers and cutting down to 370 men. Roberts and Ley told him that at least fifty or sixty of the men let go were skilled contract miners. Luckily, Roberts and Ley got along well with Quincy's head mine captain— John Cliff, another Cornishman—so they figured they'd survive the cutbacks. To get along up on Lake Superior, it never hurt to have friends around from the old country.

At the start of the month, Penhallow, Roberts, Ley, and three other team members went to John Cliff's captain's office. After some haggling, which failed to convince the captain to raise their contract rate from the month before, the men agreed to continue stoping at the same spot underground. They would receive $19 per cubic fathom of copper rock blasted free. A cubic fathom, six feet on a side, equaled 216 cubic feet. Measurement by fathoms, rather than feet, was a Cornish tradition transferred to Lake Superior, as was the custom of having miners—the men who did the drilling and blasting—work under contracts.[5]

At the start of this and every month, an assistant captain set benchmarks at the working face, showing where Penhallow's team started from. Half the team worked the day shift, which lasted about ten hours from the time the men went underground to the time they finished blasting and reappeared on the surface. The other half went to work two hours later on the night shift.

Between the two shifts, the noxious gases and dust produced by blasting had a chance to clear. After every week's work, the day and night shifts traded places. Underground, of course, it was always dark as night, regardless of the time, regardless of whether the sun or moon shone in the sky. Nevertheless, Penhallow often felt out of sorts because of the alternating weeks of day and night work. Just as his body was getting used to one, he changed to the other, upsetting his internal clock all over again.

At the end of the month, the captain measured how much rock the team had blasted out. Penhallow's team, in his first month, broke 18.71 cubic fathoms of copper rock at the $19 rate. Before settling with the men, Quincy deducted $70.25—the costs of supplies they had drawn, such as powder, fuse, candles, and drill steel. What was left over, the net settlement of $285.24, Penhallow shared equally with his partners. The contract team had no boss or foreman earning more than the rest. All the men had put in the standard twenty-six shifts that month, so all received the same amount: $47.54. That was actually a bit less than what they hoped for; $50 was about the norm for contract miners. At the pay window, Quincy held back one last bit—the mandatory monthly charge (fifty cents for a single man like Penhallow; a dollar for married men) that covered treatments and medicines administered by the company doctor.[6]

Our Cornishman's workdays started at the dry, where he changed into his miner's garb: coarse coat and pants; hobnailed boots; a resin-impregnated felt hat that protected his head from minor bonks, but little else. A lump of clay held one candle to the front of his helmet; Penhallow tied additional candles to his waist.[7] He carried a tin lunch bucket, usually with a pasty inside, as he left the dry and walked fifty yards to the man-engine shaft. There he stood in line with Roberts and Ley, waiting to go down in the mine.

Penhallow arrived at Quincy ten or eleven years after it first opened the Pewabic lode. The deepest part of the mine already reached the thirteenth level, which was 130 fathoms, or 780 feet, underground. Penhallow was happy not to have to descend a long set of ladders to get into the mine at the start of each shift, and even happier that he didn't have to climb hundreds and hundreds of rungs to carry himself to surface at the end of an arduous day. Just the year before he got there, Quincy put in a man-engine, a kind of mechanical ladder that took workers in and out of the mine.[8]

The man-engine, moved by a steam engine on the surface, was a pair of side-by-side, ten-inch-by-ten-inch rods that rested on rollers as they ran down an inclined mine shaft. The rods carried small steps about ten feet apart, and they reciprocated that same distance, always going in opposite directions. One went down ten feet while the other went up. Then the rods paused momentarily before reversing directions. Penhallow rode the man-engine underground by always stepping over to the rod that had just gone up and was now poised to descend. During every pause he moved over to the rod set to go down another ten feet on the next stroke.

At the end of his shift, Penhallow got to the surface by reversing his motion: during each pause, he stepped over to the rod that had just gone down and would next go up. Only three mines on the Keweenaw had a man-engine at this time, and Penhallow was glad he worked at one of them. It saved wear and tear on heart and lungs, on arms and legs.

It took Penhallow and his buddies about fifteen minutes to get from the surface to their work level underground. Once off the man-engine, they walked along a drift, or horizontal tunnel, that cut right through the copper-bearing lode and ran from one shaft over toward the next. The first men entering a drift sometimes caused bats to let go their hold of the rock and flutter off, or sent scavenging mine rats scurrying for cover.

The men made their way by the illumination of the candles on their helmets, which flickered as the miners walked and put them in a small pool of light that marched across the mine. If other men moved along the drift in front of Penhallow's shift team, if they were any distance away, he couldn't make out any features or details. All he'd see was their pinpoint candle flames.

At their appointed place, Penhallow, Roberts, and Ley climbed up into the stope where they were blasting out copper rock from one drift up toward the next. This was quite a climb at Quincy; the mine was very steep here. Before starting to drill shot-holes, the men practiced a couple of near rituals. They sat down to smoke their pipes and peered up at the mine's roof, or hanging wall, to see if the rock looked safe or sinister. If they saw a suspicious piece of hanging, they rapped it with a steel bar to see how it sounded and felt. If it didn't seem tight, if they judged the hanging unsound, the men stood off to the side and used a long bar to pry against the loose piece and bring it crashing down. Having tended to their pipes and hanging wall, they affixed a candle or two to the mine wall with clay balls or spikes and got to work.[9]

The three stopers attacked the rock with hand-held drills, eight-pound sledgehammers, and black powder. The drills were made of octagonal bar steel, forged and sharpened on one end to a simple chisel point. One man held the drill steel; the other two men drove it into the rock, rhythmically alternating sledgehammer strikes. While one hammerman delivered his blow, the other wound up to deliver the next. In the brief moment between strikes, the drill holder lifted the steel just a bit and turned it slightly, so the next blow cut a better chip at the bottom of the hole. The brain part of this work was reading the rock for lines of least resistance, and locating and angling the shot-holes so that when fired, they brought down the most mineral. The brawn part was swinging the sledge hour after hour—and hitting the drill squarely on the head, no matter what angle it was held at.

Fortunately, the Quincy mine at this depth was not too hot. In fact, at about sixty degrees year-round, it was about perfect for hard physical labor. The men didn't overheat when working or get too chilled when they stopped. No men could drive drill steels all day without breaks. To ease tired arms and shoulders, everybody took a turn holding the drill, and periodically all three men rested and reached again for their pipes.

Sometimes, if they saw a single candle flame coming their way, then perceived that its bearer was wearing a white coat, they knew a captain was paying them a visit. He might check to see they were taking down only good copper rock and leaving behind the copper-poor trap rock that sandwiched the lode on top and bottom. But they didn't fret about the captain's inspection. If enjoying a pipe at the time, they would continue with that, and never hop up and grab a sledge just to look busy to impress any boss. These contract miners set their own pace of work. That was an advantage they enjoyed over unskilled laborers who trammed rock or put up timbers; those work gangs often had a boss with them, telling them what to do and when to do it.

About halfway through his shift, Penhallow broke for his underground meal. He reheated his pasty by putting his lunch bucket over a candle flame for a while. The midshift break was a good time to tend to other matters, too. There were no undergound latrines, save whatever the men improvised for themselves. So they'd pee in any slightly out-of-the-way spot. For more serious business, they'd sit over an old powder keg or box, tucked off in a corner somewhere.[10]

With a few hours to go in the shift, the miners finished drilling and cleared shot-holes of rock chips. They went off to their team's iron powder magazine and took out the needed amount of explosive. They charged each hole with black powder—for safety's sake, tamping it home with a wooden rod, not a metal bar that might spark—and set the fuses. As one miner lighted the fuses, the others stood a safe distance off to the side, to protect themselves and to keep any passersby from wandering into the blast area. With all fuses lighted and all men in safe retreat, they counted the explosions as they went off. If they'd set eight charges and heard eight explosions, they were done. But if they only heard seven, they waited around until they thought it safe to go back in and detonate the missed hole.[11] Then they trooped over to the man-engine shaft and returned to the surface.

Miners like Penhallow, Roberts, and Ley broke the copper-bearing rock and left it lying on the mine floor. A series of other working men took over from there, handling, transporting, sorting, breaking, and processing the copper rock until it finally emerged as ingots.

Unskilled laborers mucked up the rock at the bottom of a stope and transported it along a drift to the shaft. Initially, they used wheelbarrows for this work. By the time Penhallow arrived at Quincy, the company had put rails along its drifts, and men trammed a ton or two of rock at a time in four-wheeled cars. Several teams of trammers, headed by bosses, went from place to place underground, going to work wherever a sufficient amount of copper rock had been broken and needed moving.

To fill the tram cars, men shoveled in the small stuff. For larger pieces weighing up to a hundred pounds, they stooped over and picked it up with coarse, calloused, thick-fingered hands. If they could move a piece of rock but not lift it, they scooted it up an inclined plank to drop it over the lip of the tram car. If they couldn't budge a big piece, they called in a block holer, a miner who blasted it into smaller fragments. After filling and pushing a heavy tram car a hundred yards or so to the shaft, the laborers returned for more.

These unskilled workers were the mine's "beasts of burden." With all the lifting, shoveling, and pushing they did, they had the hardest underground job. When not moving rock under the supervision of one of Quincy's timbermen, they might be moving heavy stulls, or long sections of tree trunks used to prop up unstable sections of the hanging wall. It was no mean feat to transport a stull, maybe two to three feet in diameter and ten or fourteen feet long, along a drift and then up into a stope.

In return for such work, unskilled underground workers received a flat wage of $40 per month, or 10 to 20 percent less than an average contract miner. The bosses who served as foremen over the work gangs of ten to fifteen men got an additional $5 per month.[12]

Underground rock wheelers had once dumped wheelbarrowsful of rock into buckets ("kibbles") that were raised up the shafts by hand-cranked windlasses or horse-powered whims. By the late 1860s, trammers dumped their loads into four-wheeled rock skips that ran on tracks laid down the shafts. Then a filler—who worked at the intersection of shaft and drift—pulled a lever, which in turn tugged on a wire that rang signal bells up on the surface. On hearing the proper signal, the engineer at the controls of a steam-powered hoist set his machine in motion. The hoist drum reeled in the wire rope that lifted the skip, and a couple tons of rock rose out of the ground at about five hundred feet per minute.[13]

Atop the mine, a lander received the copper rock within a simple board-and-batten structure built over the shaft collar. The rock dumped from the skip into small cars, which were pushed from the shafthouse to an adjacent sortinghouse. There another work gang spilled the rock out onto the floor, sorted it by hand, and put it back into cars sent off to different destinations.

The sortinghouse men worked not for a flat monthly wage but under a contract specifying a piece-rate system: they were paid so many cents per car filled, and the rate varied depending on the various types of mine product being sorted. Because their work entailed hard labor *and* making decisions about the mine product and where to send it, these men earned more money than contract miners, and far more money than unskilled laborers. With monthly contract settlements running $60 or more per man, the members of the hard-working sortinghouse crew had earnings on a par with the most skilled machinists, blacksmiths, or carpenters at the mine.[14]

On observation, some rock contained too little copper to bother with. Workers sorted out this poor rock and put it into cars that surface trammers wheeled to the back of the mine site and dumped onto waste rock piles. When men spied loose pieces of native copper the size of a walnut and up, they tossed them into a car that went to the copper house, where men packed the copper into wooden barrels. This barrel copper, along with large masses of native copper too big for barrels, went down to Quincy's docks on Portage Lake. Lake freighters picked the copper up there—including the "mineral" produced by Quincy's stamp mill—and delivered it to the Waterbury and Detroit Copper Company's smelter in lower Michigan, where furnacemen turned it into ingots.

Most of the tonnage spilled out on the sortinghouse floor consisted of "stamp rock," so called because it needed to be broken up by mechanical stamps to free its included copper. (In 1867, Quincy's eight to twelve sortinghouse workers handled 38,063 tons of this material.)[15] Copper rock no bigger than four to six inches across was already small enough to fit into the stamps, so trammers wheeled it straight from the sortinghouse to the head of the tramway running down to the stamp mill on Portage Lake. Sortinghouse men sent the bigger stuff to one of two nearby kilnhouses, where yet another gang of workers performed hard physical labor: they broke the rock another time, making it small enough for the mill.

Nine or ten men worked at each kilnhouse. Their boss made $55 per month, while they worked for $40, the same unskilled labor rate as underground and surface trammers.[16] Kilnhouse laborers used fire as a rock-breaking tool. They filled a masonry-lined pit with many cords of wood, put tons of rock atop the wood, and set the wood afire. The heat caused some rock to crack and break down. As the fire died out, workers poured water on the hot rock, causing more to split. The laborers then descended on any large uncooperative copper rock that remained, striking it with sledgehammers or picks until it was finally small enough to go to the stamps.

The stamp-mill tramway was a two-tracked, gravity-operated affair. As loaded rock cars went down one track, they drew out cable from one end of a winding drum mounted at the top of the incline. The weight of these descending, full cars turned the drum, which wound up cable on its opposite end. This second cable pulled empty rock cars back up the incline's other track. At the mill, a single man wheeled full cars into the structure and dumped their contents into the rock bins above the stamps. He worked under a piece-rate contract: two and a quarter cents for each ton of rock wheeled to the bins. For a summer month in 1867 when he wheeled in 2,325 tons by himself, he earned $52.31.[17]

By living in a boardinghouse and frequenting Hancock's saloons, Penhallow knew men who worked in all parts of Quincy's operations. He figured he'd recognize most of the company's 350 to 400 employees, just from seeing them around so much. And he knew many by name, especially fellow Cornishmen. He was on friendly terms with men ranging from underground trammers, to skilled mechanics and hoist operators on the surface, to stamp tenders at the mill. Penhallow knew several men who worked at Quincy's mill, and a couple of the boys who worked there as well, the sons of company employees.

Men and boys worked together at the mill to liberate and then capture the copper. They stamped, washed, and concentrated the metal, then dispensed with the crushed rock, which they tailed out of the mill as waste sands and dumped into Portage Lake. The stamp rock that entered the mill was about 2 percent copper; the concentrated "mineral" that left the mill in barrels was 60 to 80 percent copper and ready for smelting at Detroit.[18]

When Penhallow arrived at Quincy, the stamp mill was the most mechanized part of the copper production process. The mill used many machines, and it also used water, gravity, and troughs or "launders" to carry the crushed rock and copper from one step to the next. The work of tending machines in the mill wasn't nearly as heavy as the work done by miners, trammers, sorters, or kilnhouse workers, so the company hired boys to do some of it.

The boys provided their company with cheap labor and their families with additional income, which parents needed and welcomed. While an unskilled adult laborer typically earned $40 per month, many boys received a dollar a day, or $26 per month. (The youngest, about twelve years old, sometimes earned only $18 or $20. The oldest—sixteen or seventeen years of age—earned as much as $35.)[19] Penhallow saw nothing unusual about or wrong with putting boys to work after a bit of schooling. Back in Cornwall, he'd started earning his keep at age ten. Many of the other men from Cornwall, Ireland, and Germany now working at Quincy had done the same. And there was an added benefit to having a boy work in the mill in this district. Occasionally, he might bring home some valuable "half-breeds"—lumps of native silver attached to a bit of native copper. The mill was a good place to collect these precious-metal specimens. (Joseph Rawlings, master mechanic at the Cliff mine, noted that its vein carried a considerable quantity of silver, much of which the miners got, instead of the company. The stamps were a great place for collecting silver, too: "the 'apron' in front was frequently cover'd over with pieces the size of pin-heads, which the boys pick'd and pocketed.")[20]

Standing tall above the mill, a wrought-iron stack constantly emitted wood smoke from the steam boilers inside. Firemen stoked the mill's boilers shift after shift, feeding them five thousand cords of wood a year. Steam from the boilers went to engines that powered the mill's three basic types of machines: pumps, stamps, and concentrating equipment.

The pumps drew from Portage Lake the vast amount of water used from start to finish in the milling process. The stamps mechanically broke all the rock down to small size, liberating copper in the process. Batteries of rise-and-fall cast-iron stamp shoes repeatedly struck the rock held in a mortar box at the base of the machine. The mortar box had one or more sides formed of heavy plates laced with pea-sized holes. Water poured into the mortar box and flowed out through the plates, carrying with it all the pieces of rock and copper small enough to pass through.

Water then carried the copper and rock mixture to various machines, such as jigs and buddles, that performed gravity separations of the two materials. In one manner or another, the machines acted on the principle that copper had a higher specific gravity than rock. Jigs used a plungerlike motion to agitate a watery bath of copper and rock. When the agitation stopped, the copper sank faster and concentrated on the bottom of the jig, while the lighter rock concentrated above it. At a buddle, a wet mixture of fine copper and rock particles spilled out near the center of a horizontal, rotating disk. The water tended to carry the rock all the way across the disk, finally tailing it over the edge. The copper, meanwhile, stayed on the disk, and workers periodically stopped the machine to collect it.

It took skill and experience to set up and adjust the stamp mill's machines. The trick was to catch as much copper as possible and not let fine flecks of the metal wash right out of the building with the waste sands and flow into Portage Lake. Just tending the machines, as opposed to adjusting them, was a simpler task that an unskilled man or boy could do. So up to two dozen boys worked at the mechanized mill, while only two or three boys worked underground at Quincy, or on the surface at the mine, where most of the jobs called for more strength or skill than boys possessed.[21]

When Penhallow first arrived at Quincy in 1867, he figured that fellow Cornishmen comprised nearly half the company's employment. The Germans and Irish—he saw many of them underground and on the surface, too—each seemed to make up a bit less than a fourth of the workforce. Americans, Scots, and Englishmen (Penhallow *always* considered the English as separate from the Cornish) were there, and filling some prominent positions, but their numbers weren't great. Even more scarce were Swedes and Finns. They seemed to fill only a few contract-mining teams.[22]

Down in Hancock's bars and businesses, Penhallow ran across many French Canadians, but he didn't work with any of them, and extremely few were on the mine's payroll. They mostly worked out in the woods, converting forests into fuel and such. Most unusual to him, Penhallow occasionally encountered "colored" men, also referred to in speech and in the papers as "niggers" or "darkies." He never saw colored men work in the mines, but some got hired on at the docks and aboard lake freighters. In town, they also worked as barbers or entertainers; Penhallow once attended a "darky minstrel show" and found it most curious and foreign.[23]

Penhallow learned straightaway that who you were and who you knew counted for a lot in getting ahead in this place. The top boss at the mine was the agent, the man who oversaw all the disparate operations and communicated with company officers and directors back east. The clerk ran the mine's business affairs, such as ordering supplies, paying the bills, and making the payroll. The head mining captain supervised the underground and dictated how and where to exploit the lode. A surface superintendent, aided by a master mechanic and boss blacksmiths and machinists, looked after the boilers and hoists, the fabricating shops, and all surface equipment. Another superintendent directed operations at Quincy's stamp mill. The men filling these positions, it seemed to Penhallow, were always going to be Americans, Cornishmen, Scots, or Germans, but they wouldn't all be equally qualified for all top positions.

Americans didn't work in the mines—Penhallow never saw an American swing a sledgehammer underground—and generally they weren't technically expert. They did, however, know business practices, and they *were*, after all, Americans working for American mining companies. So although the Americans never qualified as mining captains, they might rise up the business side of a company to become the chief clerk and then the agent.

A Cornishman or Scot could get to the top post by coming up the mining side of things, by being an expert in finding and following copper and managing men. When Penhallow got to Quincy, the agent was a Scot, George Hardie; the clerk an American, James North Wright; the head mine captain a Cornishman, John Cliff; the surface superintendent a Scot, John Duncan; the master mechanic an Englishman, Fred Labram; and the mill superintendent a German, Philip Scheuermann.[24]

As Penhallow put in his first half-dozen years of work at Quincy, a bit of turnover naturally occurred, but the ethnic makeup of the company leadership didn't stray very much. Two different Americans, James North Wright and A. J. Corey, advanced from company clerk to mine agent, and Donald McCall succeeded John Duncan, a fellow Scot, as surface superintendent. The mill remained firmly in the control of Scheuermann, and the mine captaincy remained in the grasp of Cornishman John Cliff. (In fact, early in the 1870s Quincy refused Cliff's tendered resignation and wouldn't let him move on to another mine because with his knowledge of Quincy's underground works, he was too valuable to let go.)[25]

Quincy was the sort of company that liked to get good men into supervisory positions, then leave them there and leave them alone, as long as they got the job done. Captains, superintendents, and bosses enjoyed considerable autonomy over their various parts of the mine and had the power to hire and fire. So a man filling an important niche at Quincy was in a position to help his fellow countrymen out. When jobs were lost during the hard times following the Civil War, Cornish contract miners at Quincy were glad to have a Cornish mine captain because they expected John Cliff to offer them some special consideration. At the stamp mill, the one key operation at Quincy headed by a German, it was no surprise that Philip Scheuermann put many fellow Germans to work: machinists Kielen and Jegel; fireman Schon; woodpasser Wiedenhofer; carpenter Schubert; blacksmith Schintzen; barrel maker Offenbacher; and stamp tender Holzbauer.[26]

The Irish didn't fare as well when it came to having their own in high and influential places. The highest-ranking Irishman, James Quinn, served as one of two assistant mine captains at Quincy, and that was about as high as an Irishman could go—they never managed to leapfrog over Cornishmen or Scots. But the Irish, too, knew how to use what important niches they filled to advantage. Irish contract miners were especially welcome at Quincy as long as Quinn was on the job (just as German contract miners had once been plentiful at Quincy in the 1850s, when William Worminghaus served as captain).[27] And for years John McCormick did all right for himself, his company, and a dozen or so other Irishmen who worked for him in and around Quincy's sortinghouses.

In the early 1860s, a gang of Germans headed by Henry Obenhoff had contracted to receive and sort Quincy's mine product. McCormick somehow got on that crew in September 1863, and just a few months later, the Germans were gone from the sortinghouses, replaced by McCormick's Irishmen.[28] Since the end of 1863, then, McCormick put together his own crew of men and contracted with Quincy to receive, sort, and send off to mill, kilnhouse, copper house, or waste pile the rock hoisted from the mine. The monthly contract stipulated a pay rate per carful of rock, and McCormick's crew handled the entire output of the mine. Instead of taking on a large army of indifferent workers, McCormick took on a small army of hard workers. Better to divvy up the settlement a dozen ways, rather than twenty. At the end of the month, fewer men split the settlement, and each man made considerably more than an average miner as long as McCormick kept him on the team. The men McCormick kept were overwhelmingly Irish. If the stamp mill was a German stronghold under Scheuermann, the sortinghouses were an Irish stronghold, thanks to McCormick. Working alongside him were the likes of Jerry O'Neil, Michael Cuddihey, Patrick Coughlin, Peter O'Brien, and John Maloney.

Penhallow's fellow contract miners did the same sort of thing in putting together their teams. Since they set their own pace of work and shared equally in monthly settlements, hard workers looked to match up with hard workers, and slackers with slackers. That produced more harmonious teams. So did matching up with men of the same ethnic background. The men self-selected their teams and put together many that were all Cornish (such as the stoping team of Hosking, Hosking, Dunstan, Tamblin, Richards, and Sincock); or Irish (one particular stoping team contained two Caseys, two Sullivans, a Kelly, and a Crowley); or German (a four-man drifting team included Stoppart, Schultz, Schuckmill, and Kaufmann); or even Scandinavian (Solmonson, Peterson, Erickson, and Nelson).[29]

Josiah Penhallow stuck with John Roberts and Samuel Ley, and they often completed their contract team by adding more Cornishmen. They needed just one more man when driving a small five-foot by six-foot drift (which was the work they undertook most often); three more men when stoping in more open spaces; and up to five or six more men on the rare occasions when they worked as shaft-sinkers. In six years, well over two dozen individuals undertook contract work with Penhallow, Roberts, and Ley, and the team worked all over the mine, in ground tributary to four shafts, and on at least ten different levels.[30]

Over those six years, Quincy steadily grew deeper, moving from the 130-fathom level down to the 220-fathom level. Quincy was now a quarter-mile deep—1,320 feet. In the course of getting there, Penhallow recollected that the mine had killed about one man a year. A couple fell to their deaths; explosives blasted a couple; and another one or two died under rock falls.[31]

Underground technology and work hadn't changed much since Penhallow started at Quincy, but he knew that change was in the works. It was only a matter of time, he figured, before companies did away with sledgehammers, hand-drills, and black powder—all the principal tools of his trade.

Since the late 1860s, several companies had experimented with new explosives and rock-drilling machines. To date, however, the new tools hadn't worked out well. Nitroglycerine oil had scared the men; this explosive developed by Alfred Nobel was too powerful, too unstable. A couple of mines tried it, and at one, the Huron mine, angry and frightened men had blown up the nitro on the surface, just to get rid of it. Six or eight mines—including Quincy—had tried to drill shot-holes with a new machine powered by compressed air. The machine, invented by Charles Burleigh, had been very successful driving a railroad tunnel in New England (hence the Cornish nickname for the machines, "Yankee miners"). But so far, the Burleigh drill was a bust on Lake Superior because it was too big and unwieldy, too heavy to move around and set up in a steeply canted mine. So Penhallow and the majority of miners along the mineral range still broke rock with tried-and-true tools, but they sensed that drilling machines were coming, along with high explosives, like Nobel's newer and supposedly safer explosive, dynamite.[32]

Up on the surface, one new machine at Quincy was starting to make quite a difference—the Blake rock crusher. This machine broke copper rock by squeezing it between two heavy cast-iron jaws. It replaced Quincy's kilnhouses and the "burning and dressing" of copper rock by unskilled laborers. The jaw crushers went into a single new rockhouse located near the head of the stamp-mill incline. An endless-rope, steam-powered tramroad passed by the shafts and delivered all the mine product to the rockhouse, where it was spilled out over a "grizzly," a coarse screen that sorted the stamp rock by size. So the new technologies in the rockhouse not only eliminated Quincy's kilnhouses; they eliminated its sortinghouses, too.

Quincy reassigned many kilnhouse and sortinghouse workers to the rockhouse, but due to its labor-saving tramroad, crushers, and grizzly, the facility eliminated some surface workers' jobs. It also eliminated the monthly sorting contracts that had gone to John McCormick's Irish crew. For years, those men had made good money. Reassigned to tend machines in the rockhouse, and reclassified as common laborers, they now worked for a monthly wage of $40 or $45, $10 or $15 less than what they had been making.[33]

Down at Quincy's mill, the technology was little changed. Some companies had gone to using much bigger cast-iron stamps, which were both lifted and propelled downward by a steam-driven piston directly connected to the stamp's vertical stem. Quincy's bosses thought these new machines abraded and tore the copper too much. As the heavy stamp shoes pounded the rock in the mortar box, they reduced some flecks of copper to a size and weight so small that the mill's concentrating machines couldn't slow, stop, or catch them as they were being carried along in a stream of water. So Quincy still used batteries of much smaller, lighter drop stamps. These stamp heads were lifted by steam power but descended onto the rock thanks only to gravity, with no power-assist.

Quincy did make a change when it came to smelting. It no longer sent all its mineral and mass copper to Detroit, but had some of it melted and refined right on Portage Lake at Hancock, where a custom smelter operated by the Detroit and Lake Superior Company performed this service for numerous mining companies.

In the 1840s and 1850s, companies had shipped mass and mineral south and east for smelting. Over time, the smelters moved closer to the mines, moving from Boston and Baltimore, Pittsburgh, and Cleveland to Detroit and, finally, in 1860, to Hancock. By the late 1860s, the Hancock and Detroit smelters handled most of the product of the Lake Superior mines.[34]

There were a couple of reasons why smelters—or a smelting industry—hadn't proliferated on the Keweenaw during the early decades of mining. First, no mine on the lake produced enough copper to justify the expense of building a smelter just for its own product and use. While virtually every operating mine built its own stamp mill, very few companies considered building a smelter. Second, smelting Lake Superior's native copper proved a rather mysterious art or craft. Early attempts to smelt copper near the mines failed, and throughout the nineteenth century, only a few men, such as C. G. Hussey, John R. Grout, and the father/son team of James R. and James B. Cooper, ever mastered the business of setting up and running native copper smelters.

So smelters were not ubiquitous industrial features on the Keweenaw landscape, nor were they large employers of men until late in the nineteenth century. Nevertheless, the Portage Lake smelter was a very important addition to the overall copper industry—one that employed maybe a hundred men and received and smelted the mines' product year-round. The crucial work at the Portage Lake smelter took place within a main furnace building, which had four reverberatory furnaces inside, one near each corner, surmounted by a tall brick stack. Each reverberatory furnace had a removable top. Inside, a low bridge wall separated a firebox on one end from the furnace's shallow hearth. The bridge wall kept impurities in the coal from mixing with and contaminating the melt.

The smelter offered hot and heavy work. With the furnace top removed, men loaded the low hearth with a charge of mass copper and mineral. After resealing the top, workers charged the firebox with coal and lighted it. On the opposite end of the furnace, a man adjusted the chimney flue to help control the blaze. Fire and hot gases went up and over the bridge wall, reverberated along the hearth (melting the charge of mineral and mass), and then went up the stack.

As the furnace charge melted, the copper collected on the bottom of the hearth, and a bath of molten rock floated atop it. Furnacemen opened access doors, reached in with iron tools, and skimmed the molten rock off into slag buggies—cast-iron pots on wheels. The molten rock solidified into a glassy slag, and men wheeled it away. Next, the furnacemen reached long paddles into the melt to "rabble" or splash the copper around. Mixing air with the molten copper oxidized impurities. Then, to get rid of excess oxygen in the melt, the men "poled" it—they thrust small greenwood poles into the bath of copper. The wood instantly combusted, its carbon combining with oxygen to produce carbon monoxide and dioxide gases that passed up the stack. The furnacemen skimmed off the last bit of slag, then dipped cast-iron ladles into the copper, which they tipped into molds to produce ingots of various sizes and shapes. Once the men were finished with ladling, that batch of copper was done, and the furnace would soon receive a new charge of mineral, mass, and fuel. Meanwhile, men tended the other furnaces, whose heats were in various stages of completion.[35]

Josiah Penhallow didn't much care about surface work or technologies. Just so long as they didn't create bottlenecks that slowed down miners' work— that's about all he cared about. He did care about the price of copper, though. For years after the war, since Penhallow had arrived, in fact, the demand for new copper and the price paid for it had stayed low: it sold for twenty-five cents a pound in 1867, the year he arrived, and bottomed out at only twenty cents in 1870. As long as the price remained low, miners' earnings stayed low. The mining captain forced them down into the $45 to $50 range and kept them there. The men didn't like it, but the industry was struggling, jobs were tight, the contract workers weren't organized, and there was little they could do about it.

Finally, in 1872, the copper industry recovered from its doldrums, and the average price of a pound of new copper climbed 50 percent from the year before, jumping from twenty-two to thirty-three cents. Now the companies wanted to step up production and maximize profits during a long-awaited return of high prices. Problem was, after so many slow years, they were short on labor. They didn't have enough men around to accelerate the winning of copper. This gave workers an advantage over their employers they hadn't had for half a dozen years.

Miners wanted higher earnings, and to force the issue, at the Portage Lake mines and up at Calumet and Hecla, they walked off the job. Penhallow's contract team, along with fellow Quincy miners, struck for eight days in May 1872, returning only after the company raised its contract rates for drifting, stoping, and shaft-sinking. Month after month, Penhallow had regularly taken home less than $50 for twenty-six hard-working shifts per month. In the first three months following the strike, he took home $102, $73, and $82![36] Penhallow knew that this bonanza wouldn't last—that as high wages attracted more men to the mines, the companies would start cutting earnings down again. But he enjoyed it while it lasted. Why, a man could actually take it easy, maybe even take a day or two off besides Sundays, and still make more than he had in years.

By the mid-1870s, 8,250 adult males lived and worked in Keweenaw, Ontonagon, and Houghton counties (including Isle Royale). Sixty-five percent of them—5,350 men—worked in the copper industry: in the mines, the surface shops and offices, the stamp mills, the Portage Lake smelter. Michigan's state census of 1874 reported that a considerable number of skilled tradesmen worked in the region: about 210 blacksmiths, machinists, mechanics, pattern makers, or moulders. The building trades were well represented, too: over 350 men worked as carpenters, joiners, painters, masons, bricklayers, and plasterers.[37]

In a land of forests, where wood, a wonderfully versatile material, was put to so many uses by a new industrial society, it was not surprising that many men made their living with saws and axes. The population included about 450 men who worked as loggers, woodchoppers, lumbermen, sawyers, hewers, and wood dealers. Others made a living off nature—forests, fields, lakes, and streams—in different ways: the census counted nearly two hundred farmers, and seventy-five fishermen, hunters, and trappers.

Much heavy material moved across the Keweenaw. Supplies came in, copper went out, people moved about. The place was still in transition between the horse age and the steam age, and a number of men occupied themselves by outfitting and keeping horses (thirty harness makers, saddlers, wagon makers, wheelwrights, hostlers and livery keepers) and driving horses (over two hundred teamsters and stage drivers). Of course, people got around on foot, too, and a surprisingly high number of shoemakers—sixty of them—made the Keweenaw their home. (Perhaps so many were needed to make and repair miners' special hobnailed boots.)

The Keweenaw's towns supported nearly sixty hotelkeepers and boarding-house keepers; as many barbers as lawyers (eleven each); thirty physicians, six druggists and three dentists. A man who smoked and drank as a respite from his workaday world could deal with any one of seven cigar makers or tobacconists, and tip drinks across the bar from eighty men earning their way as saloon keepers.

In the 1860s and early 1870s, Houghton County paid men to perform a host of miscellaneous jobs: repair bridges, build fences, transport prisoners, kill wolves, build coffins, dig paupers' graves, transport the ill to quarantine, serve on inquests, join a sheriff's posse, and bring in dead bodies. As for the few women who worked for the county, Mrs. Nolan got paid for "cleaning jail" and Mary McCarthy and Ellen Dunn for "cleaning courtroom" and "scrubbing courthouse." Gertrude Post received the unenviable assignment of "Nurse employed in Pest House."[38]

Women up on Lake Superior had far fewer ways to earn an income than men. For many women, and for girls, working outside the home usually meant working *inside* somebody else's. Well-to-do women eased their domestic burdens by hiring other women to do household chores. "Domestics," or servants, who could either live in or live out, performed a wide range of chores, virtually anything that the woman of the house wanted done: getting up early to light the stove, cooking, cleaning, sewing, laundry, tending the children.

Instead of hiring out full-time as a domestic to one household, some women took in cleaning or sewing jobs from a variety of neighbors. In 1863, just as winter was starting, Henry Hobart availed himself of a seamstress who made him flannel drawers and a pair of pants. Lucena Brockway employed girls and women as full-time domestics; she also hired them for special chores. At various times, girls named Lizzie, Christiana, and Sarah worked as live-in domestics for Mrs. Brockway. Mrs. Brockway also paid Mrs. Loranger for sewing dresses and Mrs. Laporte, Mrs. Donner, and Mrs. Curtis for doing the Brockway family laundry.[39]

Mrs. Brockway surely needed help around the house. She was frail, and her home at the Cliff mine in the early 1870s received numerous visitors. The Brockways had many relatives living on the Keweenaw, and they knew everybody who was anybody in the copper business. People constantly stopped by, took meals, sometimes stayed a night or two. It is possible, even, that the Brockways had returned to running a small hotel out of their house, something they had done in earlier years. At any rate, in 1873 and 1874, Lucena Brockway kept close track of the comings and goings of visitors, recording them religiously in her diaries. On August 27, 1873, she had ten visitors and served twenty-two extra meals; in a three-week stretch a bit later that year, she served "161 Extra Meals for company." On January 10, 1874, seven visitors called in the afternoon. Lucena served them seven extra meals, and she recorded, "I have worked very hard all day baking and am tired out." On the very last day of 1874 she wrote in her diary: "I have kept an account of the transient meals during the year which amounts to one thousand & seventy meals— 1070." The total figure, it seems, stunned even her.

Hotels and bakeries offered limited employment to women in the towns. By the 1870s, comely young women served up food and drinks in restaurants; the *Northwestern Mining Journal* carried this tantalizing advertisement: "The staid and respectable portion of Hancock society will be shocked to learn of an Innovation in the Shape of Pretty Waiter Girls at Wern's."[40] But for the most part, shops and offices in commercial districts offered few opportunities for women because men filled most clerical and clerking positions. Along main street, in the 1860s and 1870s, the business most likely owned and staffed by women was the millinery. Millineries, run by and for women, conducted business in Eagle Harbor, Ontonagon, Houghton, Hancock, and Calumet.[41]

Women of some refinement, especially unmarried women who had special language or artistic skills, sometimes supported themselves as tutors. In 1856 in Ontonagon, in a room at Mrs. Doolittle's, Miss Gampert opened "a Class for Drawing, French, and Embroidery." In Houghton, Miss Cardell taught music. In the mid-1870s in Calumet, Miss Susie Flynn gave "lessons on the Piano, Organ and Melodeon" and also imparted "instruction in the manufacture of human hair into flower-shaped work and other forms of ornamentation."[42]

Women also served as teachers in formal schools—private, parochial, and public. Teaching was the profession most open to them. In Ontonagon in 1855, Miss Keyes opened her own small private school in what used to be a clothing store.[43] One interesting group of women teachers arrived on the Keweenaw during the Civil War era: Catholic sisters. Under the direction of Superioress Venerable Mother Magdalen Stehlenhas, an Ursuline convent opened at Ontonagon in 1862 and took over operation of a two-story Catholic school started in 1858. In 1863, Father Baraga wrote, "The . . . convent in Ontonagon flourishes visibly under the blessing of God. It contains many Sisters within its walls, has thirty-two boarding scholars and a considerable day school." Within a few years, other convent schools, conducted by sisters of St. Joseph, operated in Hancock and L'Anse.[44]

For the first ten or fifteen years of settlement, public schools were slow to establish on the Keweenaw, so they offered few positions for women teachers. But in the late 1850s through the 1870s, as mine communities matured and more families moved in, the movement toward tax-supported public education accelerated, resulting in more schools and teaching posts. In 1857, the copper district boasted only six qualified teachers and a like number of schools. By 1875, Houghton, Keweenaw, and Ontonogan Counties together supported about thirty public schools, which employed eighty teachers—fifty-four of whom were women, usually American-born, young, and single.[45]

Throughout this period, a woman needn't have the highest of credentials to qualify as a teacher. Few would have completed a full course of instruction at a "normal" or teaching college. A young woman needed to be well-spoken, able to read, write, and cipher, and of high moral character. (Teaching contracts specified that "gross immorality" was cause for dismissal by local school boards.) Since men filled the school boards that selected principals and teachers, a pleasing personal appearance no doubt helped some female teachers land a job. In 1877, school board member William S. Thomas recorded in his journal that he couldn't help but notice the attractive shape of a young woman he had just interviewed for a teaching job in Keweenaw County. She had the tiniest waist he'd ever seen. She got the job, and for a while Thomas courted her and another woman teacher, while debating which to choose—or should he choose neither of them? He was attracted to them physically, yet their womanliness seemed to scare him, and he faulted their intellects as inferior to his own. Paralyzed by indecision, Thomas finally stopped seeing both teachers. (Years later, when he married somebody else, this fretful, tentative suitor confessed in his journal, not too surprisingly, that he was incapable of fulfilling his husbandly duties.)[46]

Early public schools often had but two teachers. A man usually headed the school and taught older students; a woman assisted and taught younger scholars. This was precisely the situation at the Clifton Public School during the Civil War. Henry Hobart served as principal teacher. At first, Miss Cundy assisted him. She kept "very busy" because she had "quite a number of small ones to hear read." When Miss Cundy left to go to the normal school in Ypsilanti, Miss Nutt took her place among the younger students. Typically, at Clifton and elsewhere on the Keweenaw, younger, subordinate women teachers received half to two-thirds the pay of men.[47]

Smaller villages kept their one- or two-room schoolhouses, but after the Civil War, more prosperous villages such as Houghton and Calumet erected commodious graded schools. These schools not only offered women more teaching jobs; they also allowed a group of young, intelligent women to work *together*, which was something quite new and different on the Keweenaw. When Houghton opened its new graded school in 1866, William Sidnam served as principal and Miss Carrie Edgerton as preceptress, or head teacher. Others on staff included one male teacher and five women: Misses Kate Easton, Sophia Mabbs, Ettie Cummings, Hattie Funston, and Ellen Selley, described as "assistant teachers."[48]

Even those communities with graded schools and high school departments did not expect many older boys and girls to attend. In 1863, teacher Hobart noted that "William Benney, one of my best scholars, has gone to work in the [stamp mill] Wash House." In 1875, the Calumet township school supervisor ruefully admitted that "only a few in this community ... expect to give their children anything more than a very limited education." That same year, the Houghton County Superintendent of Public Instruction sounded a similar note: "Children permanently leave school at as early an age as they can be employed at home, or at service for wages."[49]

Children did not constitute much of a protected or privileged class on the Keweenaw. The treatment given children at the Cliff mine appalled the Yankee from Vermont, Henry Hobart:

> I have been convinced fully in my opinion that the use of kindness is the true way of governing the young. ... After witnessing the cruel practice of beating, scolding, shutting up in dark closets, tying up etc. that is generally adopted here and the character of the children, I fully believe that they are not near as well behaved as those who are managed by kindness & correct training. The practice of continually punishing a child causes him to be in a raging passion.[50]

The practice of child labor made it likely that many boys and girls suffered abuse at the hands not only of parents but also of employers. Girls perhaps fared worse than boys. Compared to boys working in industrial settings, girls may have gone to work in domestic settings at earlier ages. Some girls as young as six were "farmed out" by their families to live and work in other households. Girls seem to have earned substantially less than boys. Boys earned about a dollar a day ($26 per month). Girls working as domestics received about two dollars a week, or eight to twelve dollars per month. Boys often worked in groups, in quite open spaces, where many people came and went and could observe goings-on. Girls often worked alone, in a confined house, out of sight of the watchful eyes of others.[51]

The girls who worked in the house where Henry Hobart boarded were not out of his sight, and he recorded in his diary how Mrs. Rawlings constantly mistreated them, how she could fly into a "violent passion" and assail a girl with "an awful tirade" and go "big guns" with her over some trivial cause:

It is a fact that the English people are well versed in tyrannizing over all who come under their authority. There is an aristocratic feeling that I detest. They look upon a servant as a dog & treat them as such. Mrs. Rawlings is a fine specimen of a totally ignorant English woman. . . . She has had four girls this summer who have left rather than listen to her jawings. . . . Says Mrs. Rawlings: "If you was my girl I would beat the flesh from your bones. I would haunt the life out of you. . . ." Think of tying a little girl six years old or striking her over the head & saying you would tear her to pieces. Is this a specimen of true management?[52]

Like other American frontiers, the Keweenaw at first had a leveling effect on the society it hosted. Generally, the richest and poorest in the world below either wouldn't or couldn't make the trip to Lake Superior. The privileged rich, living in more prosperous and genteel surroundings, didn't have to live on the frontier and suffer blizzards and blackflies. If they wanted to get involved in this place at all, they could keep their bodies at home and put their money to work on the Keweenaw by investing in the new mines. The poorest of the poor stayed home, too: people who were too old or frail or disabled to work; people who didn't want to work at jobs as hard as those promised by the mining industry; and people who didn't have enough money to pay the passage to get there.

Absent the richest and poorest, the Keweenaw's first small communities were quite egalitarian. From the 1840s through the 1850s, the mining and commercial villages maintained their rough-hewn appearances from one end to the other. Everybody had the same muddy trails and stump-strewn fields to look at. Common frontier experiences and hardships blurred social distinctions, and settlers bore the impress of being workers, whether they served as bosses, merchants, or miners.

But by the 1860s and 1870s, the population had become larger and more diverse, and economic and social distinctions became much more discernible. As this new place developed, it offered settlers the chance to advance themselves, to be upwardly mobile, to get ahead faster and better than they would have if they'd stayed at home in New England, New York, or lower Michigan—or in Prussia, Cornwall, or Ireland.[53] A person could move from being a miner in Cornwall to a mine captain here, from being a store clerk in New York to a chief mine clerk on Lake Superior. Every single time an embryonic village took form on Lake Superior, it offered somebody the chance to be a land speculator, the chance to get in on the ground floor and put up the first mercantile establishment, or hotel, or livery, or brewery.

Some seized business or job opportunities at growing commercial villages or growing mines, worked hard, perhaps got lucky, and succeeded handsomely. Cornish-born Johnson Vivian served as head captain and agent for the Phoenix mine and several others. Adam Haas, Bavarian, emigrated to Lake Superior in

1852 at age thirty; he started a successful family brewery. William Lapp, Prussian, born in the mid-1820s, became a manufacturer of lubricants and mining candles on the Keweenaw. Peter Ruppe (born 1823) and Joseph Wertin (born 1818), both Austrians, became successful, influential merchants, as did the Irishman John Ryan, and the American Ransom Shelden.[54]

While many could tell their success stories, far, far more continued to work hard not to prevail in this society and place but just to get by from day to day. Those who migrated to the copper district and competed for jobs or customers or position knew well that individual abilities and initiative and ambition counted. But ethnicity, age, and gender counted, too. They set residents apart from one another and helped cast them into different roles and occupations that rewarded some with more influence, status, and money than others. Most men were destined to be laborers throughout their working lives—not stockholders, entrepreneurs, or businessmen, but men who had to strain and sweat and stay healthy to make a living. Women never had the same economic opportunities as men on the Keweenaw; the husband's place largely determined the woman's. And a sure sign of growing class differences was made evident every Monday, as women of greater means opened their doors to hired women of lesser means, who came in to do the laundry. Class differences could be seen when some boys and girls marched off to school, or off to a language or music lesson, while others marched off to the stamp mill or some better-off neighbor's house, where instead of learning, they'd wash copper sands or carry the water or firewood.

Over twenty-five years of settlement, work in the copper industry—by far the largest local employer of men—had stayed the same in some ways and changed in others. The mining companies operated with small business bureaucracies—very few men worked in offices, while thousands labored in the mines and shops. The industry continued to put a premium on practically trained experts, who'd learned their skills on the job, rather than on university-educated men. Underground captains, not geologists or mining engineers, found and followed the copper and decided how to exploit it; surface captains, not civil or mechanical engineers, laid out the physical plants and superintended the installation of boilers, hoists, and other machines.

From the start, the industry put working men on long shifts—ten hours underground, sometimes even longer in stamp mills and shops. It scheduled long workweeks, too, taking only the Sabbath off during normal weeks, and maybe just an extra day off at select holidays. And much of the work they offered remained hard, physical labor, best left to men in their twenties and thirties who could withstand it.

In terms of changes, some workers' jobs had been altered, or even eliminated, by early mechanization. One machine every underground worker had reason to like—because it made his work routine easier at the start and end of the shift—was the man-engine that carried him into and out of the mine. For raising rock, steam-powered hoists replaced human-powered windlasses. For moving stamp copper on the surface, railroad locomotives and endless-rope tramroads replaced many a man who'd made a living pushing wheelbarrows or cars full of rock. Mechanical jaw crushers broke rock that laboring men had initially split with fire, pick, and sledge. Machines, then, especially on the surface, had taken over some of the most arduous rock-breaking and rock-transporting tasks. But underground, mechanization proved slower in coming. The first air-powered machine drills had been tried—and had failed. So miners still wielded sledges and hand-steels against the rock.

As the mining companies started employing new technologies, they also started organizing workers in new ways. At the start, a mine like Quincy used contract labor extensively. Men put together their own work crews and contracted as a team to do a set job at a set rate for a set period of time. Early on, besides contracting with miners, Quincy let contracts to other men to wheel rock; hoist rock in winzes; erect timbers; break and sort rock in the mine; windlass rock and water to the surface; sort, burn, and dress copper for the stamps; tram rock to the incline; run rock into the stamp mill; and forge and sharpen drill steels.

Over time, as Quincy and other companies deployed new technologies, matured, and tried to exact greater, more direct control over their operations, they started paring down their contract work. They shifted most unskilled manual laborers off contracts, paid them a flat monthly wage, and deployed them in company-selected work gangs headed by foremen or other bosses. These men, in effect, suffered a demotion in status, usually attended by a loss of earnings. Instead of contractors, they were now hired hands, who did what the boss told them to do. The miners who drilled and blasted rock, on the other hand, got to keep their contract system. So miners became entrenched as the underground elite among the working class, a distinct cut above trammers, timbermen, or common laborers.

A job is more than just a task accompanied by the tools needed to do it. A job has many elements: pace of work, control of decisions, status, safety, sociability, earnings. A job also has an element of security: can it be counted on day after day, week after week, year after year, to deliver adequate and steady financial support to worker and family? Up on Lake Superior, job security was not a hallmark of the copper mining industry.

Observers noted that for the capitalist, for the investor, the copper mines represented a risky, "subterranean lottery." They were no less risky for workers in search of job security. Mine failures not only consumed wealth (the district lost four times more money than it made in the first two decades); they also threw men out of work. Of nearly one hundred mining corporations launched before the Civil War, two-thirds achieved little or no production, and only eight paid any dividends. After the war, the half-decade-long recession closed more of the weaker mines and forced cutbacks on the stronger ones. In this risky boom-or-bust industry, amid so many failures, for many workers job security and "rooting in" remained an elusive dream. Early settlers remained unsettled. After moving *to* the Keweenaw, they continued moving *around* the Keweenaw, hoping that instead of closing another mine out, they might find themselves at one of the few profitable ones with staying power. In the meantime they were kept "almost as migratory as birds of passage."[55]

Under the pressures of closings, booms and busts, depressed wages, work reorganizations, and the encroachment of mechanization and technological change, it was only a matter of time before men took some actions to try to wrest greater control over their lives, work, and earnings. So in 1870 at the Huron mine, they blew up nitroglycerine oil on the surface rather than suffering its use underground, and a few years later they launched a series of strikes for better wages against Calumet and Hecla and the Portage Lake mines. On the whole, however, mine workers had little in the way of collective force on the mining frontier. If a working man, a family man, just couldn't cut it on his wages, rebellion against his employer was not the usual solution. The usual solution was to take in boarders or have the wife take in laundry— or to take the children out of school and put them to work.

SEVEN

SAINTS AND SCHOLARS
Village Churches and Schools

Pupils are required in all cases to be kind and respectful in their deportment to each other and their teachers, to be neat in their persons and appearance, to refrain from the use of tobacco and from vile or profane language and other immoral conduct of every kind, to be punctual and regular in their attendance, diligent in study and faithful in the observation of every rule of the school. . . . Pupils shall clean all mud and dirt from their feet as near as possible before entering the school house, walk gently in the halls and stairways, and at no time scuffle, run, jump, or make any loud noise in any part of the building.

— "Rules and Regulations of Quincy School,"
adopted August 26, 1868

Along the Keweenaw's mineral range, the fates of mining companies, churches, and schools were inextricably intertwined. Where the mine showed the promise of profitability, the population swelled, the number of families increased, and building a school and church became a priority. If the company suddenly went bust after a few years of operation, then its failure brought down attendant social institutions that had just started to root in. Families moved out. Local schools and churches collapsed. On the other hand, if the company settled in for a long run of profitable mining, the churches, schools, and other social institutions operating on its margins grew larger and more varied over time.

After laboring hard for six days of the week, some workers caroused on the seventh, but many others chose to worship. The church was an important part of many peoples' lives, one that served their spiritual needs while offering a refuge from daily trials and tribulations. Settlers migrated from faraway places to a very different world on this northern frontier. The church provided them with an opportunity to reconnect with fellow countrymen and to reestablish important religious traditions. But churches had to adapt to frontier conditions, and worshipers had to accommodate changed circumstances. Newcomers to Lake Superior could emulate but never duplicate their earlier religious experiences.

Early arrivals at settlements, especially in the 1840s, found themselves lacking both a house of worship and a preacher or priest. To initiate religious services, like-minded worshipers congregated at a home and relied on laity to present sermons, conduct prayers, or run a Sunday school. The next step, at location after location, was to erect a small, nondescript log or frame building that served as a schoolhouse on weekdays and doubled as a church for evening prayer meetings and Sunday services. In many places, the mining companies built these structures, which might be used for awhile by Protestants and Catholics alike. The Minesota mining company built its church/school in 1852. Catholics in Houghton and at the Central mine worshiped in school buildings in the late 1850s. Out on sparsely populated Isle Royale in 1874–75, Sarah Barr Christian still found this practice in vogue: "We had a little building used for school weekdays and for worship on Sundays, and for the midweek prayer meeting."[1]

In many villages, settlers, missionaries, and mine company officers worked in concert to build churches. During the pioneer era, German, Irish, and French Canadian settlers on the Keweenaw were mostly Catholic; the Cornish, mostly Methodist. It followed that Catholic and Methodist churches went up first in the small communities along the mineral range and beside the harbors.

The Catholic Indian mission near L'Anse, originally intended to serve the Ojibwa, began serving the new mine villages just a few years after the copper rush started. Geologists, miners, and voyageurs were not the only ones to fight their way through dense forests or coast along rugged, dangerous shorelines. Father Frederic Baraga, every bit the pioneer, joined them. Baraga, born in Slovenia in 1797, was a well-educated European, versed in several tongues. He entered seminary in 1821, was ordained in 1823, and left Europe for American Indian mission service in 1830.[2]

In the mid-1830s, Frederic Baraga first traveled into the upper Great Lakes region and began learning the languages of Native Americans so that he could better minister to them. Baraga settled at L'Anse in 1843, but over the next few decades he rarely remained in one location for long. The seemingly indefatigable traveler tended to Catholics from Superior, Wisconsin, all the way across Michigan's Upper Peninsula, and down to Cross Village on the Lower Peninsula. In 1847, Father Baraga made his first two mission trips from L'Anse up to the mine camps and villages near Keweenaw Point; each trip lasted about three weeks.[3] In January 1848, he went to the mines again: "I am wont to visit them at least twice a year, in order to give them opportunity to receive the holy sacraments and to hear the word of God. The foremen at the mines are mostly Americans and belong to no particular religion, but the great majority of the miners are Catholics and exceedingly happy to see the priest once in a while."[4]

Father Baraga toured all the copper mining districts as they opened up: first

Keweenaw Point, then Ontonagon, then Portage Lake. For several years he ministered to his diverse band of Catholics while they still met in homes or schools. At the same time, he set about acquiring lots, raising funds, building churches, and finding priests.

In 1852, on a mission tour of Keweenaw Point, he purchased a church lot in Eagle Harbor. In 1853, tending to his flock on the opposite end of the mineral range, he "received a town lot in Ontonagon Village as a present from James Paul, to build a church thereon." In 1858 he took up a collection at Portage Lake for the first Catholic church to be built there; of the first $630 raised, $350 came from the Quincy and Pewabic mining company officials. That same year, he closed a contract for $1,860 to build a Catholic church at the Cliff mine. The president of the mining company, Thomas Howe of Pittsburgh, contributed $100 to the building fund. Father Baraga believed Howe's charitable act demonstrated that company officers, although Protestants themselves, were "inclined to be friendly" toward Catholics. In 1859, Baraga went to the directors of the Clark mine, whose workers were overwhelmingly Catholic, to ask them "if they would build a neat little church here."[5]

For many Catholics up and down the mineral range, the days of worshiping in makeshift churches were coming to an end in the late 1850s. In 1859, Father Baraga blessed and dedicated new Catholic churches at the Cliff mine, in Houghton, and at the Minesota mine. The Minesota mine Catholic church was just one of three on the southern end of the mineral range, which was home to "the largest congregation of Catholics in the entire diocese, Irish . . . , the French from Canada, and especially many Germans." Father Baraga was particularly proud of the Ontonagon, Minesota mine, and Norwich mine Catholic churches: "Although they are built only of wood, the interiors are plastered so that they appear as if they were of masonry and vaulted." And wonder of wonders, within the "nice, elegant and big" Minesota mine church, parishioners listened not to a small melodeon but to a real organ shipped north from Buffalo.[6]

Even with their churches built, in important ways practicing Catholics on Lake Superior settled for less than what they had experienced in their homelands. Their new churches were smaller, less grand, and far less filled with memories and traditions. Church elders were largely absent, because younger men and women came to the mines, mostly leaving their parents' generation behind. Itinerant priests were spread thinly over the Keweenaw and were not always available. And instead of each ethnic and language group having a church of its own, the Irish, French Canadian, and German Catholics *shared* a church. As his diary for 1856 made clear, Father Baraga was one of those clerics who spread himself thin, trying to cover all the mine churches in his diocese, with their diverse parishioners:

Aug. 10:   "Confirmation at Ontonagon, only 12."

Aug. 13:   "Arrived at Minesota."

Aug. 17:   "Confirmed 27 at Minesota."

Aug. 20:   "Arrived at Norwich. . . ."

Aug. 24:   "I confirmed 33 there [Norwich]."

Sept. 16:   "To the Cliff. . . ."

Sept. 17:   "I preached in 3 languages and confirmed 26."[7]

Finding dedicated, competent, and popular priests to serve on the Keweenaw was no small feat. Not all priests were cut out for the copper district's isolation, long winters, and frontier conditions, and at least one ran off, despite economic inducements to stay. In July 1858, Father Baraga sent a new priest, Rev. Moyce, to serve in Ontonagon. On October 4, Baraga wrote in his diary: "I was very much displeased in Ontonagon because I was compelled to pay Rev. Moyce $200 annually, otherwise he would not live there." Just a bit later, things got even worse: "arrived in Ontonagon!!! where I found that Mr. Moyce, who is not qualified for our poor missions, had departed with bag and baggage on Oct. 11."[8]

When Father Baraga visited any of the churches, he always had myriad religious tasks, sometimes conducted in several languages. As the only priest present at the Minesota mine church on June 15, 1862, he had himself a busy Sunday: "heard some confessions, said mass at 8, sang the 10 o'clock mass, preached in English, sang vespers in the afternoon, preached in German and English, gave benediction and administered one baptism."[9] Multilingualism was a hallmark of a good frontier priest, and Father Baraga noted that "priests who speak English, German and French are not easy to find." Catholics of different ethnicity shared a church but still wanted to hear their own language and be ministered to by a friendly and familiar priest. Father Baraga found good priests during this era in Rev. Edward Jacker, Rev. Thiele, and especially Rev. Martin Fox. Rev. Fox was a Prussian who labored with "tireless zeal" to put up the Ontonagon, Minesota, and Norwich churches. "Although he is German," Father Baraga wrote, "he speaks and preaches fairly well in English and French and he is [as] well liked by the French and Irish as he is by the German people."[10]

The same could not be said of Rev. Dennis O'Neil, installed at the new St. Ignatius church in Houghton in 1859. The "dissatisfaction of the Germans and French" toward this Irishman "showed itself immediately." After about a year, Father Baraga placated the Germans and French Canadians; he "handed O'Neil his document of interdict and removed him from the house."[11]

Father Baraga and his fellow Catholic priests had their counterparts in Rev. John Pitezel and the Methodist ministers who seeded their own churches on the Keweenaw. In 1834, well before the mine rush, the Methodists had established a Christian beachhead alongside Keweenaw Bay, amid the Ojibwa at

L'Anse. Besides trying to Christianize the Native Americans, the Methodists tutored them in literacy and agriculture. Pitezel joined the Methodist Indian mission in 1844. Late in 1846 he started taking his mission to the miners. He made the difficult tramp up toward Keweenaw Point and back, preaching eleven times over his three-week trip.[12]

Using the cooper shop as his pulpit, Rev. Pitezel preached the first Methodist sermon at the Cliff mine. In the late 1840s, when single men dominated the population and "civilization" seemed a fragile thing, the minister found that many men didn't want to hear his Christian message. Instead, they drank, sang, took sleigh rides, climbed cliffs, and otherwise frolicked on the Sabbath. Feeling both shunned and appalled, Rev. Pitezel nevertheless gathered a core of faithful Cornish Methodists about him. He helped get a Methodist church built at the Cliff mine in 1848, and that same year he moved from L'Anse up to the busy northern end of the mineral range, settling his family at Eagle River.[13]

As more families—especially Cornish families—migrated to Lake Superior, the work of Pitezel and other Methodist missionaries became easier and more popular. Between the late 1840s and the early 1870s, as the center of mining activity and population shifted from the northern tip, to the southern end, to the middle of the mineral range, Methodists established churches up and down the Keweenaw. In addition to the Cliff church, others went up at Eagle Harbor, Eagle River, the Phoenix and Central mines, Ontonagon, Houghton, Hancock, and Calumet.[14] Just as they did for Catholics, the mining companies helped early Protestant congregations erect churches. In 1869, just as its mine was proving very strong and Red Jacket village was bustling with growth and change, the Calumet and Hecla mining company provided its Methodists with a leased building lot, contributed five hundred dollars to the church building fund, and gave them use of the company's carpenter shop to hold a fundraising tea social and concert.[15]

Several early communities, after a few years of settlement, boasted two churches: one Catholic, one Methodist. At larger commercial or mining villages, additional Protestant churches sometimes joined in. Episcopalians, if they did not beat the Methodists to the punch and erect a village's first Protestant church, sometimes arrived just a few years later to build the second. Within ten or twelve years of being sited, Clifton, Eagle River, Ontonagon, and Houghton all had a Catholic, a Methodist, and an Episcopal church. Ontonagon, the Keweenaw's biggest village in the late 1850s, claimed four and then five churches, adding Presbyterian and Baptist edifices. Hancock had one of the region's earliest Congregational churches; Calumet, one of the earliest Lutheran churches.[16]

A small early church on the Keweenaw seated about 150 worshipers; a large one doubled that figure.[17] But a church started to empty out if its neighboring mine fell on hard times, causing workers to move to find new jobs. While some churches declined or even closed, other ones went up in newer or more flourishing villages. By 1870, as this ebb and flow of new construction here and abandonment there continued, the copper district claimed thirty-three churches with active congregations. About half stood in Houghton County. The Methodists and Catholics each had eleven churches; no other religious denomination then had more than four.[18]

Devout settlers went to midweek prayer meetings and attended Sunday services and Sunday schools to answer their spiritual needs. They also went for social needs—to knit together a sense of community at this strange new place; to link kindred spirits who had come from the same faraway land, be it Vermont, or Cornwall, or Germany; to enjoy a Sabbath-day respite from the workaday world; to celebrate holidays and feasts with hearty, wholesome vigor.

Having an active church life meant different things for men and women on Lake Superior. Men were the missionaries, the church founders, the spiritual leaders who offered up the prayers, sermons, and sacraments. Ordinary men sometimes stepped to the fore in church activities. In a region where true clerics were in short supply, the Methodists, especially, relied heavily on laymen—miners, engine drivers, and the like—to fill the gap and serve as "local preachers." Henry Hobart heard several Cornishmen give "pious instruction" from the pulpit at Clifton's Methodist church. He was pleasantly surprised once when a miner, James Willis, "preached a good sermon" on the subject "God forbid that I should glory save in the cross of Christ." The Yankee, surely a harsher judge than others in the pews, found most Cornish laymen horribly prepared for the task of preaching: "Nothing that I can discover goes to show that they have any education. They can exhort and groan and make a noise but there is nothing refining about them. . . . Violent gestures. Great noise, Cornish eloquence."[19]

Women on the Keweenaw had fewer opportunities than men to mingle together outside the home and join organizations. They wrote in their diaries of loneliness and their yearning for female companionship. When churches were built, women had a safe, respectable place to go and meet in groups, enjoy one another's company, and engage in cooperative, useful, and entertaining endeavors. In lieu of giving sermons, women of the church gave socials and benefits. They organized charities and church picnics. Just a few days before Christmas in 1855, the Ladies Sewing Society of the Church of the Ascension in Ontonagon held a fund-raising fair where they sold their crafts in the village's main hotel, the Bigelow House.[20] In 1870, women in Hancock worked to bring people together through their church:

> The ladies of the Hancock Congregational Church propose holding a series of fortnightly
> sociables in the new lecture-room of the church. The first will be on Wednesday evening
> next, and they invite the public to attend, without regard to creed or denomination. No
> charge for admission will be made, the design being to have the people of the district,
> both old and young, meet and pass an evening together now and then in a rational and
> pleasant manner.[21]

The ladies of the Congregational church, by tendering their invitation without regard to creed or denomination, practiced a fine ecumenicalism not always found up on Lake Superior. People in the mining villages tended to cleave to others who shared their homeland, language, and religion. Villages of just one or two thousand inhabitants had three church steeples poking up above the town precisely because it was *not* home to a homogeneous society. Different groups with different traditions, beliefs, liturgy, and dogma shared the same time and space.

The frontier did not strip Christian settlers of religious bias; they were prone to practicing exclusivity and engaging in rivalry. At the Cliff mine, the teetotaling Methodist minister, Rev. John Baughman, once delivered a temperance address that cast a local Catholic priest in an unfavorable light. An Irish Catholic took exception to the remarks and made his displeasure known to the cleric. The Catholic priest, in turn, led his flock against the Protestants and seemed to offer a threat to the "gray-headed" Methodist minister. The Irish Catholics at the Cliff also wanted to pull their children out of public school and start a parochial one so that their young scholars would not be corrupted by the Protestant teacher, Henry Hobart.[22] And God forbid that people who worshiped apart from one another in life should lie next to one another in death. So separate cemeteries—one for Catholics, one for Protestants—were notable features of the landscape at places like Clifton and Hancock.

Religion was closely tied to ethnicity, and throughout the nineteenth century on the Keweenaw, people were tagged with their ethnic identities. In this society, once Irish, always Irish, even if the family had uprooted itself and moved halfway across the globe. The same held true for the Cornish, the Scots and Scandinavians, the Germans and French Canadians. In this mining district, immigrant families did not become Americans in a year, a decade, or over one or even two generations. The children of immigrants, as they grew up on Lake Superior, hewed to their parents' ethnic identity. At the same time, however, the young did assimilate some new ways in this new place, especially if they regularly attended public schools filled with diverse classmates and taught by Yankee teachers.

Many immigrants had not attended school in their homelands and were poorly versed in reading, writing, and arithmetic. Or, if educated in French or German or another European language, they were untutored in English.

For their children, stepping out from home to attend a public school and to learn to cipher and to read and write English was an important part of the American experience. Some families seemed to cherish this opportunity; others largely turned away from it. In corresponding fashion, some settlements built adequate or even exemplary schools for their era, while others evidenced precious little concern for public education, save for minimizing its cost.

Henry Hobart, besides heading the public school at Clifton, supplemented his income by teaching a private night school for men. Sometimes it was hard to sustain an adequate enrollment. After ten-hour-long work shifts, men were just too tired for night classes. Other men dropped Hobart's instruction because they left Clifton for the new, booming Portage Lake mines, or even for far-flung California gold fields.[23] Despite enrollment problems in his night classes, Hobart believed that men of little learning, besides thirsting for knowledge themselves, were some of the staunchest supporters of public education for their children. In 1863, he taught an evening school composed of "working men" up to fifty years of age:

> Some come in unable to tell a letter—others can cipher a little or read some. How sadly they regret their misspent time while young or that they had no chance to attend school. They would give almost anything to be a good scholar. Some men are coming to me who cannot cipher any who send three or four scholars to day school. The School Inspector sends four children and comes himself to evening school [to study arithmetic]. Parents, give your children good education and they will bless you when old.[24]

In 1870, Houghton County's superintendent of public instruction sounded a similar note: "As a general thing our foreign population prize our public schools as among the dearest of their privileges, and many of their children are among our most faithful and intelligent scholars."[25] But this vaunted "prizing" of public education—on the part of immigrants and native-born Americans alike—clearly had its limits. In truth, only in a few places did good public schools, good teachers, and good students come together.

In 1864 the *Mining Gazette* severely berated the local mining and commercial communities near Portage Lake for neglecting public education. The paper called it "the quintescence of folly" to "suppose that a good school can be taught in a small, overcrowded, dirty, ill-ventilated room, unprovided with blackboards, charts, maps, etc." It railed at the inadequate schools in Houghton, Hancock, Hurontown, and Pewabic; at the latter, "for lack of seats . . . a large number of the children were seated in rows on the floor." The people, in their dozen or so years of settlement, had simply never paid proper attention to "their duty to assist in educating the rising generation," and it was "a burning shame that in a County possessing the wealth and enterprise of Houghton County such a vital interest should be so entirely neglected." The *Mining Gazette* urged communities "to do justice to themselves, their children, their country, and their God, by making the schoolhouse what it should be—commodious, well-arranged, cheerful and attractive."[26]

Teacher Henry Hobart also faulted local schools. It was a rare thing, Hobart wrote in his diary, "to find a good, well-ventilated, well-arranged, well-furnished school room. . . . [M]ost of the houses are fitted to torture the children rather than to add to their comfort and ease. Under such circumstances they dislike to go to school or when there are so uncomfortable that they cannot learn or improve at all."[27]

Proper school buildings and school reform came to some communities but not to others. Two years after the *Mining Gazette* launched its educational crusade, the effort seemed to bear fruit. Houghton opened a new, substantial school, constructed of stone, in 1866 to serve primary grades through high school—and the *Mining Gazette* properly celebrated the occasion by publishing "a correct engraving" of the structure, which was the first illustration ever to grace the paper's pages.[28] But in the 1870s, Houghton County's superintendent of public instruction still bemoaned the fact that "one school has been held in an unplastered attic over a mine office, another in an equally uncomfortable room over a saloon." He noted that "our mining officers and businessmen are not in the habit of employing good workmen at high wages without providing all the necessary appliances for doing good and efficient work, but as school officers they are continually doing this." In a similar vein, the superintendent for Keweenaw County reported that of his twelve operating schools, only four had wall maps, just three had a Webster's Unabridged Dictionary, and only one "exults in the possession of a respectable globe."[29]

At the mining villages, schools were as good or bad as the mining companies made them. The companies owned most of the land, paid most of the taxes, controlled local politics, and supplied the managers and bosses who sat on local school boards. In 1867, residents of Quincy township—home of the Quincy mine—organized their School District No. 1. All legal voters in the township received a printed notice of a first meeting to organize the new school district and elect a school board. On April 23, the office of the Quincy Mining Co. hosted this initial meeting, which was chaired by John Duncan, the mine's surface captain. Ballots were cast and counted. The newly elected three-member school board consisted of "Moderator," Thomas U. Flanner (the Quincy mine's company doctor); "Director," J. M. Foster (Quincy's chief mine clerk); and "Assessor," James North Wright (Quincy's agent, the man in charge at the mine). These mining company officials set the length of the school year (in 1868–69, "40 weeks of 5 days to the week"); selected the teachers (always one male, one female); established the school's annual budget; and determined how much money had to be raised through property taxes and other means (such as dog licensing!). They submitted the school's annual financial reports on "Office of the Quincy Mine" letterhead.[30]

A poor, struggling company inevitably had a poor, struggling school nearby. A successful mine, such as the Cliff, could afford to do better—at least as long as its profitability lasted. The deep and long recession following the Civil War hurt not only the mines but also their attendant schools: "We have suffered from a great depression in the business interests of this portion of the country. Several of our larger mines, employing large numbers of men, and having schools on their locations, have stopped work altogether, or are being worked temporarily. These changes, where they have not entirely closed the schools, have greatly diminished their numbers."[31]

The school at the Cliff started out in the late 1840s as an informal affair, taught by clerics for a brief time during the year without the aid of any textbooks. Over fifteen years, as the village expanded to a population of about 1,500, the school grew to two rooms and had two teachers, who met their students six days a week over nine months. In 1861, the annual report of the Cliff's parent company proudly boasted, "Our school is well sustained, having two very competent teachers and an average attendance of ninety-six scholars, and is supported principally by the regular two mill tax collections on valuation of property in school district."[32]

The Cliff settlement never squandered money on its school, to be sure. While he was there during the Civil War, teacher Henry Hobart had to wait months for a promised blackboard; he trudged through a swamp to get to the school's front door (because of its poor, low-lying building site); and he either did maintenance and painting himself or did without. He met up to a hundred young scholars in a single room because not until 1863 was the school "built over and two apartments made, one for the small scholars and one for the large ones," an arrangement finally adopted because it promised to allow both groups to "make much more rapid progress."[33]

But even though the company was a bit tight with the purse strings, it gave an extra helping hand to public education on occasion and nurtured civic pride in the school. In February 1863, Henry Hobart matched twenty-five or thirty of his students against a like number from the Eagle River school in a spelling and grammar competition. On this as on other special occasions, the mining captain at the Cliff provided the village's young scholars with a double team of horses, a driver, and a large sleigh to transport them to Eagle River.[34]

The Clifton students, for a week prior to the competition, had gone to extra evening sessions at the school, where Hobart drilled them in spelling and grammar. Once in Eagle River, they laid a pretty good whipping on their counterparts. In the first round of the spelling bee—each student had one chance to spell correctly a one-syllable word—twelve Clifton boys and girls were still in the contest after all the Eagle River students had been sat down. In the second round, students had two chances to spell more difficult words. Ten Clifton students remained standing when the last Eagle River child sat down. Clifton prevailed in grammar, too, when the Eagle River students declined to go to the blackboard, put up sentences, and then analyze them.

The mine company horses and sleigh returned to Clifton with a victorious group of youngsters, who flew an American flag and let people know that they'd won. They sang songs as the sleigh passed through the village. Hobart recorded in his diary, "We halted before the store where the crowd gave the school & teacher three hearty cheers. I then had the scholars give Captain Halls three cheers for his kindness in furnishing us with a team." The happy and proud teacher also recorded: "The parents are all rejoicing & the scholars are working very hard. Many of them are making remarkable progress. Much good will result from this affair."[35]

Henry Hobart, the elitist Yankee, often criticized the manners, customs, and smarts of the Cornish and Irish immigrants at Clifton. His prejudices, however, did not seem to carry over to their children. The teacher took a sincere interest in his students' well-being and education. He worked hard for them and expected the young woman teacher who assisted with younger scholars to do the same. He put in extra hours and arranged special programs. He was a nurturer, not a stern taskmaster.

Neither teaching nor learning could have been easy at any of the villages. The size and roster of classes varied greatly throughout the school year. Migratory working-class families came and went, bouncing from mine to mine, taking their children with them. Parents sent their children to school when they were a bother at home, then turned around and kept them home when extra help was needed. Students stayed home in droves when temperatures nose-dived and blizzards blew. The five- and six-year-olds, especially, quit going to school when snowbanks reached over their heads.

Children also stayed home when measles, mumps, chicken pox, and other contagions swept through their ranks. Many boys and girls left school to take on paying jobs. Others left after a short but legal stint of schooling. As late as 1871, Michigan law—which gave all children over five the *right* to attend school—mandated as little as twelve weeks of education yearly for children between ages eight and fourteen, and only six of these had to be consecutive.[36] In this society, the notion of compulsory school attendance was neither universally believed in nor strictly enforced.

The young school districts along the mineral range, like those throughout Michigan, were required to take an annual census of school-aged children within their boundaries. (The definition of "school-aged" started out as four to eighteen years old, then became five to twenty by the 1860s.) The state also required all schools to take and report attendance. Based on this information, it appears that in the mid-1850s, about 40 percent of Houghton County's enumerated children actually attended school in two organized districts. Fifty percent attended in the early 1860s. The countywide figure climbed to 65 percent by 1865; peaked at 87 percent in 1870; declined to 68 percent in 1875; and dropped to only 56 percent in 1880. (In 1880, of Michigan's seventy-seven counties, Houghton County ranked near the bottom—seventy-first—in terms of school attendance.)[37] Looking at attendance figures for all three copper-producing counties—Keweenaw, Ontonagon, and Houghton—it appears that when and where the mining industry boomed, making more money for schools available, the attendance percentage *dropped*. Conversely, during hard, recessionary times, or in places where early mines had withered or closed, attendance percentage *rose*, even as school funding probably declined. The likely explanation is that if children—especially older boys—lacked job opportunities, they stayed longer in school.

One of the problems of education in this era was that the more students showed up, the harder it was to teach them anything because of overcrowded rooms and too few teachers. In 1863 at Clifton, daily attendance over nine months averaged 80 students, but on many days more than 100 showed up. Just keeping track of them and learning their names was a chore, because 228 *different* students came to school at one time or another that year.[38] If pupils in attendance averaged 80, truants, transients, and part-time students averaged nearly 150! Given large class sizes, the mingling of younger and older children, and the spotty attendance record of many students, maintaining discipline and order in the classroom was as essential as it was difficult.

Hobart keenly appreciated his assistant teacher, Miss Nutt, because she labored "earnestly to promote the interests of every pupil under her care," and she made "the small ones toe the mark." "She is," Hobart wrote in his diary, "a lady of determination and aims to have everything conducted with a regard to order & discipline. It requires such a person to manage these small scholars who are not aware of what it is to mind. They want drilling and I am sure that they are getting that very thing."[39]

Head male teachers were authority figures. At many schools, if needed to enforce discipline, they were expected to wield their physical prowess against unruly students, especially rowdy, defiant boys. Hobart, however, did not believe in threats or physical punishments for misbehavior. He thought many of his students were already too battered at home. They needed no more abuse at school: "I hold that there should be good feeling and perfect love between pupil and teacher. The scholar should love and respect his instructor. It is false that they will learn best through fear or that success is found where the teacher exercises a tyrannical power and every pupil is afraid of him."[40]

Discipline. Order. Drills. Assigned seats. Rules against whispering and other forms of misbehavior. Constant and repeated practice in arithmetic. Memorizing the tables. Repetitive loops and other handwriting exercises. Learning to spell. Learning to read. Sitting still while others read. Doing the same tasks over and over and over again until they had been mastered. Squirming in a room that might be too hot, close, and crowded in the "nicer" months, or bitter cold and drafty during the dead of winter. Much of the learning was uninspired, rote, and mechanical. A good teacher like Hobart occasionally enlivened and enhanced it by adding spelling bees, writing and speaking contests, and even field trips. In mid-March 1864, he organized a sleigh ride for eighty scholars and treated them with seven dollars' worth of candy and nuts:

> At nine the teams were ready & with three flags flying we left the Cliff singing "Rally round the flag, boys." We went through the villages of Eagle River, Garden City, Humboldt, Copper Falls, etc. [and] arrived at the Harbor at half past twelve. Had the large hall warmed & there we took a fine lunch that we brought with us. We returned our sincere thanks to the proprietor & his wife. Sung them a song, gave them three cheers & came home in fine spirits.[41]

In 1866, sixty-two students in the upper and lower classes of Houghton's new graded school discovered their names in the pages of the *Portage Lake Mining Gazette*. This was no simple, flattering list of "All A" and "B or Better" honor-roll students. Instead, it was a full report of all students' grades in up to seven subjects, their grades in "deportment," their overall scholarship average, their rank or relative standing in school, and the number of half days they had been absent.[42] Here were the names of the sons and daughters from American, Cornish, English, Irish, German, and French Canadian families, all learning and growing up together on a copper-rich peninsula far removed from the world below. Benjamin Williams, Hattie Funston, and Della Funston all tied for top honors at the school, with 99 percent averages in their studies and 98 percent in deportment. A young "George Washington" ranked thirty-second in the school. A couple of Irish boys, Daniel Shea and Thomas Cuddihy, ranked near the very top, while two Irish girls, Katie Dunn and Katie O'Brien, brought up the rear. William Cooney might have been one of those bright boys who excelled in what interested him, tolerated the rest, and occasionally made his boredom felt by either acting up or staying away. He ranked near the very bottom of the list of scholars, although he achieved a 90 percent grade in reading. His other scores were poor or mediocre, he missed twenty half days of school, and he got the school's lowest grade for behavior or deportment—only 64 percent.

Besides collecting school census and attendance data, the state of Michigan gathered, from school inspectors around the state, uniform information on what subjects were being taught. In 1866–67, all Houghton County school districts taught certain subjects. These were the basics: spelling (using National, Sanders, Webster, or Parker and Watson texts); reading (using National, Sanders, or Parker and Watson texts); writing or penmanship (in accordance with Spencer's text); and arithmetic (using Robinson's, Greenleaf's, or Thompson's texts).

Two other subjects—grammar and geography—were nearly universally taught. But only one or two of six school districts taught algebra, geometry, bookkeeping, natural philosophy, or physiology. Nobody taught chemistry. Of a dozen subjects tracked by the state, the Portage township school district around the village of Houghton claimed to cover the most (eleven), while Adams township covered the least (only four).[43]

By 1875, Houghton County had eleven school districts; the subjects taught had changed a bit; and the state tracked instruction in a few new fields: drawing, the science of government, and American history. Universal, or nearly universal, subjects now included reading, spelling, arithmetic, geography, grammar, U.S. history, and algebra. Only one or a few districts offered bookkeeping, drawing, government, geometry, natural philosophy, or chemistry. Most districts claimed they offered instruction in about seven of fifteen possible subjects. Calumet's district covered all but drawing and government, a curriculum exceeded only by that of Houghton, which offered everything.[44]

The children who trudged off to schools up and down the Keweenaw could be pretty certain of some shared things. Large classes; little in the way of individualized instruction; few teachers; lots of repetitive drills; classmates from diverse ethnic backgrounds; and instruction in the English language (which would tend to obliterate some ethnic differences). But in many ways, the schooling received was very uneven. Some met in cramped, one-room log structures, others in attics. Still others, especially children in Houghton or Calumet, learned in larger, more comfortable, graded schools. The central school in Calumet—owned and built by the wealthiest mine in the district, Calumet and Hecla, and leased to the school district—was in the mid-1870s deemed one of the largest and best schoolhouses in the entire state.[45]

Some students received their instruction from a caring man like Henry Hobart; others were taught by a mining company's surface boss, who bolted from the classroom and abandoned his students anytime a steam engine, rock crusher, or other mechanical contrivance needed work.[46] Some students—by 1875, maybe a quarter of them, at least in Houghton County—received instruction from a graduate of a teachers' college. But most were taught by quite young instructors, especially young women, who had recently completed their own schooling and who had just enough grounding in the basics to pass a locally administered teachers' exam. Houghton's graded school, by the late 1860s, provided not only education but also educators—its graduates—for other local schools. In 1870, the superintendent of public instruction for Houghton County wrote: "The county is greatly indebted to this school, not only as furnishing an excellect model, both in appointments and in management, but in the training of teachers for our schools."[47]

By 1875, 5,500 children were enrolled in schools along the Keweenaw, including 3,650 in Houghton County alone, which then led the way in producing both copper and young scholars. After years of a postwar recession, the schools were not all in the finest of shape. In 1874, Houghton County's superintendent reported to the state that of seventeen schools under his purview, three were unfit for further use, seven were destitute of suitable outbuildings, none had an enclosed and improved playground, only two had suitable furniture in good condition, and just one, in his opinion, was properly warmed and ventilated.[48] The process of building good schools throughout this mining district was a long and difficult one, wracked by the rising and falling fortunes of the copper mines. Every time one flourishing village took a step forward in educating its children, somewhere else a mining company and a community school suffered decline together.

EIGHT

THE SINS OF THE BODY

Maladies, Medicines, and Frontier Physicians

I am now having the toothache quite hard as the Dentist is trying to separate a couple of the double ones [molars] so as to fill a hole between them. This is done by crowding in cotton batten which expands as it is moistened & crowds them apart. The pressure makes them feel very sore & painful. It is a horrible feeling.

Henry Hobart, diary,
January 20, 1863

Those who settled the Keweenaw and Isle Royale found more than copper, trees, water, and snow. With too frequent regularity, they found broken legs, fractured skulls, or crushed hands. They discovered floating bodies and frozen corpses. They had come to a new place but had not escaped old problems: contagious diseases and epidemics, mysterious fevers and influenza. They ate some bad meat and suffered gut aches and "a turn of the back door trot or 'Dictionary' [dysentery]."[1] They creaked with rheumatism and lumbago. They endured venereal sores, impotence, piles, gout, and rotten teeth. They had complicated and deadly pregnancies, unwanted pregnacies, stillborn babies, and many dead infants and young children.

In the first decades of settlement the Lake Superior population was young. The mines wanted men in their prime years to tackle the arduous labor they offered, and women of child-bearing age accompanied the men. Relative youth, however, by no means protected the population from physical and emotional trauma, from illness, disease, and death. Threats to a person's sense of comfort, security, and well-being were never far removed from everyday life.

Some threats literally came with the territory. Select risks and hazards associated with water, winter, and mining were more prevalent on Lake Superior than in the world below. The water that bounded the Keweenaw and Isle Royale, that filled up the inland lakes and streams, was not always kind. Douglass Houghton was not the only person to drown on stormy Lake Superior—he was just the most famous. Nearly thirty victims died with the sinking in 1863 of the *Sunbeam*, by far the most catastrophic shipwreck in Keweenaw waters. Not all drowning victims went down in such dramatic fashion, and not all drowned in the big lake. Some fell off docks, fell through soft or thin ice, or just suddenly found themselves in over their heads. The Houghton County supervisors occasionally paid a bounty for those who found a body in Portage Lake and fished it out. Children—boys in particular, it seems—risked drowning when they bathed, boated, or frolicked in a lake or stream despite their inability to swim. Swimming was not a skill regularly taught to children, and some paid a tragic price. Twelve-year-old Patrick Hanley died in the Portage near the Pewabic ferry dock; the little son of Connie O'Brien drowned near the Quincy mine's wood dock; and to the north a bit, the six-year-old son of John O'Brien fell into Eagle River at the Bay State Mine and was pulled out, dead, a mile downstream. The "mother of the boy has been sick for a long time, and this is a severe blow to the poor woman."[2]

Winter's snow and cold offered their own hazards. This northern world was sometimes too bright. Sunlight falling on never-ending white strained the eyes and threatened snow blindness.[3] People bundled up against the cold but still risked hypothermia and frostbite if caught outside for too long, especially at night. Getting drunk, getting lost, or getting caught in a sudden blizzard sometimes resulted in death.

Winter's hardships and hazards particularly jeopardized pioneers in the 1840s. They lived in rude shelters; traversed poorly marked, difficult trails; and if caught out in the cold, had precious few neighboring cabins in which to seek refuge. In the winter of 1846–47, a small party of miners stayed at Wheal Kate, near Portage Lake. They lived in an "ice cave," which was really a canvas tent with an open fire out front. A blazing fire melted the ice and snow on the tent, but it iced up again as soon as the fire died. One day, a premature blast of explosives severely injured one man's head: "his eye was torn out so that it lay exposed upon his cheek. The nearest surgeon was fifty miles distant, and this poor wounded wretch had to walk that long distance through the cold and snow to obtain relief."[4]

Even in later decades it was not that uncommon to find a frozen corpse along a road or on the outskirts of a village. At least five men trying to snowshoe their way off the Keweenaw in the winter of 1854–55 died of exposure. At the Cliff mine, in February 1866, Cornelius Green, missing for two days, was found dead and frozen in the mine's woodyard.[5] In December 1870, James Lynch froze to death on the road to the South Pewabic mine, just a short distance from his house. Earlier, in crossing a lake on the way home, he had fallen through the ice and gotten soaked. He stopped at a friend's house to warm up, and the friend urged the "half-frozen" Lynch to stay over night, as it was bitter cold, and there was danger in attempting so long a walk in his wet condition. But Lynch headed out into the cold again, "saying that he must go home that night, and provide wood to keep his wife and little ones from the winter's fury." Unfortunately, he never made it. Hypothermia stopped him dead in his tracks: "overcome with cold he lay down in the snow, and though a few steps would have brought him to the shelter of his own roof, where loving hands would have quickly warmed him to life, yet that seductive drowsiness which tempts unto sleep eternal, benumbed all his senses, and palsied his limbs with the icy touch of death."[6]

O. W. Robinson recalled a time in 1856 when on an extremely cold day, well below zero, he almost froze to death while driving a yoke of oxen pulling a sleigh loaded with grain. He thought he was "well dressed to resist the cold, wearing a heavy mackinaw coat with a hood," and he had tied a red knitted sash around his waist to hold the coat close and keep in his body heat. On his feet he wore moccasins over heavy woolen socks; he had also wrapped his feet in two pairs of nepes. On his hands he wore "tufted woolen mittens." The bundled-up Robinson grew tired of walking alongside the oxen, so he climbed aboard the sleigh to ride—and fell asleep. The next thing he knew, he was off in the snow.

Robinson realized that being bounced from the sleigh and awakened had probably saved his life. He knew that sleep and extreme cold were a deadly combination, so he started running to stay awake and warm: "I ran back on the road a short distance, then turning ran forward to the team, urged the cattle forward, then ran back down the road again. This I kept up about two hours until we reached the barn at home."[7]

Henry Hobart's diary recorded the pain of winter. He saw a man in January with torn, frozen hands and reckoned they'd be lost to amputation. The teacher regularly noted how the cold kept many young scholars home, and those who did trek through the cold to school were not always happy about it. On the coldest day of the winter in 1863–64, Hobart got to school early and lighted a fire. Then "the scholars begin to come in, some crying, some half-froze." In December 1863, one little boy at Clifton narrowly escaped death when he got stuck in a snowdrift on the way home from school. A man passing by found him and pulled him out; otherwise, "he would have perished as he was in up to his head."[8]

Open water and long, hard winters posed special hazards to settlers; so did the mining industry that lured them north and provided work. Through the 1860s, it is likely that about one hundred men died outright in underground accidents, with another ten or fifteen killed on the surface. They were blasted by ill-timed explosives. Tons of rock fell from a mine's hanging wall, mangling victims. Men fell to their deaths in steeply pitched openings or got caught up in machinery that crushed the life out of them.[9] At the Isle Royale company's mill for reducing and concentrating copper rock, nineteen-year-old William

Hodge took a misstep and suddenly found himself in a tragic wringer, as crusher rollers seized and pulled in his left foot and leg. Two coworkers grabbed him and held on until the engine was stopped and reversed, expelling the victim from the rollers' grasp. But by then his lower leg was crushed, and "the skin and muscles had been torn away from the cords and bones of the upper part of the thigh as if cut with a knife." Young Hodge lingered in agony for two days before "death came to his relief."[10]

For every man who was killed, dozens suffered less-than-fatal, but nevertheless serious, work injuries. In April 1863, Henry Hobart noted that "many are the cuts and bruises that men receive in mining which is very dangerous business." In September he wrote, "There has been quite a number of accidents at the mine. One man killed by tons of rock falling on him. One or two had legs broken, fingers & toes smashed." His diary entries show how work injuries and occasional deaths punctuated the rhythm of life at the Cliff:

May 8:   "A miner had a leg broke the other night in the mine."
May 31:   "The engine driver while oiling was caught in the flywheel & carried round
            & round & smashed to a jelly; he still clung to one of the arms of the wheel
            when found the next morning and was going round with it."
June 19:   "Mr. Phillips, draining the pumping engine, had his little finger taken off by
            putting it in a hole in the feed pump to remove some dirt when the plunger
            came down and took it off."
June 27:   "When he arrived at the 110-fathom level on . . . the ladder his hand missed
            the top round and he fell backwards to the bottom, a distance of seventy-
            five feet striking on his head on the solid rocks. His skull was broke in pieces
            & he was brought up senseless."[11]

Some boys worked in the copper industry, so some died there. A collapsing sand bank buried a fifteen-year-old tramroad switchtender; in the Cliff mine, a fall killed thirteen-year-old Henry Benney.[12] But a child didn't have to work in the industry to be hurt or killed by it. Living and playing around the mines was hazardous, especially in an age when people—including children—were expected to look out for themselves instead of being looked after.

Mining companies never sealed abandoned shafts or adits, and through the 1860s they were lax about keeping children out of operating mines. Daring young explorers went underground for an adventure and sometimes paid for it with their lives. Losing his light and feeling his way through total darkness, a boy stepped into a shaft and fell to his death; another caught in similar circumstances went down in a water-catching sump and drowned.[13]

Play on the surface, too, entailed risks, especially around the railroads, tramroads, and gravity inclines serving the mines. The transport systems that carried rock from shaft to rock-crushing house to stamp mill seemed to attract children, who wanted to clamber aboard the rolling stock or dash across tracks just in front of a passing train. They didn't always make it. And sometimes the industrial environment killed the innocent, even if snug in their beds. The cabins at Clifton stood at the base of the mineralized bluff that gave the place its name. Once a part of the cliff gave way: "The rocks came down the Bluff and a rock of about seven tons dashed in the side of a house standing at the foot of the Bluff and killed a little girl asleep in the bed. . . . The house was knocked to pieces and everything in it."[14]

Besides accidents and physical trauma, settlers on the Keweenaw confronted a wide range of illnesses and diseases. In March 1866, Lucena Brockway suffered the "slight shock of paralysis and general prostration of the nervous system" that stole her vitality, made her at times a semi-invalid having little mobility, and put constrictive and uncomfortable boundaries on her world.[15] Lucena, too often housebound, lonely, and engulfed in self-pity, felt that the larger sweep of life passed her by. Meanwhile, within her lesser world, other debilities, such as poor eyesight and arthritis, made a struggle out of the pastimes of reading and sewing.

At Clifton in 1863–64, Henry Hobart recorded the various ailments that he and his neighbors suffered. Snow blindness and sore throats. Vomiting at one end and diarrhea and dysentery at the other. Throbbing toothaches. Rheumatism and lumbago. Measles, influenza, scarlet fever, typhoid fever, and "some kind of fever." Dropsy and deranged livers. Bilious attacks, resulting in the jaundice that painted a body with a yellow cast. Severe colds, consumption, and inflamed lungs.[16] (Settlers often rhapsodized about the pure air they found on the Keweenaw, but sometimes it was hard to draw a breath of it.)

In 1865, physician A. S. Heaton reported on public health at the Pewabic and Franklin mines at Portage Lake. Heaton mentioned several of the same maladies recorded by Hobart and added a few other important ones, such as pneumonia, cholera, and smallpox. Linking local conditions with otherwise unidentified epidemics, Heaton noted that the "most prominent disease prevailing" was the "Portage Lake fever," which was "most virulent during the summer and fall of 1862 and 1863." Cases of "Portage Lake fever" had been "less numerous and less serious" since 1863, and Heaton opined that there was "every reason to suppose it [would] finally disappear altogether" when the "exciting causes" disappeared.[17]

In the nineteenth century, when doctors were not required to fill out death certificates, Houghton County kept very incomplete death records. Sometimes a friend or relative of the deceased duly reported the death to the township or village clerk; and sometimes that clerk duly reported the death to the county clerk, who was then expected to report countywide death statistics to the state. But often, this chain was never started or completed, so many died without an official record of their passing. The death records probably missed as many deaths as they recorded, and in an era of limited diagnostic skills, they no doubt often erred in listing an individual's true cause of death. (For example, when young children of teething age died, it was not uncommon for teething to be cited as the cause of death.) But despite errors and omissions, death records provide another window to the illnesses, diseases, and accidents that threatened or claimed lives.

In 1871, the Houghton County death records specified a cause for ninety-two of 110 recorded deaths.[18] Remittent (or malarial) fever, dropsy, tuberculosis, and convulsions claimed eight to eleven lives each. Seven died from accidental, traumatic injuries, while another six drowned. Stillbirths, premature births, and encephalitis accounted for three to five deaths each. Two deaths each were accounted for by typhoid, dysentery, rheumatism, heart disease, gastritis, teething, and childbirth. The list of causes identified as costing a single life included, among other things, measles, scarlet fever, whooping cough, cholera, erysipelas, cancer, pneumonia, and apoplexy.

In the 1840s, it behooved the pioneers to stay healthy, because if injured or ill, they had almost nobody to turn to for treatment. But in the 1850s and 1860s, conditions improved. As society evolved, it picked up the pieces of a medical delivery system: doctors, dentists, druggists, hospitals, a few nurses, and local boards of health. In this era, physicians were becoming more professional and important across the nation, while home nursing and treatment remained essential components of health care, and the burden of providing that care fell to women. So it was important, from a health standpoint, that both more doctors and more women settled on the Keweenaw.

In the mid-nineteenth century, thanks in large measure to accelerated industrialization, many single men left their families and headed off to find work in new, foreign territories. For these mobile, uprooted men, "home" nursing and treatment no longer offered succor because they had no traditional "homes," no mothers or wives to nurse them.[19] Many single men in this condition ended up on Lake Superior, and the mining companies, as they established settlements and started hiring hundreds of men, recognized a paternal obligation to obtain the services of a physician to treat them. It was the humane, "right" thing to do. It also appeased the Cornishmen, who came to the mines expecting medical service because the employment of a "bal" (mine) surgeon was a tradition back home.[20] And the companies also knew that the existence of a doctor—much like the provision of a school or church—would help them attract and keep the skilled married workers they especially wanted.

In the 1850s and 1860s, a company usually obtained the services of a doctor when employment had reached about one hundred men. Small, adjacent mines, which often shared many of the same investors, often shared a doctor as well. Two or three small mines pooled financial resources, pooled their patients, and obtained a single physician. By the time a company crossed the three-hundred-employee threshold, it usually acquired a doctor all its own, and by 1860, the Cliff mine employed at least two.

Doctoring at midcentury was not the prestigious, high-paying profession it later became. Medical science was advancing through the development of new anesthetics and such, but it was by no means to the point that doctors carried miracle medicines in their bags or magic touches in their scalpels. Doctors had no effective arsenal at all against many illnesses and diseases. The medical environment was generally unsterile, and the risks of infection great, so doctors severely limited their use of surgery. Most operated to amputate wrecked limbs or to repair traumatic injuries, such as skull or compound fractures. Doctors still treated gallstones and appendicitis as maladies to be treated medically, not surgically. Physicians, then, were still struggling to demonstrate the superiority of their treatment over the folk medicines, midwives, and patent medicines that many in the population still turned to. As a consequence, many physicians across the United States found it difficult to support themselves by doctoring alone.[21]

Doctors did not flock to the northern woods on their own as medical missionaries bent on tending to a frontier population in need. The companies *lured* doctors to Lake Superior by paying them good salaries; by treating them as important company officials; and by giving them perquisites, such as free housing. Any "physician and surgeon" who answered the call and moved to the mines had to be one of those resourceful doctors who could be happy working as a medical jack-of-all-trades. Single employees paid fifty cents a month for medical coverage; married men paid a dollar. In return, workers and their families received, for no additional charge, all needed medical attendance and medicines. So the company doctor would be the most general of practitioners, handling the ailments and needs of all the people: men, women, and children. The docket on a given day might run from delivering a baby, to preparing a prescription for a child with diarrhea, to amputating a miner's crushed leg. Some early mine doctors—like their peers elsewhere—doubled as dentists, and some, since they were the resident experts on living things, served as large-animal veterinarians and treated company work animals.[22]

Most mining companies allowed their doctors to open a private practice on the side, which benefited the general population of the Keweenaw. For a fee, these doctors treated the early settlers who weren't miners but shopkeepers, butchers, saloon owners, or their wives or children. In Houghton and Hancock, doctors George Fuller and William McCall advertised themselves in the *Mining Gazette* as "Physician and Surgeon to the Mining Companies," believing this title represented a stamp of approval that would attract private patients. Dr. McCall was "supplied with instruments and operates for most of the Diseases, Injuries and Deformities that human flesh is heir to." He was prepared to treat cross-eyes, cataracts, deafness, hare lip, club feet, crooked limbs, enlarged tonsils, tumors of all kinds, and ulcers. Armed with dental instruments, he was also prepared "for extracting all varieties of teeth." Because he was a mine physician, he had to squeeze his private practice into limited hours: weekdays, you could see Dr. McCall at his Hancock office ("first door west of the New Drug Store") from 8:00 to 9:00 A.M., and from 1:00 to 2:00 and 7:00 to 8:00 P.M. On Sunday, he held office hours at 9:00 A.M. and 4:00 P.M.[23]

As the Keweenaw's population expanded, the mine physicians were joined by others who set up wholly private practices, not at the mine villages proper but at the waterfront settlements serving as the region's commercial centers. Dr. I. M. Rhodes was an early arrival; by 1856 he had set up his office at the Bigelow Hotel in Ontonagon. In the early 1860s, Dr. Henry Geismar practiced out of Mayworm's Hotel in Houghton, and patients could also catch him at his home "on Shelden St., beside Walker's Blacksmith's shop."[24]

Itinerant doctors, too, found their way to the Keweenaw. By the 1850s and 1860s, the area was already billed as a beautiful, cool summer destination served by ships plying the Great Lakes. Doctors caught on to this opportunity; they could enjoy a vacation visit to the north and practice their craft at the same time. Thus, Dr. Jones "of New York City" set up practice at the Douglass House in Houghton from "the 10th to the 26th of July, 1866." Jones offered his services as a specialist in deafness and blindness; he would "skillfully treat" all diseases and deformities of the eye and ear.[25]

By the mid-1860s, the poor—whether residing at the public poorhouse and farm, living on their own but with assistance from the supervisors of the poor, or staying in jail—had access to medical services free of charge, as delivered by a county physician. Houghton County contracted with its first physician in 1863 and annually invited bids to provide medical attendance and medicines for "all sick and disabled persons who by law, come under the care of any officer of this county." The county supervisors, through 1871, choose five different physicians for this post, sometimes wrangling over the selection.[26]

Clearly, minimizing the cost of medical service to the poor was a major concern of the county board. By accepting bids as low as $600 to $700, they assured that the county physician would treat his public post as a part-time job and devote most of his time to private practice. But at the same time, the supervisors also evidenced a concern for quality and public trust. They rescinded the very first county physician's contract after five months' service, probably because, early in his tenure, he had angered a worried public. He had transported a girl with smallpox across Portage Lake from Hancock to Houghton on a ferryboat full of passengers, thus exposing them unnecessarily to the virulent disease. The *Mining Gazette* railed against the doctor's dereliction of duty and poor judgment, and soon the county supervisors saw to it that he was gone.[27] In 1868 they rejected high bids of $2,500 and $1,200 to serve as county physician; passed up a bottom bid of $600; and awarded the post to W. W. Perry, whose $700 offer was deemed "the lowest *responsible* bid." Even then, in a novel move, they required Perry to post a $1,400 bond "for the faithful performance" of his duties.[28]

By the 1860s, mining company workers, the rest of the public, and even the poor had quite good (for the time) access to physicians. Nobody on the Keweenaw had to trudge fifty miles anymore to get a wound sewn up. In 1865, the older villages of Eagle River and Eagle Harbor each boasted three physicians; by the late 1860s, the newer villages of Houghton, Hancock, and Calumet claimed a similar number. By 1874, the state census counted seven physicians in Keweenaw County; another seven in Ontonagon County; and twenty in Houghton County, whose mines and villages, after a slow start, were then going strongest.[29]

Mining companies led the way in bringing doctors to Lake Superior. The larger, more successful companies also pioneered in erecting the first hospitals. Typically, a profitable mining company put up its hospital about five to seven years after starting production, and maybe two to four years after employing its first full-time physician. Thus the Minesota mine erected a hospital over the winter of 1857–58 that was "well fitted up for the accommodation of the sick." Quincy erected and outfitted its hospital starting in 1859. Pewabic and Franklin, two interlocked companies, put theirs up in 1862, when "humanity, justice, and the true interests of the companies all demanded that this good work should no longer be delayed." The Mesnard mine kept a hospital by 1864, and Calumet and Hecla's hospital, with twenty beds, opened in 1870.[30]

The structures were usually two-story, wood-frame buildings whose architecture was more domestic than institutional. A company hospital looked like a large company house of the better class. (Indeed, Calumet and Hecla's first hospital was originally built as a mine agent's house.) Some hospitals kept patients in wards; others offered small, more private rooms.

These company hospitals differed in important ways from hospitals across the nation. As the nineteenth century progressed, the American hospital changed dramatically in terms of its social/medical role. Initially, hospitals were largely almshouses, not medical facilities; they served as catchalls for society's downtrodden who needed shelter, food, and help. Then hospitals assumed more of a medical role: they started offering medical care, not just alms, but they still served only the most destitute, dependent members of society. Finally, hospitals evolved into medical insitutions tending to all members of society: rich and poor; men and women; adults and children.[31]

Company hospitals on Lake Superior—dedicated to serving their male employees—did not follow the same evolutionary path. They were neither almhouses, nor medical facilities dedicated to the indigent, nor broad-based institutions treating the injured and ill from all strata of society. These hospitals had a special niche; they had special admissions and treatment policies that limited access and reflected corporate prejudices and interests.

Hospital patients usually paid their company a daily room and board fee, but nothing additional for medical attendence and medicines. Companies claimed they ran their hospitals at a loss, and restrictive admissions policies helped control costs by limiting access. In the main, the mine hospitals were most likely to admit men with traumatic injuries suffered in on-the-job accidents. A gravely ill male employee with some treatable malady might also be admitted, but that was about it. The physician for the Pewabic and Franklin hospital put the admissions policy succinctly: "Neither women nor children are received, and no married or single men except such as are so badly injured or so ill as to require the immediate and almost constant attention of surgeon and nurse."[32] The male mine worker was the most important member of Lake Superior society, and hospital admissions mirrored that corporate prejudice.

Besides employing county physicians, local governments occasionally took other actions to safeguard public health, especially when threatened by communicable diseases. In 1863, smallpox killed a few residents in Houghton, and a public flap ensued over the county physician's transporting a smallpox victim on a public ferry. In 1864, when smallpox visited again, the village of Houghton set up a Board of Health, appointed Dr. George Fuller as advising physician, and took measures to check the spread of the disease. It hired nurses to take care of the afflicted and employed guards to stand watch over every house known to have smallpox. The guards kept those with smallpox from leaving and others from entering.[33]

In the vicinity of Houghton, the Board of Health of Portage Township set up the west end of Snow Shoe Island, in Portage Lake, as a quarantine ground. The board published a regulation that "no boat or vessel, having on board any person infected with the smallpox or other contagious disease, shall pass said quarantine ground west into Portage Lake, or land at any place in said Portage Township." Houghton County, doing its part, rented and outfitted a dwelling to serve as a "pest house" to shelter and isolate poor residents suffering smallpox; secured the services of Asa Jeffry and his wife to nurse these patients; and paid for transporting and feeding those quarantined. Company doctors, too, acted in concert with public health officers to check the contagion. At the Pewabic and Franklin mines, Dr. A. S. Heaton reported two smallpox cases late in 1863. Subsequently, "three hundred children were vaccinated, and the disease disappeared in the spring entirely."[34]

Small businessmen—in the form of druggists—moved to the mining frontier to help with the medical needs of settlers and trade in sundries. By 1856, when the Ontonagon County mines, especially the Minesota, were rapidly developing, the Murdock & Crandall drugstore conducted business in the village of Ontonagon. It advertised "Drugs and Medicines as cheap as any establishment west of Buffalo." The drug store also dealt in paints, oils, turpentine, glass, perfumery, fancy soap, hair oils, trusses, supporters, cigars, and liquors for "Medicinal and Family use, embracing all the varieties and most favorite brands."[35]

By 1864, two drugstores served the Houghton environs. Druggist Thomas Smith advertised "Physicians' prescriptions carefully prepared," while his competitor, the Shelden & Sheffer drugstore, promised to "exercise especial care in the compounding and preparing of the prescriptions of Physicians." Smith offered "Family Groceries" and "all articles usually found in a first class drug store." Shelden & Sheffer stocked "pure drugs," "popular patent medicines," the "best perfumeries," and a "superior stock of stationery." By 1865, Hancock boasted its first drugstore, and by 1870, Calumet already had a druggist or two. All of them engaged in commercial hyperbole, advertising that they stocked the most and, of course, sold only the best.[36]

None of the drugstores, however, specifically advertised toothbrushes for sale, and through 1870, local general stores sold precious few toothbrushes. Most settlers neglected oral hygiene, rarely if ever brushed, and suffered tooth decay and loss. Residents' mouths offered many challenges to frontier dentists (and to doctors doubling as dentists). And going to a dentist offered great challenge to the patient, who expected to obtain long-term comfort, but often at the cost of much short-term pain.

New technologies and anesthetics were just starting to transform dentistry, and dentists themselves were starting to become more professional and "scientific," just as the copper frontier was being settled. Prior to the 1840s, patients endured all their dental work—having cavities scraped out, teeth pulled, and impacted and broken teeth dug out—without benefit of anesthesia. Dentists did all their work by hand, without the aid of drills, and false teeth remained expensive items that relatively few working-class people could afford.

Then, in the mid-1840s and beyond, inhaled anesthetics came into use: nitrous oxide (or laughing gas), ether, and chloroform.[37] These anesthetics allowed the most modern dentists to work without inflicting great pain—at least if their work was limited to only a few teeth and could be completed after a single snootful of gas. (A dental patient with an open mouth filled with fingers and tools could not continually inhale gas to produce long-term anesthesia, so if working on many teeth, a dentist often had to rush his work, and still the patient might feel much pain before all procedures were done, and afterward as well.) In addition to using first-generation anesthetics, American dentists were starting to employ lower-cost false teeth or dental plates made of vulcanized rubber by the late 1860s, and foot-powered dental engines for powering drills and burrs by the early 1870s.[38]

Big-city dentists adopted these innovations before their peers scattered along the frontier. Surely all these dental improvements seemed very remote to the earliest Lake Superior settlers. On Isle Royale in 1847, Cornelius Shaw suffered a very troublesome tooth, to the point that he could not open his jaws to eat. Finally, after more than a week of this, he "got it pulled," which made him "completely wild with pain." In his diary, Shaw didn't record who wielded the pliers in his mouth; at that very early date, it might well have been an untutored coworker, performing a charitable act of amateur dentistry.[39]

Itinerant dentists arrived on Lake Superior by the mid-1850s. These traveling men worked out of a suitcase and a hotel room, sometimes staying only a week or two, sometimes staying a full season. Dr. Cone set up dental shop at the Douglass House in Houghton in 1855; Dr. Wheeler, "Surgeon Dentist," took rooms at the Johnson House in Ontonagon in 1856. Wheeler offered "to perform all operations upon the Teeth in the most thorough and workmanlike manner, both for their beauty and preservation." Dr. Wheeler's advertisement in the *Lake Superior Miner* encouraged people to "pay a little timely attention" to dental problems now, to "present much future expense and suffering." He even put his message in rhyme:

> The raging Tooth-ache who'll endure,
> When there is found a speedy cure;
> That saves the tooth and stops the pain,
> And gives the sufferer ease again.[40]

Not all heeded the good dentist's advice; they put off dental work till they had a whole mouthful of problems. In 1863, Henry Hobart at the Cliff took an accumulation of decay to Dr. Greenlee, who filled his cavities, "three or four of the front ones with gold & others with tin foil. It is a severe task to remain quiet & let a dentist fill decayed teeth after going through the painful operation of having them dug out." Others had it even worse. In August 1874, Dr. and Mrs. Walker toured Keweenaw County while he practiced his dentistry. Lucena Brockway recorded in her diary that "this forenoon Miss Burnett had 12 teeth extracted and it was the worst job the Dr. ever had except one in his life—she stood better than expected. In the afternoon Christine had 11 pulled and was better than she expected. Both are in bed. Sick."[41]

After the pain eased, many early dental patients at least seemed better off than before. Henry Hobart allowed as how, after all his fillings, he took "great comfort with solid teeth." Dr. Greenlee prepared false teeth for an acquaintance of Lucena Brockway who was minus all her lowers, and Lucena approved of the results: "Aunt Nabby got her teeth today and it is a great improvement in her looks."[42]

At least eight dentists toured the Keweenaw between the mid-1850s and early 1870s. Some came back year after year; others were seen but once. A couple of dentists tried to set up permanent practices but with little success. Early in 1867, the *Mining Gazette* ran an article entitled "A Good Dentist

Wanted." Many people didn't trust itinerant dentists, the paper said, because the dentists' mobility left them unaccountable for the quality of their service. Many in need of false teeth costing one or two hundred dollars, for instance, instead of trusting an itinerant practitioner, traveled to a known, established dentist "down below." The paper figured that a local full-time dentist would do well, drawing patients from up and down the Keweenaw and from Marquette County, a hundred miles to the east.[43]

In June 1867, Houghton got what the *Mining Gazette* wanted; dentist E. J. Hovey took "rooms over Dallmeyer's Tobacco Store with a view to a permanent location." Hovey advertised "artificial teeth" and "teeth extracted without pain" (implying that he used anesthetics), and stuck it out in Houghton for three years. As he prepared to leave he ran a notice in the paper: "Dr. E. J. Hovey will remain here only one month longer. All who are in need of his services should avail themselves of this opportunity, as it is not likely there will be a resident dentist here again for a long time to come."[44] Once again, residents were thrown back on itinerant dentists, whether they liked and trusted them or not.

When it came to relieving toothache pain, fever, diarrhea, upset stomachs, sore muscles, and any number of other ailments, sufferers did not have to turn for help only to local physicians or dentists. There were other ways to go, including traveling to the world below to seek special attention. In 1863, Dr. McLeod, the "eminent Scotch Physician and Surgeon," hoped to attract patients to his Detroit office by advertising his speedy cures for "Blindness, Deafness, Catarrh and Chronic Diseases" in Houghton's *Mining Gazette*.[45]

If residents on Lake Superior could not travel to distant "experts," they could nevertheless write to them. Medical entrepreneurs, usually operating on the east coast, made a business of offering advice and prescriptions or "recipes" through the mail, running ads for these services in papers across the country. In 1855, Dr. Johnson Stewart Rose of New York City advertised in the *Lake Superior Miner* his expertise in curing consumption, bronchitis, and asthma through the breathing of vapors. His *Treatise on Consumption* cost $1; for $5 and up, applicants received needed medicines and apparatus. To assure proper treatment, correspondents were to "state if they have bled from the Lungs, if they have lost flesh, have a cough, night sweats and fever turns—what and how much they expectorate, what is the condition of the stomach and bowels." By the 1860s, Dr. Rose had been superseded by Rev. Edward A. Wilson of Kings County, New York, who offered his own "Sure Cure for Consumption, Asthma, Bronchitis, &c."[46]

In the 1850s and 1860s, medicine by mail had its version of the "plain brown wrapper" for those seeking help in curing problems with their private parts. If they were perhaps too embarrassed to discuss a problem face-to-face with a doctor, they could describe it in writing to a distant party who mailed back—

in a plain, sealed envelope—something guaranteed to bring relief. The Howard Association of Philadelphia advertised its services in the *Lake Superior Miner* in 1857; it offered publications and medicines to persons suffering from venereal diseases and impotence brought about by a profligate lifestyle or masturbation, which was seen as a harmful vice. In 1866, the Howard Association advertised "an essay of warning and instruction for young men" on the subjects of marriage and celibacy. It revealed the "diseases and abuses which prematurely prostrate the vital prowess, with sure means of relief."[47]

In a similar vein, Joseph Inman of New York City offered a safe and simple remedy for the cure of "Nervous Weakness, Early Decay, Diseases of the Urinary and Seminal Organs, and the whole train of disorders brought on by baneful and vicious habits." And John B. Ogden, another New Yorker, would "send the recipe and directions for making the simple remedy" for curing the "errors of youth"—"Nervous Debility, Premature Decay, and all the effects of youthful indiscretion."[48]

Wives and mothers could turn to older women, newspapers, and comprehensive books on "domestic medicine" for help in treating health problems at home. The *American Household Book of Medicine*, by no means the first publication of this kind, was advertised in the *Mining Gazette* in 1867. This "handbook for families" told "how to nurse the sick and manage the sick room." It covered the causes, symptoms, and cures of all the diseases of men, women, and children. It offered antidotes for poisons; first aid for accidents; and chapters on how to stay healthy and prevent disease through such activities as "Physical Training and Gymnastics."[49]

Lucena Brockway kept on the lookout for medical recipes and cures. At the back of her 1866 diary, Lucena recorded the fixings for a dysentery remedy, which seems to have been taken from a newpaper; the recipe had reputedly been used in New York "with rapid cures in every case." This remedy was easily concocted: Fill a teacup half full of vinegar. Dissolve as much salt in it as possible, with just a little additional salt left in the bottom. Pour boiling water into the solution till the cup is two-thirds or three-fourths full. "A scum will rise to the surface, which must be removed and the solution allowed to cool." Then take one tablespoonful, three times a day, till dysentery or protracted diarrhea is relieved. In the back of her 1867 diary, Lucena copied a recipe for "Bromide of Potasium with Camphor & Water," which promised relief from an upset tummy or gas. She also copied two different "hair restorer" concoctions, using ingredients such as sugar of lead, lac sulphur, alcohol, bay rum, borax, and rainwater.

Many who fell ill felt that their way back to health started by emptying themselves out—by ridding their entire digestive system, top to bottom, of whatever had attacked the body from within. A "severe emetic" was sure to bring on a strong, effective bout of vomiting, while a cathartic purged the bowels. Castor oil served nicely for the latter and was available in virtually all early stores on the Keweenaw. Those needing an emetic went to the store to purchase alum or tartar. Sufferers of flatulence bought camphor. Magnesium served as a laxative, as did a formulation of licorice and senna. Seidlitz pow-ders—effervescing salts—drunk while bubbling in water proved a mild ca-thartic, while flowers of zinc and sulfur became ointments and skin treatments. Quaffing cherry-flavored, syrupy pectoral relieved respiratory problems; a dose of bitters served as a tonic to stimulate the appetite and improve digestion. A whiff of smelling salts relieved faintness and light-headedness.

In an era when physicians wielded limited curative powers, both with their medicines and with their scalpels, it was not surprising that people sometimes put as much faith in themselves and in home remedies as in doctors or wanted to believe in over-the-counter or through-the-mail remedies that promised to cure anything and everything quickly and at low cost.[50] Patent medicines ar-rived on the mining frontier along with the first settlements and stores. Early Keweenaw consumers, in the main, purchased generic goods—foods, clothes, and household items bearing no brand names. But patent medicines were dif-ferent. They proudly carried brand names and were advertised and distributed nationally. Thus an ailing trammer in 1849 could go into John Senter's store in Eagle River and buy some "McAlister's All Healing Ointment."

As advertised in the local press, patent medicines could almost be expected to bring the dead back to life, so extensive were their curative claims. In the mid-1850s, Holloway's Pills operated "on the stomach, the liver, the kidneys, the lungs, the skin, and the bowels, correcting any derangement in their func-tions, purifying the blood, the very fountain of life, and thus curing disease in all its forms." Rhodes' Fever and Ague Cure entirely protected "any resident or traveller even in the most sickly or swampy localities, from any ague or Bilious disease whatever, or any injury from constantly inhaling Malaria or Miasma." And Conger's Magic Regulator and Conger's Tonic Liver Pills were supposed to be "the best, cheapest, and safest family medicines known." If taken "sometimes one, and sometimes the other, and sometimes both together," they provided a

safe, certain and prompt cure for asiatic cholera, dysentery or bloody flux, cholera mor-bus, cramps, cholic, griping, cholera infantum or summer complaint, diarrhoea of every kind . . . , vomiting, sick stomach, palpitation of the heart, sea sickness, coughs, colds, consumption in its curable stages, rheumatism, paralysis, neuralgia, tooth ache, ague in the face, sore throat or tongue, influenza, indigestion, sour stomach, loss of appetite, pains in the head, back and every part of the body—venereal complaints, scrofula, scald head, all sores and eruptions, debility, hysteric fits, convulsion fits, nervousness, delirium tre-mens, sick head ache, female complaints, all impurities of the blood, liver complaints, fever and ague, scarlet, typhus, typhoid and bilious fevers.[51]

By the mid-1860s, Portage Lake boasted a patent medicine producer of its own: Meagher's Eye Wash. John Meagher of Ripley used the testimonials of local citizens to help peddle his product. Michael Sullivan of the Huron mine had lost the use of one eye to scarlet fever. He claimed that Meagher's Eye Wash had restored his sight, after several physicians' prescriptions had failed.[52] The ads for Chicago-made Red Jacket Stomach Bitters spelled out a major attraction of many patent medicines: their alcohol content. These bitters—sold in quart bottles—strengthened and invigorated the system, assisted digestion, prevented fever and ague, and cured nervous headache. What were these marvelous bitters made of? "They are a combination of rare herbs prepared in the choicest old bourbon whiskey."[53]

A special class of medicines sold in the 1850s and 1860s was aimed at women. In an ironic turn, they were advertised not to cure but to *produce* "Monthly Sickness in all stages and circumstances." If a woman had skipped one or two periods, these medicines would restore her "monthy sickness" of menstruation by eliminating whatever "uterine obstruction" was in the way.[54] In short, these medicines—advertised in the *Lake Superior Miner* and the *Portage Lake Mining Gazette* and sold in local drugstores—promised, albeit in a veiled way, to let a woman give herself an abortion to end an unwanted pregnancy.

In mid-nineteenth-century America, the birthrate was declining. American women averaged about seven children in 1800; five to six in 1850; and only three to four by 1900.[55] This decline did not come about by chance or accident. Women throughout the century became more interested in limiting family size, and they attempted to do so by practicing birth control or by resorting to abortions.

In the 1850s and 1860s, women on the Keweenaw had access to the same means of birth control available elsewhere in the country: marriage manuals that offered family-planning advice, and drugstores and mail-order suppliers offering select rubber goods and powders. Birth control methods known about and used at the time included total or periodic abstinence (some times of the month were believed safer than others for intercourse) and withdrawal (or coitus interruptus).

If a couple found neither abstinence nor withdrawal acceptable, they could complete their sexual acts and rely on "technologies" to prevent conception. Thanks to Charles Goodyear's relatively recent work on vulcanization, many manufacturers engaged in making and distributing rubber condoms. This new product was more available to working-class men and women because it cost less than earlier sheaths imported from Europe, which were made from the ceca (intestines) of sheep and other animals. Manufacturers also fashioned the new material of vulcanized rubber into vaginal diaphrams, pessaries, or "womb veils" intended to stop the fertilization of the egg with sperm.[56] Women who had completed unprotected sex could, after the fact, hope to reduce their chances of getting pregnant by douching with a solution believed to have spermicidal qualities. In advertisements placed in the *Mining Gazette* in 1862, Dr. S. W. Smythe of Philadelphia offered the "Royal India Rubber Co.'s GUTTA PERCHA FEMALE SYRINGE . . . for Special Purposes." Society didn't openly talk or write much about sexual matters, but people knew the code. One "special purpose" alluded to in the ad was the washing away and killing of sperm after sex. The price for each syringe, "handsomely boxed, containing full accompaniments and directions for use," was $5.[57]

The knowledge and practice of birth control was hardly an exact science in the nineteenth century. Contraceptive techniques and products accounted for a reduced birthrate but by no means eliminated unwanted pregnancies. A woman who didn't want a child and who had missed a period or two or three might grasp at straws or take drastic measures to get out of her predicament, especially before she felt "quickening," or the stirring of the fetus within her.

By the mid-1850s on the Keweenaw, a woman could go to Murdock and Crandall's drugstore in Ontonagon and buy for a dollar "The Great French Remedy, Madame Boivin's Female Silver Pills." These pills could be safely taken for all kinds of "women's problems" but carried this warning (or promise?): "The Pills should not be taken by females during the FIRST THREE MONTHS of Pregnancy as they are sure to bring on miscarriage." Dr. Smythe, who offered female syringes through the mail, also dealt in "Female Regulating Powders," which he had been using on "ladies of different temperaments" since 1859, and which had "*never failed* to produce the desired effect." His No. 1 powder would "remove all obstructions and cause a safe and regular return of monthly sickness." He cautioned women "not to use my No. 1 Powder in cases of Pregnancy, as it is sure to produce miscarriage. Those whose health will not permit an increase of family will find this powder a valuable preventative."[58]

Some commercial abortifacients were fraudulent placebos foisted on desperate women. Some merely contained mild laxatives. But some contained active ingredients that could be hazardous if taken in excessive quantities, such as ergot, oil of tansy, oil of savin, aloe, or black hellibore.[59] (In lieu of buying prepared pills or powders, women could acquire many of these same ingredients from stores or apothecaries and make up their own abortifacients in accordance with recipes found in women's books or passed by word of mouth from woman to woman.) The serious, strong concoctions supposedly worked on the theory that the way to release "blocked menses" was to dose the woman with a medicine that caused "great evacuations and vomiting." If made sick enough, and heaving enough, she might abort the fetus.[60]

If an abortifacient taken orally failed to work, a woman might use other concoctions, or even just water, administered by an invasive syringe. She could overstress or physically tax her body; knead or strike her abdomen; jump from harmful heights; or turn to a physician who could use probes or newly invented suction or electrical devices to try to trigger an abortion.

It is impossible to determine the incidence of abortions on the mining frontier. Aside from newspaper advertisements for commercial abortifacients, little evidence of the practice is found. The word "abortion" is not found in any local literature. Women's diaries and physicians' reminiscences make no mention of it. Nevertheless, abortions surely took place on the Keweenaw. The years 1840 through 1880 were marked by a great increase in purposefully terminated pregnancies in the United States. Couples—and especially women—sought smaller families, and an abortion, which was not illegal at the time, was an available means to that end. It has been estimated that near midcentury, for every five or six live births, one abortion occurred. In Michigan, a special committee of physicians formed by the state Board of Health estimated in the early 1880s that *one-third* of all pregnancies in Michigan ended in abortion.[61] Abortion was part of a covert culture within this society. The act went on in the shadows, and people did it but did not talk or write about it openly and freely.

Periods of pregnancy, childbirth, and child rearing were clearly central to the lives of women on the Keweenaw Peninsula. By 1870, the population of the Keweenaw's three counties had increased to nearly 21,000 people. The census enumerated 3,700 families and a like number of women of child-bearing age (defined as years sixteen through forty-four). Of these 3,700 women, 1,000 had given birth during the previous year. These women, in their homes, tended to 9,800 children under the age of fifteen and to another 1,500 aged fifteen to nineteen, most of whom still would have remained with their parents.[62]

In the middle decades of the nineteenth century, women in America still gave birth at home, where they were often assisted by a midwife and surrounded by female friends and relatives. The trend toward physician-assisted deliveries, however, was growing, and that trend was probably accelerated on the Keweenaw because of the existence of company doctors. Working-class women on the Keweenaw had greater access to physicians than most, and by the 1860s, company doctors attended many home deliveries. In fact, in a report covering his activities from the last few months of 1862 through the end of 1864, Dr. A. S. Heaton, who served the Pewabic and Franklin mines, rated "the great number of obstetrical cases"—three hundred births—as by far "the most laborious duty of the doctor."[63] He no doubt had some help in carrying out these duties, however, because as long as childbirth happened at home, it remained largely a female activity. A pregnant woman's female friends and relatives might defer to the male doctor during the act of delivery, but they would be with the woman before the doctor arrived, and they would stay, tending to mother and child, after he left.[64]

A high infant mortality rate assured that many of those born never lived to maturity. Within Keweenaw families, the death of a child or sibling was not uncommon. At Clifton, Henry Hobart was especially attuned to the deaths of children; he was, after all, their teacher. His diary recorded them, one after the other:

> Feb. 9, 1864: "Last Sunday, while at Sunday school Mr. Souden's little boy was taken vomiting. . . . The next day he died at twelve o'clock. This is very sudden and no one can tell the cause."
>
> Feb. 13, 1864: "Mr. Souden's little boy died last night after an illness of a few hours. He has lost two this week. Scarlet fever is said to be the cause. . . . Johnny is the only child left, they have buried four or five small children. It seems impossible for some to raise a child."
>
> March 15, 1864: "James Thomas, one of my scholars, was buried. . . . Little James was not sick only a few days & died suddenly. He was a fat healthy little fellow & quite active to learn. It is sad to see so many little ones dying in a village like this. Be ye also ready."[65]

Reverend William Allen Johnson of the Grace United Church was at the Cliff mine at the same time as Hobart. The minister, like the teacher, was attuned to dying children. Between December 1862 and August 1864, he officiated at twenty-five burials. Nine of the dead were under a year, another nine between one and two years.[66] High mortality rates for infants and children can be gleaned from other sources, too. Of the thirty-three deaths reported to clerk of Houghton County in 1868, nineteen were under the age of five. Of the thousand babies born alive on the Keweenaw in 1870, one hundred expired before reaching their first birthday. In that year, the average age of the 241 persons who died in Houghton County was 10.93 years for males and 7.75 for females. Houghton County residents died at a rate of 17 per 1,000 inhabitants. Statewide, the average age of death for males and females was twenty-five, and the death rate was under 10 per 1,000.[67]

Year after year, it was no easy thing to be born on the shore of Lake Superior, to live through treacherous childhood years, and to reach adulthood. Individuals born there, and individuals who migrated there, knew pain and suffering; dealing with illness, injury, and sorrow was no rare occurrence. Some residents no doubt felt cheated by the remedies that too often offered hope but no cure, and by the physicians—company doctors and others—who performed too few miracles. Many physicians, in their turn, no doubt felt a lot like Dr. A. S. Heaton, who found himself hampered in trying to fend off disease among children and other maladies prevalent in a working-class population of numerous immigrants: "with bad hygiene, bad diet, bad nursing, and exposed to all the inclemencies of the weather and climate, medical treatment can effect but little; and to the physician is left the consolation that medicine was not intended to cure [all] the sins of the body."[68]

NINE

ICE CARNIVALS, CAMELS, AND SUNDAY TROMBONES
Pioneer Pastimes

After weeks of arduous toil, coasting in small boats many a league of stormy shore, pushing their way through tangled underbrush and almost impenetrable cedar swamps; carrying packs of provisions, tools and blankets on their backs; fording, or rafting on streams, and exposed to all the storms of heaven, tortured by mosquitoes, blackflies and sand flies, and often suffering from thirst and hunger, worn, ragged, unshorn, tanned like Indians, these indomitable explorers would return to Copper Harbor, and pitching their tents in a cool place by the side of the waters, indulge in a period of rest and recreation.

—A. P. Swineford,
"History and Review," 1877

As life and landscape transformed together on the Keweenaw between the early 1840s and early 1870s, settlers enjoyed more security, comfort, and civility. Fewer people coasted along hazardous shores in canoes or other small boats; instead, they booked passage on schooners, side-wheeler steamboats, or propeller ships. Fewer pushed their way through swamps or thickets; instead, they traveled over roads, perhaps even a turnpike or railroad. Fewer were "tanned like Indians," because frontier society, as it evolved, relocated settlers from the great outdoors to the indoors. And fewer lived like rough-and-tumble vagabonds, packing their possessions from place to place, sleeping on the ground with only a tent overhead; instead, settlers returned night after night to the same shelter and bed.

The harshest of frontier conditions eroded, and the amenities of everyday life multiplied. The days of "indomitable explorers" passed, giving way to the days of more ordinary, less colorful managers, merchants, and working-class men, women, and children. But life on the Keweenaw only became easier; it did not become easy. The explorers on Lake Superior who camped out at Copper Harbor in the 1840s were not the only ones who needed periods of rest and recreation. So did those who followed them to the Keweenaw over the next few decades.

Residents continued to endure much. Settlers altered the landscape by clearing forests and building villages, roads, canals, and mines, but they did not come close to subduing or controlling this northern woods environment and its climate. In particular, they still struggled through the long, harsh winters and too-short, buggy summers. They toiled hard, whether working with wash boilers in stifling August kitchens or with sledgehammers, drills, and explosives, eight hundred feet underground, and they needed occasional breaks from their labors. And even as the Keweenaw's population exceeded twenty thousand people, many residents—longtime settlers and newcomers alike—suffered loneliness and a sense of isolation and separation from the world below. So they needed pleasant opportunities for socializing with friends and relatives, for enjoying companionship.

Susie Childs keenly remembered her experience as an early settler:

> Woman has been found to bear her share of . . . the struggles of the pioneer. She finds herself environed by sights and sounds to her entirely new, and strange. She may be surrounded by few of her own language and manner of life. . . . At first it seems most romantic . . . , but the spell is at last broken and the scene begins to wear an aspect of monotony. Her body is in the forest, but her mind is with loved ones far away.[1]

John Forster also experienced a deep sense of isolation that wore on the pioneer's mind and spirit: "Without the stimulus of companionship and conversation it was not to be wondered at if he fell into despondency. As has been truly observed by more than one student of human nature, those persons who have been reared in the woods, on the frontier, acquire a grave cast of character verging on deep melancholy."[2]

To escape the drudgery of labor and the tedium of daily routines, and to keep melancholy, depression, and "cabin fever" at bay, Susie Childs, John Forster, and other settlers needed to develop coping skills. They needed to aspire to more than just enduring life on the lake; they had to find ways of enjoying it. Regardless of gender, age, or social class, they needed activities that promised them peace of mind, good cheer, amusement, fellowship, and entertainment.

Fortunately, these activities—these opportunities or excuses for shunning tedium, travail, hard work, and isolation—came soon and in many forms. Settlers learned to take simple pleasures in and around their house or garden. They learned to play in the snow, not just curse it, and to enjoy the woods and streams, not just damn the bugs. Small businessmen arrived to provide many commercial forms of entertainment or escape, ranging from saloons to ice-skating rinks. Sports, games, and competitions came to enliven the social scene. And importantly, a succession of festive holidays punctuated the work-aday calendar.

Holidays presented opportunities for social get-togethers and for consuming special foods and beverages. Early settlers marked New Year's Day and, a month and a half later, Valentine's Day—when "swains and sweethearts" sent each other "anonymous missives," which by 1870 had become "more and more filthy and obscene." Washington's birthday was followed by St. Patrick's Day, especially celebrated by the Irish. By the 1860s the members of the St. Patrick's Society at Portage Lake had organized a high mass on this day; after this mass, they paraded, hundreds strong, accompanied by a band, through Houghton, Hancock, and seven or eight nearby mine villages.[3]

Easter came at a time when residents longed for an end to winter. Out at the Cliff mine, adults helped children color Easter eggs, "but very few were to be had & these at sixty cents per dozen." The Fourth of July, from the first years of exploration on, was an important midsummer holiday. In November, just as they started to hunker down for winter, the Scots celebrated their holiday in homage to St. Andrew. By the late 1850s, Thanksgiving became a special November day, when people gathered to worship and then enjoyed "a real New England dinner of turkey, pudding, pumpkin pie and sweet cider." About a month into hard winter, Christmas arrived in its turn.[4]

In the first few decades of mining copper on the lake, pioneers mostly celebrated patriotism and faith; the three biggest holidays were Washington's birthday, the Fourth of July, and Christmas. Gala affairs in the dead of winter assured that the "Father of his Country" would not be forgotten. Orrin Robinson recalled in great detail the festivities that took place on February 22, 1855, at Dan Cavanaugh's large two-story log house, located about twelve miles upriver from Ontonagon. Special invitations had gone out to the "upper crust" along the Keweenaw for this particular party; Robinson himself traveled twenty-five miles by sleigh to get there.

At four in the afternoon, the ball opened with a grand march, "followed by a quadrille, for round dances such as waltz and two-step were not indulged in on Lake Superior at that time." Two fiddles, a bass viol, and a cello provided the music; "a big mulatto known as 'Ben Bolt' " played the bass and "called the changes for the quadrilles and contra-dances, now and then interspersed with the Virginia reel and 'Pop Goes the Weasel.' "

The ladies' fashions worn at Cavanaugh's were "up to date" for Lake Superior in 1855, when proper dancing attire was "buckskin moccasins and leggings, embroidered in fanciful designs with colored beads." The corresponding men's costumes, too, were not elaborate: "no white vests nor swallow-tailed coats were seen. Most of the men wore buckskin moccasins and flannel shirts, either blue or red and a few wore white or what was then known as 'biled' [boiled] shirts."

About eight o'clock, the host announced supper. The "tables fairly groaned under the weight of the feast prepared," which was served up by "waitresses, who were dusky maidens of the forest." The menu included canned oysters, pea soup, baked lake trout and fried whitefish, corned beef and cabbage, boiled pork with sauerkraut, and spiced baked ham. Diners passed baked beans, boiled potatoes, and mashed rutabaga. They ate wheat bread or saffron rolls and, for dessert, gingersnaps or dried apple pie. Celebrants drank tea or coffee, which some doctored with milk or sugar. They also drank alcohol: "Whiskey straight, Scotch, Irish, and Kentucky, all drawn from the same cask into separate bottles—take your pick."[5]

Even the earliest explorers and geologists crisscrossing the Keweenaw in search of copper stopped to celebrate the Fourth of July. They took some special food from their packs, such as a can of oysters, and maybe went hunting to make sure they could put together a particularly good meal. Lacking proper fireworks, they blew up some rocks with black powder, thus providing the exuberant bang the day required. In 1847, a party of about sixty men from the mines near Copper Harbor "held a meeting and dined together, commemorating the Declaration of Independence." Fittingly enough, the pioneers tied in the history of their new nation with the very short history of their new mining district. As recounted by geologist Charles T. Jackson, this holiday "afforded an opportunity for each of the inhabitants to give an account of his labors, privations and adventures in the first settlement of that district. This meeting enabled me to form some estimate of the enterprise and zeal of the early adventurers, and was highly instructive as well as entertaining."[6]

Fourth of July celebrations became larger and more structured as villages swelled with more men, women, and children. At the Cliff and Pennsylvania mines, by the 1860s cannons fired, flags flew, bands played, and children marched. Patriots young and old assembled at church to pray and sing. One upstanding citizen read the Declaration of Independence, then another pillar of the community (always a man) delivered a public-spirited speech. Afterward, a holiday committee, having already canvassed the village for donations, hosted a picnic, where the children, especially, enjoyed treats such as "lemonade, candy, raisins & nuts." Meanwhile, others largely ignored the official celebration of American patriotism, and used the day as an excuse to get drunk. Good Father Baraga, at Eagle Harbor on July 4, 1861, described it simply as a "day of general sinning and misfortune."[7]

Christmas also occasioned many get-togethers. Work and school were called off, and families and friends assembled to worship, feast, exchange gifts, and—quite often—to enjoy bottled good cheer. John Forster recalled that in the winter of 1846–47, before the Keweenaw was much settled year-round, he "walked forty-five miles on snow shoes" to attend Christmas dinner at Fort Wilkins.[8] By the 1850s and 1860s, people usually stayed much closer to home for Christmas. To make the season more festive for all, but especially for children, many families trimmed a tree in their cabin. The village school, too, decorated a Christmas tree, hanging from it many small presents, which would be cut off one by one and given to the young scholars, who stepped forward to fetch a gift on hearing their names called out.[9]

By the mid-1860s, residents near Houghton enjoyed the season by going to see a "laughable Christmas Extravaganza" entitled "Father Christmas," given by the English Amateur Theatrical Society. And on Christmas day, bands composed of brass and string instruments played "grand concerts" of sacred and secular music. Meanwhile, out at the Cliff mine village, carolers sounded the season, tramping through the snow from one house to the next. The working men singing Christian songs picked up more singers and more beer or ale at their stops. No solemn bunch of carolers were they: "To see a party of fifty or one hundred men with *enough down* to make them lively, all singing a song, is a very amusing sight." By the time night fell on the merry band, they'd likely all be all drunk.[10]

For some, Christmas meant well-lubricated revelry. For others, such as Lucena Brockway, it meant family: "We rode up to Charlotte's [her daughter's] & made a Christmas call." Christmas was a time for family to gather at the table to enjoy some of the best food of the year, served in extraordinary abundance. One Christmas, the Brockways indulged in "Roast Turkey & Roast Goose for dinner." Another Christmas, they had "fricassied chicken, chicken pie, fresh oysters and sweet cider first course. Then tea & coffee, mince pie & cream pie and cake & ice cream." And it was a time for exchanging "lots of Christmas presents." Perhaps a gold pen, or nice cravats, a hand-held looking glass, kid gloves, or "Annie's photograph in a nice frame."[11]

On holidays and at other times, music played an important role in the lives of many pioneers. On January 11, 1847, Father Baraga visited one of the earliest mines, where he expected to find people living a hardscrabble existence. But he was "dumbfounded at the fast spreading of civilization on these shores of Lake Superior." He wrote a friend that he "found in many places neat houses with nice carpeted rooms." And in one house, of all things, "there was even a piano on which a young American woman played very skillfully."[12]

The Catholic missionary may have stumbled upon the first—and, in 1847, perhaps the only—piano on Lake Superior. Somebody must have wanted it badly. That piano had surely sailed on at least two lake boats, surviving a portage at the Soo, and some additional land transport on the Keweenaw. It arrived at a rude mine camp, just as early as the first steam engine shipped north by a mining company to help with the work. So the piano sounded a cultural note: many pioneers kept music in their lives, whether they played instruments themselves or listened to others.

Many settlers undoubtedly brought musical instruments with them. Others special-ordered instruments at frontier stores. By as early as 1849–50, John Senter's store at Eagle River did a modest trade in musical instruments, selling an accordion, a melodion (a foot-powered organ), bass violas and bows, a violin and bow, guitars and guitar strings, flageolets and a German flute, a tuning fork, and a violin and cello instruction book.

Music enriched settlers' lives, including the sometimes lonely life of Sarah Barr Christian, who resided at a mine on Isle Royale in 1874–75. Christian ached for female companionship. She had worked hard to find a maid willing to leave Houghton or Hancock and relocate to Isle Royale: "All the women seemed to feel they would be leaving the world forever and would not venture forth, although we offered what was then a fabulous price." Finally, she secured a domestic, only to lose her shortly thereafter to a miner, who took her away as his bride: "She had about fifty stalwart young men to choose from, and I fear chose the least desirable." That left Sarah Barr Christian with just one woman to talk to for the duration of a long winter: her mother-in-law. Under such circumstances, the young, lonely wife took comfort and pleasure in playing her piano. But even that experience could not extricate her from the particulars of the unusual place where she lived:

> It had grown warm enough to have the windows open. At the end of our sitting-room was a bay window. One day while sitting at the piano, with my back to the window, playing my simple little tunes, I heard a grunt. I turned to see in every window the head and shoulders of an Indian buck and behind him his squaw. . . . I was a little startled, but quickly realized they were harmless.[13]

In an advertisement from the mid-1870s, the *Portage Lake Mining Gazette* opined that "music hath charms to soothe a savage, rend a rock and split a cabbage, and the sweetest music in the world is that of the birds." The paper announced that a local retailer was selling imported German canaries and Java sparrows, "all in song." Exotic pets had arrived at the mines to entertain and amuse the populace: first birds and then, a bit later, goldfish.[14] And in Houghton, to cash in on the market for amusement, Peter Bellehemeur kept a "Lake Superior menagerie," where the curious paid to view captive bears and wolves. But long before the arrival of caged bears and birds, man's best friend—the dog—had taken up residence on Lake Superior.[15]

Dogs arrived with the earliest settlers. They multiplied and in time ran in packs, raided trash, fouled footpaths, and howled at the moon. In 1863 a writer for the *Portage Lake Mining Gazette* christened Hancock the "Village of the Dead Dogs," after discovering nine deceased "bow-wows" at the town's main intersection. They'd all been poisoned by a citizen bent on bringing more peace and quiet to the domestic scene.[16] But if dogs ultimately became public nuisances, in the earliest settlements they offered special and welcomed companionship. Ruth Douglass left downstate Michigan with much trepidation but soon came to enjoy her new life on Isle Royale. Part of that life was a pet dog. On December 1, 1848, she wrote in her diary, "All is quiet around me except my little favorite, 'Roy,' who barks occasionally at Frank the teamster who passes by frequently with loads of wood."

A few days earlier, on a dark and rainy day late in November, Ruth Douglass had passed the time sewing and reading: "with my needles and books I find no time to get lonely. I recollect an old adage that when the hands are busily employed the mind is content."[17] For many women, especially those who made clothes for a large family, sewing was an arduous task. But for others, like the childless and well-to-do Ruth, it represented a pleasant pastime.

Many who settled on Lake Superior shared Ruth's habit of reading. The region did not go long without a local press. In 1846, John Ingersoll of Copper Harbor put out the first paper, the *Lake Superior News and Mining Journal.*[18] This paper was short-lived, but in the 1850s two important English-language weeklies established themselves: Ontonagon's *Lake Superior Miner* and Houghton's *Portage Lake Mining Gazette*. Libraries, albeit modest ones, also formed. In 1861 E. L. Baker, president of the Pewabic Mining Company donated "a valuable collection of books," which formed "the nucleus of two libraries, namely: the Pewabic and Franklin Miners' Free Library, and Pewabic and Franklin School Free Library." Stockholders in the interconnected Franklin and Pewabic mining companies were, in the companies' annual reports, "respectfully solicited to contribute [spare books] to this most useful object." By 1865, the school library was a proud owner of forty-four volumes.

At Clifton, Henry Hobart for a time kept the village's entire "public library" in a single large bookcase in his classroom. The library grew to 336 books by 1865 and to 504 by 1870. Libraries of about the same size operated in Copper Harbor, Eagle Harbor, Calumet, Hancock, and Houghton. Ontonagon boasted the largest library in the district—864 volumes by 1865—and voters that year earmarked $100 of public funds for the library's upkeep.[19]

On the frontier, reading served as more than a mere diversion. It comforted pioneers by making them feel like they were still connected to the world below and homelands left behind. On April 16, 1864, in anticipation of the opening of navigation, the *Mining Gazette* announced that the "Meteor" would be bringing up a "large supply of N.Y. and Detroit papers, illustrated Amer., German, English, French and Irish papers, illus. almanacs, magazines, novels, fashion books, Thackeray's 'Life and Works,' and more."

Henry Hobart was an enthusiastic reader who set himself to such tasks as tackling Bancroft's multivolume *History of the United States*. On a hot day late in June 1863, the teacher found a bit of quiet contentment: "I spent the day in reading and resting." Besides books, Hobart read papers mailed to him from his boyhood home in Vermont. During the Civil War, this Yankee was frustrated when he could not read up-to-date information on this great conflict, which he wanted to experience vicariously, but not in person.[20] The news in the local press was cold because papers still relied on the mail for their communications from the "world below." The telegraph did not reach Houghton until March 1866, and for some time after that the *Mining Gazette* could only infrequently print telegraphed news dispatches. The telegraph line and operators connecting the Keweenaw with Green Bay proved "confounded nuisances" that worked but half the time.[21]

Reading was vitally important to Lucena Brockway, a woman who struggled with poor health, loneliness, and depression. Lucena, a native New Yorker, married Daniel D. Brockway, a Vermonter, in lower Michigan in 1836. They migrated to Lake Superior in 1843, making them one of the first white families to settle there and raise a family. Lucena gave birth to two sons (only one lived to maturity) and to three girls. They first lived in L'Anse, where Daniel served as a government blacksmith to the Ojibwa. With the onset of the copper rush, they relocated to Copper Harbor in 1846 and opened a hotel.

Daniel Brockway, an energetic man, juggled many interests and businesses. In 1849, while still keeping hotel at Copper Harbor, he assumed the post of agent at the Northwest mine for two years. In 1861, the family moved to Eagle River and operated a hotel there. In 1863 they returned to Copper Harbor and started a mercantile business. In 1869, the Brockways went south to lower Michigan, where they farmed for a few years. Migrating back to the Keweenaw in 1872, they settled this time at the Cliff mine, where Daniel opened a general store and meat market.

In 1879, Daniel Brockway, at the age of sixty-four, ran off to the Black Hills for seven months to explore for gold. In his late sixties he assumed charge of the nearly defunct Cliff mine, and he and the once-great mine grew old and frail together. In 1895 Lucena and Daniel Brockway finally retired to a house in Lake Linden. After sixty-three years of marriage, the two pioneers died within a few months of one another in 1899.[22]

Lucena Brockway's many diaries do not depict a very happy life from the mid-1860s onward. Her children had grown and gone off. Lucena enjoyed a day in 1863 when she visited with all four children under one roof; eleven years passed before this mother saw all her family together again. Husband Daniel, too, was often absent. To Lucena, it seemed that "D. D. B." was always on the road, tending to some business matter, while she was stuck at home, often suffering poor health—specifically, the debilitating effects of an apparent light stroke that hit her in 1866.

Lucena Brockway craved companionship. She absolutely needed to be connected to a world bigger and more interesting than her quarters in Copper Harbor or at the Cliff mine. For this woman, sometimes a shut-in, reading was a passion, if not an obsession, and mail was her salvation. The spring of 1867 had been unpleasant; it had snowed several times during the first week of May. Then came the blessed mail: "In the evening we got a through mail, the first in two weeks. Got a letter from D. D. B. Two from Charlotte, one from Sarah & Scott, one from Ada Harris, one from Mrs. Broughton . . . , and a dozen papers. And I read more than I was able being so long without any news from the lower world."[23]

Often, Lucena recorded in her diary the news she had gleaned from newspapers. Having few loved ones or family to share the news with, she shared it with herself. In 1874 this lonely woman at the Cliff mine recorded this: "The marriage of the Duke of Edinburgh and the Grand Duchess Marie was solemnized on the 23rd of Jan. at St. Petersburgh. The Bride was splendidly appareled in a long crimson velvet mantle, trimmed with ermine, and wore a diamond coronet. Her train was born by four pages."[24]

Newspapers and perhaps books helped Lucena Brockway keep up with the world at large and with the rich and famous. Her diary in 1874, besides noting royal weddings, highlighted the birthdays of Commodore Vanderbilt and the Harvard scientist Professor Louis Agassiz. But what Lucena—and so many other early settlers—really wanted to read was personal mail from friends and family. Her same 1874 diary that records the comings and goings of dukes, commodores, and professors also mentions 146 letters sent out to thirty-nine different people, and 138 pieces of incoming mail, penned by forty different hands.

At times, the right thing to do was not to do much, but to stay home and relax. For the men, especially, indulging in tobacco was an important, almost ritualistic part of relaxing, of "tapering off" from work. Some of the earliest pioneers took a lesson from the voyageurs and Ojibwa and smoked local "kinni-kinnick." This creeping plant, found in sandy soil, had a deep-green velvety leaf that passed as a tobacco substitute. But soon no substitute was needed, because all early stores stocked tobacco products. James North Wright described the early miner, especially the Cornishman, as "an inveterate smoker" whose pipe was "never out of his mouth except when necessity compelled it." He "puffed steadily at a large meerschaum held firmly between his teeth . . . only removing his pipe at intervals to blow dense clouds of dark smoke." If a man didn't want a pipe, he might smoke a cigar "in quiet contentment," chomp on a chaw, or dip a bit of snuff. Settlers consumed these tobacco forms far more than cigarettes, but a few did buy cigarette papers and roll their smokes.[25]

On Lake Superior, people needed to get out and about, to take advantage of the pleasures offered by the natural environment, and not be put off by the cold, or the snow, or the bugs, or the dense forest, or the swamp, or the cold water of Superior. For the sake of their spirits, pioneers could ill afford to hold themselves hostage inside a small, dark, smoky cabin—not when outside they might discover that "the weather is delightful" and that a man's breast could "swell with a new emotion of delight as he inhaled the air of this northern wilderness."[26]

Men and women alike took pleasure in walking, in following footpaths into the forest or strolling down a beach. Along the way, they picked wildflowers or berries or pocketed colorful agates to add to a collection. Henry Hobart often took "rambles" in the vicinity of the Cliff mine. Sometimes he toted his gun, thinking he might kill "a few pigeons or pheasants." Sometimes he took fishing tackle, hoping to hook some trout.[27]

Pioneers enjoyed the waters and shores bordering their world. In 1848, coasting along Isle Royale exhilarated Ruth Douglass: "Just returned from a fine pleasure excursion thirteen miles up the Lake. . . . When we got down as far as the point where we enter the harbor, we landed and feasted for nearly an hour upon berries and wild pears, then returned home." These excursions also enhanced the young woman's sense of freedom and accomplishment. She made one trip accompanied only by Mrs. Mathews. They "returned home quite pleased with our trip feeling very independent—that we were able to go out alone."[28]

On Lake Superior, the very green world of summer inevitably turned very white, forcing a change of activities. Children (and adults, too) put away their marbles, maybe in exchange for snowballs. Henry Hobart frequently reported "fine snowballing" at the Cliff mine. He liked to battle his young scholars and thought it perfectly fine if many of them had swollen eyes after a "good round at snow balling. It is good exercise for them & will do them good."[29]

In winter, those who wanted to tramp into the woods brought out their snowshoes. Others brought out sleds. At the Cliff, Hobart noted that downhill sledding was an amusement engaged in by residents without regard to gender or age. Women came out to sled, and he "saw an old lady out the other evening, who has a family of six or eight children, enjoying the sport with the others."[30]

At Houghton, a village sitting at the foot of a steep hill, the *Mining Gazette* in 1864 enthusiastically announced the arrival of "pure, white, bright, exhilarating snow!" The village boys, especially, were jubilant:

> Visions of the hillside and swift coasting upon their favorite sleds enraptured their souls, and they could hardly await the time when the snowy mantle should be thick enough to permit them to indulge in their charming winter sports. Sleds, the renowned coursers, shod with shining steel, were soon brought into requisition, and the steep acclivity of Portage Street was the favored locality of the grand carnival.

Just a few months later, the *Mining Gazette* reported that the "grand carnival" of November had become the "dangerous amusement" of January. Men and boys disrupted traffic by sledding down two principal streets at all hours, and one coaster bowled a woman over, breaking her leg. The Houghton village board was going to have to consider banning the sport.[31]

Early in November 1848, Ruth Douglass rued the end of the boating season but looked forward to winter sleighing. Unfortunately, she was at the wrong place at the wrong time: "I would like to change the boat for a sleigh and horses if I could, but I may as well stop wishing before I commence, for if I had the sleigh and the horse, then I have not the roads." Later, as roads and horses became more common, winter sleigh rides and summer buggy rides became popular amusements. A year after suffering her mild stroke, Lucena Brockway regularly took little jaunts in the pleasant months of June and July 1867. So often frustrated by being housebound, she enjoyed getting outdoors and riding nowhere in particular.[32]

Henry Hobart opined in 1863 that "there is nothing very interesting that a man can see in this Country except some of the mines." The teacher explored the surface works of nearby mines and took several underground tours. For those who didn't work there, climbing ladders down into the foreboding yet fascinating underground was a special adventure.

A tradition passed down in the Copper Country says that women were not allowed underground because men thought they brought bad luck. But no ban existed, at least in the early decades. No women worked in the mines, but companies let women and even children accompany men on tours. V. L. Pruyn traveled the Keweenaw with a party including a woman and child in 1858. At the Cliff mine, Pruyn went underground and reported that the "agents were very civil and showed us around." At the Minesota mine, "our party consisted of Mr. and Mrs. Harvey (Mrs. Harvey having on a Bloomer), Erastus (his son), and myself. We went down about one hundred and sixty feet . . . to a large mass of native copper." At the Cliff mine in 1863, for entertainment on a Saturday night, "Misses Cundy & Harper made a trip underground . . . as far as the ninety fathom level [540 feet] on the ladders and up again." And in 1878 the *Mining Gazette* reported that "a Chicago miss of 62 descended briskly into one of our mines the other day, putting to shame a number of young lady companions."[33]

People often went out calling on friends. They sat for awhile and enjoyed a bit of dessert, a drink, some talk, and maybe a smoke. Sometimes the visit was a bit more orchestrated. John Forster remembered that during long, dark winter evenings, "dancing and card playing were the only recreations." People came "miles through the snow drifts . . . for the sake of society; and they all enjoyed themselves right heartily."[34]

As the population grew—especially the female population—dances became frequent social events. By 1856, nobody from Ontonagon had to snowshoe fifty miles to dance. The *Lake Superior Miner* reported that "we have had in

Ontonagon and vicinity during the past winter over 50 public dances." Many of these were "first class and . . . quite expensive." Dancing, early on, became a commercial entertainment, where patrons paid the piper. Dan Cavanaugh, who staged Washington's Birthday celebrations near the Minesota mine, also staged dinner dances in the mid-1850s:

> About twenty of our citizens of the male gender, accompanied by the same number of the gentler sex, met at the house of D. Cavana[ugh] . . . and tripped the "light fantastic" to the music of Scale's band until the morning following. The party was one of the finest of the season. . . . The supper was gotten up in Dan's best style and every effort made on his part to make his guests happy, in which effort he was decidedly successful.[35]

At small mine locations, carved out of the woods and huddled around a cluster of shafts, extracting copper was the community's sole order of business. These villages offered little in the way of organized entertainment. To take advantage of the greater range of amusements available on the Keweenaw by the 1860s, settlers usually had to be in one of the larger commercial villages along Lake Superior or Portage Lake.

Within these communities, enterprising businessmen erected halls (often as part of a hotel) that hosted diverse social functions. By the Civil War era, Portage Lake boasted several halls: Miller's, Mayworth's, and the Douglass House hall in Houghton, and Lapp's and Wallace's in Hancock. Owners rented halls out to organizations wanting to hold social or charitable events, such as a group of volunteer firemen who staged a fancy firemen's ball. Sixty volunteers paraded through the streets of both Houghton and Hancock in the afternoon. Then, in the evening, two hundred couples assembled at Miller's Hall, where the "arrangements were perfect. . . . The supper tables were beautifully laid, and more than bountifully provided by the ever liberal ladies of our town." The fire company cleared over $500 toward the purchase of new uniforms.[36]

The halls regularly staged their own dinner dances, "social hops," and masquerade balls, especially during winter months, when the population was more in need of inside entertainment. New Year's was a busy time for the village halls, which offered citizens extensive revelry. In 1863, Houghton celebrants could go to New Year's Eve balls at William Miller's and Frank Mayworm's, and the next night go to the Douglass House ball. As 1869 drew to a close, Miller's Hall assured that "the 'fatted calf' has been killed, and that there will be no lack of turkies, geese and chickens, with which to tickle the palates of the hungry. Go there and dance till twelve, and then sit down to your first feast in 1870."[37]

The halls hosted numerous masquerade balls and often gave prizes for best costume. Mayworth's Hall staged a masquerade on a cold Tuesday evening in February 1863. A "gentleman and a Lady," if masked, got in for a dollar, and this included supper. Without a mask, it was two dollars. A man could bring a second lady friend along, masked or not, for an additional dollar. The hall published the "strictly enforced" rules of the event: "No person allowed to dance without a mask before 12 o'clock. No person allowed to interfere with the masks of their friends. After 12 o'clock, everybody will be allowed to dance and act as they please so that propriety is observed."[38]

During summer months, entertainers from the world below came up to perform at the Copper Country's villages. A prestidigitator performed "laughable tricks and curious experiments which defied ordinary scrutiny," and black minstrel shows toured the region during the Civil War. By 1870, even traveling circuses toured the Copper Country. That year, Dan Castello's "Great Circus and Egyptian Caravan" performed at Hancock and Calumet, bringing along its equestrians, aerialists, acrobats, clowns, and "Genuine Double-Humped Bactrian Camels!" Adult admission was a dollar, about half a day's pay for a miner. Children got in for half a buck.[39]

Other exotic acts made their way north to entertain the mining population. In June 1866, the *Mining Gazette* at Portage Lake correctly noted, "There will be no lack of amusements the coming week." The entertainment included two or three jugglers' performances; three grand balls held at local halls; a touring musical family presenting five performances; one theatrical performance in German; two grand-prize wrestling matches; and last but surely not least, an exhibition, in both Houghton and Hancock, of two "Wild Men of Borneo." These "Heathenish Little Men," standing only three and a half feet tall—these "greatest living curiousities . . . part human and part animal"—would perform acts of strength and other astonishments. They would not, however, offend any one: "Ladies and children can visit the Wild Men, as there is neither word, action, nor deficiency of dress, to offend the most delicate eye or ear."[40]

In summer, the more well-to-do residents of the Keweenaw could partake of pleasure-boat excusions on Lake Superior. Schooners, propellors, and steamboats offered passage for one-day excursions—up to the tip of the Keweenaw and back—and more adventurous, expensive trips as well. For two dollars per day, a traveler could sail for up to two weeks, taking in the Pictured Rocks shoreline near Munising; Isle Royale; and Canada's northern shore of Superior.[41]

In winter, many adults and children ice-skated. They enjoyed it some on frozen ponds and lakes, but often these natural rinks were too covered with snow to permit good skating. The *Mining Gazette* noted that it was a "rare occurence in this country" when residents could enjoy good skating on Portage Lake. One such time occurred in December 1869, when hundreds of "all ages and sexes" enjoyed "several days of tolerable skating." They "were flying around and many were the sore heads and involuntary view of stars obtained by would-be 'champions.' "

Starting in the 1860s, skaters found better sport at new ice rinks, where either a roof held unwanted snow at bay or workers were paid to flood and make good ice and to shovel it off when needed. At the Pewabic Mine, "young gentlemen" turned an old kilnhouse for roasting copper rock into a rink, "for the delectation of themselves, their wives and sweethearts. They're an economical set, them boys; they make the mine pumping engine do the flooding for them."

At Houghton, by 1866 a park held a very large rink, measuring 214 by 160 feet. Such rinks were commercial ventures. Skaters bought season tickets or individual admissions to special events. Skating carnivals or masquerades mimicked masquerade balls. J. N. Scott had a "pleasant evening" in January 1869, when he dressed up as a Turk and took his wife, Annie, skating. Rinks booked bands to play at their ice carnivals and offered prizes for costumes or skating skill. By 1870, a Hancock merchant offered sharpening for all skates, "from the dandy skate, with gilded trappings, to the common fellow that is strapped." Meanwhile, a second merchant offered "elegant and gorgeous skating suits for young ladies" that "are admired by all who have seen them."[42]

By the 1860s, contests, sports, and gambling became important parts of life on the Keweenaw. If young ladies attired in skating suits anchored one end of the sporting spectrum, the other extreme end belonged to male combatants, going head to head. In what may have been the first bare-knuckles prizefight on the Keweenaw, John King and Ben Dean, for a $100 prize, pounded each other for thirty-three rounds—outside—in January 1866. Surely, the sweet science of boxing had rarely been taken up in a more unlikely setting:

> The fight took place at Edwards' meadow, on the Eagle River road, about eight miles from Portage Lake. At an early hour in the morning the crowd, in sleighs and on foot, started for the selected ground, and at nine o'clock, about twenty teams and two hundred spectators, blocked the road and crowded . . . close by the spot where the ring was formed. The snow had been shoveled away and the grass coated with saw-dust for about twenty feet for the inner ring.[43]

This prize fight, according to the *Mining Gazette*, "pleased the English but sickened the American spectators." Another English—or, especially, Cornish—favorite was wrestling, which was far more common than boxing on Lake Superior. Halls and saloons regularly offered Cornish wrestling matches, with monetary prizes and even championship belts going to the winners. While the Cornish took their wrestling seriously, the Americans in residence sometimes took a jaundiced view of the sport. The *Mining Gazette* remained skeptical of one promoter's claim that his was "to be a genuine wrestle, without humbug." And the Yankee teacher at the Cliff mine wrote disparagingly of the wrestling scene:

I witnessed a few tumbles . . . for a prize of thirty dollars. There was a crowd of men and women . . . also several barrels of ale on the ground. The wrestlers took off their shirts and put on a very loose jacket made of bagging tied with cord up & down in front. It was then a rough and tumble game, twisting each other in all shapes. Most of them were full of 'Beer,' swearing, fighting. . . . I never witnessed such a tight, rough set of men in my life.[44]

Other sports and games, less violent or brutal, did not cleave fans and detractors into opposite camps. Baseball, the first team sport played on Superior, proved a popular game enjoyed by many of different ethnic backgrounds. This up-and-coming sport in the late 1860s and 1870s provided players with exercise; spectators with entertainment; and the teams' sponsoring villages with a sense of indentity and pride.

Late in April 1864, Henry Hobart noted in his journal: "The little hillock just below the schoolhouse is bare and the boys are enjoying a game of ball." By late in the decade, many local communities had formed baseball clubs. They cleared fields of boulders and other debris; some clubs even fenced them. They scheduled practices and held fund-raising balls so they could get new uniforms. By 1870, the Houghton Baseball Club, the First National [Bank] Baseball Club of Hancock, and the German Socks of Calumet regularly played each other. The *Portage Lake Mining Gazette* duly reported game results (such as the 36-to-35 squeaker, Houghton over Hancock) and, early on, faulted some "chronic 'muffers' " who were "too easily excited, and dropped too many balls." The paper also faulted early spectators who, perhaps because they had bets down on the game, annoyed both umpire and players "by shouting decisions, which the umpire alone has the right to make."[45]

After 1870, when Hancock played Calumet on the Fourth of July, baseball became a traditional part of that holiday. By 1881, when Houghton and Calumet played an Independence Day doubleheader (one game in each village), a thousand spectators might attend. And it wasn't just men, or the residents of bigger villages, who picked up or followed the game. Lucena Brockway recorded in her diary of July 4, 1874, that "all our folks went to Eagle River to see Copper Harbor boys & Phoenix boys play Base Ball—Phoenix boys beat. In the afternoon Copper Harbor boys play with Cliff boys—the latter beat." A few weeks later, it was baseball again: "Today all have gone to Calumet to play Base Ball with the Calumet Club and got beaten, 4 white washes [scoreless innings] on each side, and Keeweenaws had scored 13 and Calumets 18." The sports team, affiliated with one particular village, had become a rooted part of local culture.[46]

There were other competitions, too. The winners of target-shooting matches returned home with turkeys or geese or, in one instance, a tame deer as the prize. Horsemen staged match races that excited much wagering. The year 1867 witnessed a couple of interesting two-horse contests. One, for a $100 purse, pitted two animals running from Hancock to Eagle River and back; the other, run in winter for two hundred dollars a side, took place on the ice and snow of Portage Lake.[47]

Within the larger villages, gaming houses that offered billiards, bowling, and shuffleboard stood among the storefronts. Saloons and other establishments encouraged card playing, and for a while the bingolike game of keno was all the rage. By the mid-1860s, at least one community—Houghton—had passed village ordinances making it an offense to bowl at any time on Sunday, and from midnight to six in the morning on all other days. Houghton also set fines for keeping a disorderly gaming house where frequenters played for money or gambled. Over the winter of 1869, Hancock native J. N. Scott found himself too engaged in such activities. Scott was a devoted family man with a "dear wife and boy," whom he described as his "jewels." On January 27 he wrote in his diary, "Swore off today . . . on billiards for one month." About a week later, he did it again: "Swore off today with Mr. Gurrin until May 1st on Billiards & Card playing in Saloons."[48]

Scott thought his personal game playing and wagering had gotten out of hand. In the late 1860s, the *Mining Gazette* thought the same was true of society at large: betting had "run wild." Experienced gambling men had said of a recent Tuesday spiced with billiards and horse racing:

> never in their life have they seen such wild, reckless betting as was indulged in at the race . . . and the billiard matches. . . . Thousands of dollars changed hands on that day alone. Two match games of billiards were played for twenty-five dollars a side, while the side bets on each game amounted to from one to two thousand dollars, several of one hundred dollars being made, while ten dollar bills were flying around like leaves in autumn. Everybody seemed crazy to bet something; what, they did not seem to care; all they wanted was an opportunity to show their nerve. Of course, large quantities of the ardent were imbibed.[49]

In this emerging society on Lake Superior, ardent spirits showed up early and played an important, albeit controversial and sometimes disruptive, role in the social life of villages. Pioneers incorporated drinking into all sorts of activities, even those conducted on the Sabbath. Joseph Rawlings, a master mechanic at the Cliff mine, remembered that in the 1860s, "Sundays were truly days of rest, and the churches were well attended." Everybody "had to be 'as good as they knew how,' or woe to the transgressor; for the 'good people' were very 'goody,' 'goody.' "[50] But Rawlings's description of a straight-laced, pious Sabbath contrasted sharply with life as recorded by others. John Forster described the "festive character of Sunday": "The saloons are all wide open on that sacred day and well patronized. . . . Bands of music and parades of firemen and guilds enliven the morning hour as the pious are wending their way to church. The sound of church bells is drowned in the blare of the trombone."[51]

Imbibing alcohol became commonplace in conjunction with sports and games, holidays, elections, paydays, and long winters infected with cabin fever. Early stores carried alcohol; several breweries soon dotted the local landscape; hotel bars, main-street saloons, and scrub taverns opened. Mine bosses, temperance societies, religious leaders, and even military men at Fort Wilkins tried to slow or halt the consumption of alcohol, but with modest success. While temperance orators preached to the converted, heavy drinkers put away as much as they wanted.

In 1834, Congress passed legislation permitting military commanders to regulate trade in Indian territories. They could even banish ardent spirits, if necessary, to preserve order. In 1845, Capt. R. E. Clary at Copper Harbor acted under this law, as he informed General George Gibson:

> No sooner had this command reached the site destined for its future garrison than numbers of that base and unprincipled class who prey upon our frontier post established themselves in our immediate neighborhood; and would have most seriously interferred with our duties and labors, inundating the Camp with the Whiskey which they were provided with, had I not in self defense . . . seized and destroyed some 250 gallons; thereby obtaining temporary alleviation from the evil.[52]

The U.S. Army was not alone in worrying about alcohol on the frontier; the mining companies worried, too, and banned the sale of intoxicants on the property.[53] But no ban on alcohol could last or be effective, and early stores on the margins of the mines stocked up on alcoholic beverages.

In 1849–50, John Senter's store in Eagle River peddled several brandies and wines, sherry, champagne, whiskey, gin, rum, and "Jamaican spirits." Other stores added ale, beer, schnapps, bourbon, and rye. Typically, they sold some "best" or "premium" brandies or whiskeys, along with lesser-priced varieties, and they also sold in several different containers and quantities. Whiskey, for instance, could be purchased in pints, gallon jugs, kegs, and barrels. An exception to this brisk booze trade was the company-owned and-operated store at the Minesota mine, which traded very rarely in brandy, wine, and rum. The Minesota Mining Company did not encourage inebriation among its working men, and its store seems to have reserved alcohol sales for managers or for "medicinal" purposes.

The early stores sold more liquor and wine than beer and ale, but the latter were soon made available by local breweries. Frank Knivel brewed the first commercial beer on the Keweenaw at Eagle River in 1855. The Union Brewery opened in Houghton in 1857, and two years later the A. Hass Brewery joined it. By 1870, seven breweries operated on the Keweenaw and produced a total of seven thousand barrels of beer per year. In 1871 Joseph Bosch & Co. started up at Lake Linden and in short order shipped four thousand barrels annually.[54]

Retail establishments dispensing alcohol by the drink also quickly went into business, not at the company-controlled mine locations but in neighboring commercial villages. In the early years—and, in fact, all the way through the mid-1870s—these bars and saloons operated in a freewheeling, unregulated market. Michigan's state constitution specifically barred its legislature from passing any liquor licensing acts, so saloons peddled alcohol when they wanted, to whom they wanted, and paid no liquor taxes.[55] In this unrestricted environment, many a house served part-time as a tavern. When occupants wanted to announce that they were open for business, they ran a flag or banner up a pole, as noted by an author for *Harper's* magazine in 1853:

> As I approached the village of Eagle River, which consists of some 20 or 30 houses, I was much struck . . . with the great number of poles which rise up everywhere. . . . Almost every house on top of the hill appeared to be provided with one of these appendages, to which was also attached a cord, as if for running up a flag. It was soon shown that these houses were "groceries," a sort of scrub-tavern quite common in the western world, where very cheap and very bad liquor is sold to the miners. . . . Each one has its flag-staff from which on particular occasions, as Sunday, they hoist their respective colors, like ships of different nations. The Eagle River House where I stop, I soon perceived has the tallest and most conspicuous of this sort of sign in the place, indicating that it is a sort of man-of-war in the business.[56]

Some scrub taverns stood alongside the Keweenaw's primitive roads and trails. They served as halfway stops between distant settlements, and many a weary traveler rejoiced at finding a crude cabin in the woods, banked high with snow, warmed by a wood fire, where a man and his wife offered drink, food, and roof overhead. Within the larger commercial villages, the scrub taverns competed with fancier, full-time, main-street saloons opened to tap the workers' trade. By the mid-1860s, Eagle River boasted three such saloons, Houghton five, and Hancock six.[57] The just-developing village of Calumet soon saw a proliferation of bars, too. Scrub taverns, saloons, hotels and halls, breweries, and stores made alcohol readily available to anyone who wanted it. While a growing number of "goody-goody" templars condemned alcohol's use altogether, most settlers saw no harm in the pleasantries of tipping a few now and again. The trouble was, some drank too much and too often, abusing themselves and those around them. If social drinking made life on the frontier more pleasant, excessive drinking made it more woeful. Heavy drinking contributed to much of the mayhem and violence found in the streets and homes of the Keweenaw during the first quarter century of settlement.

SHATTERED HOPES AND
BROKEN PROSPECTS

Lunatics, Larcenists, and Lives of Woe

Has not Keweenaw a stock of tales waiting to be worked over . . . ? Slip
up alongside of some old settler and gain his confidence. Read in the empty
stare of vacant houses the story of shattered hopes and broken prospects,
of life, of death, of love, of courtship, of friendship, of marriage, of happy
homes and sacred memories. Go among the tombs, the silent resting places
of the dead; read there the story of agony and mourning.

J. A. Ten Broeck,
"Old Keweenaw," 1906

Those who joined the ranks of the earliest pioneers on Lake Superior risked
life, limb, and security. At first, "beyond the boundaries appointed for the
residence of man," virtually no social safety net existed to catch the victims
of misfortune. The tales of woe coming from the 1840s and early 1850s were
particularly poignant, because sufferers endured so much while so *alone* in the
wilderness.

The coming of more settlers, the pushing away of the wilderness, and the
planting of villages did not bring an end to stories of agony and mourning.
These stories in fact multiplied as the years passed and more men, women,
and children took up lives on the Keweenaw or Isle Royale. It was axiomatic:
the more people lived there, the more people were exposed to myriad sources
of harm: physical, mental, social, and economic. But one thing was quite different: later settlers, when beset with troubles, weren't so alone anymore.

This new industrial society, as it matured, knitted together means of coping
with misfortune. It offered measures of protection and restoration to individuals
and families jeopardized by all sorts of problems. These measures ran the
gamut from simple acts of kindness, tendered from neighbor to neighbor; to
charitable assistance provided by mutual aid societies, mining companies, and
other groups; to government programs at the local and state level.

Diverse persons needed help: Johnny Butler, a "poor little blind boy";
Robert Ellis, a blinded mine worker; and Mary Ann Holland, a deaf-mute. At

the Copper Falls mine, a wife and "five pretty children" watched George Wilbury, once a skilled master mechanic, lie on his bed "more helpless than an infant," because falling machinery had crushed his back and wasted his legs. At the Albany and Boston mine, a woman with six children coped with her disabled man, who had been "blown up in the mine" but not quite killed. At Portage Lake, Samuel Thompson, an otherwise likable fellow, suddenly went daft while serving as wheelsman on a ferryboat. After bellowing out temperance lectures, he jumped overboard, swam ashore, and ran to his boardinghouse and hid. Discovered, he wildly tore his clothes to shreds.[1]

In the northern part of the copper range, "Widow" Toy, "Widow" Cole, and "Widow" Shea were too poor to get by—as were four other women with a total of thirteen children, whose husbands had abandoned them. At the Huron mine, the family of a man "out of work for a long time" subsisted almost wholly on potatoes. In Houghton, a man with a weakness for gambling deserted his wife and four children, leaving them destitute. The wife joined a sizable cadre of poor women at Portage Lake who were widowed, abandoned, or single and too ill to work.[2]

Afflicted men, women, and children who'd fallen on hard times on the mining frontier *through no fault of their own* wrung sympathy from family, friends, bosses, public officials, and the press. They merited compassion and help, which others delivered in various amounts and ways. Meanwhile, other individuals in trouble earned little for themselves except wrath, disdain, derision, or punishment: able-bodied beggars, men and women, who shirked paying jobs; drunks, some who just sat in a stupor, some who raged at others; and thugs, thieves, and other criminals who preyed on fellow citizens. Keweenaw society, as it became more populated, dealt with more of these misfits, too.

Frontier society put a premium on young, vigorous, and strong individuals. But society did not include just colorful voyageurs, skilled immigrant miners from Cornwall and Germany, woodsmen from French-speaking Canada, and merchants and managers from New England and New York. It did not include just civil, hard-working, and self-sufficient men and women. As frontier society evolved, it also included the blind, the deaf, and individuals with paralyzed or missing limbs. It included the chronically ill, including mentally ill or deficient persons, deemed insane or idiotic. It numbered among its ranks poor widows, frail men, and orphans. Society included sixteen-year-old prostitutes, youthful street bullies, and occasional thieves, as well as habitual drunks and hardened criminals.

In the mindset of the times, some of these troubled or troublesome people deserved sympathy and charity; some needed saving and a severe scolding; and some needed a sheriff's cell. But they all *needed* something, and that's what linked them. They were all seen as living other than "ordinary" or "normal" lives. They either couldn't or wouldn't support themselves at honest work. At midcentury on the Keweenaw and elsewhere in Michigan, there was a growing sense that society had to do more with these individuals. That might mean putting them in a special home, school, or reformatory. It might mean sending them to a poorhouse or jail. If all else failed, it might mean burying them at public expense in a no-frills pauper's coffin.

Among the early pioneers on Lake Superior, John Forster was one of the keenest observers. In his published reminiscences, Forster portrayed life on this northern frontier as being less wide-open and rough-and-tumble than life on more notorious western frontiers: "The mining classes in my judgment are very quiet and law abiding, considering their occupation and surroundings. There is a good deal of the freedom of the frontier, and, although a world of beer is drank, the amount of drunkenness and crime is much less than one would expect to find."[3]

Forster was right, to a point. The Lake Superior copper district had the reputation of being home to "happy peoples" who steadfastly conducted their lives without the lawlessness, violence, labor strikes, and debauchery attributed to other frontiers and mine camps.[4] They lived, many claimed, in remarkable harmony in their new industrial society. But this was still a long way from utopia, and Lake Superior contended with its share of criminals and malcontents.

At the start, the U.S. Army at Fort Wilkins represented law, order, and authority on the frontier. The garrison had a bit of a mollifying influence on pioneer behavior, but not for long. When the army abandoned the fort in the mid-1840s after a short occupation, the retreat largely removed the federal government from the scene. Local and state government, as well, had hardly any toehold on the Keweenaw for the first decade or so of settlement. Pioneers lived virtually free of government in the many small mine locations. In this situation, not surprisingly, the mining companies filled the breech. Just as they stepped up to build needed public works when government wasn't there to do it, they stepped up to police society when small communities lacked constables, courts, and jails.

In 1853, *Mining Magazine* noted that in the absence of ordinances or laws, "the several companies enforce such rules as they deem necessary for the punishment of disorder, drunkenness, violence, etc." In making their rules, the companies started with a ban on alcohol: "No ardent spirits or other intoxicating liquors are sold to the miners, nor allowed to be sold upon the premises of the companies." The companies, like the temperance groups soon to follow, closely associated liquor with crime and mayhem, and they based this association not on social theory but on experience. The ban on ardent spirits was "brought about by sheer necessity, as their use among large bodies of wild and ignorant men, was found to lead to constant riots, rendering the condition of the officers and their families disagreeable, and at times precarious."[5]

Mine bosses hoping to keep the peace in their little industrial fiefdoms sometimes sat as judge and jury. They punished drunken, disorderly, or violent men by firing them and putting them off the property, or by withholding a fine or damages from their pay. Some potential transgressors—men who showed "a disposition to disorderly behavior"—actually *prepaid* their fines for unseemly acts. They posted a kind of bond with their employer when first hired. If they caused trouble, they lost their money; if they hewed to "good conduct," they got it back.[6]

Companies also took measures to reduce social friction over money matters and keep men from walking away from indebtness at one location and going to work at another mine down the road. On monthly settlement day, men collected their net earnings, not their gross. Money had already been taken out. On behalf of third parties—sometimes dozens of them—companies regularly garnisheed wages in order to pay employees' boarding charges and store bills throughout the community.[7]

Michigan started establishing county governments on the Keweenaw in 1845. It first formed Houghton County, which initially included the northern two-thirds of the peninsula. Next, in 1846, the state organized Ontonagon County, comprising the Keweenaw's southern base. In 1861, Michigan separated the tip of the Keweenaw from Houghton County, linked it governmentally with Isle Royale, and formed Keweenaw County. By the Civil War era, then, the Keweenaw had three county seats serving as centers of government and legal matters: Ontonagon in Ontonagon County; Houghton in Houghton County; and Eagle River in Keweenaw County. The Keweenaw Peninsula also gained resident judges. (Until 1865, itinerant judges from lower Michigan, who only summered on Lake Superior, had wielded courtroom gavels.)[8] Besides getting county seats, courts, and judges, the maturing society on the Keweenaw erected other symbols of civilization: county jails.

In 1861, Houghton County erected its two-story, thiry-by-fifty-foot, wood-frame jail, containing sixteen cells for men and four for women. All the cells (formed not of iron bars but of two-by-six lumber planks) measured five by eight feet. Ontonagon built a two-story log jail with two twelve-by-fourteen-foot planked cells and no separate provisions for women. Keweenaw, the smallest of the three counties, made do with two small, wooden cells, only six feet by eight feet, framed into a third story over a boardinghouse and saloon.

The counties surely did not coddle their prisoners. In 1873, Houghton County's supervisors authorized their sheriff to "employ all persons sentenced to the County Jail at hard labor." That same year, Michigan's state commissioners of "Charitable, Penal, Pauper, and Reformatory Institutions" reported that "the general appearance of the [Houghton County] jail as to cleanliness was good, but the cells were somewhat infested with vermin, and the ventilation was bad. There was no bathing facilities for the prisoners." A year later, the jail's rather meager inventory listed one and a half dozen tin cups, ten tin dishes, four new mattresses, fourteen old mattresses, five straw pillows, and fifteen and a half old blankets.[9]

The majority of the men incarcerated in the Houghton County jail mirrored the male population at large: they were young (in their twenties and thirties), mostly single, and mostly foreign-born. Only a few were charged with such crimes as fraud, embezzlement, forgery, or, by the mid-1870s, with violating state liquor or state hunting and fishing laws. A few went to jail for the likes of indecent exposure or cruelty to animals, while more were arrested for larceny or "keeping a house of ill-fame."

Most male arrests, however, involved liquor or violence, or some combination of the two.[10] They often resulted from street or saloon fisticuffs or brawls involving different ethnic groups, or they followed from domestic or family disputes. Without doubt, the excessive consumption of alcohol contributed to much of the rage and violence found in frontier streets and homes.

Teacher Henry Hobart was hardly an unbiased observer of the effects of alcohol on life in and around the Cliff mine. He was a goody-goody teetotaler and strong supporter of temperance, as well as a Yankee elitist who believed that the Irish, Cornish, and other immigrants were "born with a natural love for the beer and whiskey." Still, other more moderate supporters of civility on Lake Superior often agreed with Hobart's observations. He believed that overindulgent sots ruined all paydays by returning from "some beer shop . . . beastly drunk." They spoiled the Fourth of July and Christmas with their carousing, and when liberally plied with "a drop of the critter" by those seeking votes at election time, they turned a celebration of American democracy into an intemperate circus. Hobart noted, "Such fights, betting, bragging, dancing, working for votes *I never saw.*"[11]

Not until 1875 did the Michigan senate and house pass a resolution to amend the state constitution to allow for liquor licensing and control. Citizens ratified that amendment in the general election of 1876, and in 1877 the Michigan legislature passed laws that required licenses and operating bonds, imposed special taxes, restricted the sale of alcohol to minors, closed bars on Sundays and election days, and limited their hours on weekdays.[12] Long before these statewide restrictions were enacted, many local initiatives had pressed for the control or abolition of alcohol on the Keweenaw.

These local attempts started in the 1840s when the Army confiscated whiskey at Copper Harbor and the early companies banned the sale of alcohol at their mine locations. A public temperance movement started at least as early as 1857, when a crusade to abolish liquor played for ten days in Ontonagon.

In 1862 a High Moral Reform Society was organized in Houghton, and one of that village's early ordinances stated, "No person shall appear in the streets in a state of intoxication."[13] In the 1860s temperance lectures abounded and Good Templars established lodges at the Cliff, Central, and Copper Falls mines. Some had affiliated juvenile temperance societies for children. At Hancock, the Portage Lake Lodge of the Grand Templars, just a year after being organized in 1863, boasted 165 members and erected a three-story hall "to the cause of temperance and good order in this community."[14] At the same time, Keweenaw teetotalers pushed for greater enforcement of a recent federal act forbidding the sale of spiritous liquors to Native Americans, who were sometimes reported as walking Ontonagon or Houghton streets in an intoxicated state.[15]

Measures to discourage or control the use of alcohol steered some, for whom respectability and civility counted, down the path of sobriety and righteousness. But during the Civil War era, at the same time that the goody-goodies formed temperance groups, rowdies in the bars and streets of Houghton and Hancock created "a veritable pandemonium, where all the bad passions of embruted and lawless human nature had full swing."[16]

Social relations became decidedly less civil during the Civil War, and the orderly advance of an industrial society on Lake Superior seemed not only to stop in its tracks, but also to retreat. "Insubordination against legitimate authority became the rule," and the "steady citizens and mine managers had a hard time of it." The *Portage Lake Mining Gazette* complained that its office was being surrounded by saloons. "God defend us!," the paper wrote. "We will either have to move our office or hear the cry of drunkards on all sides." The paper regularly reported on drunken street brawls, often involving the Cornish and Irish, groups always described as having little or no regard for one another. "They were inveterate enemies" whose "feuds were endless." Drinking led to belligerence and fights, which resulted in eyes being shot out, faces "pounded almost to a jelly," stab wounds, stonings, and once in a while, death. Most brawlers were men, but sometimes the women joined in.[17]

On December 27, 1862, the *Mining Gazette* chronicled a Christmas week of mayhem on Portage Lake. On Monday, a bunch of Cornish and Irish had gotten into it. On Wednesday a congregation of the Sullivan clan had an all-in-the-family brawl, which left two men and one woman badly injured. Then, on Friday,

> there were several rows on both sides of the Lake, and six or eight men pretty badly used up. On this side [in Houghton], one man was shot through the hand and thigh, and is in a critical condition. Several others had their heads pretty badly bruised and cut up. At Hancock, a Scotchman, named McDonald, was stabbed in three or four places, his bowels protruding from one of the wounds. Others were pounded and maltreated in a shameful manner.

The excessive use of alcohol that prompted street violence also resulted in domestic violence. At the Cliff mine, Henry Hobart did not find wife-beating at all uncommon, especially at times when men predictably got drunk, such as when celebrating the reopening of navigation. A celebration meant drinking more than usual, and that was attended "by many sad and disgusting scenes": "I have seen them abuse their wives and kick them & beat them, pursue them from one place to another until they would hide in some house until the man was no longer drunk. I can witness such scenes from my window now and then. To see these poor women cry and lament their fate is very sad indeed."[18]

Hobart observed Clifton's Richard and Annie Carter—both described as drunks—torment each other. Hobart figured the well-educated Mrs. Carter was from "a very high family in Ireland," and he guessed she may have fled to America in shame over a youthful indiscretion and an out-of-wedlock child. At any rate, in America she had married beneath her station (or so Hobart thought) by wedding Richard, an uneducated, hard-drinking carpenter. Annie ended up drinking heavily, too. When on a week-long bender, she used "the most obscene and vulgar language" and was "the nastiest thing that can be found." But in truth, the husband was even nastier. When he came home "beastly drunk," he smashed things up and chased his wife away. Once they tangled in the street as they came home from drinking together: "He commenced abusing her and soon struck & caught hold of her, tearing her dress & pulling out her hair."[19]

Hobart recorded how bad life was for Annie Carter in 1863, but at least she lived out the year. Another unnamed woman, from the nearby Phoenix mine, didn't survive December's cold. The *Mining Gazette* reported that "she and her husband were in the habit of drinking pretty freely, and it is supposed they had . . . a spree and a quarrel, and she was turned out doors by the stronger brute." She was later found "lying against a stump with her babe in her arms, both frozen stiff." Hobart's diary recorded the same incident in more passionate terms:

> A drunken husband drove his wife outdoors at midnight with a little boy at the Phoenix mine. The mother and child were without clothing and were found the next morning frozen in the cold snow a few rods from the house. . . . How that little boy must have felt taken from a warm bed out into the cold to be frozen to death on the body of his mother. This is one of the results of drinking.[20]

The brute at the Phoenix mine in Keweenaw County unfortunately escaped charges in the death of his wife and son. But down in Houghton County, during the era of Civil War mayhem the sheriff jailed record numbers of men in an attempt to maintain law and order. The year 1863, in particular, was a banner one for arrests. Houghton County hauled 208 persons off to jail, about five times its annual average. It charged 94 with drunk and disorderly conduct;

40 with drunkenness; 44 with assault and battery; and 10 with assault with intent to kill. These four charges alone accounted for 90 percent of all arrests. By comparison, in 1875, a more typical year, Houghton County held only 48 men and women in its lockup. Of the 30 men whose alleged offenses are known, 10 were charged with drunk and disorderly conduct, 5 with assault and battery, and 3 with murder. One to 3 men each were charged with the remaining offenses of rape, larceny, fraud, forgery, slander, and running a brothel.[21]

While men fairly regularly pummeled one another with their fists, they did not often arm themselves with deadly weapons to commit assaults or murders. A rare and notorious instance of premeditated murder with a firearm occurred at a miner's home in Clifton in 1862. Mr. and Mrs. Harris took in male boarders, including Mr. Richards, a blacksmith. Besides sharing a roof, Mrs. Harris and Mr. Richards shared one another; they could not resist the temptation of an adulterous tryst. Word of their liaison got out, and Mr. Harris booted his wife's "seducer" from the house. But Mr. Richards kept coming back to visit Mrs. Harris when Mr. Harris worked the night shift. Word of this got out, too, as did news of the brazen couple's daytime sleigh rides.

Mr. Harris set a trap for the pair. He hid his shotgun under the inside stairs. An evening or two later, he pretended to go off to work, but doubled back to the house and hid beneath it. When he heard amorous conversation, he burst into the house to confront the lovers. He shot Mr. Richards in the chest with one blast and then sank an axe into his face, splitting it open from forehead down to mouth. Other boarders rushed to restrain him and kept him from killing his wife. A year later, Mr. Harris was still sitting in the Keweenaw County jail, waiting for the wheels of justice slowly to turn. His much faster wife, meanwhile, was back to sharing her bed with yet another man.[22]

The common practice of accepting male boarders into family households almost surely increased the incidence of adultery in this society, but adultery was a rarely charged crime. In 1870, the court did find Napoleon Gautier and Juliene Parquette guilty of adultery. He was sentenced to one year in the state prison at Jackson; she received *two years* at the House of Correction for women in Detroit.[23]

Child molestation and rape were two other infrequently prosecuted crimes. In 1863, a man was charged with "carnally knowing a child," and in 1870 the *Portage Lake Mining Gazette* reported the arrest of "Old Monkey Joe," a peddlar, "who attempted to outrage the little girl" at the Quincy mine. In the 1860s and 1870s, Houghton County tried at most about three rape cases per year, which the press sometimes reported with heated prose:

A MAN ACCUSED OF COMMITTING A VERY HEINOUS CRIME ON A WOMAN. . . . The lovers of sensational reports were electrified, on Wednesday last, by flying rumors that a rape had been committed on or near the village of Houghton. . . . Lapoint suddenly seized his victim, threw her violently upon the ground, and stifling her cries by forcing his ruffian hand into her mouth, accomplished his diabolical purpose.[24]

Diaries and newspaper accounts make it clear that domestic violence—men battering women—was not uncommon. Many in this society, if they didn't outright condone it, seemed to tolerate the idea of a man using an open hand, fist, whip, or harness to "straighten out" a woman. Lucena Brockway watched an Irishman box a woman in the street. Henry Hobart, out for a pleasant day-trip one Sunday, stumbled on a noisy altercation between husband and wife that had drawn a crowd of gawkers. The husband had caught his wife out walking with another man, her presumed lover. The suitor ran off, "taking leg bail," leaving the wife to cope with her angry mate. Now the woman was having an apparent fit—ranting, raving, and rolling in the dirt—while her husband tried to force her to her feet to walk home. Finally, "she was thrown into our wagon and taken home. The next morning the husband applied the horse whip which soon cured the fit." Hobart personally condemned such behavior and said, "Shame on such families," but most men went unpunished for it.[25]

At the Houghton County jail, women made up maybe 10 percent of the inmates. Like their male counterparts, they usually ranged in age from their late teens through their thirties, and they were most commonly charged with drunk and disorderly conduct. Far fewer showed arrests for assault, but the female combatant—whether flailing her husband to drive him out of a bar, or tagging a rival woman—was not unheard-of. In fact, society seemed to have a bit of sport with females who resorted to fisticuffs, portraying them as saucy characters. In 1867, the *Portage Lake Mining Gazette* reported with some humor and admiration the conviction of Ellen Driscoll, who had been charged with assualt and battery on Mrs. McEvoy. McEvoy had "the most pugnacious appearance of the two, for she is muscular, homely and heavy." Ellen Driscoll, on the other hand, "has not the appearance of a good fighting woman, being delicately formed, and rather comely." But it was the pretty one who wiped up the floor with Mrs. McEvoy, "winding up the last round by taking a mouthful out of her fat purple arm." For her victory, Ellen Driscoll won some jail time and a $30 fine.[26]

The sheriff locked up a woman or two a year for larceny, and about once a decade, maybe after an infant's body had been found in a lake, the court charged a woman with infanticide. Periodically the sheriff marched two or three women to jail, charging them with prostitution or with keeping a house of ill fame. (Sometimes husband and wife went to jail together for running a brothel.) But prostitutes in Houghton County did not live under the threat of constant or repeated arrests, as long as they went about their business without raising a ruckus. Only infrequently did local officials go on a cleanup campaign and round up local prostitutes, and when they did, they often charged them with disorderly conduct, not selling sex.[27]

Without any doubt, Keweenaw society always included more paupers than prisoners. For many on the mining frontier, financial security was an elusive dream. The descent into poverty could be swift for members of the working class with scant savings, who lived from payday to payday. If a mine closing, illness, or accident befell a breadwinner, economic calamity quickly followed unless some helping hand reached out.

That helping hand often belonged to an individual, perhaps a coworker, friend, or relative, who tendered aid in the face of need. A butcher in Houghton, encountering an unemployed family man out of food and money, filled the man's eyes with appreciative tears by giving him salt and meat enough to last a week. One Christmas, Lucena Brockway traveled throughout her village taking food and clothes "to poor children." On a February day she wrote in her diary, "Was cold & stormy all day and I went about doing good."[28]

Sometimes, concerned groups orchestrated acts of charity. Lucena Brockway made baked goods for a church benefit to raise funds for the needy. At Hancock, those not hurting for money danced for those who were. They held a Poor Fund Ball and "every dollar spent there is a fount of blessing to the needy poor." During the Civil War, bands played benefit concerts, with proceeds going to "suffering soldiers," and women formed a Portage Lake Aid Society, which at one of its first parties raised $130 for "sick and wounded soldiers." At the Copper Falls mine, managers and workers together gave considerable help to the paralyzed mechanic George Wilbury, his "nearly broken down wife," and their five children. They tended to them on site, then raised money to transport the entire family back to Buffalo, where relatives assumed the family's care.[29]

The uncertainties, risks, and physical demands of the mining industry caused much financial hardship. Mines closed or slowed, throwing all or many men out of work. Rock cascaded down from the hanging wall over workers' heads, or black powder detonated too early, killing, crippling, or wounding men and, in an instant, jeopardizing families. Some men grew too old, ill, or frail to hack the hard work anymore and lost their traditional means of earning a living. Prior to 1875, these various victims of circumstance struggled because they lived in an era when benefits were meager and welfare capitalism and government social programs were just getting started.

By the 1850s, mining companies provided employees with company doctors, medicines, and hospitalization at low cost. But working-class families, through their government or employer, had no unemployment compensation, no compensation for injuries or disabilities that temporarily or permanently kept breadwinners from work, no death benefits to survivors, and no retirement plans or pensions. Individual mining companies—those that survived themselves in this risky business—eschewed catering to the needs of all unfortunates. Often, however, they patched together a paternalistic social safety net and offered succor, if not to all, then at least to some.

By the 1860s, the mining companies staunchly supported patriarchy. These male-run organizations wholeheartedly embraced the view that a father properly headed his family and served as its chief provider. Fulfilling the husband-father-worker-provider role gave a man dignity and self-esteem.

In accordance with patriarchy, mine managers gave preference in employment and housing to family men, and in economic hard times companies first laid off or fired single workers. If a loyal company man grew too frail or disabled to perform his normal, arduous job—swinging a sledgehammer or putting up timbers—a mine manager might protect his provider's role by giving him an easier job, something like underground watchman or keeper of a dryhouse. If a man couldn't even do that, a company might offer preferential employment to his oldest son, letting the boy serve as a surrogate for his father, who would work if he could.

Companies did not offer employment to the needy wives or daughters of disabled or deceased workers; that did not square with patriarchy. If a dead miner's widow already occupied a company house, a charitable mine manager might let her stay there rent-free for maybe a year. She could stay even longer, perhaps, if she had boys old enough to go to work, or if she agreed to take in male workers as boarders. In addition, the company might take up a collection for her destitute family, give her an enlarged garden plot, and deliver free or cheap wood to her door for heating and cooking. But that was about it. A company always limited its largesse and never obligated itself to provide perpetual care.

The managers who ran the mines were not flinty-hearted, uncaring men who wrung all the work they could from a family and then sent them packing. Yet at the same time, they were discriminatory and uneasy caregivers. They decided what alms they would give and who would get them. So some workers received more humane treatment than others. And the mine managers were uneasy when reaching out to help because they didn't want their villages to become refuges for the afflicted and because their charitable acts, however needed and appropriate, seemed somehow to undercut the work ethic and the values of self-reliance and independence. As William Daniell, agent of the Osceola mine, admitted in the 1870s, a man in charge of a mine always felt relieved when one of his troubled, poor families got up and left.[30]

To obtain a greater measure of personal and family security, many settlers wisely chose not to be too independent or self-reliant. They partook of communal life and become joiners. Men and women joined churches, which provided not only worship but also close associations with others living similar lives, who might be counted on for care and assistance in times of need. Many men also joined fraternal organizations. Two of them, the Independent Order of Odd Fellows and the Free and Accepted Masons, drew their members from the ranks of Americans and Englishmen. Between 1859 and 1870, the Odd Fellows formed lodges in at least seven Keweenaw villages, while the Masons established themselves in at least three.[31]

In the early 1860s, Henry Hobart was a joiner. He belonged to both the Odd Fellows and the Independent Order of Good Templars. His Odd Fellows lodge held regular meetings every Saturday evening. Hobart described the IOOF's principles as "Truth, Love and Friendship" and its purpose, or "good object," as the "assistance of brothers in want and sickness." The main purpose of his Good Templars lodge was to "prevent the use of any liquors," but the Templars, too, served another important social function:

> as a Society their efforts extend to deeds of charity. Every member of the order is bound to assist another in distress, to extend the hand of sympathy, etc. I have a case in point. Our worthy Brother William Osborne is sick. He is supplied with watchers and all he wants by the Good Templars of this place. The committee visit him and he has whatever he wants. If I were in a strange land and in trouble, I should make myself known as a Templar and any Brothers present are bound by the most solemn ties to render me assistance. It is a noble order and has a noble object.[32]

Hobart was one of the Templars who sat alongside the sickbed of Brother William Osborne. When Osborne died, he sat with the corpse. When Osborne was buried, he served as a pallbearer. True to the last to their "brother," both the Odd Fellows and the Good Templars walked in procession to Osborne's grave at the burying ground at Eagle River.

In the 1850s and 1860s, Germans at Rockland, near the Minesota mine, organized a Germania Society, while their fellow countrymen at Hancock established a lodge of the Order of Hermann's Sons and a German Benevolent Society. In the 1870s, German-speaking men organized the Portage Lake Laborers Benevolent Society and a St. Joseph's Society, for Catholics. Britishers could join the likes of the St. George Society of Calumet, while Hancock's Irish formed a St. Patrick's Society. In Houghton County, the "sons of auld Scotia" could join the St. Andrew's Society, which listed charity as its "first and most important object." Such ethnic associations grew only more numerous and diverse over time. In 1875, Calumet became home to two new benevolent societies—one formed by Polish Catholics and another by Scandinavians.

Fraternal and benevolent societies often fulfilled multiple social purposes. They were tradition-bearers and helped preserve customs and the "mother tongue" of members. They provided camaraderie, amusement, culture, and entertainment. In 1858, Rockland's Germania Society staged a "grand concert" to celebrate the opening of its new hall, and the St. Patrick's Society hall in Hancock was "well arranged and finely furnished inside, and is used for theaters, lectures, and other public purposes."[33]

Importantly, when their members fell on hard times, these associations did more than just encourage acts of kindness and charity; they functioned much like insurance programs and paid out specified monetary benefits, usually derived from members' initiation fees (ranging from $1 to $5) and monthly dues (usually fifty cents to a dollar). Most had multiple membership criteria, and some criteria, apropos of the interests of insurers, involved a man's fitness and habits.

Besides living in a particular locale, belonging to a particular ethnic group or religion, and sometimes to a particular trade, members usually had to be of a certain age. The Portage Lake Miners and Mechanics Benevolent Society admitted men under forty years of age, as did Calumet's Polish and Scandinavian societies. A few admitted men as old as fifty-five, but older fellows paid higher initiation fees than younger ones. A man wanting to join usually had to meet other standards: to be of "good health," "good character," and, sometimes, "good morals."[34] (Benefits could be withheld if a man's misfortune was his own doing, resulting from drunkenness or crime or, in some cases, suicide.)

The Keweenaw's earliest known mutual aid and benefit society operated on the southern end of the mineral range. This Miners' Club had 216 members by 1857. If an injured or ill man could not work, the club's bylaws said he was to receive $12 a month. When member John Nicholas died, each member of the club was to pay his closest relative two dollars, which added up to a death benefit of $430.[35] Like the Miners' Club, later societies typically paid monthly benefits when a man was unable to work because of sickness, accident, or general misfortune. And in the event of a member's death, any surviving widow or children got a death benefit and help in burying the deceased, which included a trail of mourners at the funeral.

Prior to the 1860s, individuals, churches, nascent charities, mining companies, and mutual aid and benefit societies erected an important yet imperfect social safety net on the mining frontier. The net didn't catch all who suffered misfortune, by any means, and while proffered benefits or alms provided a cushion against absolute disaster and despair, they often provided only temporary relief at a low level of subsistence. The afflicted, if they could not bounce back quickly from whatever ailed them, had little to look forward to but trouble.

During the 1860s, government—especially local government, responding both to national events and state legislation—became more responsive to the needs of less fortunate citizens. County government, in particular, reached out a helping hand and implemented new assistance programs, one of which was tied directly to the Civil War. During that long, deadly, watershed conflict, government asked citizens to make great sacrifices and had to give something in return. The war helped make social welfare the business of a more active government.

Besides fostering a decline in civility that led to a record number of arrests, the Civil War had other widespread social effects on the Keweenaw. During the war, things were changing and on the move. The demand for copper was up. The price of copper was up. Established mines pushed to ship as much copper to market as possible. Inactive mines raced to get back into production. Wages shot up, but not as fast as the prices local stores charged for pork, salt, flour, clothes, and boots. Boarding charges doubled. Mobility marked the day. Workers moved from mine to mine; men marched off to war; new immigrants arrived from Cornwall, Ireland, Canada, and Scandinavia, filling in behind them. In very unsettled times, money seemed to matter more. People needed more of it to get by because of inflation, and nobody wanted to do something for nothing. It took a $300 or $400 bounty to get a man to enlist in the Union army.[36]

Houghton County sent some 460 men off to the Civil War; Ontonagon County contributed 254 soldiers; and Keweenaw County, 119. After paying bounties to many of these men, the counties drew on their treasuries to create a Volunteer Relief Fund for soldiers' families. The three counties together, starting by late 1862, paid out nearly $17,000 to support the wives and children of county residents who'd gone off to war.[37]

In addition to providing assistance for soldiers' dependents, in the 1860s the supervisors of Houghton, Keweenaw, and Ontonagon counties initiated other important social welfare work. Each county named superintendents of the poor, who used public funds to help relieve private problems, who supported "the paupers in our midst who were unable to provide for themselves."[38]

Each superintendent of the poor was a successful man who, on behalf of the county, tended to the needy within his own village or township. When individuals or families asked him for help, he could provide it in one of two ways. If the supplicant had a place to live and a way of earning some income, and was mentally and physically strong enough to sustain independence, then the superintendent provided "outside relief" while the pauper stayed with society at large. In more extreme cases, he sent dependent men, women, and children to the county poorhouse.[39]

The counties preferred putting people on outside relief. Providing only partial support for a pauper (or an entire family) was often cheaper than assuming full care at the poorhouse. Also, outside relief encouraged work, thrift, and self-reliance among the poor. If they gained some mastery over those virtues, they might learn how to pull themselves up and out of pauperism.

At a time when a healthy miner or other skilled laborer earned roughly $50 per month, outside relief payments typically ran from $8 to $20 per month.

The village's superintendent of the poor set the amount, based on his evaluation of the situation. Just after the Civil War, in Hancock, Superintendent Robinson provided assistance that benefited, altogether, fifty-three "souls." He allowed fifteen dollars monthly for a blind man with a wife and five children; the same amount went to a widow with four children and an "old mother-in-law" to support. And "two infants cost each $10.00 per month for their maintenance."[40]

Across the Portage at Houghton, Superintendent Pryor's allotment of relief orders covered a total of forty-seven individuals. One widow with two children received $18 monthly; another widow with two children, only $10. Superintendents Robinson and Pryor, besides providing money for recipients to spend on their own for food, rent, or clothes, sometimes provided goods and services directly. In Houghton, while two old men received $10 each month, two old widows received no payment, but a free cord of wood. Others received barrels of flour. Mr. Robinson managed to keep Hancock's flour budget beneath Mr. Pryor's budget in Houghton, because he "succeeded in purchasing condemned flour at $7 per barrel, while Mr. P. had to pay the full price asked by the merchants."[41]

Superintendents of the poor sometimes provided special outside relief; one used public funds to purchase the lumber needed to rebuild a Calumet woman's house that had burned. In lieu of providing for a pauper month after month, which could end up being year after year, the superintendents occasionally shortcut the system: they'd pay up to $200 in transport costs to return paupers "to their friends 'below' " after first extracting a promise that the pauper would never again wash up on the Keweenaw's shores. If a pauper went "below" in another sense—if he or she died—the poor-relief fund picked up the tab for grave-digging and a coffin.[42]

County supervisors and superintendents of the poor found it too expensive to provide outside relief for the most needy. Instead of putting them up in dwellings scattered in numerous villages, paying their rent, providing them with orders good at local stores for clothing and food, and giving them fuel and flour, they admitted them to poorhouses.

At first the counties rented dwellings to serve as their poorhouses, and they contracted with a keeper who tended to the facility and its inhabitants. Later, Houghton and Ontonagon Counties built their own poorhouses, which were deemed especially suited to the task of sheltering a wide range of troubled individuals, male and female, as well as families with children.

Keweenaw County operated a poorhouse starting in 1861. Two men resided there that first year, along with Mrs. Kaufman and her four children; Mrs. Stanton and three children; Mrs. Finnigan and four children; and Mrs. Sullivan with her two children. In 1868, in need of more space, the superintendents of the poor for Keweenaw County rented a dwelling at the centrally located Pennsylvania mine, which had shut down operations the previous year.

Keweenaw County contracted with George Jones to keep its poorhouse. Jones was to "furnish the house with all necessary bedding, stoves, and firewood," serve up a plain and healthy menu, keep the "inmates" and their rooms clean and decent, and do their washing, if they couldn't manage it themselves. For providing these services, Jones received $13.87½ per month "for each person large and small." A year later, James Cocking became the keeper, at the reduced rate of $13.50 per month. In the mid-1870s, another keeper received just $13 "for the board, washing, nursing, fuel and lights and sewing of every person maintained in the county poorhouse." That keeper, however, received an additional $10 per month if fewer than six paupers occupied the poorhouse.[43]

By the early 1870s, Ontonagon County had erected its own substantial poorhouse:

> All buildings are in good condition. No facilities for bathing. Buildings warmed by wood stoves, and ventilated by windows. Treatment of paupers good. Food: fresh and salt meats, fish, bread, vegetables, tea and coffee, all well cooked by women. Clothing sufficiently comfortable. Care of the sick is kind and good. No accommodations for the insane and idiotic. Children are sent to the district school.[44]

At Ontonagon, the poorhouse operated in conjunction with a farm, because the facility was not just to sustain the poor but to rehabilitate them, to reeducate them in the value of self-reliance and the work ethic. This philosophy of rehabilitation was well stated in 1871 by the "Special Commissioners to Examine the Penal, Reformatory, and Charitable Institutions of the State of Michigan." The commissioners believed that a poorhouse should also be a workhouse: "all inmates of poor-houses should be sternly required to work to the extent of their ability." It was the "settled conviction of all thoughful persons" that "there is no such foe to order and morality as idleness, this prolific parent of all vice, and there is no duty upon the part of the public to support any one in idleness, who can work. There is also a well recognized moral power in work, as an element in both the building up and the reformation of character."[45]

Accordingly, Ontonagon's poorhouse had its able-bodied occupants open a new farm. The reported results for one year included: "Six acres of land logged off; one thousand rails put on fences; four acres underbrushed and chopped; twenty rods of ditch made; eighty rods new rail fence made; one barn built, and house repaired."[46]

In 1865, Houghton County purchased a farm. The next year it put up and furnished a forty-by-eighty-five-foot, two-and-a-half-story, wood-frame poorhouse that had "twenty-four large rooms." The county hired a keeper to run the $6,000 facility. He received an annual salary of $750 to $900, plus free room and board for his family. The superintendents of the poor then sent the keeper each village's most needy residents—if they could be made to go. Whenever people asked for full support from the county, they were given not money, not rent, not food, but a ticket to the poorhouse: "instead of giving applicants an order good for so much money or goods, they are given an order *on the keeper* of the poorhouse for admission. In many cases this kind of order is quickly refused; only those absolutely destitute accept them."[47]

The first inhabitants of Houghton County's poorhouse, besides the keeper and his family, were six men, five women, and sixteen children. Of the six men, two were blind, two were "worn out by excesses and disease," one was old and infirm, and another young but idiotic. Between 1867 and 1875, about one out of ten of those receiving welfare assistance from Houghton County lived in the poorhouse; the others received outside relief. The poorhouse typically boarded forty-five to seventy-five different paupers per year, keeping from thirty to forty at any one time. It tallied 11,000 to 15,000 days of boarding and up to 45,000 meals per year.[48]

In the early 1870s, when state commissioners inspected the facility, thirty paupers happened to be in residence, including three insane adults and seventeen children. The commissioners reported that "the house is roomy, well built, and kept, as far as we could judge, in a good condition. We saw the paupers at table, and can bear witness that the table, with its neat oil-cloth covering and good crockery dishes, and well scoured knives and forks, presented a very inviting appearance." A few years later, Houghton County's own Building Committee gave the facility a rave review, describing it as a prosperous poorhouse (as if there were such a thing): "We . . . proceeded to the poorhouse and farm and report with pleasure that we found all buildings and apartments in perfect order and prosperity seemed to reign in the community there assembled."[49]

The poorhouse sat three miles removed from Houghton, "on the summit of a beautiful elevation, from which can be seen the villages of Hancock and Houghton and surrounding mines on the one side, and the head of Portage Lake and Lake Superior on the other." At this picturesque spot, the poorhouse farm (which by the early 1870s had grown from 100 to 240 tillable acres) presented plenty of opportunities for men, women, and children to work. The farm regularly produced vegetables (especially potatoes), oats, and hay; needy women and their children were sent out in midsummer to pick strawberries and raspberries. The poorhouse kept as much farm produce as its people and animals needed, and sold off the rest, putting the revenue back into the county poor-relief fund.[50]

County supervisors and superintendents of the poor believed that a poorhouse conserved taxpayers' dollars while fulfilling a social need and providing alms to the poor. The stigmatized poorhouse was supposed to scare or shame people off the public dole and back to work. No self-respecting person wanted to go there. And for those who went regardless, a county could keep them within a central institution "cheaper than when scattered in the various towns." Houghton County boasted that in its first year of full operation, the poorhouse and farm clothed, fed, and sheltered a pauper for only fifty-five cents per day; by 1874–75, that cost had been driven down to only seventeen or nineteen cents.[51]

But at the same time, the overall costs of county-provided welfare had risen dramatically. In the early 1860s, the supervisors of the poor in Keweenaw and Houghton counties received annual appropriations of only $1,200 to $1,500. By 1870, Keweenaw County's annual poor fund had increased nearly fourfold, to $6,000. Houghton County's expanded even more, reaching $12,000 by 1870 and $17,000 by 1875. Those figures made Houghton County one of the largest welfare providers in the state.[52]

Several factors explained the need for expanding county poor funds in the 1860s and 1870s. There simply *were* more poor, in part because there were more people. The Keweenaw's population nearly doubled between 1860 and the mid-1870s, rising from 14,000 to 27,000 inhabitants. During the Civil War, inflation pushed the prices of shelter and many goods beyond people's reach. Then, after the war, the recession in the copper mining industry forced employment cutbacks. And finally, a national economic crisis, the Panic of 1873, hit the region hard, causing the price of copper to plummet from thirty-three cents a pound to just twenty-two. That downturn shook up even the newest and richest of the mines, Calumet and Hecla: "The outlook is so black that we must husband every resource we can lay hold of. It is absolutely impossible to sell any copper."[53]

The years from 1860 to 1875—just when the counties assumed a growing welfare role—were tumultuous ones in general, so it was no surprise that welfare spending became a controversial issue. In 1866, the *Portage Lake Mining Gazette* had published articles very supportive of better treatment of Houghton County's poor. But in 1879, the *Hancock Journal* looked back over welfare spending since 1870 and condemned it:

> Thirty-three percent of all the money raised by taxation for nine years, gone for the support of paupers! One hundred and forty-eight thousand dollars, or over $17,000 a year, in a county of less than nineteen thousand population. And the burden grows heavier every year. . . . If it goes on increasing at the same rate in the years to come, the best thing the people of Houghton county can do is to get the county set apart as a pauper's reservation, invite the indigent from the four corners of the earth, to come and settle here, and take care of themselves—and then get out of this pauper-ridden corner of God's green earth as quick as they can. We have been entertained with the comedy of the Jolly Beggars quite long enough . . . , and the people demand a change of programme.[54]

While some started to chafe at the amount of public assistance provided by Michigan's counties, others argued that those counties—not just on the Keweenaw, but throughout the state—were not doing enough for residents needing care, protection, or rehabilitation. The counties relied too heavily on jails and poorhouses to serve as human catchalls, where they tucked away all of society's problems (except, perhaps, for the chronically ill, who might be sent to a county hospital instead). In 1871, Michigan's "Special Commissioners to Examine the Penal, Reformatory, and Charitable Institutions of the State" roundly condemned jails and poorhouses for breeding problems, instead of solving them.

The special commissioners described county jails as "hot-beds and nurseries of vice and crime." In their "wretched" cells,

> there is no separation of the convicts from persons merely accused of crime. Here, often, are gathered those old and hardened in villainy, lost to shame, proud and boastful of their crimes; those who have committed their first crime under the influence of some strong temptation; those who have committed some venial offense while under the influence of intoxicating liquors or some sudden passion; mere children, new in the paths of vice; those who are accused, but are entirely innocent of any crime; and those who are arrested on civil process and are unable to find bail.

The special commissioners sardonically concluded, "If the wisdom of the State had been exercised to devise a school of crime, it would have been difficult to devise a more efficient one." Then the commissioners condemned county poorhouses on similar grounds. In poorhouses, "degraded, debased, and thoroughly corrupted" paupers, totally wasted by "drunkenness and licentiousness," mixed with other unfortunates more worthy of sympathy and, sometimes, more likely to turn their lives around:

> There are those who, from old age, accident, disease or infirmity, and without fault of their own, are unable to support themselves, and are driven to the poor-house. There are weak-minded and imbecile persons and idiots and the incurable insane; some harmless and some not. Then there are children, some young and helpless, and others of such an age that their characters are becoming rapidly formed, and who are receiving life-long impressions that must shape their whole being. The mingling of all these classes together can only result in unmixed evil.[55]

Instead of placing all troubled individuals into just a poorhouse or jail, counties were advised to send them to state facilities. Michigan had started creating specialized institutions for handling different problem cases in 1838. Just a year after achieving statehood, it opened the state prison at Jackson. Jackson took the worst offenders out of local lockups. Then, in the 1850s, Michigan started building schools, asylums, and reformatories targeted at specific parts of the population. Instead of just being contained, troubled individuals received treatments—moral and medical ones—intended to cure or lessen their problems.

In 1854 Michigan opened a School for the Deaf, Dumb and Blind in Flint; then, in 1880, it divided it, splitting off a special School for the Blind in Lansing. These two schools took in children only and, through special education, sought to make them fit for "honorable, *useful* citizenship."[56]

In 1855, troubled youths started doing time in a House of Correction for Juvenile Offenders, located in Lansing. This prisonlike institution evolved into a reformatory, called the Industrial School for Boys, which was matched in the very early 1880s by Adrian's Industrial Home for Girls. The reformatories took in youths who had already run afoul of the law and tried to straighten them out by teaching them reading, writing, and arithmatic, plus moral lessons and discipline, as well as a useful trade.[57]

The insane, too, attracted special attention. In 1871, Michigan's special commissioners argued very strongly that the insane should not be put away in poorhouses:

> There is no chapter in the history of our charitable institutions so fraught with painful and revolting interest, as that which relates to the treatment of the insane and the idiotic in our poor-houses. . . . Their utter helplessness excites our commiseration, and their want of reason and self-control excites our fears. . . . They require the tender guardianship of the State.

A few years later, another board of state commissioners found that "the insane and idiotic are proper subjects for treatment of a very different kind from that which the jails afford, and a humane and just regard for these unfortunates . . . demands, by every consideration of humanity, that they should not be confined in jails." Instead of putting them in a poorhouse or jail, counties should send their mentally ill to Kalamazoo, where Michigan had established its first Asylum for the Insane in 1859.[58]

In 1874, the state turned its attention back to the needs of children and opened the doors of a new state public school in Coldwater to "little 'waifs and strays.'" The school reached out "to rescue those friendless and destitute children . . . from the evil practices and vile associations of the street." It bunked them in cottages on thirty-six acres "tastefully divided into playgrounds, orchard, gardens, and meadows." It prepared them "by education and industry for respectable and useful lives"—and for adoption, or "distribution among private families."[59]

So the counties on the Keweenaw could turn to the state for help in taking care of diverse, troubled individuals. But none of this help came free. All the state's institutions were nearly five hundred miles distant from the Keweenaw, and escorting persons to a prison, asylum, school, or reformatory was an expensive proposition. In 1866, Houghton County paid its sheriff $538.15— "Fees for bringing John Thomas (nigger) to Jackson and three boys to reform school." Once they received a county resident, state institutions charged for board and treatment. In the early 1870s, the expense to Houghton County of keeping its "cranks" in the Kalamazoo insane asylum about doubled the cost of boarding them in the local poorhouse.[60]

Due to cost considerations and the many miles separating Lake Superior from the likes of Kalamazoo, Flint, Lansing, and Coldwater, the counties through 1875 made only limited use of downstate institutions. Their jails and poorhouses generally remained catchalls, and the superintendents of the poor often treated local cases in their own way rather than resorting to state help. The counties sometimes acted generously, sometimes miserly.

The counties sent few youthful offenders to state reformatories and very few orphans or neglected children to the state public school at Coldwater. Children remained a large part of the local poorhouse population, although superintendents of the poor or other county agents did occasionally arrange for adoptions or other arrangements. In 1876, rather than carry him on their poor fund, the superintendents of the poor of Keweenaw County apprenticed out a six-year-old orphan pauper. Until the boy reached age twenty-one, he would work with James Cocking—who sometimes contracted to keep the county's poorhouse.[61]

Very few went from the Keweenaw to the state School for the Deaf, Dumb, and Blind. Up in Keweenaw County, after spending nearly all day with Johnny Butler and reading to him till her eyes hurt, Lucena Brockway wrote in her diary in 1867, "Poor little blind boy, how I pity him." While Johnny remained in his community, in 1870 Houghton County sent Mary Ann Holland, "a deaf-mute," to the state school in Flint, and at about the same time, the county poor fund paid for special help for a blind man, Robert Ellis. In 1869–70, the county paid out about $550 to send him to Chicago's Cook County Hospital for eye treatments, which allowed him to resume work at the Quincy mine with "one good eye." Other blind men, meanwhile, languished sightless in the poorhouse.[62]

Of all the state institutions (including the prison at Jackson), Houghton County made most use of Kalamazoo's Asylum for the Insane. It sent patients there in the 1860s, as did the other local counties. In 1869, when the likable ferryboatman, Samuel Thompson, "manifested symptoms of insanity," he went to jail for a few weeks, where he may have been restrained for a time in a straitjacket. Then the sheriff escorted him and two other insane persons to Kalamazoo. The public followed this tale of woe, step by step, in the pages of the *Portage Lake Mining Gazette*. Two months after Thompson went to Kalamazoo, the paper carried a hopeful report "From Our Lunatics"—Thompson was "improving as fast as could be expected." After another three months, the paper advised that "Sam. Thompson, whose sudden insanity and curious performances enlisted the deep sympathy of many of our people, has so recovered that he will come back before the close of navigation."[63]

By 1875, Houghton County sent a total of ten to fifteen men and women per year down to Kalamazoo. But the first destination for anyone caught acting peculiar remained not a medical or treatment facility but the county jail, and from there many of the "insane" went to the poorhouse. The jail remained a catchall for "lunatics" and larcenists alike. (Even in a later era, from 1875 through 1900, one-fourth of all women taken to the Houghton County jail were charged not with an alleged crime but with alleged insanity.)

It took all kinds to make up the population on the mining frontier, and some who lived there fared far better than others. As the local society came of age and settled in for decades of large-scale mining, an important part of its evolution included the stringing up of a social safety net to provide a greater sense of security for Keweenaw residents and to break the falls of individuals and families in trouble through no fault of their own. The underpinnings of that net were several: neighborly acts of kindness and goodwill, freely offered in times of need; company paternalism; fraternal organizations, churches, and charities; mutual aid and benefit societies; county superintendents of the poor; and state institutions such as a reformatory, an orphanage, or a school for the deaf and blind.

The trend through 1875 was to make the social safety net larger over time, to enable it to provide more coverage for more people. It expanded because people believed in the social redemption of some troubled souls and in the essential fairness of giving the afflicted a chance to lead lives as "normal" as possible, and a *working* life, at that. Society was just now starting to single out children as a class needing more help and protection, and people approved of state and local government playing more active roles in shepherding citizens and intervening in their lives in order to improve their conditions. Institutionalization and treatment gained in favor: government intended to pull the afflicted out of their usual environment, offer rehabilitation, then return them more hale and hearty to society.

Of course, there were limits; counties, companies, and charities had finite resources to expend on welfare. And many on the Keweenaw, as in the rest of the country, were never that comfortable serving in the brother's-keeper role. That role provided absolutely essential services but at the same time seemed to run contrary to the values of self-responsibility and self-reliance. Many of the troubled, surely, brought on their own problems. They lived profligate lives. They were liquored up, licentious, or lazy. Too much help for them only undercut the work ethic, and hard work was what the copper district was all about.

TRANSFORMATIONS
A Long-Lived Frontier

1867 has arrived and 66 has gone into oblivion, never to return. Time flies,
O how swiftly—and soon we shall pass away and be forgotten.
—Lucena Brockway, diary,
January 1, 1867

In the 1840s, a wave of pioneers washed up on the shores of Isle Royale and the Keweenaw Peninsula on Lake Superior. Armed with precious little accurate knowledge of the region but fired by enthusiasm and high hopes, investors launched speculative mining companies. The companies in turn hired voyageurs, explorers, geologists, miners, woodchoppers, cooks, clerks, and young, strong-backed laborers. Together, they set about the difficult business of finding commericial quantities of native copper in the ground beneath a remote and rugged wilderness.

The nascent copper mining industry met with scant success on Isle Royale, and the flow of capital and people to that island slowed. But the Keweenaw Peninsula proved a different story. To be sure, most ventures there soon ended in failure and discouragement. But by the late 1840s the Cliff mine on the northern end of the Keweenaw worked a rich fissure vein of mass copper and rewarded its investors with the region's first dividends. The success of the Cliff helped rekindle enthusiasm and restore confidence in the industry, and soon a second great, profit-making success, the Minesota mine, emerged on the southern end of the hundred-mile-long mineral range.

A bit later, in the late 1850s, several mines that would become strong copper producers took shape near the peninsula's midpoint, at Portage Lake. And by the late 1860s, ten miles north of Portage Lake, the Calumet and Hecla (C&H) mines started up. C&H, sitting atop the richest lode ever discovered on the Keweenaw, quickly became the region's biggest producer, employer, and dividend-payer.

In its first three decades of operation, the copper mining industry sorted itself out. It abandoned regions of poor ground, exhausted some paying ground, and all the while kept looking for new lodes to exploit. The industry, as it matured, expanded in size and scope. Going beyond just the mining of copper, it engaged in milling and smelting. And individual operations—at least the richest ones—grew considerably larger. When the Cliff mine paid the first dividends totaling $60,000 in 1849, it produced approximately one million pounds of copper while employing fewer than two hundred men. In 1875, C&H's dividends amounted to $1.6 million; the company produced 21.5 million pounds of copper and employed 1,780 men.

As the mining industry evolved and changed, so did the landscape. Many early settlers rhapsodized about the Keweenaw's beauty. It was a special place and quite unlike the world below. They admired its stands of virgin timber, its craggy bluffs, rolling hills, and river valleys. They praised the fresh air and beautiful skies. They remarked about the beauty of inland waterways and especially appreciated the grandeur of Lake Superior. Yet praise and appreciation did not suggest protection or preservation. Up here, settlers slated the environment for use and exploitation. They accepted as perfectly proper the transformation of a beautiful woods into a field of stumps; the remaking of a picturesque lakeshore into a bustling scene of stamp mills, smelters, warehouses, and docks; and a water-body's demotion from pretty lake to industrial dump.

After twenty-five or thirty years of mining activity, some stretches of the Keweenaw looked as wild and untamed as when seen by the exploring parties of the 1820s, or 1830s, or 1840s. These stretches tended to be away from the Keweenaw's copper-charged central spine and away from the natural harbors and river valleys nearest the operating mines. Not surprisingly, the cultural landscape most altered the natural one near those places found to be richest in copper.

By the mid-1870s, about twenty mine locations scattered along the mineral range worked their lodes sporadically at best and produced less than half a million pounds of copper a year. Seven other mines produced one to two million pounds each. One yielded two to three million pounds, and Calumet & Hecla, the new giant in a class by itself, produced over twenty million pounds annually (nearly 90 percent of the region's total production). In addition to the shafts, hoists, boilers, rockpiles, houses, churches, and farm plots associated with the ongoing twenty to thirty operations, dozens of abandoned ventures dotted the mineral range. Some were marked by no more than a shallow shaft or short adit, by some trenches and piles of poor rock, and by some discarded tools and equipment. At others, the forest was taking back once-cleared fields; grasses tried to obliterate signs of trails; and whole neighborhoods of mine houses stood empty and silent.

Changes to the Keweenaw's land, water, and sky wrought by white settlers bent on mining copper were perhaps most visible and dramatic at Portage Lake. Early visitors had glided along this waterway in canoes, paddles out of the water, relaxing and taking in the vista of dark green forests blanketing steep hillsides that ran down to water's edge. Autumn only made things more beautiful because much of the green turned yellow and red.

By 1875, the Portage waterway had itself been greatly altered. One end had been dredged and improved to allow passage of the biggest ships navigating Superior. On the other end—the western side of the Keweenaw—a new canal cut across ground that had once kept the Portage Lake and Lake Superior waters apart. Mines lined the hilltops along the lake. Several tramroads and one railroad, the Mineral Range, ran down the hills—now virtually barren of trees but littered with stumps and poor-rock piles—to deliver rock to mills. Inside the mills, ponderous stamps noisily hammered away at rock. Outside the many mills, each of which burned thousands of cords of wood a year, smoke almost continuously streamed from boilerhouse smokestacks. Meanwhile, the mills released their slimes and tailings, washing them out along wooden troughs or launders and sending them into Portage Lake. The lake water ran red near the Osceola mill, because that was the color of its stamp rock.

A major smelter complex, iron foundries, warehouses, and docks lined the busy waterway, which was flanked on one side by Houghton and on the other by Hancock. Each village boasted several churches and hotels; large boarding-houses for single workers; neighborhoods of single-family homes; and quite well-rounded commercial districts, which included the offices of professionals, general stores, tobacconists, confectioners, tailors, saloons, and other tradesmen and merchants.

Numerous agents of change had participated at different times and in different ways in this transformation of life and landscape on the copper mining frontier. To be sure, government—at any and all levels, federal, state, and local—maintained quite a low profile on the Keweenaw during the first twenty years of settlement, and especially for the first ten or so years. For a time, symbols of government authority seemed lacking, such as law enforcement agencies and courts, and so were improvements done with public monies in the name of the common good, such as schools and much-needed roads. Yet government was not merely a laissez-faire observer of change on the Keweenaw; it made some things happen that helped move this new society along.

The federal government negotiated the treaty to obtain the copper lands. It sponsored several important geological explorations of the region. It paid Michigan to conduct a linear survey that divided the land up into units, then opened a land office that first leased and then sold mineral properties to speculative investors and companies. It erected Fort Wilkins, which for a brief but perhaps critical period of time represented order and protection in a wilderness state. It made land grants in support of essential transportation improvements, such as the canal and locks at Sault Ste. Marie. It erected lighthouses that made sailing to, from, and around the Keweenaw safer. And importantly—albeit very irregularly, especially in winter—mail carriers under contract with the federal government brought the mail up to this northern outpost. For many ordinary citizens, providing mail delivery to local postmasters was probably the most highly valued and visible thing that the federal government did.

Michigan, too, under the direction of the ill-fated state geologist, Douglass Houghton, ran important mineral surveys of the Keweenaw. In the 1840s it set up the first counties on the peninsula, and later it modified old county lines and created new ones, putting them in step with the ebb and flow of population and industry from place to place. State government also helped facilitate and encourage the construction of the Soo Locks, as well as the Keweenaw's Portage Lake and Lake Superior Ship Canal. Monies finally released from the state to the local counties in the mid-1860s made possible the construction of much-needed and long-delayed wagon roads running the length of the Keweenaw and off toward distant population centers.

State and local government became much more visible, active, and involved in settlers' lives after about 1860. Judges and sheriffs became more prominent officials, and new courthouses and jails were built. Townships and villages formed more school boards and erected far more public schools. Villages such as Houghton passed and published ordinances that put more controls over the behavior of individuals and businesses alike. Boards of supervisors hired county physicians and tended to public health concerns in other ways, such as by establishing and enforcing quarantines. The county supervisors also oversaw and funded the work of superintendents of the poor, who ran outside relief programs as well as poorhouses and farms. County almsgivers also interacted with Michigan officials and institutions to decide if select Keweenaw residents should be transported downstate to an insane asylum or school for the deaf, dumb, and blind—or kept at home in the jail or poorhouse.

In many regards, the most dynamic agents of change on the copper frontier were the mining companies themselves. To start a fledgling, highly speculative mine, they built a camp; to operate a paying mine, they built a community. The mining companies used their capital in numerous ways, not only to win metal from the ground but also to accelerate the social development of the region.

The mining companies built much of the early housing. They cleared fields, platted land, and helped establish commerce and agriculture on the margins of the mines. When all levels of government were initially slow to make internal improvements to the region, the companies filled the breech by blazing trails, then horse paths, then wagon roads and plank roads, and by improving harbors, building docks, dredging rivers, and making canals. When sheriffs, courts, and jails were yet scarce, mine officials at their various isolated locations kept the peace and represented order and authority. Mining companies lured the earliest doctors to the region and built the first hospitals. By making do-nations to building funds and providing land and sometimes materials, they supported the construction of early churches. Importantly, mining companies' paternalism, together with their housing and hiring policies, actively encour-aged families to take up residence on the Keweenaw. The arrival of women and children domesticized the frontier and dramatically altered the social life of the region.

Some agents of change accelerated industrial and social development on the Keweenaw without ever setting foot there. Instead of sending themselves, they shipped their products to Lake Superior. Distant manufacturers supported the mining industry by providing drill steel, explosives, steam boilers, hoisting engines, chain, wire rope, steam locomotives, lubricating oils, and much more in the way of equipment, tools, and supplies. Similarly, other producers in the world below provided much of the foodstuffs, furniture, clothes, and other personal and domestic items that settlers bought and used. The availability of these commodities distinctly enhanced the quality of life experienced in the mid-nineteenth century on this frontier.

Settlers were fortunate that their diets were not limited to what they could hunt, gather, or grow locally. Shortly after the mine rush began, a waterborne supply line connected the Keweenaw with far-flung growers and food produc-ers. Admittedly, this supply line was tenuous at first because few large ships sailed on Lake Superior prior to the opening of the locks at Sault Ste. Marie in 1855. And every winter, storms and ice kept all lake boats away from Keweenaw docks. Nevertheless, lake shipping played a vital role in supplying stores and family larders with foodstuffs that permitted a more healthy and varied diet. Settlers consumed canned oysters and lobsters from the eastern seaboard; spices and sweeteners gathered from around the world; preserved meats from the likes of Cincinnati and Chicago; fresh fruit from New York and Ohio; plus such staples as flour, butter, and cheese.

This same supply line provided other goods that blunted the frontier ex-perience and made life in the copper lands more like life in the world below. North came milled building materials, such as flooring, doors, and windows. Lake boats delivered cast-iron stoves, kitchenware, tableware, furniture, plaster, wallpapers, and curtains. They brought up shoes and bonnets, store-bought clothes for men, and a wide array of dry goods. Not long after the rush began, dock workers in Copper Harbor, Eagle River, or Ontonagon were unloading patent medicines and an occasional piano. In fact, from the late 1840s on, settlers could pretty much get anything they wanted on the Keweenaw, as long as they could afford it and were willing to wait for its delivery, which some-times was delayed over a long winter. The supply line pierced the frontier line to deliver books, magazines, newspapers, musical instruments, soaps, lamps, cure-alls, combs, and coffee.

The market economy that reached out to alter life on Lake Superior involved distant producers, a network of interconnecting transporters, and local merchants. Economic opportunity on this frontier came in many forms, and so did the settlers. Merchants, tradesmen, shopkeepers, small businessmen, and professionals followed on the heels of voyageurs, geologists, and miners and played key roles in shaping social and economic life in the region.

Doctors, dentists, druggists, tailors, and tinsmiths set up shops. Hotelkeepers provided accommodations and helped commercialize entertainment by staging festive holiday celebrations, dances, and masquerades. Other settlers brewed beer, ran saloons, staged horse races and wrestling matches, ran boat excursions, and operated ice rinks. Some women gave lessons in languages and the arts, while others set up millineries. Frontier society had first coped with providing the necessities of life; as an industrial society took shape, it added embellishments.

Of course, ordinary settlers, men and women, did much to enhance their own quality of life. Families did not depend solely on store-bought foods and other goods; they still produced much of what they wanted or needed. They went berry picking, hunted and fished, tended to gardens, and kept domestic fowl, hogs, or an occasional cow. Women made clothes, performed a multitude of household tasks, and labored hard to transform a new domestic scene into something that felt more familiar and comfortable.

Many pioneers were not rugged individualists. On the contrary, they felt the urge to form and join organizations. With the aid of the mining companies and Catholic and Methodist missionaries, they established churches. In several early villages they launched fraternal organizations and joined the likes of temperance societies, the Odd Fellows, or the Masons. They created their own social safety nets—mutual aid and benefit societies that provided moral and financial support to members and their families who were in harm's way due to illness, injury, or death. They performed individual and group acts of charity, from reading to an unfortunate blind boy to feeding the poor on holidays.

Acknowledging that work and worry were not all of life, communities formed baseball teams for sportful entertainment. They orchestrated civic celebrations to commemorate special days, such as the Fourth of July. Individuals coped with cabin fever and arduous labor in myriad ways of their own. Some walked the woods and beaches while collecting agates, wildflowers, or berries. Some went to minstrel shows, circuses, plays, and dances. Others headed to the billiard hall or saloon. Still others quietly read, or sewed, or wrote letters, or smoked their pipes.

Over time, life at the mine locations and in the commercial villages became less harsh and more comfortable and secure. But transforming this environment did not come easily or quickly. Even as forests fell to the ax, lodes yielded millions of pounds of copper, harbors filled with lake boats, and village streets filled with shops, settlers continued to sense that this was a special place that only slowly surrendered its wilderness. The Keweenaw was a long-lived frontier, and settlers here felt they were living beyond the boundaries for a number of years, for at least a decade and a half after the mine rush began. And in the Keweenaw's smaller, more isolated settlements, people still sensed that they were pioneers living on a frontier even into the 1870s—a full three decades after Copper Harbor had first become a mecca for adventurers and speculators.

Several factors prolonged the frontier experience on the Keweenaw. Pioneers in this region keenly felt a sense of separation from what they continued to call "the world below." In settling the Keweenaw, they did not locate along a frontier line that was just a bit west of civilization. Instead, they leapfrogged over several hundred miles of unsettled or sparsely settled territory to get to the south shore of Lake Superior. They went to a place that was as distant from Detroit as Detroit was distant from the nation's capital, Washington, D.C. Here they created an isolated node of settlement surrounded by wilderness and water. Other population centers arose in Upper Michigan (such as on the Marquette iron range) and in Wisconsin, but good wagon roads and telegraph lines did not lead off toward Marquette or Green Bay until the Civil War era, and direct railroad service through to Portage Lake did not start until the 1880s. In the meantime, the Keweenaw remained a small world unto itself.

The frontier experience lingered here because it kept being recycled or repeated. Along the hundred-mile mineral range, not all mines started at once. Each passing decade brought new attempts in new places, and each attempt followed the same general pattern. A small crew of men went into the forest in search of copper. They lived in a camp, absent women and children, domiciled in rude huts or boardinghouses. The camp evolved into a community only if the lode showed signs of being extensive and profitable. Then came the cabins and houses, the families, churches, schools, and other trappings of civilization. Until those trappings were in place, residents lived in a new, frontierlike settlement, and it didn't much matter if the calendar read 1850, 1860, or 1870. They were still in a rough-and-tumble mine location, out in the woods.

Without any doubt, the single most important factor in prolonging the Keweenaw's frontier era was winter. It was exceedingly long. Because of Superior's lake-effect snow, it was exceptionally white. People wrote of being buried up in snow. And most important of all, because of winter settlers were "frozen out" from the world below each year from November till May. The long closing of navigation worked considerable hardship on the people of this region. Throughout the 1860s and into the 1870s, they still worried about securing their winter larders of food and about running out of wholesome, palatable food before next year's boats arrived. They still felt cut off from other valued supplies and amenities; they felt alone, isolated, and deprived.

Surely, the Keweenaw copper frontier was more than just a place. "Frontier" was also a state of mind bound up with ideas or feelings of risk, deprivation, separation, and isolation. On the Keweenaw, such feelings did not soon go away. They did not totally disappear even as the population along this peninsula rose to a thousand, then to ten thousand, and even to twenty thousand persons. Even if these worrisome feelings diminished in the glories of summer that followed the reopening of navigation, they came back in haunting fashion late each autumn, year after year, as the closing of navigation loomed.

Still, the frontier experience did soften over time. In the 1840s and 1850s, settlers coped with a difficult and remote wilderness, with a natural environment seemingly bent on thwarting the smooth progress of a developing industry and society. By the 1860s, settlers had not really tamed or subdued this far north environment, but they had learned how to cope with it and get by. Simultaneously, they had surrounded themselves with ever more of the trappings of civilization. Interestingly, however, just as the wilderness state had brought its peculiar problems, so did the accumulation of more and more civilization. Select social and economic problems came to demand attention, such as the Civil War era's increase in drunkenness, assaults, and other crimes. The long and harsh postwar recession shut down mines and communities, while driving up unemployment and pauperism. Villages of two thousand inhabitants debated the need for better public schools, or coped with the unsightly grime and garbage that blighted lots and lanes, especially each spring, when snow no longer hid the sight and smell of offal and other wastes. Growing communities started to face the problems of inadequate water, sewer, and firefighting facilities. Greater class distinctions and rivalries began to show themselves within this industrial society, and the mine industry encounted its first serious labor disputes: over the use of nitroglycerine oil in one case, over wages in the next.

As this region went through its broad, collective social transformations in the first two or three decades of settlement, individuals on Lake Superior lived out their separate lives. Some flourished, some failed. Some had nothing but praise for this place; others found it damnable.

Lucena Brockway, one of the earliest white settlers, raised her family here and lived to a ripe old age but spent much of her time in poor health and lonely. Ruth Douglass, on the other hand, left behind a diary that captured her more upbeat, accommodating spirit. She hadn't wanted to go to Lake Superior in the first place in 1848, but she soon became happy there, "even," as she wrote, in this solitude. . . . We have as many comforts of life here as we should enjoy in almost any place. Many more than I would suppose that had no experience in this new country. We have as yet a plenty of fresh meats such as beef, fish, fowls, rabbits, etc., etc., together with as good vegetables as one could wish to find in any place, also a sufficiency of nick-nacks. In short everything for our health and comfort."[1]

Unfortunately, Ruth Douglass's health didn't last long on the northern mining frontier. The spirited woman did not raise a family there, or live to old age. She died a young pioneer in 1850.

Those who succeeded and those who suffered shared a common attitude over the years: Lake Superior was indeed a special place—one you might love or loathe but could hardly take for granted. In 1866 the *Portage Lake Mining Gazette* extolled the virtues of the place: "This is indeed the country for tourists. Scenery wild, magnificent and unequalled; rich deposits of minerals, splendid fish and fishing, the purest and most bracing of atmospheres, a go-a-headitive people—in short a thousand and one things to make a trip here pleasant, profitable, and desirable."[2] Surely the ancient and dead *Mining Gazette* editor of 1866 would only approve of this tourist-historian, over a century later, borrowing his words and echoing his sentiments.

NOTES

AIME *Trans.*   American Institute of Mining Engineers *Transactions*
A.R.   *Annual Report*
C&H   Calumet and Hecla
CCJ   *Copper Country Journal: The Diary of Schoolmaster Henry Hobart, 1863–1864*
CMU   Central Michigan University
CS   Cornelius Shaw
DMG   *Daily Mining Gazette*
E&MJ   *Engineering & Mining Journal*
HAER   Historic American Engineering Record
HCBS   Houghton County Board of Supervisors
KHSC   Keweenaw Historical Society Collection
LB   Lucena Brockway
LSJ   *Lake Superior Journal*
LSM   *Lake Superior Miner*
LSMI *Proc.*   Lake Superior Mining Institute *Proceedings*
MCJ   *Mining Congress Journal*
MH   *Michigan History*
MMC   Minesota Mining Company
MPHS   *Michigan Pioneer and Historical Society Collections*
MTU   Michigan Technological University Archives and Copper Country Historical Collections

NMJ	*Northwestern Mining Journal*
OM	*Ontonagon Miner*
PLMG	*Portage Lake Mining Gazette*
PMC	Pewabic Mining Company
QMC	Quincy Mining Company
RD	Ruth Douglass
WHC	Western Historical Company

ONE *Water, Woods, and Winter*

1. This account of Ruth and C. C. Douglass's trip to Isle Royale, and their stay there, is based on her 1848 diary. The original is held at the Clarke Historical Library, CMU; a copy is held by MTU. Once attributed to Lydia Smith Douglass (a later wife), the diary is now attributed to Ruth Douglass, based on recent research into Douglass family history conducted by Robert L. Root of CMU.

2. John R. Halsey, "Miskwabik—Red Metal: Lake Superior Copper and the Indians of Eastern North America," *MH* (Sept.–Oct. 1983), 32–41.

3. For a brief, readily understood account of the region's geology, see T. M. Broderick and C. D. Hohl, "Geology and Exploration in the Michigan Copper District," *MCJ* 17 (Oct. 1931), 478–81, 486. Also see B. S. Butler and W. S. Burbank, *The Copper Deposits of Michigan*, U.S. Geological Survey Professional Paper 144 (Washington, 1929); and George N. Fuller, ed., *Geological Reports of Douglass Houghton, First State Geologist of Michigan, 1837–1845* (Lansing, 1928). For an excellent account of how the copper deposits came to be understood by early geologists, especially Henry Rowe Schoolcraft, Douglass Houghton, and Charles T. Jackson, see David J. Krause, *The Making of a Mining District: Keweenaw Native Copper, 1500–1870* (Detroit, 1992).

4. Krause, *Making of a Mining District*, 19–43.

5. Sydney W. Jackman and John F. Freeman, eds., *American Voyageur: The Journal of David Bates Douglass* (Marquette, Mich., 1969), 58; and Henry Rowe Schoolcraft, *Narrative Journal of Travels through the Northwestern Regions of the United States* (Albany, 1821), 175–76. (Schoolcraft's delineation of the copper boulder is found on pp. 176–77.) For an account of the removal of the Ontonagon Boulder to Washington, see Krause, *Making of a Mining District*, 136–38.

6. James H. Lanman, *History of Michigan* (New York, 1841), 16.

7. Schoolcraft, *Narrative Journal*, 178.

8. Charles Whittlesey, *Fugitive Essays upon Interesting and Useful Subjects* (Hudson, Ohio, 1852), 316. For discussions of how American attitudes toward the wilderness changed (from seeing it as a wasteland to seeing it as picturesque and sublime), see Roderick Nash, *Wilderness and the American Mind*, rev. ed. (New Haven, 1973), 23–66; and Bernard C. Peters, "Revolt from the Wilderness: Romantic Travellers on Lake Superior," *Michigan Academician* 13, no. 4 (spring 1981), 491–501.

9. Whittlesey, *Fugitive Essays*, 314.

10. John Harris Forster, "Early Settlement of the Copper Regions of Lake Superior," *MPHS* 7 (1886), 186–87.

11. Philip P. Mason, ed., *Copper Country Journal: The Diary of Schoolmaster Henry Hobart, 1863–1864* (Detroit, 1991), 201 (hereafter cited as *CCJ*).

12. Charles T. Jackson, *Report on the Geological and Mineralogical Survey of the Mineral Lands of the United States in the State of Michigan*, Senate Exec. Doc. 1 (31st Cong., 1st sess., 1849), 454.

13. Bernard C. Peters, ed., *Lake Superior Journal: Bela Hubbard's Account of the 1840 Houghton Expedition* (Marquette, Mich., 1983), 54.

14. Jackson, *Report on the Geological Survey*, 419–20.

15. Forster, "Early Settlement," 189.

16. James L. Carter and Ernest H. Rankin, eds., *North to Lake Superior: The Journal of Charles W. Penny, 1840* (Marquette, Mich., 1970), 42.

17. Horace Greeley, *Recollections of a Busy Life* (New York, 1868), 246.

18. Jackson, *Report on the Geological Survey*, 428.

19. Krause, *Making of a Mining District*, 144, 146–48.

20. Lewis Marvill, "First Trip by Steam to Lake Superior," *MPHS* 4 (1883), 68.

21. John N. Dickinson, *To Build a Canal: Sault Ste. Marie, 1853–54 and After* (Miami, Ohio, 1981), 24.

22. Orrin W. Robinson, *Early Days of the Lake Superior Copper Country* (Houghton, Mich., 1938), 10.

23. Sarah Barr Christian, *Winter on Isle Royale: A Narrative of Life on Isle Royale during the Years of 1874 and 1875* (n.p., 1932), 5–6.

24. "Family Histories of Pupils in High School of Houghton," KHSC no. 183, MTU.

25. Regis M. Walling and Rev. N. Daniel Rupp, eds., *The Diary of Bishop Frederic Baraga* (Detroit, 1990), 45.

26. Whittlesey, *Fugitive Essays*, 318.

27. Robert E. Clarke, "Notes from the Copper Region," *Harper's New Monthly Magazine* 6 (March 1853), 441.

28. Greeley, *Recollections*, 244.

29. "From Allegheny to Lake Superior: Journal of George M. McGill," *Moorsfield Antiquarian* 1 (1937–38), 260.

30. CS's diary is found in the Ben Chynoweth collection (Box 6, Item 291), MTU.

31. *CCJ*, 154–55.

32. Charles Lanman, *A Summer in the Wilderness Embracing a Canoe Voyage up the Mississippi and around Lake Superior* (New York, 1847), 129–30.

33. An extensive run of LB's diaries is found in the Brockway Family collection, MTU.

34. LB, diary, 8 Dec. 1866.

35. RD, diary, 7 Nov. 1848; *CCJ*, 240.

36. CS, diary, for all given dates.

37. Ralph D. Williams, *The Honorable Peter White: A Biographical Sketch of the Lake Superior Iron Country* (Cleveland, 1905), 127–30. For another acount of the Motts' fate, see poem, "Angelique," by Rev. George Duffield, typescript in KHSC no. 363A, MTU.

38. *OM*, 8 April 1876. On 3 March 1902, the *DMG* published a list of dates documenting the opening of navigation at Sault Ste. Marie from 1855 to 1901. 11 April marked the earliest opening; 12 May, the latest.

39. LB, diaries, 26 April 1867 and 9 April 1889.

40. CS, diary, 27 July 1847.

41. Alexis de Tocqueville, *Democracy in America*, trans. George Lawrence, ed. J. P. Mayer (New York, 1965), 485.

42. Alfred P. Swineford, *History and Review of the Material Resources of the South Shore of Lake Superior* (Marquette, Mich., 1877), 44–45.

43. For a discussion of the meaning of "wilderness," see Nash, *Wilderness and the American Mind*, 1–7; for a discussion of using and/or subduing the wilderness as a frontier is settled, see Ray Allen Billington, *America's Frontier Heritage* (Albuquerque, 1974), 39–44.

44. Robert E. Lang, Deborah Epstein Popper, and Frank J. Popper, " 'Progress of the

Nation': The Settlement History of the Enduring American Frontier," *Western Historical Quarterly*, 26, no. 3 (Autumn 1995), 291–93.

45. Charles K. Hyde, "From 'Subterranean Lotteries' to Orderly Investment: Michigan Copper and Eastern Dollars, 1841–1865," *Mid-America: An Historical Review* 66 (Jan. 1984), 8. For an economic history of the early development of the region, see William B. Gates, *Michigan Copper and Boston Dollars: An Economic History of the Michigan Copper Mining Industry* (Cambridge, Mass., 1951), 1–63.

46. For copper production statistics, see William Gates, *Michigan Copper*, table, 197. The Keweenaw's population statistics are based on census records for Houghton, Keweenaw and Ontonagon counties; Baraga County is *not* included.

47. Frederick Jackson Turner noted that the frontier had "come to mean the edge of settlement." Hence, "living on the edge" seems an appropriate metaphor for what settlers on Lake Superior experienced and felt. See Turner, *The Frontier in American History* (reprinted. with foreword by Ray Allen Billington, New York, 1962) 41.

TWO   *Heaving up Jonah*

1. This account of Cannon's travel experiences with the American Exploring and Mining Company is based on George M. Cannon, *A Narrative of One Year in the Wilderness* (Ann Arbor, 1982). For his trip from Detroit to the Soo, see pp. 7–10; his stay at the Soo, pp. 11–14; his voyage from the Soo to L'Anse, pp. 14–17; his travel from L'Anse around Keweenaw Point, past Isle Royale to the landing on Superior's north shore, pp. 18–23; his overland explorations and coasting along present-day Minnesota and Wisconsin, pp. 23–41; his stay at Ontonagon and passage up the west branch of the Ontonagon River, pp. 42–47; his overland expeditions in the Ontonagon area, pp. 48–55; his winter on the Keweenaw, p. 67.

2. James P. Barry, *Ships of the Great Lakes: 300 Years of Navigation* (Berkeley, 1973), 15, 30; Karl Kuttruff et al., *Ships of the Great Lakes: A Pictorial History* (Detroit, 1976), not paginated.

3. Cannon, *A Narrative*, 16.

4. Ibid., 51.

5. Ibid., 55.

6. The discovery and unsuccessful development of Cannon's mine site is covered in American Exploring, Mining and Manufacturing Company, *Report* (1847); Norwich Mining Company, *Report* (Aug. 1855); "Charter of the American Mining Company" (New York, 1852); "A Statement of the Condition and Prospects of the Norwich Mine," (1 July 1853); and "To the Stockholders of the American Mining Company," (10 Feb. 1854). Several of these sources can be found in the Norwich mine vertical files, MTU.

7. Charles Whittlesey, "Pioneers of Lake Superior," 188, ms. held by the Western Reserve Historical Society, Cleveland.

8. Charles Lanman, *Summer in the Wilderness*, 141–42; Robert James Hybels, "The Lake Superior Copper Fever, 1841–47," *MH* 34 (1950), 36–37.

9. John H. Forster, "Life in the Copper Mines of Lake Superior," *MPHS* 11 (1887), 177.

10. Charles Lanman, *Summer in the Wilderness*, 146.

11. John R. St. John, *A True Description of the Lake Superior Country* (New York, 1846), 13, 15.

12. For quote about the "hardiest sailors" looking upon the Keweenaw shoreline "with dread," see Whittlesey, "Pioneers of Lake Superior." An unpaginated, unattributed newspaper clipping entitled "The Early Settlers of the Copper Region" that is included in this manuscript quotes a Nov. 13, 1845, letter from Cyrus Mendenhall on this subject. Also see Swineford, *History and Review*, 29–33.

13. Clipping, "Early Settlers of Lake Superior," found in Whittlesey, "Pioneers of Lake Superior."

14. Ruggles to Gibson, letters, 29 June and 30 Sept. 1844, R.G. 192, National Archives.

15. Swineford, *History and Review*, 32.

16. Edwin Henwood, "Early Reminiscences," KHCS no. 192, MTU; for a published description of activities at the Soo in 1852, see Clarke, "Notes from the Copper Region," 437.

17. An account of these explorations is given in Krause, *Making of a Mining District*, 66–70, 95–96, 103–17.

18. See Fuller, *Geological Reports of Douglass Houghton*, and John W. Foster and Josiah D. Whitney, *Report on the Geology and Topography of a Portion of the Lake Superior Land District in the State of Michigan, Part 1, Copper Lands*, U.S. House, Exec. Doc 69 (31st Cong., 1st sess., 1850).

19. William Gates, *Michigan Copper*, 2–3, 6; Thomas Friggens, "Fort Wilkins: Army Life on the Frontier," *MH* 61 (Fall 1977), 221–50; Whittlesey, "Pioneers of Lake Superior," 189.

20. Charles K. Hyde, *The Northern Lights: Lighthouses of the Upper Great Lakes* (Lansing, 1986), 17, 158–84.

21. Dickinson, *To Build a Canal*, p. xiii, 28–29, 48.

22. Ibid., 54.

23. The most thorough narrative of the canal's troubled construction history is Dickinson, *To Build a Canal*; also see William Gates, *Michigan Copper*, 18–19.

24. *PLMG*, 2 April 1864; *LSM*, 14 Nov. 1857.

25. Graham Pope, "Some Early Mining Days at Portage Lake," LSMI *Proc.* 7 (1901), 27.

26. Ibid., 24.

27. Ibid., 27; WHC, *History of the Upper Peninsula of Michigan Containing a Full Account of Its Early Settlement; Its Growth, Development and Resources* (Chicago, 1883), 254; William Gates, *Michigan Copper*, 19.

28. Pope, "Some Early Mining Days," 27–28; P. H. Agan diary, 8 Aug. 1862, found in Steere Special Collection, Bayliss Public Library, Sault Ste. Marie, Mich.

29. Alex Campbell, "The Upper Peninsula," *MPHS* 3 (1881), 258–59; Dickinson, *To Build a Canal*, 134; *Michigan State Gazetteer and Business Directory for 1863–1864* (Detroit, 1863), 347.

30. WHC, *History of the Upper Peninsula*, 253; *PLMG*, 17 Nov. 1870; Arthur W. Thurner, *Strangers and Sojourners: A History of Michigan's Keweenaw Peninsula* (Detroit, 1994), 81–82.

31. William Gates, *Michigan Copper*, 61.

32. Agan, diary, 7 Aug. 1862; Pope, "Some Early Mining Days," 28.

33. Frederick Stonehouse, *Keweenaw Shipwrecks* (AuTrain, Mich., 1988), 33–65; WHC, *History of the Upper Peninsula*, 518; *CCJ*, 201.

34. *LSJ*, 9 July 1853.

35. Walling and Rupp, *Diary of Bishop Baraga*, 72n; J. G. Kohl, *Kitchi-Gami: Wanderings Round Lake Superior* (1860; reprint, Minneapolis, 1956), 168–69.

36. A letter written by J. G. Kohl to his sister on 24 Sept. 1855, describes this trek; the letter appears in Walling and Rupp, *Diary of Bishop Baraga*, 72n.

37. The maps are included within the annual reports of these companies for the given years.

38. Copper Falls Mining Company, *A.R. for 1852*, 11–12; *LSJ*, 9 July 1853.

39. William Gates, *Michigan Copper*, 21.

40. Forster, "Life in the Copper Mines," 176.

41. William Gates, *Michigan Copper*, 20; Toltec Mining Company, *A.R. for 1852*, no page, and *for 1855*, 12–14.

42. *LSM*, 16 June 1857.

43. *First A.R. of the Northwest Mining Company* (1849), 9; *Second A.R. of the Toltec Mining Company* (1855), 13; Robinson, *Early Days*, 9.

44. *PLMG*, 16 Dec. 1865 and 6 Jan. 1866.

45. Christian, *Winter on Isle Royale*, 22–23.

46. John Harris Forster, "Lake Superior Country," *MPHS* 8 (1886), 143.

47. *CCJ*, 238; *PLMG*, 24 Feb. 1870; *LSM*, 22 Dec. 1855.

48. Pope, "Some Early Mining Days," 19; *PLMG*, 17 March 1866 and 16 Dec. 1869.

49. *PLMG*, 1 April 1880.

50. Forster, "Lake Superior Country," 143.

51. Joseph W. V. Rawlings, "Recollections of a Long Life," ms. in KHSC no. 156, MTU. For a published version, see Roy W. Drier, ed., *Copper Country Tales* (Calumet, Mich., 1967), 75–127.

52. *CCJ*, 235, 259.

53. Robinson, *Early Days*, 13–14.

54. Quotations from the *OM* are found in WHC, *History of the Upper Peninsula*, 512; Swineford, *History and Review*, 25–26.

55. Robinson, *Early Days*, 19.

56. William Gates, *Michigan Copper*, 20–21; Orrin W. Robinson, "Recollections of Civil War Conditions in the Copper Country," *MH* 3 (Oct. 1919), 606–7; *PLMG*, 24 Sept. 1864.

57. See advertisement for Crooks stage, *PLMG*, 14 April 1870. See other stage-related ads and stories in the same paper for 6 Nov. 1864, 3 Feb. 1866, and 24 Nov. 1870. Henry Hobart (*CCJ*, 7 Dec. 1863) and Lucena Brockway (diaries, 3 Feb. 1866, and 10 Nov. 1874) make mention of winter stage service along the northern Keweenaw.

58. William Gates, *Michigan Copper*, 26, 61; C. Harry Benedict, *Red Metal: The Calumet and Hecla Story* (Ann Arbor, 1952), 67; Frank H. Haller, "Transportation System and Coal Dock," *MCJ* 17 (Oct. 1931), 515; *PLMG*, 18 April 1867.

59. John F. Campbell, "The Mineral Range Railroad Company," *The Soo* 2 (Oct. 1980), 16–20.

THREE   *Settling In*

1. Cannon, *A Narrative*, 62; for other descriptions of camping out, see pp. 51–53, 59, and 63.

2. Ibid., 54; also see pp. 58–59, 63, and 67. From Cannon's descriptions, it is not clear if his company's "shantees" had walls of laid-up logs, or if the structures were merely framed of logs, then covered or sided with cedar bark.

3. John H. Forster, "Some Incidents of Pioneer Life in the Upper Peninsula of Michigan," *MPHS* 17 (1892), 336; Swineford, *History and Review*, 24.

4. St. John, *True Description*, 29.

5. Clarke, "Notes from the Copper Region," 441, 443.

6. Friggens, "Fort Wilkins," 224–25.

7. Ibid., 233; Preservation Urban Design Incorporated, *Architectural Analysis: Fort Wilkins Historic Complex, Fort Wilkins State Park, Copper Harbor, Michigan* (Ann Arbor, Mich., 1976), 46–50.

8. Preservation Urban Design, *Architectural Analysis*, 27.

9. Ibid., 22, 27–29, 46–50.

10. Friggens, "Fort Wilkins," 225–26.

11. Forster, "Life in the Copper Mines," 177.

12. For a discussion of the leasing and subsequent sale of mineral lands, see Krause, *Making of a Mining District*, 179–82.

13. Pope, "Some Early Mining Days," 21; PMC, *Report* (March 1858), 7; MMC, *Report* (1858), 13; Phoenix Mining Co., *Report* (1865), n.p.

14. Pope, "Some Early Mining Days," 21; MMC, *Report* (1858), 13.

15. Foster and Whitney, *Report on Geology*, 146–51.

16. *Mining Magazine* 1 (1853), 295; Pope, "Some Early Mining Days," 27.

17. Whittlesey, "Pioneers of Lake Superior," 190.

18. Larry D. Lankton and Charles K. Hyde, *Old Reliable: An Illustrated History of the Quincy Mining Company* (Hancock, Mich., 1982), 16; PMC, *Report* (1858), 7, and *Report* (1859), 13.

19. North American Mining Co., *Report of the Directors* (1857), 15.

20. Michigan, *A.R. of the Commissioner of Mineral Statistics for 1880* (Lansing, 1881), 44–46, 58, 77, 82; Lankton and Hyde, *Old Reliable*, 92.

21. This transition from boardinghouses to single-family housing, from single men to married men, is perhaps best documented in the annual reports of the PMC published between 1858 and 1862. Also see Larry D. Lankton, *Cradle to Grave: Life, Work, and Death at the Lake Superior Copper Mines* (New York, 1991), 149–50.

22. William Gates, *Michigan Copper*, 208, 228; Michigan, *Statistics of the State of Michigan, Collected for the Ninth Census of the United States, June 1, 1870* (Lansing, 1873), 36, 50, 76. Population statistics used in this book cover Houghton, Keweenaw and Ontonagon Counties but always exclude Baraga County.

23. See Terry G. Jordan, *American Log Buildings: An Old World Heritage* (Chapel Hill, N.C., 1985), 14–15. The description of early cabins is based primarily on numerous photos of early mine villages at MTU, and also on discussions with archaelogist Patrick Martin, who has investigated Keweenaw housing at various sites.

24. This enlargement of the company cabin or house is shown in numerous nineteenth-century photos of mine locations; it is also documented by many maps or plans of the mine locations (that show house outlines), and by bird's-eye views of the Quincy Hill and Calumet locations done in the early 1870s.

25. Virginia McAlester and Lee McAlester, *A Field Guide to American Houses* (New York, 1992), 84.

26. For a description and construction history of various house types at the Quincy mine, see Sarah McNear, "Quincy Mining Company: Housing and Community Services, ca. 1860–1931," HAER report, Library of Congress, 1978.

27. For a fuller discussion of company houses at mine locations, see chapter 9, "Homes on the Range," in Lankton, *Cradle to Grave*, 142–62.

28. James North Wright, "The Development of the Copper Industry of Northern Michigan," *Michigan Political Science Association* 3 (Jan. 1899), 135, 139–40.

29. Lankton and Hyde, *Old Reliable*, 35.

30. Ibid., 35; Lankton, *Cradle to Grave*, 151–52. Cost data covering housing construction are sometimes found in mining company annual reports. For instance, the PMC *A.R.* (March 1858), 7, shows that boardinghouses cost slightly over $500 each to build (and more to furnish); the company's next *A.R.* (10 May 1859), 14, indicates that the company had eight log houses valued at $800. An "Inventory of Phoenix Mine," Aug. 31, 1865, appended to the *Directors Report* for 1865, lists an agent's house ($1,000); engineer's house ($1,200); twenty-four log houses at new mine ($300 each); four old log houses at old mine ($100 each); and seven tenements in old stamp building ($100 each).

31. For the opening up of various districts, and the movement from fissure veins of mass copper to the mining of amygdaloid and conglomerate lodes, see Krause, *Making of a Mining District*, 221–38. Production figures covering the fortunes of the various early mines from 1855

to 1880 are found in Michigan, *A.R. of the Commissioner of Mineral Statistics for 1880*, 152; also see production figures in Butler and Burbank, *Copper Deposits of Michigan*, 64–98.

32. Although the Cornish miner, Josiah Penhallow, is a fictitious character, the depiction of the Portage Lake shoreline, of Hancock, and of the Quincy and Pewabic mines is based on historical fact, as documented by a variety of sources, such as period photographs, maps and bird's-eye views, business directories, mining company annual reports, and newpaper advertisements and stories.

33. The Hancock waterfront, the board sidewalk leading up to town, and the town itself are shown in the photograph "Old view of Hancock, ca. 1865–68," Reeder collection, no. B2 202, MTU. For Cornish Hotel, see *PLMG*, 26 April 1866.

34. See photograph cited in note 33.

35. The mentioned artisans, tradesmen, professionals, and mercantile establishments in Hancock were largely identified through newspaper advertisements of the period; through the *Michigan State Gazetteer and Business Directory* (1865), 158; through QMC, *Invoice Books*, ca. 1865–70, MTU, which show the mine trading with several Hancock businesses; and through the 1870 U.S. Census, which lists the occupations of Hancock residents.

36. See ca. 1865 map of the Quincy mine in Lankton and Hyde, *Old Reliable*, 29. In the same source, also see the photographs of Quincy/Hancock environs, pp. 31, 42; an 1873 bird's-eye view of the Quincy, Pewabic, and Franklin mines, p. 53; and a discussion of Quincy's log houses in 1859, p. 35.

37. *PLMG*, 27 June 1867, and 15 April and 1 July 1869.

38. Ibid., 3 Dec. 1864.

39. This depiction of Pewabic housing is based on PMC, *A.R.* (31 Dec. 1862), 13, and *A.R.* (31 Dec. 1866), 17, 19.

FOUR   *A Lapful of Apples*

1. Greeley, *Recollections*, 244–45.

2. *PLMG*, 7 July 1870; *OM*, 14 July 1877.

3. Bela Hubbard, *Memorials of a Half-Century in Michigan and the Lake Region* (New York, 1887), 54. Hubbard recalled that the Douglass Houghton expedition of 1840 had one revolver and "one rusty shot-gun." Account books from local general stores from 1849 to 1870 show very little in the way of sales of weapons, ammunition, hunting equipment, or fishing tackle.

4. Jackman and Freeman, *American Voyageur*, 62; Peters, *Lake Superior Journal*, 52.

5. Cannon, *A Narrative*, 19.

6. *PLMG*, Jan. 6, 1870.

7. Whittlesey, *Fugitive Essays*, 313; Carter and Rankin, *North to Lake Superior*, 40, 42. Whittlesey (p. 342) also discusses pheasants, partridges, squirrels, bears, moose and other small and large game; Peters, *Lake Superior Journal*, 72, discusses gulls, loons, ducks, and pigeons.

8. Carter and Rankin, *North to Lake Superior*, 42; Greeley, *Recollections*, 244–45.

9. Cannon, *A Narrative*, 59.

10. Hubbard, *Memorials of a Half-Century*, 52–53.

11. Forster, "Early Settlement," 191–92.

12. This tale was told by Mrs. Robert Grierson in *DMG*, March 28, 1915.

13. Mrs. W. A. Childs, "Reminiscences of 'Old Keweenaw,'" *MPHS* 30 (1906), 154–55.

14. *Calumet News*, 17 March 1913.

15. For white settlers' accounts of Ojibwa serving as berry pickers, boatmen, and fishermen, see Robinson, *Early Days*, 6, 7, 9; CS, diary, 11 July 1847; *PLMG*, 19 April 1866 and 17 and

24 August 1882. For maple sugar, see Christian, *Winter on Isle Royale*, 25, and *PLMG*, 19 April 1866; for spruce beer, Kohl, *Kitchi-Gami*, 171.

16. *Laws of Michigan, 1863*, 411–13; *Laws of Michigan, 1865*, 717–18; *Compiled Laws of the State of Michigan* (Lansing, 1872), 679–82.

17. See unattributed newspaper clipping included in manuscript, Whittlesey, "Pioneers of Lake Superior."

18. Ruggles to Gibson, 29 June 1844, R.G. 192, National Archives.

19. *Mining Magazine* 7 (1856), 311; MMC, *A.R. for 1858*, 13, and *A.R. for 1861*, 15; and Michigan, *A.R. of the Commissioner of Mineral Statistics for 1880*, 74. Also see Lankton, *Cradle to Grave*, 15–16, 163–64.

20. MMC, *A.R. for 1858*, 13; PMC, *A.R. for 1862*, 19; *CCJ*, 145.

21. For figures on acres of improved land and for agricultural production, see Michigan, *Census and Statistics of the State of Michigan, May, 1854*; Michigan, *Statistics of the State of Michigan* (compiled from federal census data) for 1860 and 1870; and Michigan, *Census of the State of Michigan, 1874*. For the "Great Turnip," see *LSM*, 27 Oct. 1855. For a mining company's early production of hay, oats, cornstalk (for fodder), potatoes, and turnips, see Ohio Trap Rock Co., *Report of the Directors, Manager and Treasurer* (1855).

22. Clarke, "Notes from the Copper Region," 582; *OM*, 2 Nov. 1872.

23. *CCJ*, 121; *PLMG*, 15 Sept. 1870.

24. *PLMG*, 2 May 1867 and 25 May 1876.

25. Daniel J. Boorstin, *The Americans: The Democratic Experience* (New York, 1974), 307.

26. Edwin Henwood, "Early Reminiscences," KHSC no. 192, MTU.

27. For a detailed treatment of antebellum agricultural production, see Paul W. Gates, *The Farmer's Age: Agriculture, 1815–1860* (New York, 1960).

28. Boorstin, *The Americans*, 322.

29. Paul Gates, *Farmer's Age*, 197–201, 206–7.

30. Ibid., 191–96; Charles B. Kuhlmann, "The Processing of Agricultural Products in the Pre-Railway Age," in Harold F. Williamson, ed., *The Growth of the American Economy* (New York, 1944), 194.

31. Kuhlmann, "The Processing of Agricultural Products," 201–3; Gates, *Farmer's Age*, 201–3.

32. Boorstin, *The Americans*, 309–16; Earl Chapin May, *The Canning Clan: A Pageant of Pioneering Americans* (New York, 1937), 152.

33. For biographical material on Ransom Shelden, see WHC, *History of the Upper Peninsula*, 285–86; and Alvah L. Sawyer, *A History of the Northern Peninsula and Its People*, vol. 2 (Chicago, 1911), 1012–14. For John Senter, see T. A. Ten Broeck, "Sketch of John Senter," *MPHS* 30 (1906), 156–62. For a general discussion of the socioeconomic role of frontier merchants, see Lewis E. Atherton, *The Frontier Merchant in Mid-America* (Columbia, Mo., 1971), 9, 16.

34. All store records are held by MTU; undergraduates enrolled in a class on "Everyday Life in the Nineteenth Century" inventoried their contents. The store account books were: John Senter's store (1849); Ransom Shelden's store (1859–60); J. Hoar & Bros. store (1862–63); Minesota mine company store (1864); Quincy mine store (1864–65); Perkins & Co. store (1864–65); Foley & Smith store (1866); MFS & Co. store [M. Frend & Son] (1867); and unidentified store (1869–71).

35. See, for instance, Michigan, *Statistics of the State of Michigan, June 1, 1870*, 530–31, 622.

36. Michigan, *Census of the State of Michigan, 1874*, 405.

37. "Family Journal," Clarence Bennetts coll., MTU.

38. Childs, "Reminiscences of 'Old Keweenaw,' " 153–54.

39. LB, diary, 20 Aug. 1874; also see 16 Sept. 1867 and 5 Aug. 1889. On various years,

around the Fourth of July, LB usually spent some time picking strawberries. Also see RD, diary, 8 Sept. 1848; and *CCJ*, 164.

40. Nancy Fisher, unpublished graduate seminar paper written at Michigan Tech, "Heating and Cooking in the Keweenaw."

41. Ransom Shelden's store, account book, entry for 15 Nov. 1859; MFS & Co. store, account book, sales made between June and August 1867.

42. Ruth Schwartz Cowan, *More Work for Mother: The Ironies of Household Technology from the Open Hearth to the Microwave* (New York, 1983), 54.

43. Ibid., 55.

44. Jeanne Boydston, *Home and Work: Housework, Wages, and the Ideology of Labor in the Early Republic* (New York, 1990), 106.

45. Ibid., 106; also, Susan Strasser, *Never Done: A History of American Housework* (New York, 1982), 36, 40–41.

46. Cowan, *More Work for Mother*, 49–50, 62; Boydston, *Home and Work*, 107.

47. *CCJ*, 241; LB, diary, 8 Oct. 1889.

48. LB's 1873 and 1889 diaries are both at MTU.

49. *CCJ*, 239.

50. *PLMG*, 8 June 1876.

51. Jinny Penhale, "Letter 1," enclosed with Rawlings, "Recollection of a Long Life," MTU.

52. *CCJ*, 177–78.

53. Ibid., 177–78, 200, 241, 292.

54. Ibid., 200, 209.

55. Ibid., 200.

56. See ad for "Queen Refrigerator and Plain Ice Chests," *PLMG*, 5 Aug. 1869. For local ice harvests at Portage Lake, see *PLMG*, 4 March 1865, 10 March 1870, 13 Jan. 1876, and 21 Feb. 1878. For a general description of ice harvesting, see Joseph C. Jones, Jr., *America's Icemen: An Illustrative History of the United States Natural Ice Industry, 1625–1925* (Humble, Tex., 1984), 20, 24.

57. *PLMG*, 16 May 1867.

58. Friggens, "Fort Wilkins," 235.

59. Robinson, "Early Days," 10–11.

60. Christian, *Winter on Isle Royale*, 7. The greatest delicacy, she wrote (p. 8), was "canned French mushrooms."

61. *CCJ*, 111, 282–83.

62. Dr. A. I. Lawbaugh, "A Physician's Life in the Copper Country Early Days," KHSC no. 189, MTU; Forster, "Lake Superior Country," 144.

63. Robinson, *Early Days*, 6; LB, diary, 7 May 1874.

64. *PLMG*, 16 Dec. 1869. Also, see *PLMG*, 20 Feb. 1864, and 3 Feb. and 3 March 1870.

FIVE   *Keeping House*

1. Michigan, *Census and Statistics of the State of Michigan, May, 1854*, 125–27, 281–83; *Mining Magazine* (1857), 576, 585. For additional data on women and children at early mine locations, see *Report of the Directors of the North American Mining Co.* (1857), 9; *Mining Magazine* (1853), 131–32, and (1854), 553, and (1855), 40; MMC, *A.R. for 1858*, 13; and Michigan, *A.R. of the Commissioner of Mineral Statistics for 1880*, 74, 77.

2. See Michigan, *Statistics of the State of Michigan, June 1, 1870*, xxxiii, and *Census of the State of Michigan, 1874*, xxi–xxxviii.

3. Michigan, *Census of the State of Michigan, 1874*, xlii–xliii, 3–4.

4. George Buehler, "Family History," KHSC no. 183, MTU.

5. *PLMG*, 8 Dec. 1870 and 2 March 1876.

6. Cowan, *More Work for Mother*, 18–19; Strasser, *Never Done*, 180–201.

7. Childs, "Reminiscences of 'Old Keweenaw,'" 154.

8. RD, diary, 31 Aug. 1848.

9. Thomas J. Schlereth, *Victorian America: Transformations in Everyday Life, 1876–1915* (New York, 1991), 116–30.

10. "Family Journal," Clarence Bennetts collection, MTU.

11. Strasser, *Never Done*, 63; Schlereth, *Victorian America*, 112–16; Jack Larkin, *The Reshaping of Everyday Life, 1790–1840* (New York, 1988), 140–42.

12. Strasser, *Never Done*, 58–60. Michigan's 1874 *Census*, p. 405, lists three candlemakers in Houghton County; at least two had been in business for a decade or more.

13. Strasser, *Never Done*, 60–61.

14. Larkin, *Reshaping of Everyday Life*, 122; Strasser, *Never Done*, 63.

15. Strasser, *Never Done*, 95–96.

16. *PLMG*, 9 and 23 Sept. 1880 and 15 June 1882.

17. *CCJ*, 213. For the work of getting (and getting rid of) water, see Strasser, *Never Done*, 86–90.

18. *PLMG*, 14 June 1866.

19. Ibid., 29 April 1869.

20. Strasser, *Never Done*, 90–92; ewers and basins were sold out of many local stores.

21. None of the general or company stores, which operated from 1849 to 1870, and whose merchandise was inventoried as part of this research, carried an appreciable amount of furniture or toys for children. (For stores, see Chapter 4, note 34.) In 1866, the Foley & Smith store sold an occasional high chair or crib, and in 1867 the M. Frend, Son & Co. store sold a cradle.

22. *PLMG*, 2 May 1870.

23. Factory-produced chairs were available by the time of the Keweenaw's settlement, and all stores whose merchandise was inventoried carried and sold wooden chairs. See discussion of chairs in Larkin, *Reshaping of Everyday Life*, 137–40.

24. LB, diary, 20 Oct. 1873; "Family Journal," Bennetts collection, MTU.

25. *CCJ*, 124.

26. Boydston, *Home and Work*, 86.

27. "Family Journal," Bennetts collection, MTU.

28. CS, diary, 25 July 1847.

29. "Hon. Samuel Worth Hill," *MPHS* 17 (1890), 51–53.

30. Rawlings, "Reminiscences," KHSC no. 156, MTU. For common male dress, also see *CCJ*, 206; Childs, "Reminiscences of 'Old Keweenaw,'" 151; and James North Wright, *When Copper Was King: A Tale of the Early Mining Days on Lake Superior* (Boston, 1905), 7, 12, 15, 29.

31. See drug store ads, *LSM*, 12 Jan. 1856, and *PLMG*, 17 Jan. 1867. For Hocking's, see *PLMG*, 16 May 1867.

32. *LSM*, 3 Oct. 1857; *PLMG*, 10 and 17 Nov. 1870.

33. *OM*, 19 May 1877.

34. *LSM*, 3 Nov. 1855.

35. See, for example, LB, diaries, 12 Jan. and 30 Sept. 1867, 31 Dec. 1872, 15 Jan. 1874, and 16 Feb. 1875.

36. The "latest styles of the patent clothes-wringer" were advertised for sale in *PLMG*, 14 Oct. 1869.

37. Boydston, *Home and Work*, 84–85; Strasser, *Never Done*, 104–5, 109.

38. Strasser, *Never Done*, 104–8.

39. *PLMG*, 28 Oct. 1869.

SIX   *Tasks at Hand*

1. William Gates, *Michigan Copper*, 39–43. Also, Rodney R. Michael and Larry D. Lankton, "Accounting Innovations: The Implications of a Firm's Response to Post Civil War Market Disruptions, " *Accounting Historians Journal* 21, no. 2 (Dec. 1994): 41–84; this article has numerous tables depicting the effect of the recession on the Quincy mine's labor force and operations.

2. William Gates, *Michigan Copper*, 15–17, 203.

3. Ibid., 43–45; Benedict, *Red Metal*, 28–76.

4. The fictive Penhallow has been joined to two actual Quincy miners, John Roberts and Samuel Ley. This account is based on factual data concerning the places Roberts and Ley worked, the types of contracts they took up, and the wages they earned, as found in QMC *Contract Books* for the period (MTU). Further information on the Roberts-Ley team is found in Lankton, *Cradle to Grave*, 68–69.

5. For Cornish traditions and contracts, see Roger Burt, ed., *Cornish Mining: Essays on the Organisation of Cornish Mines and the Cornish Mining Economy* (Newton Abbot, U.K., 1969).

6. Lankton, *Cradle to Grave*, 182; Wright, "Development of the Copper Industry of Northern Michigan," 136.

7. *CCJ*, 206; Wright, *When Copper Was King*, 30–31.

8. Lankton and Hyde, *Old Reliable*, 22–23. The master mechanic who installed the first man-engine in the district was Joseph Rawlings; see his "Recollections of a Long Life," 115.

9. See Larry D. Lankton, "The Machine *under* the Garden: Rock Drills Arrive at the Lake Superior Copper Mines, 1868–1883," *Technology and Culture* 24 (Jan. 1983), 6–7.

10. Lankton, *Cradle to Grave*, 35–36.

11. For a discussion of miners' safety precautions (barring down loose rock, handling explosives), see ibid., 114–15, 119, 132.

12. The wages/salaries/earnings of skilled and unskilled workers, as well as of bosses and managers, are found in QMC *Contract Books* and *Time Books*, MTU.

13. Lankton and Hyde, *Old Reliable*, 25–27.

14. QMC, *Contract Book* (1866–69), MTU.

15. QMC, *A.R. for 1867*, 11.

16. Descriptions of kilnhouse labor are found in Clarke, "Notes from the Copper Region," 578, and in Robinson, "Recollections of Civil War Conditions," 598–99. Other data regarding kilnhouse wages and work are found in QMC *Time Books* and *Annual Reports*.

17. See QMC, *Contract Book* (1866–69), entry for June 1867.

18. The definitive treatment of stamp-mill technology is C. Harry Benedict, *Lake Superior Milling Practice* (Houghton, Michigan, 1955).

19. The boys' wages were taken from QMC *Time Books* and *Contract Books*, MTU.

20. Rawlings, "Recollections of a Long Life." MTU.

21. QMC *Time Book* covering June 1872 indicated just two boys working underground (at $18 each per month), and twenty-four boys working at the stamp mill at rates ranging from $20 to $30 per month.

22. Lankton and Hyde, *Old Reliable*, 39; QMC *Payroll Accounts* for June 1865 show that of 594 employees, 289 were Cornish, 138 German, 130 Irish, and 29 Scottish or English.

23. *CCJ*, 184–85; *PLMG*, 9 Aug. 1862, 2 and 29 Sept. 1869, and 20 July 1876.

24. Lankton and Hyde, *Old Reliable*, appendix, "Quincy Mining Company Officials," 151; also see p. 20.

25. A. J. Corey to William Rogers Todd, letter, 24 May 1873, Quincy Mine collection, MTU.

26. See QMC, *Time Book*, 1872.

27. Lankton and Hyde, *Old Reliable*, 8; QMC, *Time Book*, 1855.

28. See contracts to sort and break rock, QMC *Contract Book* (1861–63), entries for Sept.–Nov. 1863.

29. All are actual mining teams recorded in Quincy's *Contract Book* covering 1872.

30. Lankton, *Cradle to Grave*, 68–69.

31. Quincy's fatal accidents over these six years were documented as part of an overall study of mine fatalities on the Keweenaw. See Lankton, *Cradle to Grave*, chapter 7, "The Cost of Copper: One Man per Week," 110–125; and Larry D. Lankton and Jack K. Martin, "Technological Advance, Organizational Structure, and Underground Fatalities in the Upper Michigan Copper Mines, 1860–1929," *Technology and Culture* 28 (Jan. 1987), 42–66.

32. *PLMG*, 5 Aug. 1869, and 24 April 1870; Lankton, "The Machine *under* the Garden," 1–37.

33. The last of the higher-paying contracts to "break rock and fill cars for stamp mill" were for October and the first part of November 1873; subsequent contracts were for much reduced rates, once the jaw crushers were in operation.

34. William Gates, *Michigan Copper*, 28–30; Lankton and Hyde, *Old Reliable*, 31–32.

35. See Thomas Egleston, "Copper Refining in the United States," AIME *Trans.* 9 (1879), 275–312.

36. See entries for Roberts-Ley team in QMC *Contract Book* covering 1872.

37. This enumeration of laborers, tradesmen, and businessmen is based on *Census of the State of Michigan, 1874*, 405, 411–12, 421.

38. HCBS, *Proceedings, 1861–69*, entries for 10 April and 10 Oct. 1866, and *Proceedings, 1869–87*, entries for 1 Feb. 1869 and 25 July 1871. Found in Houghton County Public Records collection, MTU.

39. *CCJ*, 227; LB, diaries, 22 Dec. 1866, 4 and 17 Sept. 1867, 21 Aug. 1872, 19 Jan. and 6 July 1874.

40. *NMJ*, 10 Jan. 1877.

41. Several of these are listed in *Michigan State Gazetteer and Business Directories* for 1863–64 and 1865. *PLMG*, 10 June 1865, noted the opening of a millinery store in Hancock; and on 16 Dec. 1869, *PLMG* announced a similar opening in Houghton.

42. *LSM*, 5 Jan. 1856; *PLMG*, 7 April 1870 and 2 Nov. 1876.

43. *LSM*, 27 Oct. 1855.

44. Rev. Antoine Ivan Rezek, *History of the Diocese of Sault Ste. Marie and Marquette*, vol. 2 (Houghton, Mich., 1907), 309; P. Chrysostomus Verwyst, *Life and Labors of Rt. Rev. Frederic Baraga* (Milwaukee, 1900), 341, 347, 363.

45. Data drawn from Michigan, *A.R. of the Superintendent of Public Instruction* (Lansing), for years 1857 and 1875.

46. William S. Thomas, journal, 1877–1897, MTU.

47. See male and female teachers' salaries as reported in Houghton County, *Annual Reports of the School Inspectors*, for the years 1866–1879, Houghton County records collection, accession 77–105, MTU.

48. *PLMG*, 23 Aug. 1866.

49. *CCJ*, 80; see Calumet township supervisor's report and Houghton County's superintendent's report, included in Michigan, *A.R. of the Superintendent of Public Instruction* for 1875.

50. *CCJ*, 168.

51. Ibid., 212–13; LB, diaries, 22 Dec. 1866, 21 Aug. 1872, 19 Jan. and 12 June 1874.

52. *CCJ*, 212–13, 228, 253, 264, 277.

53. Billington, *America's Frontier Heritage*, 97, 99, 106.

54. WHC, *History of the Upper Peninsula*, 280, 292, 309.

55. Michigan, *A.R. of the Superintendent of Public Instruction for 1869*, 90.

SEVEN   *Saints and Scholars*

1. Christian, *Winter on Isle Royale*, 17; *Mining Magazine* 1 (1853), 132; Walling and Rupp, *Diary of Bishop Baraga*, 144n.

2. Walling and Rupp, *Diary of Bishop Baraga*, 21–25.

3. Verwyst, *Life and Labors*, 230–31.

4. Rezek, *History of the Diocese*, vol. 1, 88.

5. WHC, *History of the Upper Peninsula*, 335; Walling and Rupp, *Diary of Bishop Baraga*, 46–47, 132, 143–44; Rezek, *History of the Diocese*, vol. 1, 250–51.

6. Walling and Rupp, *Diary of Bishop Baraga*, 129n and 145n.

7. Ibid., 83–84.

8. Ibid., 131–32.

9. Ibid., 146, 267–68.

10. Ibid., 129n and 146.

11. Ibid., 172.

12. Thurner, *Strangers and Sojourners*, 54, 57.

13. Ibid., 58; *CCJ*, 38.

14. Arthur W. Thurner, *Calumet Copper and People: History of a Michigan Mining Community* (by the author, 1974), 21; *Michigan State Gazetteer and Business Directory for 1863–64*, 291, 297, 336, 347, 429; *LSM*, 10 Oct. 1857 and 30 Jan. 1858; WHC, *History of the Upper Peninsula*, 336, 343.

15. Thurner, *Calumet Copper and People*, 21.

16. See sources cited in n. 14. Also see *Mining Magazine* 1 (1853), 294, and Pittsburgh and Boston Mining Co., *A.R. for 1860*, 21.

17. Michigan, *Statistics of the State of Michigan, June 1, 1870*, 636.

18. Ibid., 636, 639, 645.

19. *CCJ*, 148, 156, 208–9, 289.

20. *LSM*, 22 Dec. 1855 and 5 Jan. 1856.

21. *PLMG*, 6 Jan. 1870.

22. *CCJ*, 90, 108.

23. Ibid., 79–80.

24. Ibid., 229.

25. Michigan, *A.R. of the Superintendent of Public Instruction for 1870*, 74.

26. *PLMG*, 24 Sept. and 26 Nov. 1864.

27. *CCJ*, 143.

28. *PLMG*, 23 Aug. 1866.

29. Michigan, *A.R. of the Superintendent of Public Instruction for 1872*, 71, and *A.R. for 1873*, 147.

30. See School District No. 1, Quincy Township, *Minutes of Meetings* (1867–), QMC collection, MTU.

31. Michigan, *A.R. of the Superintendent of Public Instruction for 1870*, 72.

32. Donald Chaput, *The Cliff: America's First Great Copper Mine* (Kalamazoo, 1971), 93; Pittsburgh and Boston Mining Co., *A.R. for 1861*, 16.

33. *CCJ*, 80.

34. Ibid., 91.

35. Ibid., 92–93.

36. Michigan, *Public Acts, 1871*, 170–76, 251–53.

37. The number of children attending school, and the overall number of school-aged children in each of the counties, is found in Michigan, *A.R. of the Superintendent of Public Instruction* for the cited years. The *A.R.* for 1880 ranks Houghton as seventy-first out of seventy-seven counties.

38. *CCJ*, 203.

39. Ibid., 237, 250.

40. Ibid., 212.

41. Ibid., 276; also see pp. 229, 262.

42. *PLMG*, 5 April 1866.

43. Houghton County, *School Inspector Reports* for 1866–67, MTU.

44. Houghton County, *School Inspector Reports* for 1875, MTU.

45. Michigan, *A.R. of the Superintendent of Public Instruction for 1875*, 96.

46. Michigan, *A.R. of the Superintendent of Public Instruction for 1877*, 190–91.

47. Michigan, *A.R. of the Superintendent of Public Instruction for 1870*, 73.

48. Houghton County School Superintendent, "General Statistics for School Year 1873–74," found in *School Inspector Reports*, MTU.

EIGHT   *The Sins of the Body*

1. *CCJ*, 214.

2. *PLMG*, 19 July 1866, 14 April and 30 June 1870.

3. *CCJ*, 270.

4. Forster, "Some Incidents of Pioneer Life," 337.

5. Pope, "Some Early Mining Days," 24–25; *PLMG*, 10 Feb. 1866.

6. *PLMG*, 29 Dec. 1870.

7. Robinson, *Early Days*, 12.

8. *CCJ*, 240, 249, 264.

9. Twelve men are known to have been killed in the mines in the 1850s, fifty-four men in the 1860s. For a full accounting, see Lankton, *Cradle to Grave*, 110.

10. *PLMG*, 7 March 1867.

11. *CCJ*, 121, 140, 156, 163, 171, 201.

12. *PLMG*, 21 July 1870; *CCJ*, 264.

13. *LSM*, 21 Nov. 1857.

14. *CCJ*, 285; *PLMG*, 25 May 1876 and 12 Sept. 1878; *LSM*, 15 Aug. 1857.

15. LB, diary, 1 and 6 March, 7 and 16 April and 5 May 1866.

16. *CCJ*, 109, 152, 167, 172, 199, 214, 225, 227, 234, 243, 258–59, 262, 263, 269, 280, 292–93, 301, 308.

17. *PLMG*, 29 April 1865.

18. See Houghton County's death statistics in Michigan, *A.R. on the Registration of Births and Deaths, Marriages and Divorces, 1871.*

19. Paul Starr, *The Social Transformation of American Medicine* (New York, 1982), 73.

20. Lankton, *Cradle to Grave*, 181–82.

21. Starr, *Social Transformation*, 47, 65, 156.

22. Lankton, *Cradle to Grave*, 183; Starr, *Social Transformation*, 85.

23. *PLMG*, 9 Jan. 1864, (ad for Dr. McCall), and 17 May 1866.

24. *LSM*, 6 Dec. 1856; *PLMG*, 14 Nov. 1863.

25. *PLMG*, 12 July 1866.

26. HCBS, *Proceedings* (1861–69), 151, R.G. 89–464, MTU.

27. Ibid., 161; *PLMG*, 31 Oct. 1863.

28. HCBS, *Proceedings* (1861–69), 327–28.

29. *Michigan State Gazetteer and Business Directory for 1865* (see entries for the various villages); Michigan, *Census of the State of Michigan, 1874*, 405, 411, 421.

30. *Mining Magazine* (1857), 576; MMC, *A. R. for 1858*, 13; PMC, *A.R. for 1862*, 13; Lankton and Hyde, *Old Reliable*, 36; WHC, *History of the Upper Peninsula*, 299; *PLMG*, May 7, 1864.

31. Starr, *Social Transformation*, 147–50.

32. *PLMG*, 29 April 1865.

33. Ibid., 2 Jan. 1864.

34. Ibid., 14 May 1864 and 29 April 1865; HCBS, *Proceedings* (1861–69), entry for 7 March 1864.

35. *LSM*, 31 May 1856.

36. *PLMG*, 9 Aug. 1862, 25 Feb. and 2 Sept. 1865, 12 April 1866, 17 Jan. and 11 April 1867, and 10 Feb. 1870.

37. M. D. K. Bremner, *The Story of Dentistry* (Brooklyn, 1954), 184–95, 201.

38. Ibid., 202, 209, 228.

39. CS, diary, 18 and 25 Aug. 1847.

40. *LSM*, 1 Dec. 1855 and 16 Aug. 1856.

41. *CCJ*, 83; LB, diary, 21 Aug. 1874.

42. *CCJ*, 83; LB, diary, 13 Aug. 1874.

43. *PLMG*, 10 Jan. 1867.

44. *PLMG*, 20 June 1867 and 21 July 1870.

45. Ibid., 26 Sept. 1863.

46. *LSM*, 6 Oct. 1855; *PLMG*, 11 Oct. 1862 and 3 Oct. 1863.

47. *LSM*, 28 March 1857; *PLMG*, 31 May 1866.

48. *PLMG*, 31 May 1866.

49. Ibid., 2 May 1867.

50. Starr, *Social Transformation*, 127–28.

51. *LSM*, 23 Aug. 1856.

52. *PLMG*, 23 April 1864.

53. Ibid., 22 July 1865.

54. Ibid., 23 Aug. 1862.

55. James Reed, *From Private Vice to Public Virtue: The Birth Control Movement and American Society since 1830* (New York, 1978), 4.

56. Ibid., 13–16.

57. *PLMG*, 23 Aug. 1862.

58. *LSM*, 17 May 1856; *PLMG*, 23 Aug. 1862.

59. James C. Mohr, *Abortion in America: The Origins and Evolution of National Policy, 1800–1900* (New York, 1978), 55–58.

60. Ibid., 53, 60–61, 67.

61. Ibid., 50, 81.

62. Michigan, *Statistics of the State of Michigan, 1870*, 4–6.

63. *PLMG*, 29 April 1865.

64. Judith Walzer Leavitt, *Brought to Bed: Childbearing in America, 1750 to 1950* (New York, 1986), 87.

65. *CCJ*, 262–63, 274.

66. "List of official acts performed at Grace Church, Clifton (The Old Cliff Mine), Keweenaw County, Michigan, by Reverend William Allen Johnson, Rector, 1862–64," KHSC no. 196, MTU.

67. Michigan, *Statistics of the State of Michigan, 1870*, 217, 219, 224, 244–45.

68. *PLMG*, 29 April 1865.

NINE   *Ice Carnivals, Camels, and Sunday Trombones*

1. Childs, "Reminiscences of 'Old Keweenaw,' " 154.
2. Forster, "Life in the Copper Mines," 176.
3. *PLMG*, 21 March 1863, 19 March 1866, 17 March 1866, 10 Feb. 1870.
4. *CCJ*, 278; *LSM*, 24 Nov. 1855 and 13 Nov. 1858; *PLMG*, 25 Nov. 1869; LB, diary, 26 Nov. 1874.
5. Robinson, *Early Days*, 33–34. Also see *PLMG*, 20 Feb. 1864.
6. Jackson, *Report on the Geological Survey*, 410.
7. *CCJ*, 172, 180, 301–2; *PLMG*, 11 July 1867; Walling and Rupp, *Diary of Bishop Baraga*, entry for 4 July 1861.
8. Forster, "Early Settlement," 192.
9. "Family Journal," Bennetts collection, MTU; *CCJ*, 242–43.
10. *CCJ*, 78; *PLMG*, 13 Dec. 1866.
11. LB, diaries, 25 Dec. 1874 and 1876.
12. Rezek, *History of the Diocese* vol. 1, 83.
13. Christian, *Winter on Isle Royale*, 11–12, 25–26, 28.
14. *PLMG*, 16 Nov. 1876, 19 Oct. 1863.
15. Ibid., 4 Aug. 1870.
16. Ibid., 4 Oct. 1862 and 28 March 1863.
17. RD, diary, 22 Nov. 1848.
18. Swineford, *History and Review*, 28.
19. PMC, *A.R. for 1861*, 19; *CCJ*, 199; *PLMG*, 8 Oct. 1864; Keweenaw county superintendent's report in Michigan, *A.R. of the Superintendent of Public Instruction for 1870*; Thurner, *Strangers and Sojourners*, 86, 97.
20. *CCJ*, 78, 81, 171.
21. *PLMG*, 24 March and 3 May 1866.
22. Brockway biographical data from Sawyer, *History of the Northern Peninsula*, 1326–28; and *Red Jacket and Laurium Weekly News*, 12 May 1899.
23. LB, diaries, 1 March 1866, 27 April and 7 May 1867, and 21 June 1874.
24. Ibid., 23 Jan. 1874.
25. Schoolcraft, *Narrative Journal*, 21; Wright, *When Copper Was King*, 25, 29, 55; Alfred Nicholls, "Glimpse of Mining Life in the Days of Yore," ms., KHSC no. 190, MTU.
26. Charles Lanman, *Summer in the Wilderness*, 130; RD, diary, 28 Oct. 1848.
27. *CCJ*, 118, 127, 149–52, 161, 164, 169, 210.
28. RD, diary, 11 Sept. and 4 Oct. 1848.
29. *CCJ*, 125, 234, 265; Robinson, *Early Days*, 6.
30. *CCJ*, 112.
31. *PLMG*, 12 Nov. 1864 and 7 Jan. 1865.
32. RD, diary, 2 Nov. 1848; LB, diary, 28 and 30 June, 1, 6, 7, 13, and 21 July 1867.
33. *CCJ*, 91, 169, 170–71; Jerome Mushkat, "Mineral and Timber Prospects in Upper Michigan: The 1858 Diary of John V. L. Pruyn," article (no source) discovered in "Remembrances" file, MTU; *PLMG*, 1 Aug. 1878.
34. John H. Forster, "War Time in the Copper Mines," *MPHS* 18 (1892), 377.
35. Pope, "Some Early Mining Days," 22; *LSM*, 22 March 1856.
36. *PLMG*, 21 April 1870.
37. Ibid., 26 Dec. 1863 and 30 Dec. 1869.
38. Ibid., 7 Feb. 1863, 20 Feb. 1864, 20 Jan. 1866.
39. Ibid., 15 Oct. 1864 and 23 June 1870; *CCJ*, 184–85.
40. *PLMG*, 26 June 1866.

41. Ibid., 2 and 16 Aug. 1866 and 15 July 1869.

42. *CCJ*, 272; *PLMG*, 20 Dec. 1866; 16 Dec. 1869; 6 Jan., 17 Feb., 8 and 15 Dec. 1870; J. N. Scott, diary, 9 Jan. 1869, Brockway Family collection, MTU.

43. *PLMG*, 20 Jan. 1866.

44. Ibid., 29 July 1869; *CCJ*, 285–86. See ads for "Grand Wrestling Matches" in *PLMG*, 10 May 1866 and 13 June 1867.

45. *CCJ*, 282; *PLMG*, 22 April and 6 May 1869; 2 and 26 May, 9 June, and 4 and 25 Aug. 1870.

46. *PLMG*, 7 July 1870 and 9 July 1881; LB, diary, 4 and 22 July 1874.

47. *PLMG*, 14 Oct. 1865, 14 Feb. and 30 May 1867, and 24 Nov. 1870.

48. Ibid., 27 Sept. 1866, 2 May 1867, 9 Dec. 1869; Scott, diary, 11, 12, and 27 Jan. and 6 Feb. 1869.

49. *PLMG*, 21 March 1867.

50. Rawlings, "Recollections of a Long Life," MTU.

51. Forster, "Life in the Copper Mines," 185.

52. Lawrence T. Fadner, *Fort Wilkins, 1844, and the U.S. Mineral Land Agency, 1843, Copper Harbor, Michigan* (New York, 1966), 58.

53. *Mining Magazine* 1 (1853), 294.

54. WHC, *History of the Upper Peninsula*, 276, 313, 339–40; Michigan, *Statistics of the State of Michigan, 1870*, 522–23.

55. *Compiled Laws of the State of Michigan* (Lansing, 1872), 59. For information on the 1875 and 1877 legislative actions regarding liquor control, see *NMJ*, 14 July 1875; *Public Acts of Michigan, 1875*, 270–71, 283–85, 417; and *Public Acts of Michigan, 1877*, 72–73, 180, 207, 212–15, 232–39, 311.

56. Clarke, "Notes from the Copper Region," 583.

57. *Michigan State Gazetteer and Business Directory for 1863–64*, 292, 336.

TEN   *Shattered Hopes and Broken Prospects*

1. LB, diary, 22 Feb. 1866; *PLMG*, 20 May and 30 Sept. 1869; HCBS, *Proceedings* (1869–87), entries for 12 Oct. 1869 and 13 June 1870.

2. Keweenaw county, *Minutes of the Superintendent of the Poor* (1863–81), entries for 1861 and 1868 (pp. 284–85 contain records *prior* to 1863), accession 67–60–A, Agency Lot No. 1, MTU; *PLMG*, 27 Jan. 1870.

3. Forster, "Life in the Copper Mines," 185.

4. Lankton, *Cradle to Grave*, vii–viii.

5. *Mining Magazine* 1 (1853), 294–95.

6. Ibid., 132, 294; Clarke, "Notes from the Copper Region," 581.

7. Lankton and Hyde, *Old Reliable*, 35.

8. The organization of the counties is related in WHC, *History of the Upper Peninsula*; for judges, see Forster, "Lake Superior Country," 144.

9. Michigan, *Report of the Board of State Commissioners . . . of Charitable, Penal, Pauper, and Reformatory Institutions, 1873*, 89; Michigan, *Sixth Biennial Report of the Michigan State Board of Corrections and Charities, 1881–82*, 60; HCBS, *Proceedings* (869–87), entry for 27 Feb. 1873; Houghton County jail, "Inventory," 31 Dec. 1874, R.G. 89–464, MTU.

10. *PLMG*, 23 Jan. 1864; Houghton County, *Jail Records* (1874–1902), accession 77–105, MTU.

11. *CCJ*, 114–15, 155, 180.

12. See Chapter 9, note 55.

13. *LSM*, 29 Aug. 1857; *PLMG*, 6 Dec. 1862 and 2 May 1867.

14. *CCJ*, 99–100, 270, 280, 286, 288; *PLMG*, 27 Feb. and 4 June 1864.

15. *PLMG*, 2 Aug. 1862, 27 Sept. 1866, and 20 Oct. 1870.

16. Forster, "Lake Superior Country," 141.

17. Forster, "War Time in the Copper Mines," 377–78, and "Lake Superior Country," 141; *PLMG*, 16 Aug. and 27 Dec. 1862, 31 Dec. 1864, 2 Sept. 1865, and 5 April 1867.

18. *CCJ*, 136.

19. Ibid., 144–46, 152, 220.

20. *PLMG*, 19 Dec. 1863; *CCJ*, 236.

21. *PLMG*, 23 Jan. 1864; Houghton County, *Jail Records* for 1875.

22. *PLMG*, 13 Dec. 1862; *CCJ*, 107.

23. *PLMG*, 21 Aug. 1870.

24. Ibid., 23 Jan. 1864, 20 Jan. and 4 Aug. 1870.

25. *CCJ*, 211.

26. *PLMG*, 25 May 1867.

27. Only infrequently, for instance, were women charged with prostitution in the mid-1870s, although there was a spate of arrests for keeping a "house of ill-fame" in 1878. See Houghton County, *Jail Records*, MTU.

28. *PLMG*, 21 Jan. 1870; LB, diaries, 1 Feb. 1866 and 25 Dec. 1875.

29. LB, diary, 10 Jan. 1873; *PLMG*, 2 April, 24 Sept. and 17 Dec. 1864, 5 March 1866, and 30 Sept. 1869.

30. For mining company patriarchy and paternalism, see Lankton, *Cradle to Grave*, 142–98.

31. Richard A. Bartlett, *The New Country: A Social History of the Frontier, 1776–1890* (New York, 1974), 345–46; WHC, *History of the Upper Peninsula*, 274, 290, 307, 337, 339.

32. *CCJ*, 79, 293–95.

33. *LSM*, 23 Oct. 1858; *PLMG*, 21 Jan. 1867; WHC, *History of the Upper Peninsula*, 290.

34. For documentation on the establishment and membership requirements of mutual aid and benefit societies, see Houghton County, *Articles of Association*, vols. 1–5.

35. *LSM*, 9 May 1857.

36. Forster, "War Time in the Copper Mines," 380; William Gates, *Michigan Copper*, 97–98, 100, 105.

37. WHC, *History of the Upper Peninsula*, 253, 517; HCBS, *Proceedings* (1861–69), entries for 12 Feb. 1863, passim.

38. *PLMG*, 28 March 1867.

39. Houghton County's "Annual Reports of the Superintendents of the Poor" for the 1860s and 1870s (found in HCBS, *Proceedings*) recorded the number of paupers in the poorhouse, the number on outside relief, and the amount of money spent to send paupers away to be cared for by "friends below."

40. *PLMG*, 17 Feb. 1866.

41. Ibid., 17 Feb. 1866.

42. Keweenaw County, *Minutes of the Superintendents of the Poor* (1863–81), entries for 1867; HCBS, *Proceedings* (1869–81), entry for 11 Oct. 1870; *PLMG*, 28 March 1867.

43. For various years, see Keweenaw County, *Minutes of the Superintendents of the Poor* (1863–81), MTU.

44. *OM*, 14 July 1877.

45. Michigan, *Report of the Special Commissioners to Examine the Penal, Reformatory, and Charitable Institutions of the State of Michigan* (Lansing, 1871), 12–13.

46. *OM*, 14 July 1877.

47. *PLMG*, 28 March 1867; HCBS, *Proceedings* (1861–69), includes "Annual Reports of the Superintendents of the Poor," entries for 6 June 1866 and 14 Oct. 1867.

48. *PLMG*, 28 March 1867; see "Annual Reports of the Superintendent of the Poor," included in HCBS, *Proceedings*.

49. Michigan, *Report of the Board of State Commissioners for the General Supervision of Charitable, Penal, Pauper, and Reformatory Institutions* (Lansing, 1873), 107; HCBS, *Proceedings* (1869–87), entry for 10 Oct. 1876.

50. The "Annual Reports of the Superintendents of the Poor" provide information on poor-farm produce and its sale. In its first year of operation, the poor farm received $14.75 for turnips; $578 for potatoes; $5.00 for raspberries; and $78.00 for vegetables.

51. Ibid.

52. See Keweenaw County, *Minutes of the Superintendents of the Poor*, and Houghton County, "Annual Reports of the Superintendents of the Poor."

53. Lankton and Hyde, *Old Reliable*, 52; William Gates, *Michigan Copper*, 54.

54. The *Hancock Journal* article was reprinted in *OM*, Oct. 18, 1879.

55. Michigan, *Report of the Special Commissioners*, 7, 11.

56. Michigan, *Fourteenth Biennial Report . . . of Corrections and Charities for 1897–98*, 139; this source lists all state-supported institutions and provides the year in which they opened.

57. Michigan, *Sixth Biennial Report . . . of Corrections and Charities for 1881–82*, 119.

58. Michigan, *Report of the Special Commissioners*, 14–15; *Second Biennial Report of the Board of State Commissioners . . . of Charitable, Penal, Pauper . . . Institutions for 1874*, 32. Also see Starr, *Social Transformation*, 72–73, for a discussion of how American society shifted from the idea of merely containing or restraining the insane to the idea of curing them.

59. Mich., *Second Biennial Report of the Board of State Commissioners . . . of Charitable, Penal, Pauper . . . Institutions for 1874*, 32–33.

60. HCBS, *Proceedings* (1861–69), entry for 1 Feb. 1866. For treatment and boarding costs for the insane, see Medical Superintendents of the Michigan Asylum of the Insane at Kalamazoo, "Statements," Houghton County records, R.G. 89–464 (Box 17, File 13), MTU.

61. Keweenaw County, *Minutes of the Superintendents of the Poor* (1863–81), entry for June 1876.

62. LB, diary, 22 Feb. 1866; HCBS, *Proceedings* (1869–87), entries for 12 Oct. 1869 and 13 June and 11 Oct. 1870.

63. *PLMG*, 22 July and 21 Oct. 1869.

ELEVEN   *Transformations*

1. RD, diary, 25 Dec. 1848.

2. *PLMG*, 14 June 1866.

BIBLIOGRAPHY

Archival Records

Bayliss Public Library, Sault Ste. Marie, Michigan
  Steere Special Collection: P. H. Agan diary
Clarke Historical Library, Central Michigan University
  Ruth Douglass diary
Library of Congress
  Historic American Engineering Record Collection, Quincy Mining Company materials
Michigan Technological University Archives and Copper Country Historical Collections
  Clarence Bennetts Collection
  Brockway Family Collection
  Calumet and Hecla Mining Co. Collections
  Ben Chynoweth Collection
  Roy Drier Collection
  Houghton County Public Records Collections
  Keweenaw County Public Records Collections
  Keweenaw Historical Society Collections
  Quincy Mining Company Collection
  William S. Thomas Collection
National Archives
  Records of Commissary General of Subsistence, R.G. 192

Western Reserve Historical Sociey
     Charles Whittlesey manuscript, "Pioneers of Lake Superior"

Newspapers

Calumet News
Daily Mining Gazette
Lake Superior Journal
Lake Superior Miner
Ontonagon Miner
Portage Lake Mining Gazette
Red Jacket and Laurium Weekly News

Mining Company Annual Reports

American Exploring, Mining, and Manufacturing Co.
Calumet and Hecla Mining Co.
Central Mining Co.
Franklin Mining Co.
Lake Superior Copper Co.
Minesota Mining Co.
Norwich Mining Co.
Ohio Trap Rock Co.
Pewabic Mining Co.
Phoenix Mining Co.
Pittsburgh and Boston Mining Co.
Quincy Mining Co.

Government Documents/Publications

Butler, B. S., and W. S. Burbank. *The Copper Deposits of Michigan*. U.S. Geological Survey
     Professional Paper 144. Washington, 1929.
Crane, W. R. *Mining Methods and Practice in the Michigan Copper Mines*. U.S. Bureau of Mines
     Bulletin 306. Washington, 1929.
Foster, John W., and Josiah D. Whitney. *Report on the Geology and Topography of a Portion of
     the Lake Superior Land District in the State of Michigan, Part 1, Copper Lands*. U.S. House,
     Exec. Doc. 69 (31st Cong., 1st sess.), 1850.
Jackson, Charles T. *Report on the Geological and Mineralogical Survey of the Mineral Lands
     of the United States in the State of Michigan*. Senate Exec. Doc. 1 (31st Cong., 1st sess.),
     1849.
Michigan. *Annual Reports of the Commissioner of Mineral Statistics.*
————. *Annual Reports on the Registration of Births and Deaths, Marriages and Divorces.*
————. *Annual Reports of the Superintendent of Public Instruction.*
————. *Biennial Reports of the Board of Control of the Michigan School for the Blind.*
————. *Biennial Reports of the Board of Corrections and Charities.*
————. *Biennial Reports of the Board of Trustees of the Michigan School for the Deaf at Flint.*
————. *Biennial Reports of the Michigan State Industrial Home for Girls.*
————. *Biennial Reports of the Trustees of the Industrial School for Boys of Michigan.*
————. *Census and Statistics of the State of Michigan*. Lansing, 1854.
————. *Census of the State of Michigan, 1874*. Lansing, 1875.

————. *Report of the Board of State Commissioners for the General Supervision of Charitable, Penal, Pauper, and Reformatory Institutions*. Lansing, 1873.

————. *Report of the Special Commissioners to Examine the Penal, Reformatory, and Charitable Institutions of the State of Michigan*. Lansing, 1871.

————. *Reports of Sheriffs Relating to the Jails in the State of Michigan*.

————. *Statistics of Michigan*. Lansing, 1850.

————. *Statistics of the State of Michigan, Collected for the Ninth Census of the United States, June 1, 1870*. Lansing, 1873.

————. *Statistics of the State of Michigan, compiled from the Census of 1860*. Lansing, 1861.

Articles, Books, Theses, and Dissertations

Alanen, Arnold R. "The Planning of Company Communities in the Lake Superior Mining Region." *Journal of the American Planning Association* 45 (July 1979): 256–78.

Atherton, Lewis E. *The Frontier Merchant in Mid-America*. Columbia, Mo., 1971.

Barry, James P. *Ships of the Great Lakes: 300 Years of Navigation*. Berkeley, 1973.

Bartlett, Richard A. *The New Country: A Social History of the Frontier, 1776–1890*. New York, 1974.

Benedict, C. Harry. *Lake Superior Milling Practice*. Houghton, Mich., 1955.

————. *Red Metal: The Calumet and Hecla Story*. Ann Arbor, 1952.

Billington, Ray Allen. *America's Frontier Heritage*. Albuquerque, 1974.

Boorstin, Daniel J. *The Americans: The Democratic Experience*. New York, 1974.

Boydston, Jeanne. *Home and Work: Housework, Wages, and the Ideology of Labor in the Early Republic*. New York, 1990.

Bremner, M. D. K. *The Story of Dentistry*. Brooklyn, 1954.

"A Brief Account of the Lake Superior Copper Company," by "an original shareholder." Boston, 1845.

Broderick, T. M., and C. D. Hohl. "Geology and Exploration in the Michigan Copper District." *Mining Congress Journal* 17 (Oct. 1931): 478–81, 486.

Burt, Roger, ed. *Cornish Mining: Essays on the Organisation of Cornish Mines and the Cornish Mining Economy*. Newton Abbot, U.K., 1969.

Campbell, Alex. "The Upper Peninsula." *Michigan Pioneer and Historical Society Collections* 3 (1881): 247–65.

Campbell, John F. "The Mineral Range Railroad Company." *The Soo* 2 (Oct. 1980): 12–35.

Cannon, George M. *A Narrative of One Year in the Wilderness*. Ann Arbor, 1982.

Carter, James L., and Ernest H. Rankin, eds. *North to Lake Superior: The Journal of Charles W. Penny, 1840*. Marquette, Mich., 1970.

Chaput, Donald. *The Cliff: America's First Great Copper Mine*. Kalamazoo, 1971.

Childs, Mrs. W. A. "Reminiscences of 'Old Keweenaw.'" *Michigan Pioneer and Historical Society Collections* 30 (1906): 150–55.

Christian, Sarah Barr. *Winter on Isle Royale: A Narrative of Life on Isle Royal during the Years of 1874 and 1875*. N.p., 1932.

Clarke, Robert E. "Notes from the Copper Region." *Harper's New Monthly Magazine* 6 (March 1853): 433–48, and (April 1853): 577–88.

Cowan, Ruth Schwartz. *More Work for Mother: The Ironies of Household Technology from the Open Hearth to the Microwave*. New York, 1983.

Dickerson, Don Willis. "Theatrical Entertainment, Social Halls, Industry and Community: Houghton County, Michigan, 1837–1916." Ph.D. diss., Michigan State University, 1983.

Dickinson, John N. *To Build a Canal: Sault Ste. Marie, 1853–1854 and After*. Miami, Ohio, 1981.

Drier, Roy W., ed. *Copper Country Tales*, Calumet, Mich., 1967.

Dunbar, Willis. *All Aboard! A History of Railroads in Michigan*. Grand Rapids, 1969.

Egleston, Thomas. "Copper Mining on Lake Superior." American Institute of Mining Engineers *Transactions* 6 (1879): 275–312.

———. "Copper Refining in the United States." American Institute of Mining Engineers *Transactions* 9 (1880–81). 678–730.

Fadner, Lawrence Trever. *Fort Wilkins, 1844, and the U.S. Mineral Land Agency, 1843, Copper Harbor, Michigan*. New York, 1966.

Forster, John Harris. "Early Settlement of the Copper Regions of Lake Superior." *Michigan Pioneer and Historical Society Collections* 7 (1886): 181–93.

———. "Lake Superior Country." *Michigan Pioneer and Historical Society Collections* 8 (1886): 136–45.

———. "Life in the Copper Mines of Lake Superior." *Michigan Pioneer and Historical Collections* 11 (1887): 175–86.

———. "Some Incidents of Pioneer Life in the Upper Peninsula of Michigan." *Michigan Pioneer and Historical Society Collections* 17 (1892): 332–45.

———. "War Time in the Copper Mines." *Michigan Pioneer and Historical Collections* 18 (1892): 375–82.

Friggens, Thomas. "Fort Wilkins: Army Life on the Frontier." *Michigan History* 61 (Fall 1977): 221–50.

Fuller, George N., ed. *Geological Reports of Douglass Houghton, First State Geologist of Michigan, 1837–1845*. Lansing, 1928.

Gates, Paul W. *The Farmer's Age: Agriculture, 1815–1860*. New York, 1960.

Gates, William B. *Michigan Copper and Boston Dollars: An Economic History of the Michigan Copper Mining Industry*. Cambridge, Mass., 1951.

Greeley, Horace. *Recollections of a Busy Life*. New York, 1868.

Haller, Frank H. "Transportation System and Coal Dock." *Mining Congress Journal* 17 (Oct. 1931): 515–18.

Halsey, John R. "Miskwabik—Red Metal: Lake Superior Copper and the Indians of Eastern North America." *Michigan History* (Sept.–Oct. 1983): 32–41.

Hollingsworth, Sandra. *The Atlantic: Copper and Community South of Portage Lake*. Hancock, 1978.

"Hon. Samuel Worth Hill." *Michigan Pioneer and Historical Society Collections* 17 (1890): 51–53.

Hubbard, Bela. *Memorials of a Half-Century in Michigan and the Lake Region*. New York, 1887.

Hybels, Robert James. "The Lake Superior Copper Fever, 1841–47." *Michigan History* 34 (1950): 97–119, 224–44, and 309–26.

———. "A Narrative of the Lake Superior 'Copper Fever,' 1841–1847." M.A. thesis, University of Chicago, 1948.

Hyde, Charles K. "An Economic and Business History of the Quincy Mining Company." Historic American Engineering Record report, Library of Congress, 1978.

———. "From 'Subterranean Lotteries' to Orderly Investment: Michigan Copper and Eastern Dollars, 1841–1865." *Mid-America: An Historical Review* 66 (Jan. 1984): 3–20.

———. *The Northern Lights: Lighthouses of the Upper Great Lakes*. Lansing, 1986.

Jackman, Sydney W., and John F. Freeman, eds. *American Voyageur: The Journal of David Bates Douglass*. Marquette, Mich., 1969.

Jenkin, A. K. Hamilton. *The Cornish Miner, An Account of His Life Above and Underground from Early Times*. London, 1927.

Jones, Joseph C., Jr. *America's Icemen: An Illustrative History of the United States Natural Ice Industry, 1625–1925*. Humble, Tex., 1984.

Jordan, Terry G. *American Log Buildings: An Old World Heritage*. Chapel Hill, N.C., 1985.

Karamanski, Theodore J., et al. *Narrative History of Isle Royale*. Chicago, 1988.

Kohl, J. G. *Kitchi-Gami: Wanderings Round Lake Superior.* 1860. Reprint, Minneapolis, 1956.

Krause, David J. *The Making of a Mining District: Keweenaw Native Copper, 1500–1870.* Detroit, 1992.

Kuhlmann, Charles B. "The Processing of Agricultural Products in the Pre-Railway Age," 189–209, and "The Processing of Agricultural Products after 1860," 432–66, in *The Growth of the American Economy,* edited by Harold F. Williamson. New York, 1944.

Kuttruff, Karl, Robert E. Lee, and David T. Glick. *Ships of the Great Lakes: A Pictorial History.* Detroit, 1976.

Lang, Robert E., Deborah Epstein Popper, and Frank J. Popper. " 'Progress of the Nation': The Settlement History of the Enduring American Frontier." *Western Historical Quarterly* 26, no. 3 (Autumn 1995): 289–307.

Lankton, Larry D. *Cradle to Grave: Life, Work, and Death at the Lake Superior Copper Mines.* New York, 1991.

———. "The Machine *under* the Garden: Rock Drills Arrive at the Lake Superior Copper Mines, 1868–1883." *Technology and Culture* 24 (Jan. 1983): 1–37.

Lankton, Larry D., and Charles K. Hyde. *Old Reliable: An Illustrated History of the Quincy Mining Company.* Hancock, Mich., 1982.

Lankton, Larry D., and Jack K. Martin. "Technological Advance, Organizational Structure, and Underground Fatalities in the Upper Michigan Copper Mines, 1860–1929." *Technology and Culture* 28 (Jan. 1987): 42–66.

Lanman, Charles. *A Summer in the Wilderness Embracing a Canoe Voyage up the Mississippi and around Lake Superior.* New York, 1847.

Lanman, James H. *History of Michigan.* New York, 1841.

Larkin, Jack. *The Reshaping of Everyday Life, 1790–1840.* New York, 1988.

Leavitt, Judith Walzer. *Brought to Bed: Childbearing in America, 1750 to 1950.* New York, 1986.

McAlester, Virginia, and Lee McAlester. *A Field Guide to American Houses.* New York, 1992.

McCracken, S. B. *Men of Progress: Embracing Biographical Sketches of Representative Michigan Men.* Detroit, 1900.

McGill, George M. "From Allegheny to Lake Superior: Journal of George M. McGill." *Moorsfield Antiquarian* 1 (1937–38): 256–66.

McNear, Sarah. "Quincy Mining Company: Housing and Community Services, ca. 1860–1931." Historic American Engineering Record report, Library of Congress, 1978.

Maltby, Lawrence J. "The Quest for Michigan's Ontonagon Boulder." *Chronicle: The Magazine of the Historical Society of Michigan* 18, no. 3 (Fall 1982): 5–9.

Martin, Patrick. "Frozen Out from the World: The Archaeological Perspective on Fort Wilkins in the Nineteenth Century." *Michigan History* 74, no. 1 (1990): 12–19.

Marvill, Lewis. "First Trip by Steam to Lake Superior." *Michigan Pioneer and Historical Society Collections* 4 (1883): 67–69.

Mason, Philip P., ed. *Copper Country Journal: The Diary of Schoolmaster Henry Hobart, 1863–1864.* Detroit, 1991.

May, Earl Chapin. *The Canning Clan: A Pageant of Pioneering Americans.* New York, 1937.

Michael, Rodney R., and Larry D. Lankton. "Accounting Innovations: The Implications of a Firm's Response to Post Civil War Market Disruptions." *Accounting Historians Journal* 21, no. 2 (December 1994): 41–84.

Michigan State Gazetteer and Business Directories. Detroit, 1863 and later years.

Mohr, James C. *Abortion in America: The Origins and Evolution of National Policy, 1800–1900.* New York, 1978.

Nash, Roderick. *Wilderness and the American Mind.* Rev. ed. New Haven, 1973.

Peters, Bernard C., ed. *Lake Superior Journal: Bela Hubbard's Account of the 1840 Houghton Expedition.* Marquette, Mich., 1983.

————. "Revolt from the Wilderness: Romantic Travellers on Lake Superior." *Michigan Academician* 13, no. 4 (Spring 1981): 491–501.

Pope, Graham. "Some Early Mining Days at Portage Lake." Lake Superior Mining Institute *Proceedings* 7 (1901): 17–31.

Preservation Urban Design Incorporated. *Architectural Analysis: Fort Wilkins Historic Complex, Fort Wilkins State Park, Copper Harbor, Michigan.* Ann Arbor, Mich., 1976.

Rawlings, Joseph W. V. "Recollections of a Long Life." In *Copper Country Tales*, edited by Roy Drier, 75–127. Calumet, Mich., 1967.

Reed, James. *From Private Vice to Public Virtue: The Birth Control Movement and American Society since 1830.* New York, 1978.

Rezek, Rev. Antoine Ivan. *History of the Diocese of Sault Ste. Marie and Marquette.* 2 vols. Houghton, Mich. 1906 (vol. 1) and 1907 (vol. 2).

Rickard, T. A. *The Copper Mines of Lake Superior.* New York, 1905.

Robinson, Orrin W. *Early Days of the Lake Superior Copper Country.* Houghton, Mich., 1938.

————. "Recollections of Civil War Conditions in the Copper Country." *Michigan History* 3 (Oct. 1919): 598–609.

Rowe, John. *The Hard Rock Men: Cornish Immigrants and the North American Mining Frontier.* New York, 1974.

Rowse, A. L. *The Cousin Jacks: The Cornish in America.* New York, 1969.

St. John, John R. *A True Description of the Lake Superior Country.* New York, 1846.

Sawyer, Alvah L. *A History of the Northern Peninsula and Its People.* (3 vols.) Chicago, 1911.

Schaddelee, Leon. "The Mineral Range Railroad." *Narrow Gauge and Short-Line Gazette* 7 (Jan.– Feb. 1882): 54–58.

Schlereth, Thomas J. *Victorian America: Transformations in Everyday Life, 1876–1915.* New York, 1991.

Schoolcraft, Henry Rowe. *Narrative Journal of Travels through the Northwestern Regions of the United States.* Albany, 1821.

Starr, Paul. *The Social Transformation of American Medicine.* New York, 1982.

Stonehouse, Frederick. *Keweenaw Shipwrecks.* AuTrain, Mich., 1988.

Strasser, Susan. *Never Done: A History of American Housework.* New York, 1982.

Swineford, Alfred P. *History and Review of the Material Resources of the South Shore of Lake Superior.* Marquette, Mich., 1877.

Ten Broeck, Joseph A. "Old Keweenaw." *Michigan Pioneer and Historical Society Collections* 30 (1906): 139–49.

————. "Sketch of John Senter." *Michigan Pioneer and Historical Society Collections* 30 (1906): 156–62.

Thurner, Arthur W. *Calumet Copper and People: History of a Michigan Mining Community.* By the author, 1974.

————. *Strangers and Sojourners: A History of Michigan's Keweenaw Peninsula.* Detroit, 1994.

Tocqueville, Alexis de. *Democracy in America.* Trans. George Lawrence; ed. J. P. Mayer. New York, 1969.

Todd, Arthur Cecil. *The Cornish Miner in America.* Glendale, 1967.

Turner, Frederick Jackson. *The Frontier in American History.* 1920. Reprint with foreword by Ray Allen Billington, New York, 1962.

"The Upper Peninsula of Michigan." *Harper's New Monthly Magazine* (May 1882): 892–902.

Van Buren, A. D. P. "Our Temperance Conflict." *Michigan Pioneer and Historical Society Collections* 13 (1889): 388–407.

Veness-Randle, April Rene. "The Social-Spatial Lifecycle of a Company Town: Calumet, Michigan." M.A. thesis, Michigan State University, 1979.

Verwyst, P. Chrysostomus. *Life and Labors of Rt. Rev. Frederic Baraga.* Milwaukee, 1900.

Walling, Regis M., and Rev. N. Daniel Rupp, eds. *The Diary of Bishop Frederic Baraga.* Detroit, 1990.

Western Historical Co. *History of the Upper Peninsula of Michigan Containing a Full Account of Its Early Settlement; Its Growth, Development and Resources.* Chicago, 1883.

Whittlesey, Charles. *Fugitive Essays upon Interesting and Useful Subjects.* Hudson, Ohio, 1852.

Williams, Ralph D. *The Honorable Peter White: A Biographical Sketch of the Lake Superior Iron Country.* Cleveland, 1905.

Wright, James North. "The Development of the Copper Industry of Northern Michigan." *Michigan Political Science Association* 3 (Jan. 1899): 127–41.

———. *When Copper Was King: A Tale of the Early Mining Days on Lake Superior.* Boston, 1905.

Young, Otis. "The American Copper Frontier, 1640–1893." *The Speculator: A Journal of Butte and Southwest Montana History* 1 (Summer 1984): 4–15.

INDEX